The Complete
SAILING
Handbook

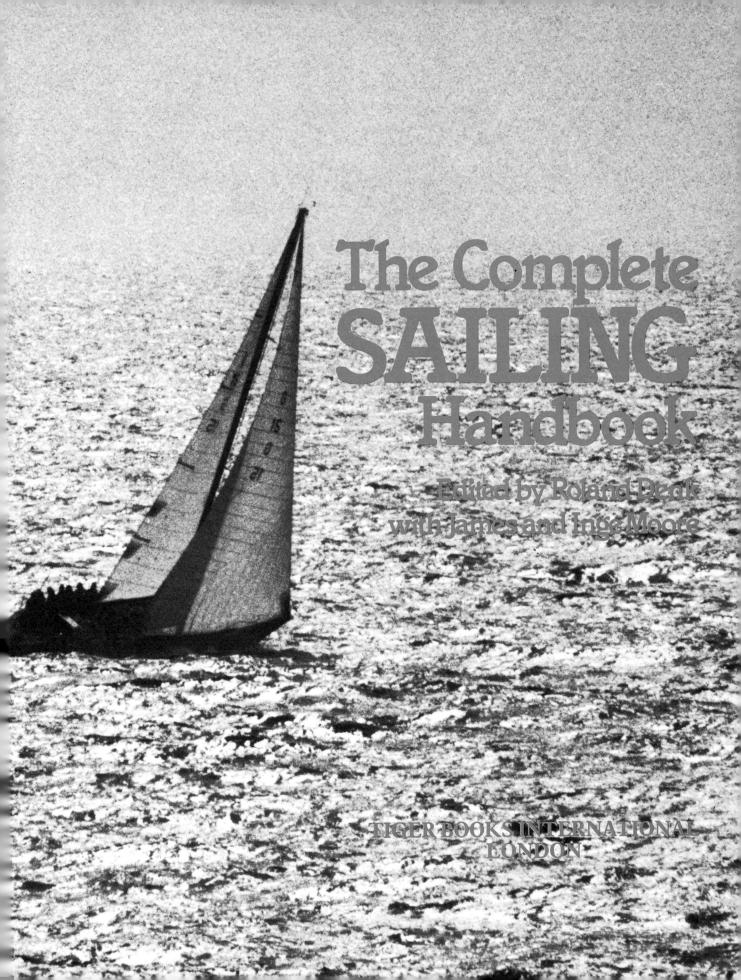

The Complete
SAILING
Handbook

Edited by Roland Denk
with James and Inge Moore

TIGER BOOKS INTERNATIONAL
LONDON

© BLV Verlagsgesellschaft mbH,
Munich 1976

English translation © Martin Dunitz
Limited 1979

This edition published in 1990 by
Tiger Books International PLC, London

ISBN 1-85501-077-1

Printed and bound in Singapore

The Complete Sailing Handbook

Preface

Sailing is a sport with many facets. It encompasses all kinds of racing, round the buoys, hot classes and offshore, coastal and blue water cruising, and just messing about in boats from gunkholing to sailing simply for the love or excitement of it. You can sail in a great variety of craft — monohulls, multihulls or sailboards. But deciding what particular aspect you will be attracted by and then acquiring a knowledge of it is not easy. This is where this book will really help you. *The Complete Sailing Handbook* combines in one volume what the interested sailing man would otherwise have to extract from at least four or five separate books on different subjects. Besides being an invaluable reference book even for experienced yachtsmen it is ideal for all those who want to find a systematic introduc-

tion to the sport, enabling them to move on to even more detailed study of individual sailing subjects if they are ambitious.

Each chapter has been written by an expert in their own particular field. Every one has presented the latest information in a straightforward way, backed up by clear, instructive diagrams with many beautiful and highly relevant photographs, which are one of the outstanding features of this book. Not only is the team of writers made up of experts, but all the editors and artists are sailing people too. In this way every effort has been made to see that only first-hand knowledge is passed on to you.

We hope you will enjoy using *The Complete Sailing Handbook* and will turn to it again and again during the course of your sailing career.

Contents

Racing

Navigation

Weather

Navigation rules

About boats

The layman often finds the many different types and designs of boat bewildering to say the least.

For a start we have to distinguish between monohulls and multihulls (catamarans and trimarans). There are a good many more monohulls and their main distinguishing feature (apart from having only one hull!) is their deeper draft. The underwater part of the hull viewed from the side is called the lateral plane and provides lateral resistance, thus counteracting leeway. A fixed keel also plays a part in providing stability. Monohulls can be divided into boats with a fixed keel and those with a centre or daggerboard which can be retracted. There are, however, variations on this theme.

Small centreboard boats

These are also described as dinghies or centreboard dinghies and are generally smaller and lighter than keelboats. The one obvious advantage is that they can sail in shallow waters and run ashore on beaches without damage, as the board is simply pulled up into a trunking (daggerboard) or pivoted around a pin (centreboard). Both retract flush with the hull, either by hand or by means of some sort of purchase or tackle. The advantage of a centreboard over a daggerboard is that if it touches bottom it will kick up of its own accord. Centreboards are rarely made of metal as they used to be, but are made of plywood or fibreglass.

Centreboards, for obvious reasons, have to be carefully shaped, like aerofoils, being rounded at the leading edge and having relatively sharp trailing edges as this not only reduces turbulence, but also helps to give the hull lift when sailing closehauled. This again helps to reduce leeway. Usually, the centreboard is located in the centreline of the boat, an American idea dating back to the early nineteenth century. Previously leeboards were used, as are still seen on Dutch craft today and, occasionally, on dinghies such as inflatables. Larger dinghies fitted with small cabins or cuddies are normally described as day sailers or trailer sailers. In a dinghy the hull shape and beam play an important part in the stability of the craft. Owing to a relatively broad beam the average dinghy is, initially, fairly stable, but after a certain point stability rapidly decreases as the boat heels. The dinghy can then capsize since its centre of gravity is higher than that of a keelboat. Crew weight is used to keep the boat upright and this is the important difference between dinghies and small keelboats.

The advantage of a centreboard in a dinghy is that it can be retracted by any amount — in this picture it is about half way up — and the boat can be brought in close to a landing stage in shallow water.

The E-Boat, a popular trailer-sailer.

Keelboats

Keelboats usually have a fixed ballast keel under the hull and, as this means the centre of gravity is well below the surface of the water, the yacht is virtually safe from capsize although it can of course still sink if holed, or if water pours in through an open hatch when the boat is knocked down by a strong wind, or if the cockpit is filled by a wave. In general, the more the boat heels the greater the righting moment becomes.

There are various hull profiles. Keels can be long, short, cut away, shallow or deep. Until recently cruising yachts generally had long underwater profiles since this was thought to give greater directional stability.

Lateral plan of modern racing yacht. This is a One Tonner.

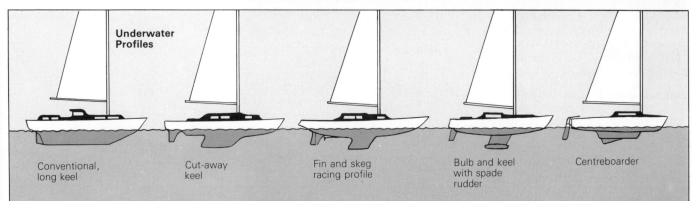

Underwater Profiles

Conventional, long keel

Cut-away keel

Fin and skeg racing profile

Bulb and keel with spade rudder

Centreboarder

Over the last ten years or so there has been a trend in racing yachts away from this towards deep, narrow fin keels, with rudders either free standing or attached to a narrow support or skeg. So successful is this development in racing yachts that most cruising yachts have followed suit.

Dragons, an Olympic keelboat now replaced.

Other hull forms

There are various specialized hull forms which belong to the keelboat family and are uncapsizable, if properly designed.

Keel centreboarders These boats have shallow stub keels, as well as centreboards so that, without losing too much stability, they can retract their boards and sail in shallow water with a reduced draft. Trailer sailers are usually keel centreboarders of between eighteen and twenty-four feet (6-8m) length. In Australia and New Zealand trailer sailers have proved very popular, as they provide low-cost yachting with the ability to trail the boat to different launch sites.

Lifting keel Boats with lifting or pivoting keels combine the advantages of centreboarders and keelboats since the ballast keel can be hydraulically or mechanically withdrawn like a centreboard. Lifting such a heavy weight up into the boat presents design problems. Under IOR rules they must be fixed during a race.

Ballasted centreboarders This is a fairly recent development for larger dinghies. The centreboard is heavily constructed to give a reasonable amount of stability. This type of craft should be handled with care when it comes to considerations of capsizability and must not be regarded as true keelboats.

Twin Bilge keels Popular in tidal waters. They enable the boat to remain upright resting on her keels when the tide has gone out. Draft is less than with a centre keel. Some yachts even have a third keel along the centre line, usually ballasted, as well as the two bilge keels. They do not sail as well under most conditions as a single fin keel, particularly when going to windward, but the advantages are obvious. A boat can be left safely on a drying mooring where a fin keel boat would take the ground and rest on her bilge, possibly causing structural damage.

The main characteristics of a hull are expressed by its sections. Hull shape, especially in keelboats, has

Development from traditional hull section to modern offshore yachts

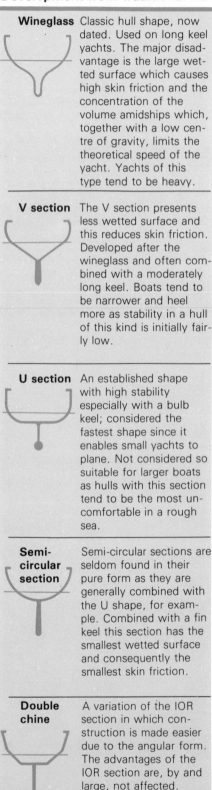

Wineglass Classic hull shape, now dated. Used on long keel yachts. The major disadvantage is the large wetted surface which causes high skin friction and the concentration of the volume amidships which, together with a low centre of gravity, limits the theoretical speed of the yacht. Yachts of this type tend to be heavy.

V section The V section presents less wetted surface and this reduces skin friction. Developed after the wineglass and often combined with a moderately long keel. Boats tend to be narrower and heel more as stability in a hull of this kind is initially fairly low.

U section An established shape with high stability especially with a bulb keel; considered the fastest shape since it enables small yachts to plane. Not considered so suitable for larger boats as hulls with this section tend to be the most uncomfortable in a rough sea.

Semi-circular section Semi-circular sections are seldom found in their pure form as they are generally combined with the U shape, for example. Combined with a fin keel this section has the smallest wetted surface and consequently the smallest skin friction.

Double chine A variation of the IOR section in which construction is made easier due to the angular form. The advantages of the IOR section are, by and large, not affected.

IOR hull section This has come about as a result of the IOR Rule Mark III. Today it is the best hull section, having the biggest advantages. In spite of a small wetted surface the righting moment is big. At high hull speed the yacht is very seakindly. Also with an angle of heel of around 30° a certain hull symmetry is maintained. The construction is complicated and expensive.

evolved in recent years and there have been dramatic changes.

Most dinghies are either built round-bottomed or hard-chined. The latter can be built most easily at home. Typical hard-chine boats include the Star, Enterprise, Snipe, Wayfarer, Lightening and Optimist.

The Star, an Olympic class boat and a typical example of hard-chine construction.

Technical expressions used in boat building

Before we take a closer look at boat-building itself, here are some basic expressions and technical terms used:

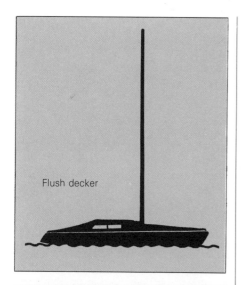

Flush decker

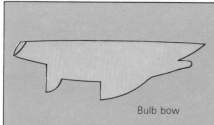

Bulb bow

Conventional, pronounced overhang.

Moderate overhang on a modern ocean racer. This is Saudade, *a German Admiral's Cup yacht.*

Auxiliary   Most reasonably sized sailing yachts rely on an inboard engine. Smaller yachts usually have outboards on special brackets, but they really are auxiliaries and are normally only used when leaving moorings or entering crowded anchorages where the use of sails is impractical or downright dangerous. During races·engines are not allowed to be used.

Ballast keel   In keelboats the ballast keel is fitted below the keel proper. Many yachts have ballast keels which are integral with the keel and are cigar-shaped with an aerofoil section. The ballast keel in a wooden boat is bolted to a wooden keel. The bolts are very long and come through the deadwood. Ballast usually takes the form of an iron or lead casting although metal punchings or lead shot encased inside a fibreglass keel are commonly used.

Beam   a. The measurement of a boat across its widest part. b. Supports for the deck that run athwartships.

Bilge   The curve in the hull which joins the topsides and the bottom.

Bilges   The very lowest part of a boat's interior below the floor or sole.

Boot top   A painted band running the full length of the hull just above, and parallel to, the waterline.

Bulkhead   An athwartships dividing partition in a yacht that separates parts of the vessel. It is usually integral with the hull construction and is used to strengthen it. It can run fore and aft or athwartships.

Cabin   Living accommodation in a yacht. Small yachts may have anything up to four berths in a single cabin. There are usually two cabins on a small yacht, the main cabin and the fore cabin.

Ceiling   The inside lining of a vessel.

Coaming   A small bulwark or ledge, usually around a cockpit, to repel water and provide a back rest for those in the cockpit.

Cockpit   A recessed area in the deck or deckhouse in which the tiller or steering wheel is located and which acts as a shelter for the crew. It is usually open.

Cruiser   A yacht with a cabin, suitable for extended voyages or cruises.

Dinghy   Broadly speaking a small, open boat either with oars or sails. It often has a centreboard.

Floors   The frames under the cabin sole, connecting the frames across the keel.

Forecastle   A compartment in the bows of a small boat. In larger vessels there may be room to sleep and in large sailing ships it usually formed the crews' quarters.

A selection of modern transoms.

A sturdy, traditional motor sailer capable of going anywhere.

Frame	A rib which goes from the keel to the deck to which the planks are fastened.
Freeboard	The height of the side of the boat from the waterline to the deck.
Galley	The cooking and food storage area in a boat.
Gunwale	Pronounced 'gun'l' this is the rail of a boat, the upper and outer edge of a boat's side where the deck meets the topsides.
Keel	A fixed or retractable fin under the hull that provides lateral resistance to counteract leeway. A keel may or may not include ballast.
Keelson	A long doubling piece which runs fore and aft above the keel, the structural 'backbone' of a wooden vessel.
Knee	An L-shaped bracket of wood or metal which joins various timbers in a vessel's structure and named from the position in which it is placed.
Lines or lines drawing	The yacht designer's two-dimensional drawings showing the outline of a boat's shape in sections — fore and aft (profile), athwartships (sections) and plans. Normally they consist of a body plan, profile and half-breadth plan. A sail plan outlines the shape of the rig and the sail area. There will also be a deck plan, accommodation plan and table of offsets to enable the builder to loft (reproduce full size) the drawings.
LOA	Length overall, or the absolute distance between the foremost and aftermost part of the vessel. This is not to be confused with the waterline length or LWL.
Motor sailer	A cross between a sailing yacht and a motor yacht. A motor sailer will probably have more power and less sail than a similarly sized sailing yacht proper and will often use both sail and power at the same time.
Ocean Racer	Offshore sailing yacht designed for racing.
Overhang	The amount by which the bow and stern extend beyond the waterline.
Planks	In a wooden hull these are the timbers which make up the outer skin of the vessel and which are attached to the frames. Carvel-built vessels have flush hulls, the planks butting against each other, whereas a clinker-built boat has overlapping planks. Another form of carvel construction is called double-diagonal in which two layers of planking are glued diagonally on top of each other. Where the planks meet edge to edge the join is called a seam. Where planks meet end to end they are said to butt together.
Rudder	A flat, wide and deep wooden, metal or fibreglass blade hung under the hull which, in response to the movement of the tiller or steering wheel, changes the boat's direction. The rudder installation consists of the blade, stock, head and, of course, tiller or wheel. Dinghies usually have retractable rudders. Types include spade rudders, transom-hung rudders and skeg-hung rudders.

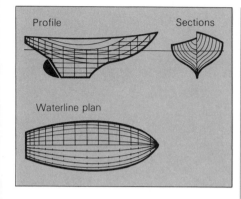

Profile · Sections · Waterline plan

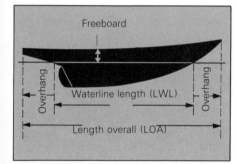

Freeboard · Overhang · Waterline length (LWL) · Overhang · Length overall (LOA)

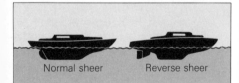

Normal sheer · Reverse sheer

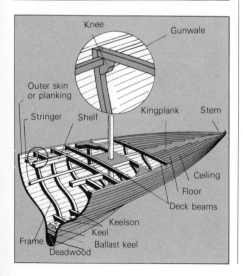

Knee · Gunwale · Outer skin or planking · Stringer · Shelf · Kingplank · Stem · Ceiling · Floor · Deck beams · Keelson · Keel · Frame · Ballast keel · Deadwood

Sheer, Sheerline	The line of the gunwale viewed from abeam in profile. Most boats have a sheer that has a concave curve, the lowest point of which is just aft of amidships.
Single-hander	A vessel designed to be crewed by one person, or a lone sailor.
Stability	There are various ways of measuring a boat's ability to resist the heeling forces imposed by wind and sea conditions. The shape of the hull and position of the centre of gravity are decisive factors in this. A beamy hull will have good initial stability although, ultimately, stability depends on the weight and position of the centre of gravity, kept low in a keel boat by the addition of a heavy keel.
Stern	The aftermost part of the hull. As with the bow or stem there are many types: overhanging, transom, counter and reverse. Some boats have canoe sterns, that is pointed sterns which are considered better in heavy seas as they tend to divide the waves. The design of a vessel's stern is crucial in allowing the water to flow cleanly away from the sides and the IOR has led to some very strange shapes in an attempt by designers to optimize their boats' rating under that rule.
Sternpost	The aftermost structural member of a wooden boat or point on which the rudder is often hung.
Stringers	Fore and aft members connecting the frames or, in the absence of frames in some fibreglass hulls, attached to the inside of the skin to give the hull rigidity.
Tender	Applied to a yacht, it means that she has low initial stability. This may be because she was built with insufficient ballast and a high centre of gravity, or merely an unusually narrow beam giving a strong tendency to heel earlier and more than normal. The opposite is a stiff boat with exceptionally high initial stability. If designed properly both are safe but exhibit different sailing characteristics. A tender boat may be easier in a seaway whereas a stiff boat may have a quick, uneasy movement. Tender is also the nautical term for a yacht's dinghy, used to ferry stores or crew.
Waterline, (designed waterline)	A boat should float on or near its designed waterline as calculated on the drawing board.
Yacht	General term for a sea going vessel used for pleasure, though a small boat without a cabin, or with only rudimentary accommodation, is referred to as a day sailer or dinghy. It can be either a sailing or motor yacht.

Boat construction

Wood

Until fibreglass took over, wood was considered to be the boat-building material par excellence. Woods used in traditional boat building include mahogany, iroko, gaboon, teak, oak, larch, pitch, pine, spruce and elm. Masts and spars were usually made from fir or spruce. In a wooden boat the keel is usually laid first and the stem- and sternposts attached to it. Next come the structural members (the frames, floors and lower deck beams), followed by the fore and aft members (the stringers) and deck beams, making up the skeleton of the boat. This is then planked up. Wooden boats can have a long working life, forty years or more is not uncommon, if the yacht is cared for. A modern method of construction which has been used mostly for dinghies like the Flying Dutchman, but has also found favour for individually built offshore racers, is moulded plywood. Veneers of wood, usually three-five, are laid diagonally across a jig or mould and glued together under pressure, either with or without the application of heat.

Steel

Steel is another material commonly used for the construction of large-and medium-sized yachts. Steel yachts are strong but can be heavy. Corrosion in a steel hull has always been a problem especially in warm, salty conditions. This means that a steel vessel can deteriorate quickly in areas like the Mediterranean, although the problem has been partially solved by using special paints and corrosion-resistant steels. Corrosion is accelerated by electrolysis, a galvanic effect which will eat away one or two dissimilar metals. This is what happens. If two dissimilar metals are in close proximity underwater, e.g., a steel hull and a bronze fastening, or a light alloy rudder blade and iron rivets, the more electro positive metal becomes an anode in the presence of sea water and the other a cathode. The electropositive, or baser metal, the anode, will disappear. As a protective measure, one or more small plates of a highly electropositive metal are bolted to the underside of the hull in places where corrosion is likely to occur and these sacrificial anodes are eroded in the course of a season's sailing rather than the more important areas of the hull and stern gear. In theory, it would also be possible to use an electric current as a form of cathodic protection, but as

this would make excessive demands on the battery, it is not practical.

Aluminium

Aluminium alloys are ideal boat-building materials combining lightness and strength, together with a freedom from most forms of corrosion. Aluminium up until now has been considered too expensive for all but the largest racing yachts and power boats, as its welding involves special techniques. Many smaller runabouts and workboats are rivetted, but it is important that they are made of the same material as the plating or, once again, electrolysis can occur.

Ferro-cement

A steel mesh skeleton of the yacht is built upside down and special cement is trowelled on to form a shell. With skilful application a very fair hull can be achieved. The method is favoured by home constructors since it is easier to build a good hull than by other methods.

Fibreglass

Most yachts nowadays are built in fibreglass and it has taken over the role of wood in the boat-building industry. The first fibreglass boats appeared in 1943 in the USA and fibreglass became increasingly widespread in the boat-building world from the middle fifties onwards. Fibreglass is an excellent material. It consists of a resin, a polyester-unsaturated component, which is dissolved in the unsaturated solvent styrene. A chemical process turns the viscous material into a hard polyester resin, a process known as polymerization. Curing is triggered off by the use of an accelerating

Building a boat in a Greek boatyard. The powerful frames and fore and aft members are clearly visible.

agent, cobalt in solution, for example, and a hardening agent in the form of peroxide. Hardening takes place between 50-70°F (10-20°C) or, if heat is applied, between 175-285°F (80-140°C). Not until the brittle polyester resin is combined with some sort of reinforcement is it suitable as a boat-building material, when the combination of plastic resin and glass-fibre strands form a laminate known as fibreglass.

Fibreglass reinforcements come in many forms. The strongest is the continuous roving which can be woven together to make loose fabric. Many types are available according to strength required and ease of handling. Chopped strand mat is probably the most common although not the strongest due to the short fibres used. Fibreglass boats have many outstanding properties including resistance to water, imperviousness to most chemicals and, above all, ease of maintenance. They are unaffected by temperature changes, do not rot, corrode or leak. They are also remarkably strong and repairs are fairly straightforward. Epoxy resins with similar properties are also coming to the fore in boat building and they are already used in the manufacture of skis and in the aeroplane industry. The mechanical properties of epoxy resins are even better than polyesters, but they are most expensive and harder to work with, taking longer to cure.

Fibreglass boats are built in temperature-controlled factories to ensure proper curing with low humidity. A wooden plug is first built in the exact form of the hull shape and this has to be primed, sandpapered and polished to a mirror-like finish. It is then treated with several coats of wax which act as a separating agent. The mould is then taken off this plug.

Then the actual building begins. First a separating agent, usually wax, is spread over the mould, so that the resin will not stick to the mould. Then, using a brush, spatula or spray gun, a fine layer of gel coat is applied to form the outer surface of the boat. This is usually a layer of polyester resin 0.3 to 0.6mm thick with a high catalytic- and accelerating-agent content. It is usually coloured with some

sort of pigment and the ultimate appearance of the boat will depend very much on this gel coat and how it is applied. The rest of the hull is built up of layers of fibreglass mat impregnated with resin until the desired thickness is reached. Finally the laminate is allowed to harden and additional layers are laid around stress points, such as the bilges and chain plates. Wood is often bonded in to give added strength to engine mountings and bearers. Stringers are usually made from glassed-in foam or wood.

The finished shell should then be left to cure finally at a temperature of around 45-60°F (7-15°C) and, although this post cure is not essential, some classification and survey societies insist on the process, which makes the boat even stronger. Any stickiness on the surface is eliminated as is the pervasive smell which often lingers round newly built fibreglass boats.

After curing, the boat is removed from the mould, the edges are trimmed and fitting out can begin as soon as the hull has been set up. The deck is sometimes bonded to the hull at this stage. Various methods are used, including bolting and a quick-setting sealant glue to full glassing over the joint. The deck and superstructure are made in exactly the same way on another mould.

An improved process involves spraying the resin and fibre into the mould under pressure. Further variations are the vacuum process in which male and female moulds are used, and a new injection moulding process which operates at a pressure of several atmospheres.

Other methods include foam or balsa sandwich and C flex, the latter being a process whereby a mat of fibreglass rods is laid longitudinally over a temporary frame before being covered in laminate in the normal way. The hull is then removed from the male mould or plug and the inside is glassed over. Finally, the hull is smoothed down and filled. It is ideal for one-off construction and was first developed in the USA.

In sandwich construction a light core of some suitable material is sandwiched between two layers of laminate. The core consists of

materials like PVC rigid foam, polyurethane foam, cellular sheeting, balsa wood or plywood. The method is frequently used for one-off hulls and especially for large yachts, where series production would not be in order. The main disadvantage of the method is the risk of water absorption if the outer skin is damaged.

Recently, materials like Kevlar and carbon fibre have appeared on the boat-building scene, enabling the builder to produce even lighter, stronger hulls. Several classes allow boats to be built in carbon fibre and it undoubtedly has a future once its high price can be reduced. The hair-fine strands of carbon can be made into sheets, blocks and ribbons. To bend a heated piece of composite carbon fibre takes several times as much force as a similar piece of steel. The strands can be made into rovings and woven like fibreglass and then laminated with polyester and epoxy resins. A hull of carbon fibre is thinner than an identical one made in fibreglass, but has the same rigidity. Experiments have been made with carbon fibre masts and it will no doubt become popular as a material in the boat-building industry. At present the main use is confined to reinforcing stress points in fibreglass hulls and, even so, the cost is still prohibitive for all but racing yachts.

Gear and fittings

All kinds of specialised fittings, locks, shackles and other gear, are used in fitting out boats. Some are reviewed here.

Basic fittings

Shackles Shackles are U-shaped links made from galvanized iron, bronze or stainless steel and they come in all shapes and sizes. They are the most common method of joining things on board whether it be sail to halyard or anchor to chain. Some shackles have a captive pin of some form or another to prevent loss but the most common is the simple shackle with a screw pin. A snap shackle is one which springs open and is especially valuable where speed is important; for example in releasing the spinnaker sheets in a hurry from the tack or clew of the sail. Shackles are often attached to some sort of swivel to enable them to take the pull of a rope in any direction.

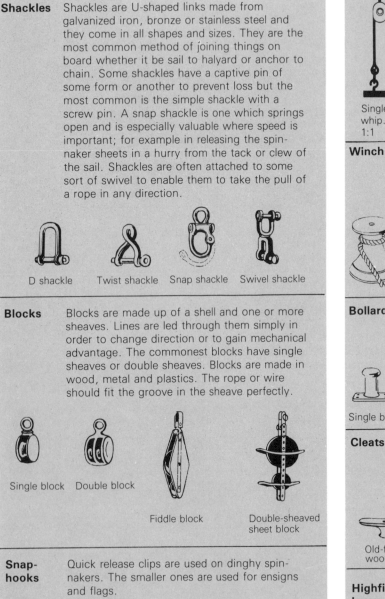

D shackle Twist shackle Snap shackle Swivel shackle

Blocks Blocks are made up of a shell and one or more sheaves. Lines are led through them simply in order to change direction or to gain mechanical advantage. The commonest blocks have single sheaves or double sheaves. Blocks are made in wood, metal and plastics. The rope or wire should fit the groove in the sheave perfectly.

Single block Double block

Fiddle block Double-sheaved sheet block

Snap-hooks Quick release clips are used on dinghy spinnakers. The smaller ones are used for ensigns and flags.

Tackles A tackle is a combination of blocks through which ropes run. Tackles found on sailing boats include, for example, the mainsheet tackle, the boom vang and the centreboard tackle. The running part is defined as the part of the rope which actually runs through the block; and the standing part, the part of the rope which is made fast to a point. The power exerted depends on the number of blocks used. They all have different names and the most common are:

Single whip. 1:1 Burton 2:1 Double whip. 2:1 Watch tackle. 3:1 Luff tackle. 3:1 Reverse luff takle. 4:1

Winch A geared drum around which sheets and halyards are wound and which is turned by a winch handle. The gear ratio and the length of the handle determine the power of the winch. Many winches have two speeds with a high- and a low-gear ratio; some have three. A ratchet stops the drum slipping back under load. Winches are used where the power needed to trim sheets and tighten halyards is too great to allow them to be brought in by hand alone.

Bollard On a pier vertical posts or bars of wood or metal to which mooring lines are attached. On a boat a samson post performs the same function.

Single bollard Double bollard Cross bollard Double-cross bollard

Cleats Metal, wood or plastic devices to which a line under load is secured. The line is wrapped several times round a traditional cleat but only once around a jam cleat which has a V on one side. They should be securely mounted. Reinforcement under the deck is advisable.

Old-fashioned wooden cleat Modern cleat Cleat with solid base-plate

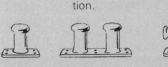

Highfield lever A device which enables a rope to be brought in a set amount in one movement. Used on jib halyards and runners where precise, immediate adjustment is required.

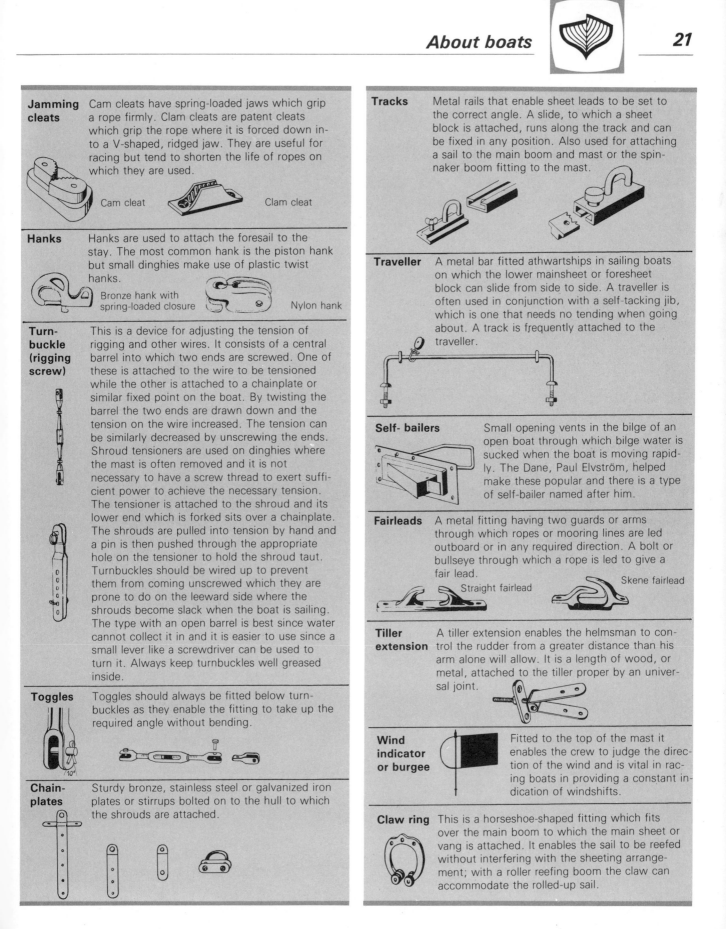

Jamming cleats Cam cleats have spring-loaded jaws which grip a rope firmly. Clam cleats are patent cleats which grip the rope where it is forced down into a V-shaped, ridged jaw. They are useful for racing but tend to shorten the life of ropes on which they are used.

Cam cleat   Clam cleat

Hanks Hanks are used to attach the foresail to the stay. The most common hank is the piston hank but small dinghies make use of plastic twist hanks.

Bronze hank with spring-loaded closure   Nylon hank

Turn-buckle (rigging screw) This is a device for adjusting the tension of rigging and other wires. It consists of a central barrel into which two ends are screwed. One of these is attached to the wire to be tensioned while the other is attached to a chainplate or similar fixed point on the boat. By twisting the barrel the two ends are drawn down and the tension on the wire increased. The tension can be similarly decreased by unscrewing the ends. Shroud tensioners are used on dinghies where the mast is often removed and it is not necessary to have a screw thread to exert sufficient power to achieve the necessary tension. The tensioner is attached to the shroud and its lower end which is forked sits over a chainplate. The shrouds are pulled into tension by hand and a pin is then pushed through the appropriate hole on the tensioner to hold the shroud taut. Turnbuckles should be wired up to prevent them from coming unscrewed which they are prone to do on the leeward side where the shrouds become slack when the boat is sailing. The type with an open barrel is best since water cannot collect it in and it is easier to use since a small lever like a screwdriver can be used to turn it. Always keep turnbuckles well greased inside.

Toggles Toggles should always be fitted below turnbuckles as they enable the fitting to take up the required angle without bending.

Chain-plates Sturdy bronze, stainless steel or galvanized iron plates or stirrups bolted on to the hull to which the shrouds are attached.

Tracks Metal rails that enable sheet leads to be set to the correct angle. A slide, to which a sheet block is attached, runs along the track and can be fixed in any position. Also used for attaching a sail to the main boom and mast or the spinnaker boom fitting to the mast.

Traveller A metal bar fitted athwartships in sailing boats on which the lower mainsheet or foresheet block can slide from side to side. A traveller is often used in conjunction with a self-tacking jib, which is one that needs no tending when going about. A track is frequently attached to the traveller.

Self-bailers Small opening vents in the bilge of an open boat through which bilge water is sucked when the boat is moving rapidly. The Dane, Paul Elvström, helped make these popular and there is a type of self-bailer named after him.

Fairleads A metal fitting having two guards or arms through which ropes or mooring lines are led outboard or in any required direction. A bolt or bullseye through which a rope is led to give a fair lead.

Straight fairlead   Skene fairlead

Tiller extension A tiller extension enables the helmsman to control the rudder from a greater distance than his arm alone will allow. It is a length of wood, or metal, attached to the tiller proper by an universal joint.

Wind indicator or burgee Fitted to the top of the mast it enables the crew to judge the direction of the wind and is vital in racing boats in providing a constant indication of windshifts.

Claw ring This is a horseshoe-shaped fitting which fits over the main boom to which the main sheet or vang is attached. It enables the sail to be reefed without interfering with the sheeting arrangement; with a roller reefing boom the claw can accommodate the rolled-up sail.

Special fittings for racing yachts

Hull and deck fittings

Deck leads – deck fairleads
Sockets set into the deck through which lines are led to blocks below deck. To reduce windage many adjustable tackles in the racing yacht are led this way.

Adjustable fairleads
These are used to regulate the setting of the jib by making it possible to adjust the sheeting angle rapidly. The slides illustrated are held in position by a small spring-loaded plunger which engages in holes drilled in the track along which they run. A block is usually attached to the slide. In a dinghy, which will have no winch for the jib sheets, it is not uncommon to fit a ratchet block so that much of the strain is taken off the crew when the sheets are pulling hard in a strong wind.

Barber-haulers
Devices used to adjust the sheeting position of jibs athwartships. The slot between the mainsail and the jib is an important factor in correct sail trim and some method of adjustment is essential. In light wind the slot can be reduced in width, whereas in stronger winds it needs to be wider. They are used for fine tuning.

Coffee-grinder winches
Winches on the modern racing boat are made of bronze, light alloy or even, in larger boats, of stainless steel. They often run on needle or Teflon bearings. There are winches geared for one, two or three speeds. On the larger racing yachts coffee-grinder winches are often used. These enable crew members to operate the same winch or winches through cranks which are situated remote from the drum.

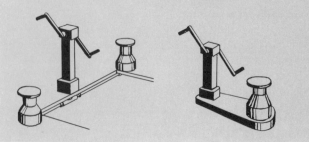

Ratchet blocks
The first ratchet blocks were made with Tufnol sheaves and a clamping device to take the strain off a loaded sheet. Modern ratchet blocks have ball-bearings to minimize friction. The sheaves themselves are ridged to grip the rope so that a sheet can be brought in easily but prevented from slipping back. The sheave, of course, revolves in one direction only when the ratchet mechanism is engaged.

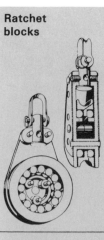

Stoppers
In the modern racing boat the tendency is to concentrate all lines on the cockpit and this is where the stopper comes in useful. It is a spring-loaded cam that acts like a jamming cleat and is usually placed in line with a winch so that a halyard, for example, can be secured and the winch then used for another purpose. The cam can be released by operating a small lever. Often banks of stoppers are seen clustered around the mast and labelled to show which lines they control.

Centreboard tackle
This enables the centreboard to be raised or lowered by the required amount and is usually only seen in boats with heavy metal boards like the Finn. Wooden centreboards can usually be raised and lowered by hand.

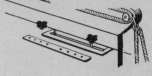

Compass
The compass in a racing yacht is a vital piece of equipment as it enables the helmsman to steer a course or, perhaps more important, to plot wind changes and directions of currents. Racing compasses are called tactical compasses as they have special markings and sectors as well as the usual compass card. The card must be clear and easy to read and well damped so it will react to the heading of the ship smoothly. Racing boats frequently have two compasses, one on either side, usually mounted in the main bulkhead so that the helmsman can see the card from whichever side he is sitting.

Mainsheet jammer

This enables the mainsheet to be brought in and let out quickly without uncleating it. It consists of a block and jam cleat mounted on a swivel. Once again ball bearings are often used to reduce friction. The helmsman can only make full use of the jammer if the jaws are at the right angle for him to be able to cleat and uncleat quickly. It is important to be able to make an adjustment rapidly in gusty winds and avoid undue heeling or even a capsize.

Water-tight compart-ments

The latter can also be used to store items needed on a race and spare gear, but it is essential for you to be able to examine inside the compartment to check for leaks and condensation. Lids to buoyancy compartments should be left off after the boat has been used to allow the air to circulate freely.

Roller jib

This allows the jib on smaller racing yachts and some cruising boats to be rolled up neatly instead of having to be dropped and unhanked. When the boat is being used frequently there is no reason why the sail should not be left attached to the roller until the boat is used again. There are a number of systems on the market but few allow the jib to be tensioned properly and thus they are not found on larger racing boats. It is useful to be able to take in a headsail in a hurry when coring into a tight berth or when beaching as it allows the helmsman an unobstructed vile to take in a headsail in a hurry when coming into a tight berth or when beaching as it allows the helmsman an unobstructed view. Some systems allow the sail not only to be rolled up completely, but reefed, which saves the trouble of using a number of different sails. The best sail shapes will not necessarily furl well, another reason one seldom sees large racing yachts using roller jibs. Control lines are led back to the cockpit which means that the crew need not venture on to the foredeck at all.

Mast, boom and rigging fittings

Cunning-ham hole

An eye sewn into the luff or leech of the sail a short distance up from the boom through which a line is rove, usually to a purchase of some sort, which enables the luff or leech of the sail to be tightened. This flattens the sail and moves the deepest part of the camber of the sail aft. In strong winds a flatter sail holds less wind and the boat heels less when sailing to windward. The tension is released for sailing off the wind where a full sail is of advantage.

Clew outhaul

This is a device which will alter the tension on the foot of the sail. In strong winds where a flat sail is desirable it will be tensioned to draw the sail out to the black limiting bands marked on the boom and stipulated by the class rules.

Shroud lever

In racing craft it is common to adjust the tension of parts of the rigging according to the point of sailing or the weather conditions. So that this can be done, rapidly adjustable levers, as illustrated here, are fitted. When the lever is open the tension is released and vice versa.

Halyard lock

Once the mainsail is hoisted the halyard, in theory, can be dispensed with as long as the head of the sail can be gripped in some way at the top of the mast. The halyard lock not only grips the last few inches of the halyard thus taking the tension off the rest of it but, in singlehanders like the Finn or boats with bendy masts, it also releases some of the compression from the mast. Basically it consists of a ball crimped on to the halyard which engages in a V-shaped fitting on the mast.

Headfoil

The grooved forestay is fitted commonly on racing yachts which are continually changing headsails, as it enables the new sail to be hoisted up the same groove, or up a parallel one to the existing sail thus making sail changes both quicker and easier. As a groove and not hanks are used, time is saved, which can be vital in a race, and as there is always a sail set even during the change (they fly together for a while) the boat loses little speed through the water. Added to this the headfoil is usually lenticular in shape which reduces windage and the luff can be set up straight. Hanking on a new sail and unhanking the old one takes up valuable time and the grooved forestay obviates this. Cruising boats could also benefit by the example of racing boats as it is also in their interests to keep sail changes quick and easy, but there are additional vibration problems, and the headfoil is more prone to accidental damage from minor knocks.

Power, muscle or magic boxes

Enclosed multi-part purchases are now used extensively to adjust forestay, jib and halyard tension. Back stays and shrouds are sometimes fitted with power boxes and the power gained is proportionate to the number of parts inside the box. They are once again a convenient way of altering the tension on a line, halyard, outhaul or shroud with the minimum of effort. Care must be taken to keep them lubricated properly and keep sand and grit out or they become hard to work involving, as they do, many blocks and sheaves.

Line drums

In order to keep the many lines on racing yachts tidy, line drums are in common use. These can be open or enclosed. Line drums sometimes automatically take up slack in the lines by means of a spring.

Mast ram

This is a device used with a bendy mast which operates at deck level and is used to bend the mast back or forward. Sailing to windward, the boat normally requires a flatter sail and, therefore, the mast is bent aft. On courses before the wind the mast is bent forward giving a fuller sail.

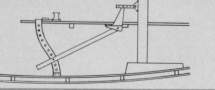

Spinnaker pole and fittings

The choice of spinnaker pole fittings is very extensive, ranging from simple dinghy fittings with snap attachments to cup fittings as used on ocean racers. The most common is the piston action fitting. Today, automatic snap fittings are being used extensively in which the outboard fittings are activated by the pressure of the spinnaker sheet. On larger yachts cup fittings have become popular. They have a universal joint which enables them to respond exactly to the movements of the spinnaker boom.

Spinnaker pole fittings on the mast

The old-fashioned fixed eyes on the front of the mast have fallen out of favour in racing because it is impossible to adjust the height of the boom. Instead tracks with slides have been developed. Today roller bearings are used for the slide which takes the considerable pressure from the boom. Some very large yachts utilize a gear train operated by a handle to adjust this. A further version is the spinnaker boom cage developed by Elvström. The cage is clamped right round the mast and rides up and down the mast on Teflon bearings.

Wind indicator

On racing yachts a simple wind indicator in the shape of a small burgee at the masthead is no longer sufficient. Instead a wind direction indicator with reference tabs is used. By using the tabs as points of reference, the sailor can compare how the boat sails to windward on one tack as against the other. In addition the angle of the following wind on downwind courses can be accurately assessed. The devices are very strongly built and work with very little friction due to needle bearings. They also work at any angle of heel. Electronic wind indicators are to be found on many large racing yachts (see chapter on electronics on board, page 50).

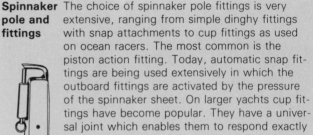

Basic sail handling

Mast and main boom

The rig consists of the mast, boom and rigging. Originally mast and boom were made of wood. Entire tree trunks chosen for their straightness were used, and fir trees were cultivated for their excellent mast-making properties. Incredible skill was shown by the sparmakers in making larger masts for merchant-men and fighting ships which consisted of sections joined together and bound by iron hoops. By the six-teenth century enormous masts were being built for merchantmen con-sisting of three parts: mainmast, top-mast and upper topmast. At the beginning of the twentieth century a great deal of knowledge was gained by the aircraft industry in the use of special glues and in building hollow spars with several laminations. This technical knowledge was applied to the making of much lighter, laminated masts in the 1920s.

The metal mast was introduced in America's Cup racing and the first yacht to use advanced metal technology was *Enterprise* whose mast was made of two thicknesses of duralumin. She proved to be decisively faster than the British yacht, *Shamrock V,* over which she won a convincing victory in 1930. Originally masts were built to be straight and rigid, but in 1936 the German/Brazilian Star Class sailor Pimm von Hutschler and the German Olym-pic Star medalist Bischoff introduced the bendy mast. The advantages of an easily adjusted rig were at once realized. It was seen that the mainsail could be made to take up different shapes for varying wind strengths. In strong winds, it could be flattened by bending the mast forwards in the middle and vice versa in light winds when a fuller sail could be achieved. The importance of matching sail to spar became obvious. Flexible masts must not be confused with per-manently bent masts as used in a number of older racing and Skerry

cruiser classes from about 1925 to 1930. Typical flexible masts can be seen in the photograph above.

Alloy masts and booms are com-monplace nowadays and in the 1972 Olympic games the German organizers even provided the Finn dinghies with alloy masts. Today masts are commonly made from ex-truded alloy and wood is seldom seen in racing. Naturally, masts are flexi-ble, although this is less true of the masts on large offshore yachts. Developments, however, are taking place in this field as well.

Alloy masts and booms are stronger than wooden ones and can be made lighter and smaller in diameter, thus decreasing wind resistance.

The following are the properties of masts of differing shape and thickness:
- Large cross-section and thin wall. This produces a light mast but, as the cross-section is large, the wind resistance is higher.
- Masts with a small cross-section offer less wind resistance but they need thicker walls and are heavier.
- Narrow cross-section and thin wall. Ideal for racing craft, but such masts require staying.
- Pear-shaped section versus round; contrary to what was originally thought the pear-shaped section does not have an advantage aero-dynamically. On the contrary it causes greater turbulence unless it can be allowed to pivot freely.

These Finn dinghies illustrate very clearly what is meant by bendy mast.

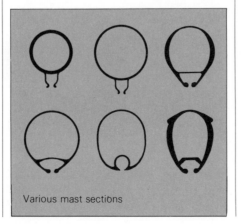
Various mast sections

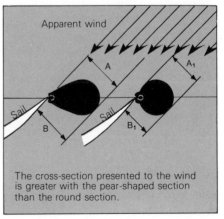
The cross-section presented to the wind is greater with the pear-shaped section than the round section.

In most racing boats the mast is a compromise between lightness and strength. The very light thin mast is less popular today since it needs more attachments, like diamonds and jumpers, to stiffen it than thicker masts and these add to wind resistance. Halyards are led down the inside of the mast to lessen windage in all but the oldest of boats.

As the wind does not strike the boom side on except before the wind, where it does not matter, it does not have to have an aerodynamic section. Booms still have to be as light .as possible in racing boats and a certain amount of flexibility allows the sail shape to be adjusted.

The mast itself is usually set up with a slight fore or aft rake according to how the boat balances. This angle is critical in the balance of a boat as it alters the position of the centre of effort of the sails, thus affecting the way the boat performs. A boat which is heavy on the helm may profit from having her mast raked slightly forward and vice-versa, but this is only part of the vast subject of sail trim and boat tuning.

The mast is stepped on the keel in most boats and there are a number of ways of doing this:

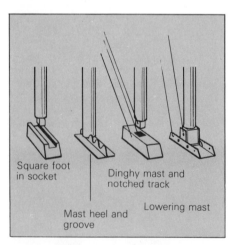

Square foot in socket

Dinghy mast and notched track

Mast heel and groove

Lowering mast

- A square foot, fitting into a corresponding socket in the keelson.
- An adjustable mast step, which locates in any of a number of positions.
- An adjustable step, which is free to move fore and aft, and which is retained by a split pin or a wedge.
- A mast stepped in a tabernacle on

Some advantages and disadvantages of groove and slide luff systems

System	Advantages	Disadvantages
Luff groove	Luff more effective from aerodynamic point of view. The load is more evenly distributed up the mast.	After lowering the sail it is no longer attached to the mast.
Luff slides	The mainsail remains attached to the mast after lowering.	Air flow between mast and sail decreases efficiency by allowing pressure to drop on windward side of sail. Uneven load and danger of slides wearing out or chafing.
Grooved main boom	No space through which air can pass. Even distribution of load. Roller reefing is more even.	Reef pennants must be tied under boom.
Slide track on main boom.	None. Reef pennants may be tied under bolt rope, evening out the strains.	Wind flows through space between boom and sail. Roller reefing can become lumpy and irregular with added disadvantage of wear and tear. Sail may become dirty if slide is lubricated.

This ocean racer has slides on both boom and mast securing the luff and foot of the mainsail.

the cabin roof, or deck, with a bolt through its base so that it can be lowered, for example for passing under bridges. A strong reinforcement under the mast is essential.

Sails are attached to mast and boom by means of bolt ropes or slides. Most boats today have sails with bolt ropes, though some older craft still have slides and track. The groove in the mast or boom takes the bolt rope of the sail, which is a rope sewn into or onto the tabling of the sail. This method of attachment gives better aerodynamic results as there is no gap between the mast and sail for the air to escape to the leeward side of the sail.

Standing and running rigging

Many small singlehanded dinghies (e.g., Finns, Lasers, OKs) have completely unstayed masts which, in some cases, are free to rotate in their mast steps. Usually there is some form of rigging in larger craft unless they are cat- or una-rigged. Standing rigging usually comes in the form of stranded stainless steel wire, 1 × 19, for example, but rod rigging is used on many racing yachts.

Stays support the mast fore and aft (forestay, backstay, and possibly inner forestay or baby stay), whereas the shrouds give lateral support. Running backstays, or preventers, are sometimes rigged which give more support aft and these can be adjusted, if needed, while sailing. The taller the mast the more complicated is the staying arrangement. Spreaders attached to the mast at intervals along its length spread the shrouds wide to increase the angle to the mast and thus improve the amount of support they give. Setting up a mast is a tricky operation involving minute adjustments to the shroud and stay tension, until the mast is absolutely straight along its length, although it may as a whole have a rake aft. Sideways bend is worse than fore and aft bend which may be induced

deliberately to improve the set of the sails. It is not uncommon for ocean racing yachts to have a hydraulically adjustable backstay and, sometimes, even hydraulically adjustable forestay. This enables the rake of the mast to be adjusted. On smaller boats the spreaders may be pivoted so that they automatically take up the load on a flexible mast. Jumpers (which project forward), cross trees and spreaders are all terms used to describe the struts which jut out from the mast to equalize the load. The shrouds and stays themselves are attached to the boat by means of adjustable turnbuckles, otherwise known as rigging screws, or bottlescrews, and these in turn are fixed to strong straps, called chainplates, through-bolted to the hull.

The running rigging is used to hoist the sails and trim them. Various individual names are used and these include the sheets fore and main, the kicking strap (from boom to mast or deck, used to hold the boom down and also called a vang), the topping lift (from the end of the boom to the masthead, used to hold the boom up when the mainsail is lowered) and the various outhauls, halyards and control lines which regulate sail shape and sail tension. Halyards must have little stretch or they will allow the sail to sag once hoisted and for this reason they

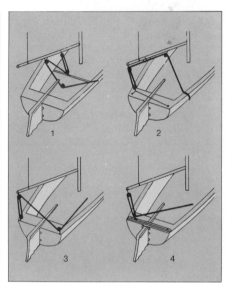

1 Centre mainsheet. 2, 3. and 4 Two types of stern-sheet adjustment with and without traveller.

are usually made from pre-stretched synthetic rope or wire. Wire halyards are hard on the hands so a rope tail is usually spliced into the end to make up just more than half the length.

Mainsheet adjustment

The mainsheet controls the angle of the boom to the centreline of the boat

Types of rigging in different sizes of yacht.

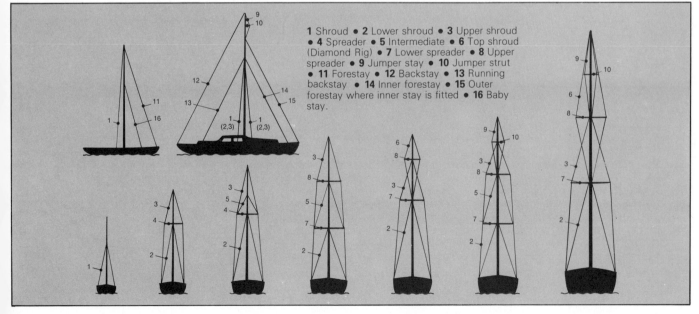

1 Shroud • 2 Lower shroud • 3 Upper shroud • 4 Spreader • 5 Intermediate • 6 Top shroud (Diamond Rig) • 7 Lower spreader • 8 Upper spreader • 9 Jumper stay • 10 Jumper strut • 11 Forestay • 12 Backstay • 13 Running backstay • 14 Inner forestay • 15 Outer forestay where inner stay is fitted • 16 Baby stay.

and so controls the angle between the sail and the wind. The centre mainsheet system is often seen on dinghies. An eye is attached to the boom, near the middle, to which a purchase is attached, the other end of which is attached to a block directly below it on the centreline or to a sliding block running on a traveller athwartships. The latter enables the helmsman to control the boom to a much greater extent. In light airs he may pull the traveller, with the mainsheet purchase attached, up to windward to allow him to trim the

sail along the centreline of the boat, whereas in heavier winds he may decide to spill wind and reduce the power of the sail by letting the traveller go down to leeward. The other system is to have the mainsheet attached to the end of the boom and there are various ways this can be set up. A compromise often seen is where the sheet is led up to a block at the end of the boom, thence to a block in the centre of the boom and finally down to a block immediately below it, as in the centre-mainsheet system. The Laser has such a system.

Advantages of the centre mainsheet

A centre mainsheet and a flexible boom can be made to flatten the sail if the helmsman can pull the centre part of the boom downwards in strong winds. If a traveller is fitted the balance between vertical and horizontal pull can be altered; efficient control of the main-

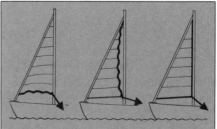

Foot of the sail shivering: move lead block further aft.

Leech fluttering: move lead block further forward.

Correct lead

sail demands constant adjustment to both traveller and sheet. In strong winds the first step that is taken by the helmsman is usually to let the traveller down the track. This will ease the pressure on the main in rather the same way as reefing.

Disadvantages of the aft mainsheet

With a flexible mainboom and strong sheet pull, the boom will bend in a convex manner, giving the sail a bad shape for windward performance. In addition, as the sheet is eased it will no longer pull vertically on the boom and the boom vang will duly partially compensate for this deficiency.

Jib sheet adjustment

The jib, whether genoa, working jib or storm jib, is no less important to the performance of the yacht than the mainsail and must be capable of being trimmed to the same extent. The sheets are attached to the clew of the sail and then led through a fairlead or block on the deck. They are then taken, sometimes by way of other blocks, to a winch or in smaller boats, to a cleat.

The angle at which the jib sheets are taken from the clew affects the set of the sail and is usually adjustable. This is done by making the sheet lead moveable, fore and aft. By fitting a Barberhauler the lead may be adjusted athwartships as well.

If the sail is trimmed correctly it must be just on the point of shaking — but not quite. The adjustment is made while going to windward, when the indications of incorrect trim are clearly seen. Should the foot of the sail begin to shake while the rest is pulling well, then the sheet lead needs moving aft until the shaking stops. This will stretch the foot and open the luff. If, on the other hand,

Diagram showing stern or midships traveller.
1 Aft mainsheet with the traveller at the stern. A vertical pull on the sheet brings the end of the boom down to the corner of the transom.
2 Centre mainsheet running on a midships traveller. With this arrangement it is possible to get a vertical pull on the boom with the boom much further out. Sail is less.

Curvature of the boom with different sheeting systems.

Centre mainsheet: when the sheet is pulled in hard the middle of the boom bends downwards, flattening the sail.

This is an advantage in strong winds when the boat is closehauled. A full sail in a strong wind will result in the yacht being overpowered whilst a flat sail will prevent this. In the former case the yacht will heel and lose speed or be forced to reef.

Aft mainsheet: a hard pull on the sheet will tend to cause the boom to curve upwards, often causing the sail to become fuller than is desirable when closehauled.

Laser-type mainsheet: here the boom is supported along its length and the bend is controlled.

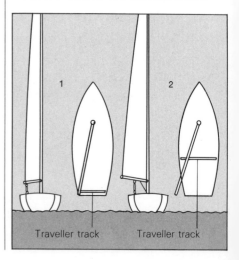

Traveller track   Traveller track

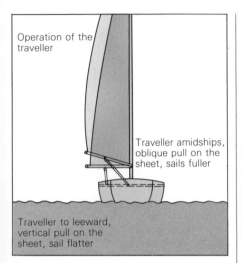

Operation of the traveller

Traveller amidships, oblique pull on the sheet, sails fuller

Traveller to leeward, vertical pull on the sheet, sail flatter

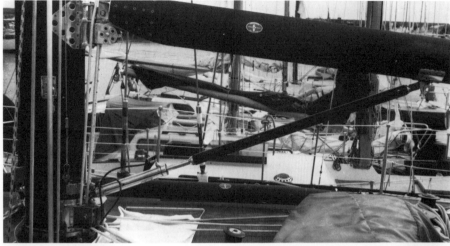

the leech shakes then the lead must be moved forward, resulting in an increased pull on the leech. A very small movement of the foot and leech is unavoidable, of course, but if a persistant shaking occurs you should consult your sailmaker. It is probably time you got a new sail.

The slot between the jib and the main can also be adjusted using a Barberhauler which moves the sheet lead athwartships. Since the flow of air through the slot is instrumental in determining the performance of the mainsail it is *essential,* for top performance, to be able to regulate it. The basic rule is that the slot is opened in strong winds and closed in light ones. A narrow slot in a strong wind will result in considerable turbulence on the lee side of the mainsail, thus upsetting its ability to generate maximum power on that side. In light winds a narrower slot will cause the airflow to accelerate and so improve the mainsail's ability to generate power on the lee side.

Traveller

As has been touched upon earlier, the traveller is considered an essential factor in the control of the mainsail. It consists of a track fitted athwartships along which a block runs on a slide. The slide usually has ball bearings or guide wheels to ease the friction and the position of the block is set by means of lines which can be made fast in jamming cleats.

The traveller can be adjusted as follows. The slide is pushed down to

Simple kicking strap or vang on a Laser dinghy.

ABOVE: Hydraulic vang on an offshore racer.

Adjustable vang worked by means of a wheel.

BELOW: Curved track for the vang on a Star. One-time Tempest World Champion Owe Mares is at the tiller.

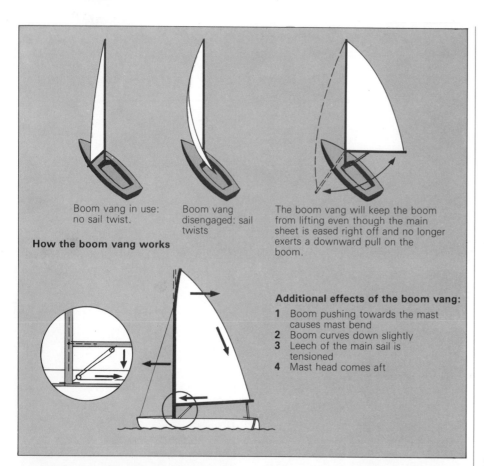

How the boom vang works

Boom vang in use: no sail twist.

Boom vang disengaged: sail twists

The boom vang will keep the boom from lifting even though the main sheet is eased right off and no longer exerts a downward pull on the boom.

Additional effects of the boom vang:

1 Boom pushing towards the mast causes mast bend
2 Boom curves down slightly
3 Leech of the main sail is tensioned
4 Mast head comes aft

leeward, thus causing the load on the mainsheet to be more vertical. This means that the boom can be hauled down, the mainsail becoming flatter and the mast bending more. This is the classic heavy-weather setting.

The traveller is moved more amidships, the opposite can be achieved. In light airs the sail can be fuller. If the track is given a convex shape then this action becomes even more pronounced. A concave track will act rather differently. In this case, if the slide is pushed to leeward some of the load is automatically taken off the leech of the sail and the mast does not bend so much.

Weathering a squall is simply a matter of pushing the traveller to leeward, the sheet remaining fast.

Main boom vang or kicking strap

The boom vang is an essential feature on any boat. The simplest form of vang or kicking strap is a tackle attached at one end to the heel of the mast and the other to the underside of the boom at an angle of about 45°. In large racing yachts rigid steel rods are often used instead of a tackle. They have the added advantage that they will hold up the boom without the need for a topping lift. The struts are either solid, their function being simply to hold the boom down without regulating it, or adjustable by means of a wheel or hydraulic device. Some boats, notably Stars and 6 and 12 Metres, are fitted with a curved track so that the load is taken vertically by the vang and the strain is taken over the whole deck.

The object of the vang is to hold the boom down and decrease the twist in the sail when not required. The boom must also be held down while running to prevent it lifting and causing a Chinese gybe. With a flexible boom, the vang can affect the mast bend considerably, thus affording another weapon in the trimming armoury.

An example of a curved vang track on an IOR racer.

Sails

The sailmaker has become one of the most important figures in the sport for, without good sails, even the best boat will prove slow and fail to win races. Competition among sailmakers is intense. Before we take a look at the cloth used in sailmaking and how it is cut, here is a brief description of sail types.

Square sails and fore-and-aft sails.

There are basically two different kinds of sails, the old square sails and the more modern fore-and-aft sails. The former were, of course, seen on all merchantmen and square riggers and can still be seen on a few training ships. They were only efficient when the wind was coming from abeam or aft. Modern sails allow a vessel to point within twenty degrees of the apparent wind.

Working sails

The standard rig used by boats on the wind, usually consisting of a jib and a mainsail.

Mainsail

The sail is carried on the main mast. It is usually kept on the boom and, whereas smaller jibs are hoisted in stronger winds, the main is merely reefed. Certain single-handed dinghies, like the Finn, have only one sail and this is a main.

Mizzen

The sail at the stern of boats which have two or more masts, carried on the after-most one, which is usually shorter than the main mast. The most common rigs of this type are the yawl and ketch. Both have two masts, a main and a slightly smaller mizzen. If the higher mast is aft the boat is schooner rigged and the after mast becomes the main, and its sail the mainsail.

Headsails

The standard headsails carried on a boat are working jib, genoa, reaching and storm jibs, but a racing boat will carry anything up to a dozen different headsails to suit the conditions. Each can be hoisted in turn up the forestay or headfoil if fitted. The cutter rig consists of the jib, the staysail and possibly a flying jib. Modern racing yachts sometimes set a more up-to-date version of this old rig and it is now called a double-headed rig. The square riggers would carry anything up to four or more jibs as they were vital in allowing the vessel to go about.

Staysails

Staysails are those additional sails which are carried below and in addition to the working sails. They are normally set 'flying', that is not attached to a stay like the jib proper. The staysail schooner rig uses a staysail between the two masts.

Storm sails

In severe winds, only the tiniest sails may be carried and these are made from heavy sail cloth, reinforced at the seams and double or treble stitched. Once the main can be reefed no more it is time to set the trysail.

Spinnaker

A parachute-like sail, mostly brightly coloured, which is supported by a pole to windward and which can be carried downwind and on a reach. There are a number of different types and weights for different points of sailing. The flat star-cut can be carried close to the wind (on a fetch). This is easily recognizable by the star-shaped panels emanating from the centre. Another type commonly used is the tri-radial. This has panels radiating from all three corners while the centre panels are cross-cut. This combination of cuts makes for a good all-round spinnaker.

Spinnaker staysails or slotsails

These are sails which are set, especially by racing yachts, in addition to the spinnaker and can be very effective. Firstly, when sailing with the wind on the quarter, yachts set the standard spinnaker staysail of 110% foot length, that is 10% more than the forestay/mast measurement. If the wind is more astern this sail tends to be blanketed by the mainsail too much and so, instead, a tall, slim staysail with a narrow foot is used. This sail is called a tallboy and is set to windward so as not to interfere with the mainsail. Since the early seventies other sails have been developed for use with the spinnaker and these are set flying in the lee of the mainsail where they can balloon out. They are nicknamed bloopers or big boys. These are similar to spinnakers in weight and cut but come into the category of foresails for measurements purposes. One special point is worth mentioning about bloopers as, contrary to some opinion which believes that a sail ballooning out too far produces instability, the opposite is the case. If a skipper is having difficulty controlling his yacht downwind he will often steady her by flying a blooper as this will counteract the broaching effect of a spinnaker in heavier wind.

Bermuda rig

Today most yachts have tall triangular sails with the luff attached to the mast along its whole length. The foot of the sail is stretched along the boom to extend it. This shape has proved to be best for sailing closehauled. These sails were used in the Bermuda islands before the end of the last century but it was only in the Olympic games of 1920 that the superiority of the Bermuda over the gaff rig was finally recognized. In that year, in Amsterdam, both gaff and Bermuda rig were tried on the R class and the Bermudan came out on top.

Gaff rig

A gaff sail is a rectangular sail with the head attached to a spar called a gaff. It is set with the aid of two halyards. It proved more effective than earlier forms of sail but has now largely been superseded by the Bermuda rig.

Gunter rig

This is essentially a variation on the gaff rig with a steeply angled gaff, almost parallel to the mast. It was named after Edmund Gunter. The rig is useful on small cruising yachts in countries with numerous bridges as these can often be passed under simply by lowering the peak.

Lugsail

A lugsail is very easy to handle and is particularly suitable for small dinghies. It is similar to a gaff sail since its upper edge is attached to a spar. This, however, extends a little way forward of the mast which improves the balance. It is hoisted with one halyard. The sail is loose-footed.

Lateen sails

The lateen rig is found on fishing and commercial craft of the Mediterranean and Indian ocean. A long spar which extends much farther forward than the spar of a lug sail is carried on a short mast. The sail itself is of a triangular cut.

Spritsails

A spritsail is a rectangular sail without boom or gaff, spread only by a diagonal spar called a spirit. This rig is rarely seen nowadays but was once used widely on the Thames (Thames barge) and in East Prussia. A spritsail, though with the addition of a main boom, is used today on the Optimist dinghy.

Sailcloth

Cloth for sails used to be made of flax and cotton until, at the beginning of the fifties, man-made fibres began to appear. Today only man-made fibres are used for sailcloth since they have obvious advantages. These advantages are: higher stress co-efficient, good form stability, high tensile strength, high resistance to moisture, considerable imperviousness to the passage of air, high resistance to abrasion, minimum-surface friction and chemical stability. Today's sailcloth is mainly woven from polyester fibres with different trade names: Dacron in the USA, Trevira and Diolen in Germany, Tergal in France, Terital in Italy, Tetoron in Japan, Lavsan in Russia, Terylene in the United Kingdom. The cloth is made on looms in the usual way but with a very tight weave. Once woven, the cloth undergoes a number of finishing processes. First it is heat-processed to stabilize and shrink it. Then it is treated with fillers, commonly a type of resin, by immersion in a bath of chemicals. This process is aimed at reducing bias stretch and further stabilizing the cloth. It may then be finished by the application of polymers to reduce porosity. Finally, it may be calendered between two rollers which apply heat and pressure. This further straightens the fibres and gives the cloth a smooth, shiny surface. Considerable research has gone into the application of fillers and finishes because, apart from their beneficial properties, they make the cloth stiff and brittle which can be an obvious disadvantage. Sailcoth which has not been filled and/or finished is softer, less slippery to handle and more elastic. The type of cloth chosen for any particular sail depends on the purpose for which the sail is going to be used. Sails for heavy weather, for instance, are made of the softer cloth since hard sails with chemical fillers would be difficult to handle in strong winds and tear more easily. Incidentally, if a sail is allowed to slat for a long period for no good reason (for instance, when a boat is left moored for some time with her sails set), there is a danger that the chemical fillers may break away and the original shape of the

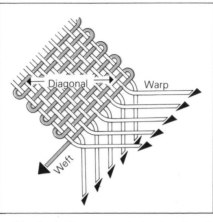

sail be lost. One cannot give hard and fast rules as to which cloth (with or without fillers) is better. Every sailmaker has his own ideas and his own trade secrets on which cloth to use for which purpose.

Every professional sailmaker subjects the cloths in question to precise tests before making use of them. He will, for example, determine the stretch along the warp and weft, and most particularly on the bias, i.e., at an angle of 45° to the threadline. Many sailmakers use special testing devices for these checks and also test the durability and finish of the cloth. Tests are often made before a cloth is used to find out what influence the

chemical reinforcement has had and how good the finish is.

Spinnaker cloths are not made from polyester fibres but from polyamide fibres, generally known as nylon. Nylon is lighter and more elastic than other sailmaking cloths. A certain elasticity is desirable in cloth used for spinnakers since the desired balloon effect is more easily achieved. Though nylon is unsuitable for sails used on the wind, it can be employed for light-weather sails set with the wind on the quarter or abeam, e.g., mizzen staysails, spinnaker staysails and ghosters. One disadvantage of nylon is its sensitivity to ultra-violet rays. The cloth deteriorates seriously after prolonged exposure to the sun.

The cut of the sails

A sail has to have a curvature, or camber. To achieve the desired camber the sailmaker has the following means at his disposal:
● Rounding the edges of the sail.
● Overlapping, widening or tapering the panels.
● Stretching the edges by rope or wire.
● The arrangement of the individual panels.

Mitre-cut genoa

The most usual cut for a sail, especially a mainsail, employs panels of cloth running at right angles to the leech of the sail, i.e., roughly horizontally. This means that the threadline (usually the weft), along which the cloth stretches least, is parallel to the leech. The leech, being unsupported, needs the most support from the cloth. The bias, on the other hand, is along the foot and luff where the sail is supported. The bias stretch along the luff comes in useful when using a Cunningham hole. Another cut often seen in jibs is the mitre cut. Here the panels run at right angles to the foot and leech and meet at a diagonal centre seam. Other cuts sometimes seen in jibs are the radial cut, the spider-web cut and the mini-mitre.

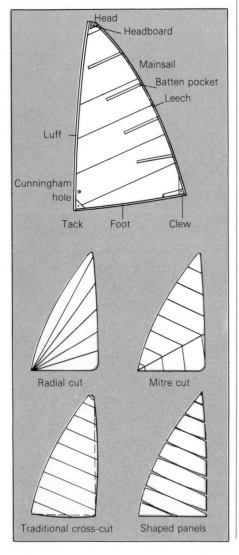

When it comes to building a camber into the sail we must distinguish between two basic methods: the traditional edge-cut method and the modern seam-dilation method.

Traditional edge-cut method - The individual panels are sewn together parallel to each other and the camber is built in by adding excess cloth in a curve along the luff and foot of the sail. This will be pushed into the sail by wind pressure to form the camber. This type of cut is typical of low-priced, mass-produced sails and it is the method of construction still used by many sailmakers. Some sailmakers also employ a refinement of this method by taking a tuck in some of the panels at the luff or leech.

The disadvantage of this method of cutting is that draft formation depends on the bias stretch of the

The deepest camber is in the first third of this foresail.

Regular fullness in a mainsail at its greatest depth in the centre. The flat leading edge of the cut in the first third of the sail is clearly visible.

cloth, which means that it can only really be used with high-stretch materials. It also means that the point of maximum draft in the sail tends to move further aft the stronger the wind becomes, which is precisely what is not wanted. It is difficult to make a good all-round sail by this method.

Modern cutting techniques (seam-dilation method) With modern cutting techniques every individual panel of cloth is shaped according to its own particular position in the finished sail. Its shape is designed according to the amount of fullness, or draft, required at any given point. This type of sailmaking is rather more costly and time-consuming but it is more likely to yield a sail with the ideal camber. To be commercially successful modern cutting techniques must be backed by efficient production methods, in-

volving the use of a large number of templates, and this is frequently beyond the ability of the smaller sailmaker.

Mainsail shape

A mainsail must have an even camber if it is to perform effectively in all wind strengths and on all points of sailing. The point of maximum draft should lie just forward of centre. In very light winds, contrary to the old-fashioned view, the sail should be flatter than under average conditions in order to produce more driving power and it should be allowed to twist, or open. In strong winds, with the mainsheet hard in, the Cunningham cringle tensioned and the mast bent to flatten the luff, the camber should also be flatter than average, but not to the point where all camber is lost. There should be no twist but, on the other hand, neither must the sail be allowed to close up, which means that the upper battens must not curve to windward. The point of maximum draft must not move aft, even in strong winds (this can happen with old, worn-out sails), and it must not move forward in light airs. This can only be achieved by the use of modern, stable sailcloths.

Modern foresail cut

There have been great changes in the cut of foresails in many classes of boat in recent years. The sheeting positions no longer lie right along the edge of the deck but between 7.5° and 12° from the midships line. Jibs have flatter leading edges to present to the wind with the line of maximum draft at a point about 35-50% of the chord from the luff. Such jibs go closer to the wind and are faster in light and moderate breezes.

Sailmakers have a certain amount of freedom when it comes to the size of jibs, since it is not usually the actual sail surface but the triangle formed by forestay, forward side of the mast, and the deck which is measured. A jib's size is usually expressed in relation to the length of the

Sail shape of a 12 Metre yacht seen from astern.

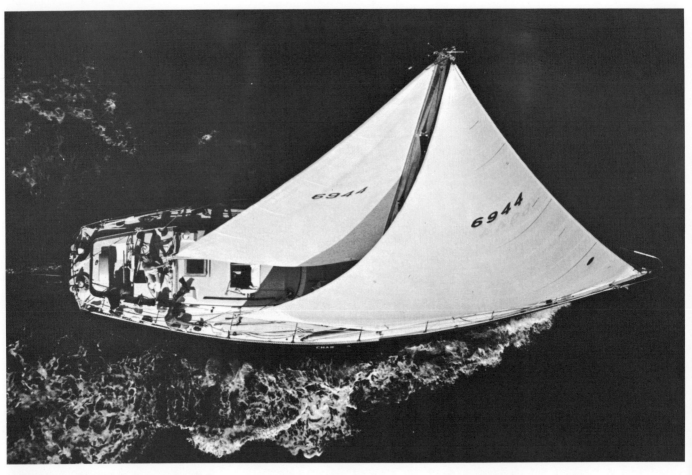

foot given as a percentage of the distance from the forestay to the forward edge of the mast. This is said to represent 100%. A normal jib on a yacht will thus, for instance, measure 110% (the foot of the sail has an extra 10%).

A standard suit of sails would comprise a jib of 110%, a medium-sized genoa of 130%, and a large genoa of 150%.

Under the IOR the largest genoa that may be used in racing without being penalized is 150% of 'J' (forestay to forward edge of mast measurement), i.e., the genoa may be half as long again as the distance from mast to forestay. If a larger sail is used, say one of 160%, the extra 10% which exceeds the IOR rule will entail a penalty when the rating of the yacht is worked out.

A racing yachtsman who wants to make his yacht as fast as possible, outside the IOR rating, will do well to

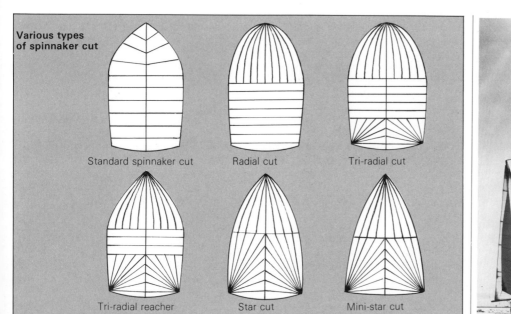

Various types of spinnaker cut

Standard spinnaker cut   Radial cut   Tri-radial cut

Tri-radial reacher   Star cut   Mini-star cut

TOP LEFT: This bird's eye view shows clearly how the genoa overlaps the mainsail.

BOTTOM LEFT: Showing the slot between mainsail and foresail

BOTTOM RIGHT: This photograph taken in 1930 shows the type of spinnaker with vertical panels and straight-cut foot which is now out of date.

Star cut spinnaker.

bear in mind that on most boats a jib with a foot exceeding 180% ceases to provide any additional drive. Bigger is not always better.

Spinnaker cuts

Spinnakers are symmetrical sails (asymmetrical spinnakers are forbidden in almost all class rules). Many experiments have been made, and are still being made, by sailmakers in the cut of spinnakers, and so there are many kinds. A spinnaker needs to have more or less fullness according to the point of sailing. It used to be thought that when sailing dead before the wind the extremely full balloon spinnaker, with its hemispherical cut, was ideal. We now know, however, that on all courses on which it is likely to be set a spinnaker does not derive its drive from the forward push of the wind but by the airflow from the luff to the leech. Hence modern spinnakers are all cut less full. They are also taller and narrower. After spinnaker width was restricted in most classes the surface offered to the wind by a spherical cut would have been less than that offered by a taller cut. With the apparent wind on the beam spinnakers with a particularly flat cut, such as the star-cut and tri-radial types, are used. Today, however, attempts are being made to cut spin-

Ketch carrying a standard-cut spinnaker.

Tri-radial spinnaker.

nakers which are, as far as possible, all-round sails, and present trends incline strongly to star-cut or tri-radial cut.

Spinnakers come in all shapes and sizes. The sail area may be considerably more than the total area of the remaining sails. According to the IOR the two luffs of a spinnaker correspond roughly to the 'I' measurement (= height above deck of highest point to which the largest jib can be twisted), and the breadth may be 180% of 'J' (= the measurement from forestay to forward edge of mast) which corresponds to the length of the spinnaker boom. A spinnaker may therefore be, at its widest, 80% wider than the 'J' figure.

Sail fittings

Sails carried on a mast and boom have a headboard at the top which these days is made of aluminium or plastic. Metal eyes, known as cringles, are pressed into the material at the head, tack, clew and for the Cunningham hole. If the sail is to have slab reefing, which is now coming into wider use, there will also be reef points at the luff and leech and sometimes two rows of reef cringles. The luff and the foot are provided with a bolt rope and batten pockets are sewn in the roach to take the battens, which are made of wood (hickory or ash) or of fibreglass. If the sail concerned is not to be set in a groove in the mast and boom, slides must be attached to the bolt rope.

Jibs also have eyelets or thimbles at the corners. They usually have stainless-steel wires or pre-stretched synthetic ropes in the luffs. The more sophisticated sails, whose shape is capable of considerable adjustment, have what is known as stretchy or vary luffs. This kind of luff consists of a sleeve which fits loosely over the luff wire and is secured only at the top. A downhaul control line is used to stretch the sleeve down over the wire thus tensioning the luff of the sail.

Both jibs and mainsails are frequently fitted with panes of transparent plastic so that the crew can have improved visibility to leeward.

Mainsails of class boats carry their class insignia and sometimes their nationality letter as well as their registration number. These letters and numbers are made of spinnaker cloth and usually sewn on. Generally they are placed higher on the starboard side of the sail than on the port side. The height and breadth of the figures and letters must correspond to IYRU regulations. The rule is that they should be placed in the top third of the sail area so that they remain visible even when the sail is deeply reefed.

Apart from their obvious use in racing, sail insignias and numbers are useful for identifying yachts in case of distress or when it is necessary to establish nationality. Any sailboat may carry sail numbers, which are normally allocated by the national class association. You should not invent your own insignia or numbers, as this can lead to confusion. Sailboats which cruise extensively are advised to have sail numbers on their mainsails, as this aids identification by such organisations as the coastguard, who may have been specially requested to keep watch and report progress.

All fittings on sails should be subject to careful check at regular intervals and especially after the sails have been used in strong winds. Points for particular attention are the headboard and batten pockets. If an external boltrope is fitted, the stitching of this should be checked frequently. A few broken stitches may mean nothing, on the other hand such small beginnings may end up with a sail being badly damaged or rendered useless. Have repairs done immediately the damage becomes apparent. Gear failure usually occurs in bad weather, which is just the time when you least want it to happen.

A sailmaker's loft; working with special templates for making sails from computer data.

National letters used by the main sailing countries:

BA	Belgium	KA	Australia
BA	Bahamas	KC	Canada
BL	Brazil	KH	Hong Kong
CZ	Czechoslovakia	KZ	New Zealand
D	Denmark	L	Finland
E	Spain	M	Hungary
F	France	N	Norway
G	West Germany	OE	Austria
GO	East Germany	PZ	Poland
GR	Greece	S	Sweden
H	Holland	SA	South Africa
I	Italy	SR	USSR
IR	Ireland	US	USA
IS	Israel	Y	Yugoslavia
J	Japan	Z	Switzerland
K	Great Britain		

Telltales
(see following page)

Windward side of genoa

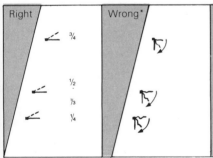

1st thread in 1st quarter 2nd thread rather higher 3rd thread in 3rd quarter acts as indicator for correct positioning of sheeting block. Slight rise correct during gusts.
*Airflow broken, pointing too close.

Leeward side of genoa

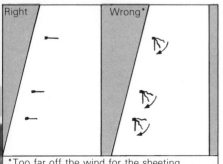

*Too far off the wind for the sheeting.

Summary of sails in use today

1 Working Sails

Name of sail	Description
Mainsail	The most important sail on board, carried on all points of sailing and in all winds (reefed on occasions). It is made from a normal, average-weight sail cloth.
Mizzen	The small sail on the mizzen mast on a ketch or yawl, cut flatter than a mainsail and sheeted in closer, as the apparent wind meets it at a smaller angle due to the airflow off the mainsail. A rather lighter cloth is used than for the mainsail.
Working jib	Once used for the foremost headsail of a craft with two or more headsails, and set to the bowsprit end, often flying, the term is now mostly used for headsails set on the forestay that are smaller than a genoa. Made of the same weight of cloth as a mainsail, cut relatively flat. A jib for light airs has more fullness.
Club jib (Boomed jib)	Jib equipped with a boom, usually sheeted to a traveller, used on many cruising yachts. Useful when short- or singlehanded as the boat may be tacked without the need to tend headsail sheets.
Staysail	A foresail carried with the normal jib on a cutter-rigged boat. The slot between the two sails gives an aerodynamic advantage. If the clew of a staysail is set very high the sail is called a yankee. A lighter weight of cloth is used than for mainsail and normal working jib.
Standard (No 1) genoa	A genoa is a foresail with sufficient length along the foot to allow the clew to be sheeted to a position aft of the mast. Aaprt from the mainsail it is the most important sail carried aboard yachts. Made of strong cloth. With modern sailing techniques there is a tendency to reef the mainsail and keep the overlapping genoa up even in strong winds.
Small (No 2) genoa	About 25 to 35% smaller than a normal genoa; for use in fairly strong winds, usually Force 5 to 7, according to the yacht's design. A sail in between a normal genoa and a jib.
Reefing foresail	Nowadays, foresails which can be reefed are available. They give the cruising sailor the advantage of not having to change foresails under way. He has the advantage of a No 2 genoa (135%) with a jib (110%) all in one sail. In modern racing yachts a foresail which can be reefed is an interesting development because of the limitations of the foresail. Modern foresails cut with parallel panels like a mainsail, and using modern sailcloth, make it possible to reef the sail without distorting it. In reefing the sail is lowered to engage a second tack cringle on the luff, a second sheet passes through a second clew cringle, and the loose cloth at the foot of the sail is tied up with reef pennants as with a mainsail.

Racing sails often have woollen streamers or telltales attached, usually three or more stuck on to the sail near the luff. These telltales give us an idea of the airflow over the surface of the sail and thus indicate whether the foresail and mainsail are correctly trimmed and whether the helmsman is making the best use of the wind. The telltales, both on the windward and leeward side of the sail, should stream horizontally backwards on the sail if it is correctly trimmed. If the telltales on the windward side flutter, this means that the boat is being sailed too close to the wind; the sail is stalling and the weather side is not really making use of the wind any more, i.e., the smooth airflow on the weather side had broken down. Off the wind, a fluttering of the windward telltales usually means that the sail has not been sheeted in hard enough. If the leeward telltales droop, the boat is being sailed too far off the wind which is no longer reaching the lee of the sail so that the airflow over the sail on that side is interrupted. If this happens the sheets must be eased until the lee telltales stream correctly again.

Half-tonner with tri-radial spinnaker.

2 Light weather sails

Light-weather mainsail	Usually made of lighter cloth, and with maximum camber further aft, halfway back along the sail chord. The depth of camber will be varied according to whether the sail is to be used for inland or offshore sailing, and the type of boat. Should only be used in light airs below Force 3 as it will otherwise quickly lose its shape.
Ghoster or drifter	A lightweight jib for use in light airs. Easily deformed and spoilt if carried in strong winds.

3 Storm sails

Trysail	A storm sail which is carried in heavy weather in place of the mainsail. It is loose-footed and cut with the clew lower than the tack. Area usually about one third that of the full mainsail. Owing to its smaller size, the weight of cloth used is not normally heavier than that of the mainsail but of course the relative strength over the smaller area is much greater. Trysails are not battened.
Swedish storm mainsail	Cut much the same size as a storm trysail but designed to be used on the boom. The sail is cut flat with a hollow leech and has no battens. Cloth as for storm trysail.
Storm jib	For use in gales or worse. Cloth is of about standard mainsail weight. The sail is half or less the size of the working jib and cut with the clew high up the sail.

4 Reaching staysails and spinnakers

Genniker, spanker or flasher	All of these names, some of them coined by particular sailmakers, are used to describe a genoa-spinnaker made of heavier material: a cross between a genoa and a spinnaker. It is flat-cut and will set almost as close to the wind as a genoa. Must only be used with a spinnaker boom in racing. Also suitable for use as a heavy-weather spinnaker.
Normal spinnaker	For use when the wind is free, in conditions up to about Force 4. Available either as the standard type, conventionally cut with a central seam, or as a radial spinnaker with the panels of cloth in the upper third of the sail radiating from the head.
Tri-radial spinnaker	A combination of star-cut and radial spinnaker with conventionally cut panels in the centre and panels radiating from the corners. This type of spinnaker, introduced in 1975, may replace the star-cut spinnaker and also has good all-round qualities. A flatter version, more pointed at the head, is the tri-radial reacher.
Storm spinnaker	Large storm spinnakers are made of heavier polyester cloth instead of nylon. In dinghies a storm spinnaker is the same size as a normal spinnaker but it is stronger and sets flatter. In yachts it is smaller than the normal spinnaker.

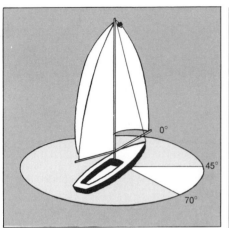

Area in which the star-cut spinnaker is set.

Yacht with tri-radial spinnaker and blooper carried together (left).

Radial-head spinnaker (right).

Light-weather spinnaker	Made of special light nylon cloth.
Star-cut spinnaker	A spinnaker for use with the wind on the beam, with load lines radiating from the corners towards the centre. The wedge-shaped centre sections form a star. This sail can also be used on a close reach when it should take up an evenly rounded shape.
Blooper or big boy	A very full, high-clewed staysail set between the mainsail and the spinnaker and trimmed to leeward, opposite the spinnaker. Made of lightweight cloth. Carried downwind, it helps to steady the boat and provides additional drive. Sometimes the mainsail is reefed to get more wind to the blooper.

Reacher can be recognized by the high-cut clew.

Reacher	A high-clewed genoa with a rather fuller cut. Serves two purposes: 1 As a heavy-weather sail for use with the wind on the quarter when a spinnaker cannot be used. Because of the high clew, which sheets well aft while the mainsheet is eased, the slot between foresail and mainsail remains as nearly parallel as possible. In a genoa with a sheeting point amidships the slackened mainsheet would cause the sail to be backwinded because of the V-shaped gap. IOR yachts often use a reacher together with a staysail. 2 As a light-weather sail. This is its more general use and for this purpose it is made of lighter material.
Jib topsail	A sail similar to a reacher. In a cutter rig it is carried together with a second foresail, a staysail, and this is then described as a double-head rig. It can also be used for cruising yachts and it bridges the gap between genoa and star-cut spinnaker.
Tallboy	A very tall, narrow staysail, especially effective on large boats in light winds. It is always carried with a genoa, a reacher or a spinnaker and is set between it and the mainsail. Its function is to accelerate the airflow on the leeside of the mainsail and thereby add more drive to it.
Spinnaker staysail	General term for a variety of different staysails which are set under the spinnaker instead of the foresail. Many years ago there was only one such sail which came halfway up the mast.
Mizzen staysail	A large staysail set foreward of the mizzen. Usually set flying as a light-weather sail but occasionally made of heavier material and used as a working sail, in which case it is hanked to the mizzenmast forestay.

Sail wardrobe

Today, big yachts usually carry between fifteen and thirty sails which can be changed according to the prevailing conditions. For instance, the standard sail wardrobe of a One-Tonner comprises the following (figures in brackets give the weight of cloth used in ounces per square yard):

1 mainsail with 3 reefs (8.0 oz); 1 No. 1 genoa 150% (4.5 oz); 1 heavy No. 1 genoa, also available as a heavy-weather reacher using a second clew cringle (6.5 oz); 1 No. 2 genoa 130% with maximum luff, can be used on occasion as a staysail if equipped with the necessary fittings (7.25 oz); 1 No. 3 genoa 105% with maximum luff, can be used on occasion with 1 or 2 reefs as a reduced jib (8.0 oz); 1 storm jib (8.0 oz); 1 trysail (8.0 oz); 1 drifter (0.75 oz); double-head combination consisting of 1 jib top or reacher (3.4 oz) and 1 staysail (or tallboy) which can be reefed (3.4 oz); 1 blooper or big boy (0.75 oz); 1 light radial spinnaker (0.5 oz); 1 all-round tri-radial spinnaker (0.75 oz); 1 heavy-weather tri-radial spinnaker (1.5 oz); 1 tri-radial spinnaker for reaching (1.5 oz); 1 star cut (1.5 oz).

Naturally, an ordinary cruising sailor need not go in for so much canvas! He will be well equipped if, for instance, he has the following sails on board his sloop:

Mainsail with two reefs (8.0 oz); 1 105-110% jib (8.0 oz); 1 130-150% genoa (7.25 or 4.5 oz resp.); 1 storm jib (8.0 oz) and 1 all-round tri-radial spinnaker (0.75 oz). He might consider using a 130% reefing genoa instead of a jib and genoa.

There is no reason, of course, why a cruising sailor should not try a blooper or big boy, too, provided he can face the expense of such a sail and has an adequate crew on board to handle it.

Various types of spinnakers used in conjunction with staysails and foresails*

Speed of apparent wind in knots	Angle of incidence of apparent wind								
	45°-60°	60°-75°	75°-90°	90°-105°	105°-120°	120°-135°	135°-150°	150°-165°	165°-180°
0-5	drifter			radial spinnaker, tri-radial spinnaker in larger yachts					
	light genoa or reacher			standard spinnaker; better still, radial spinnaker					
5-12	double-head rig or star-cut with Spi-staysail	tri-radial spinnaker or radial spinnaker							
		with tallboy or light genoa			with tallboy			with blooper (big boy)	
	light genoa or reacher	standard or radial spinnaker						with blooper (big boy)	
12-18	double-head rig	star-cut with tallboy	tri-radial spinnaker (reacher)		tri-radial spinnaker				
					with tallboy or genoa, also double-head rig		with tallboy	perhaps with blooper (big boy)	
	all-round No 1 genoa				radial or tri-radial spinnaker			perhaps with blooper (big boy)	
18-24	double-head rig		star cut	tri-radial spinnaker (reacher) with tallboy		tri-radial spinnaker			
						with tallboy		with blooper (big boy)	
	all-round No 1 genoa					tri-radial spinnaker		perhaps with blooper (big boy)	
24-30	No 2 genoa		mini-star cut or double head rig		star cut	tri-radial spinnaker (reacher)		tri-radial spinnaker with blooper (big boy)	
	No 2 genoa		all-round genoa		tri-radial spinnaker (or small heavyweight spinnaker)			perhaps with blooper (big boy)	
30-36	No 2 genoa			double-head rig		star cut or mini-star cut		mini-star cut or star cut or tri-radial spinnaker (reacher)	
	jib (perhaps storm jib)		No 2 genoa (perhaps jib)		perhaps small heavyweight spinnaker with reefed mainsail				
over 36	jib				double-head rig or No 2 or No 3 genoa		mini-star cut or No 2 genoa boomed-out		
	storm jib				jib		boomed-out jib with reefed mainsail (unless tacking downwind)		

*Applicable particularly to yachts of half-ton to two-ton size. White band for racing yachts, blue band for cruising yachts.

Treatment and care of sails

Sails made of synthetic fibres do not need any special treatment but you should observe a few basic rules.

- A new sail does not have to be stretched like a cotton sail. We recommend, however, that before you let it take a full load you sail for half or three-quarters of an hour with it, with a light wind on the quarter, to let the seams settle.
- Do not reef a new sail until it has been in use for several hours.
- Reefing should be even and no creases should be rolled into the sail because this will spoil its shape. Slab reefing is to be preferred to roller reefing and is regaining popularity because it lessens the wear and tear on the sail. With roller reefing there is always the risk of sail distortion and even of burst seams.
- When lowering a sail do not pull at the leech, but at the luff.
- A sail which is furled for a long time should be protected from sun and weather by a cover.
- Normally, a sail should be stowed in a bag into which its fits easily. When folding it up pull it into a series of accordion-pleated folds and then roll it up. (See p. 44, photographs.) Don't forget to remove the battens! A small foresail can be rolled up on its luff wire. The resulting tube is then simply folded up. Spinnakers should be folded neatly (see series of pictures on right); the larger ones can also be tied in stops ready for use.
- A wet sail can be stowed in a bag for a short period of time. It will normally need to be hung out to dry, however, since even man-made fibres may develop mildew if left folded up wet.
- Cleaning the sails will seldom be

Folding up a small spinnaker after use. One person takes the head, the other the tack and clew. Then the spinnaker is folded lengthwise. Finally it is rolled up into a parcel and put away in its bag.

Folding, or flaking, a sail. After the removal of the battens the sail is folded as shown and finally rolled up, beginning at the luff.

necessary but, if it is, use a mild household detergent. As polyester fibres are resistant to chemicals, stubborn stains can be removed by special chemical cleaning agents (e.g. tri-chloroethylene).

- Do not on any account put sails in the washing machine! Ironing them is also inadvisable.
- It is bad for a jib to be left rolled up on a jib roller for a considerable length of time, especially if it is wet. If you do leave a jib rolled up for long do not be surprised if it begins to stick together after a while. It is better to take it off and stow it. Jib rollers should also be rolled in the other direction after a while to stop the foresail from becoming permanently distorted.
- Loosen the leech line after use, particularly if you are using a jib roller.
- Spinnakers are inclined to tear, or at least get badly chafed, if you use a spinnaker launcher. There is one thing you can do about this: use a Teflon spray on your laun-

ching chute. Check first that there is no roughness anywhere.

- It is fatal to leave damp sails in the trunk of your car and then let the car stand in the sun. This results in a cooking process and no sail is any the better for being well steamed!
- When laying up for winter you should inspect the sails carefully so that any necessary repairs can be made. They should be stored for winter as open and loosely as possible in a clean, airy place. On no account should they be folded up tightly in a bag which can then be squashed up against other objects.
- Take any sails requiring repairs or overhauling to the sailmaker in autumn and winter. Do not wait for spring. Sailmakers have to plan their work time in winter.

Ropes

Ropes and lines have a multitude of applications on board, and they all have different names depending on the use to which they are put. There are halyards and sheets, painters, warps, mooring lines and even hawsers, which would be very thick lines, in excess of 3 in (7.5 cm) circumference. Rope is usually described and sold by circumference (in inches), which is just over three times the diameter.

Ropes may be made of fibres, natural or artificial, or wire. While fibre ropes used to be made of hemp and cotton, today they are almost exclusively made of synthetic fibres (90-95%). The following materials are used:

1 Polyester. This has low stretch properties and is ideal for sheets and halyards.
2 Polyamide (nylon). This has great strength and high stretch properties and is good for anchor lines and warps.
3 Polypropylene. This has medium stretch, is light and buoyant and suitable for heaving and water-skiing lines, as well as fair-weather sheets. It is cheaper than polyester and polyamide.
4 Recently some ropes (first of all sheets and halyards) have been made of Kevlar, a fibre whose resistance to breaking may bring it more to the forefront in the next few years. Kevlar is a trademark of Du Pont. The material has even higher tensile strength than steel rope. Its outstanding qualities mean that thinner, and thus lighter, lines can be used. The high-grade raw material is still very expensive, however.

Formerly, galvanized steel wire was used for wire ropes but today the wire rope used on boats is more usually made of stainless steel or austenite (chrome-nickel base alloys with the addition of molybdenum).

Recently, rods have been used for rigging (especially for the forestay) instead of twisted wire rope. The material used for rod rigging is stainless, cold-drawn steel, often with the addition of cobalt or titanium. The advantages of rod rigging are its aerodynamic qualities and the almost total absence of stretch. Rods for special aerodynamically forestays are also made of aluminium.

In the manufacture of fibre ropes the smallest thread is the filament. If this is thinner than 0.1 mm it is referred to as multifilament; if it is thicker, as monofilament.

A number of filaments are spun or twisted to form a yarn, usually right-handed. A yarn intended for further working is called cable yarn, two or more cable yarns being twisted together to make a strand. This is laid left-handed. The strands are now laid to make the finished rope. Sometimes they are plaited. For laid ropes, three or occasionally four strands are laid together, the lay being right-handed.

With plaited ropes, eight or sixteen or, depending on the manufacturer, sometimes ten, twelve, twenty or thirty-two strands are plaited together to form a tubular rope, with or without a central core. Plaited lines are less resistant to abrasion than laid ropes, but they are softer. They are mainly used for sheets.

Wire rope is made up of individual

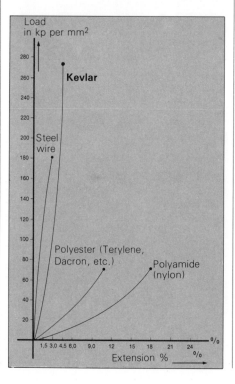

wires. Several of these are twisted round a core wire to form a strand. According to the purpose for which they will be used several strands can now be further twisted round a core strand, usually right-handed, to form a wire rope. A hemp core was used

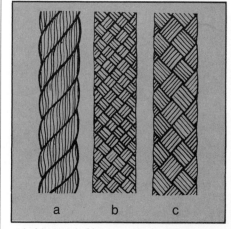

a Laid rope; b Sixteen-strand plaited rope; c Eight-strand plaited rope.

for the old galvanized steel ropes.

For standing rigging it is not unusual to use *strand* because it is so rigid. The most usual construction of strand used for standing rigging is 1 × 19 which means one single strand of 1 + 6 + 12 = 19 wires. At first, six single wires are twisted round one core wire, then another twelve wires are twisted round these.

Halyards, on the other hand, have to be very flexible and for this reason wire *rope,* as distinct from strand, is used. Rope is made by twisting several strands round a central strand; 7 × 19 rope, for example, means that seven strands of nineteen wires each are twisted together.

Wire rope can also have a plastic coating. Plastic coated wire is commonly used for lifelines and topping lifts on racing boats.

Some characteristics of synthetic fibre rope

Synthetic fibre ropes are characterized as a rule by their high breaking strength, their lack of stretch (though where stretch is desirable it can be obtained), their ease of handling, their resistance to chafe, their ability

Construction of wire rope

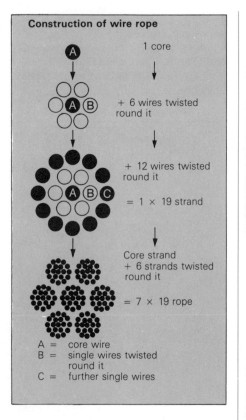

1 core

+ 6 wires twisted round it

+ 12 wires twisted round it

= 1 × 19 strand

Core strand + 6 strands twisted round it

= 7 × 19 rope

A = core wire
B = single wires twisted round it
C = further single wires

to retain the original colour and withstand the effects of seawater. The polyethylenes and polypropylenes are more brittle, however, and do not handle so well. They can be very uncomfortable on the hands once they are frayed. Synthetic fibre rope is very resistant to breaking but, when it does break, it does so without warning. Thus, for instance, a very long and elastic polyamide towing line may at first stretch quite happily. It may, however, break quite suddenly and, if it does, it will rebound with considerable impact. If it hits someone the injury could be fatal. Synthetic lines do not need any particular kind of care but they should not come into contact with chemicals (solvents, thinners, acids, alkaline solutions), especially nylon. Avoid exposing them to the direct rays of the sun for a long period. Polypropylene, in particular, is sensitive to ultra-violet rays. On the other hand it does them no harm to be put away wet occasionally. It is worth keeping in mind that in synthetic fibre ropes knots cannot be tightened so well.

Eye splices in three-strand line

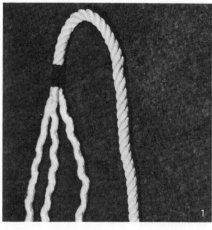

With modern artificial-fibre ropes, it is best to tape the rope as shown before unravelling the separate strands. At least twelve times the diameter of the rope should be unravelled.

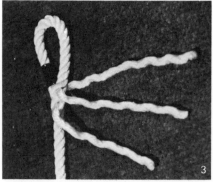

Insert the two top strands under the strands of the standing part over which they were lying.

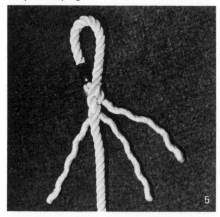

Each strand should then be taken over one, under way, as far as possible parallel with the line of the standing part . . .

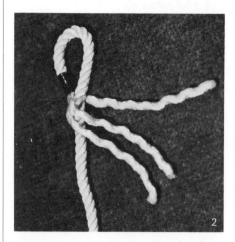

Lay two strands over, one strand under so as to give a loop of the required size.

Turn the rope over and repeat the process with the third strand.

. . . until at least three insertions have been made with each strand.

Anchors and anchor gear

The anchor is one of the most ancient pieces of equipment in the history of the sea. Over the centuries it has developed from a primitive stone anchor to the modern lightweight anchor in various forms. There are a great many different kinds of anchor available today. We will only briefly list the types of anchors used in sailing as a sport, however.

Basically, we have to distinguish between two types of anchor: firstly, the type in which weight is the primary consideration (i.e., the traditional fisherman's anchor) and secondly, the type in which the design of the actual holding surface is the first consideration (i.e., the more modern patent or lightweight anchors).

A fisherman's anchor with folding stock (and recently with collapsible flukes too) can still be a most useful piece of equipment. Its advantage is that it will hold well on stony or weedy sea bottoms. Its disadvantage is that it must be fairly heavy since it can only dig itself in with one fluke, which means the holding surface area is relatively small. One fluke is left sticking up from the sea bed with the risk of being fouled by the anchor chain or rode, or even piercing your own or another boat's hull, should the boat ground on a falling tide. Also, you cannot be sure of your final position, as the anchor often has to

be dragged some way before holding.

The patent anchors most used in yachting are the plow (CQR type) anchor, the Danforth-type anchor, and the recently developed Bruce anchor. Their advantages are that they have flukes suitably angled for holding, and a tendency to bury themselves deeper when pulled along. Their large flukes give more holding power than those of the fisherman's anchor. They have no parts pointing upwards which might foul the anchor rode and they can be dropped immediately without previous preparation.

Dinghy sailors generally use small folding grapnels or umbrella anchors, which can be folded up and neatly stowed away. In principle, there should be at least two anchors on board cruising yachts, of different kinds. Most studies suggest that, if

only two are carried, one should be a Fisherman, and the other a plow or Danforth type. The advantage of the Danforth is that it folds flatter than a plow, which is often a determining factor in yachts with shallow deck lockers for the anchor. The CQR and Bruce are of more awkward shape but are generally considered more efficient for a given weight.

A common fault of many sailors is to use too small an anchor. To assist in the correct choice of anchor size, and size of cable and hawser, we give here a table which covers sailboats from 5 to 45 tons.

Racing yachts have to meet special requirements for anchors and ground tackle and, if you are going to race, it is best to consult the safety regulations put out by the relevant national or international yachting federations.

Table of recommended anchor weights and anchor rode sizes

Tonnage displacement	Fisherman (stock type) anchor	C.Q.R. (plough type) anchor	Danforth anchor	Chain (short link)	Nylon rope
tons	lb	lb	lb	dia., in	dirc., in
Up to 5	40 (18 kg)	35 (16 kg)	30 (14 kg)	1/4 (6 mm)	1½ (38 mm)
5-8	45 (20 kg)	35	30	5/16 (8 mm)	1¾ (45 mm)
8-10	50 (22 kg)	35	30	3/8 (10 mm)	2 (52 mm)
10-15	60 (27 kg)	35	30	3/8	2¼ (58 mm)
15-20	70 (32 kg)	45 (20 kg)	40 (18 kg)	7/16 (12 mm)	2½
20-28	80 (36 kg)	45	40	7/16	2½ (65 mm)
28-35	100 (45 kg)	45	40	1/2 (13 mm)	2½
35-40	120 (54 kg)	60 (27 kg)	65 (30 kg)	1/2	2¾ (70 mm)
40-45	130 (60 kg)	60	65	9/16 (15 mm)	2¾

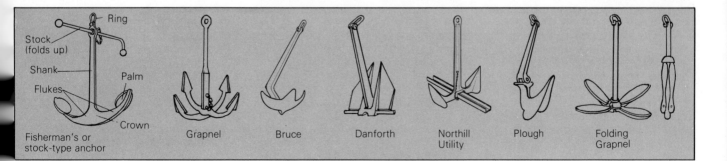

Fisherman's or stock-type anchor (Ring, Stock (folds up), Shank, Flukes, Palm, Crown) — Grapnel — Bruce — Danforth — Northill Utility — Plough — Folding Grapnel

The anchor and rode and everything that goes with it, i.e., anchor weight and buoy, are called ground tackle.

Every ocean-going yacht must be equipped with an anchor. See the table on p. 47 for recommended lengths and diameter of chain. A rope line (nowadays made of synthetic fibres) is often used for an anchor rode on smaller boats. It is not as heavy as chain but not as effective either (see chapter on Anchoring, p. 144). A compromise is to have two-five fathoms of chain attached to the anchor rode.

In order to show how much chain has been paid out it should be marked with coloured paint every five fathoms. Similar marks can be made

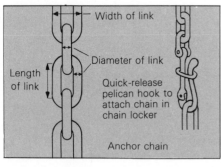

Width of link
Diameter of link
Length of link
Quick-release pelican hook to attach chain in chain locker
Anchor chain

on a rope anchor or sewn on. Small anchors and chains of small diameter can be worked by hand. With anchors over 50 lb (25 kg) and chain over 5/16 in (8 mm), an anchor winch is used to haul in or pay out the anchor. The individual links in the chain are so arranged that they will fit the chain wildcat on the winch.

Whether to use chain or rope is often discussed. Chain is much heavier and must be used in conjunction with a windlass. On the other hand it has more spring, and less scope will be necessary for comfort if you anchor in rough water and the boat tends to snatch at the rope. If you cruise extensively in a heavy boat, you might compromise with a chain on the main anchor and a strong synthetic rope with a couple of fathoms of chain on the kedge anchor. Chain is not necessarily stronger than rope, but wet rope can be difficult to handle on a bucking foredeck even with the help of a windlass.

Some technical terms:

Chain length
Chain over 1.25cm (½ in) thick is delivered in lengths of 15 fathoms. The individual lengths of chain are connected by rivetted links or special chain shackles.

Chain locker
The compartment on board where the anchor chain is stowed. The bitter end of the chain (the end away from the anchor) should never be made fast with a shackle in the chain locker. Shackles can rust and become immovable and you may need to let the chain go in an emergency. It should be secured by a lashing or a quick-release pelican hook.

Hawse pipe
The tube between the opening on deck (which can be closed) and the chain locker through which the chain runs.

Pawl
Catch on the wildcat, or gipsy, of a winch or on the stemhead, which holds the chain link by link as it is hauled in.

Anchor ball
A black signal ball which must be set in the rigging, when anchoring in daylight, instead of the white anchor light.

Miscellaneous fittings and equipment

Ventilators

Ventilators are important pieces of equipment on yachts, helping to combat rot in wooden boats and condensation in plastic or steel boats. In addition, the engine space and the bilges, where fuel vapour or gas might collect, must be well ventilated. A ventilator should fulfil the following requirements:
- It should provide sufficient ventilation in normal weather conditions.
- It should make at least a certain amount of ventilation possible even in bad weather.
- It should be safe and waterproof in very bad weather.

The commonest types of ventilators:

Venturi ventilator: this consists of a venturi tube mounted on a pipe. Air passing through the venturi causes air to be sucked up from below.

Cowl ventilators: today these are mostly made of soft plastic, are strong, and are considered the most efficient type. The head of the ventilator can be turned into or away from the wind. Thus it works either by suction or by pressure. The head is often removable and the opening is then sealed by a special cap.

Mushroom ventilator: probably the simplest type of ventilator with a head which can be rotated to open it up. When opened wide there is a danger that someone may tread on it and break the spindle, so be careful! This ventilator should not be installed in places where it can be snagged by sheets or lines and torn away.

Tannoy ventilator: a flat ventilator made of plastic and stainless steel, sometimes with a plastic cover. It works on the venturi ventilator principle and can be sealed off and remain waterproof.

Dorade ventilator: here the ventilator is mounted on a box. Air streams over an internal baffle, while any water which has got in flows out of the scuppers.

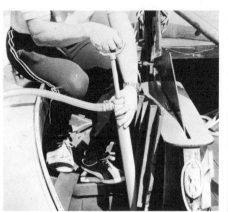
Bilge pump

Bilge pumps

On any yacht water gets into the bilges from rain, waves washing over the deck, small leaks, or through the stern gland of the propeller shaft. There must be at least two bilge pumps on board. Diaphragm pumps, plunger pumps and rotary pumps (seldom used on yachts) are the types available. A plunger pump consists of a cylinder with a plunger sliding up and down inside it to extract the water. A diaphragm pump consists of a housing — usually circular — with a diaphragm made of a material like neoprene inside it. There are single acting versions of this pump where water is drawn out on every other stroke of a lever, and double acting versions which work on every stroke. Diaphragm pumps suitable for yachts can pump between eight and twenty gallons (thirty-five and hundred litres) of water a minute. Bilge pumps can be worked by the engine, by an electric motor, or by hand. If a yacht is fitted with a motor-driven or engine-driven pump there must also be a hand-operated bilge pump on board in case the motor breaks down. As one does not want foreign bodies sucked in and stopping up the pump, a strainer should be fitted to every pump intake.

Points to remember Before buying an electric bilge pump get all the information you can about its performance, quality and method of fitting. Some pumps, for example, must not be run dry, while others can run dry

for a short time without suffering damage. Many pumps will only begin to work when they are submerged completely.

If the galley pump has to deal with salt water as well as fresh water make sure that it is made of material completely resistant to sea water otherwise it may one day fall apart!

Marine heads

The IOR guidelines lay down that yachts in categories 1 and 2 (on open-sea passages or on longer coastal passages) must be fitted with a built-in marine head. Similar built-in heads are prescribed for yachts which come into categories 3 and 4 (engaged in coastal passages and short passages in sheltered waters near land), but these may be substituted by a suitable container fitted firmly in place.

Heads are either of the flushing kind with a pump or chemical toilets which do not require special installation.

Where a flushing head is fitted make sure the crew knows exactly how to operate it. This will prevent embarrassing overflows or a broken pump. Make sure, too, that everyone understands how to turn the sea cocks off so that this can be done when the boat is underway.

Conventional head with pump fitted in the forepeak.

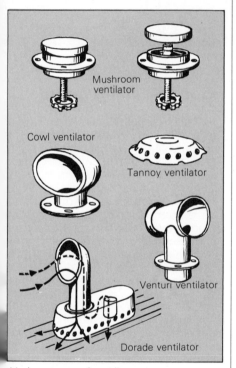
Various types of ventilator

Small butterfly ventilator: suitable installation for galley and head. Sometimes called bulkhead ventilation.

NB Do not forget to open the forehatch at any suitable opportunity, e.g., when in harbour. It is the best way to give the boat a really good airing.

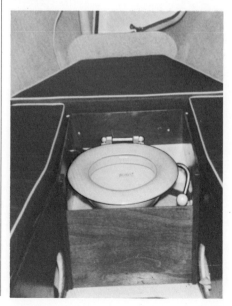

A flushing head needs two skin fittings, one for the outlet and the other, the smaller, for the water inlet. Installation of such heads must be carefully carried out for reasons of safety and no mistakes must be made in using them or water might get into the yacht — in an extreme case it might even sink it.

Galley fittings

The IOR regulations lay down that every sea-going yacht must also have some kind of galley arrangement.

There are various kinds of stoves available, working on different fuels. Kerosine stoves with two rings are very popular. The fuel they use is rich in energy and there is less chance of explosions. Alcohol stoves are also popular but alcohol does not generate as much heat as other fuels.

Gasoline stoves are not to be recommended because of the danger of explosion. Gas stoves operated on bottled propane or butane are also widely used, although butane is not allowed in USA. Compressed natural gas is becoming widely available in USA; the advantage is that it is lighter than air, hence safer. Cylinders of these gases can be bought in most harbours. As propane gas is heavier than air, however, and

Modern offshore racing yachts have instrument panels like this.

quite a small amount can produce an explosive gas and air mixture, safety precautions must be carefully observed. The gas cylinders must be kept either on deck or in a gas-tight locker with a vent to the outside. The rings must be fitted with safety burners and the supply tubes or connections made of copper.

A galley also needs a sink. If it is placed high enough the water may drain out by gravity. If the height available is not adequate then the water can be pumped out by means of a diaphragm pump or can be siphoned off into a holding tank for dirty water and then pumped overboard.

Water tanks are also required. For reasons of stability these are often fitted near the keel and water must be pumped up out of them. When there is no water tank fitted to a small yacht water must be carried in suitable containers. The minimum daily requirement of water per person (not counting water for washing and washing-up) is 4-5 pints (2.5-3 litres).

Electronics on board

As well as a depth sounder and radio direction finder most large modern racing yachts have a number of other pieces of electronic equipment. Electronics feature in the design of many instruments which give all kinds of numerical information. You will find more instruments in a racing yacht than on an ordinary car dashboard and the instruments on larger offshore yachts, which may have two cockpits, are installed in duplicate or triplicate. Sometimes there are additional repeater sets of instruments below for the navigator.

While small boats can be steered perfectly well with the aid of a wind direction indicator, electronic instruments make things much easier on large yachts. For instance, with the help of data about wind direction, wind speed, and boat speed gathered during test sails, the crew can draw up sail selection charts. During a race, these sail selection charts are then referred to and give information on which combination of sails is most effective under the given conditions.

The following individual instruments are used:

Speedometer: for measuring boat speed. On large yachts a low speed scale is added to the speedometer to show very small variations in speed. A distance measuring device called a log may be fitted to the speedometer to record nautical miles sailed.

A very neat galley lay-out on a Moody 40, a substantial cruising yacht.

Anemometer: for measuring wind speed in knots. Especially important for choosing the right sails. Used in conjunction with compass and speedometer, the instrument also enables you to determine the direction and strength of the true wind.

1 anemometer. 2 apparent wind indicator. 3 close-hauled wind indicator. 4 depth sounder.

Wind direction indicator: this instrument, provided with a 360° scale, shows the angle from which the wind is coming. An expanded scale is used to supplement this and give information on close-hauled wind direction.

Sailing performance computer: computers of this description, which store and process data and indicate the correct course to sail to windward to give the best performance, do exist, but are forbidden for racing.

Relative speed indicator: such instruments which register changes in boat speed have recently become available even for dinghies. Although forbidden for racing they can be very useful for keeping a check during practice and tuning. The transducer is fixed temporarily to the inside of the boat's hull.

Depth sounders and direction finders, as well as radio equipment, are discussed in other chapters.

It is important to remember that all electronic gear adds appreciably to the drain on your batteries, and you must calculate accurately your consumption so that you carry sufficient battery capacity for all your needs. It is common for larger yachts to have three banks of batteries, one for the electronics, one for the lights and domestic use and the third for starting the motor.

Modern yacht rigs and their characteristics

There are various types of rig according to the way in which mainsails and foresails are combined, and the number and arrangement of the masts.

The simplest single-masted rig is called a cat or una rig and consists of a mainsail alone. Boats with this rig are mostly small single-handers, for instance Finn dinghies, Lasers, Contenders and A class catamarans. Occasionally you come across small cat-rigged cruising yachts. If a foresail is added to the mainsail we have a sloop rig, as found in the majority of sailing yachts today. If the rig employs two foresails (a jib and a staysail), we describe it as cutter rig, a very interesting rig for cruising sailors, since it offers a number of possible sail combinations. For example, if the wind increases it is easy to reduce the sail area by handing either the jib or the staysail. The old cutter rig, which set three foresails (jib, staysail and flying jib) as well as a gaff topsail, is hardly seen today and certainly not used for racing.

On large yachts a rig with two masts is more practicable, particularly for cruising, because the individual sails are smaller and the sails are thus easier to handle. The description of these two-masted rigs depends upon the size and position of the aft mast. If this mast — the mizzen mast — is a small one, people often call the boat a one-and-a-half-master, but the correct term for most two-masted rigs is either ketch or yawl. In the yawl rig the mizzen mast is relatively small and is stepped aft of the rudder post. In the ketch rig the mizzen mast is rather larger than in a yawl and is stepped forward of the rudder post. A

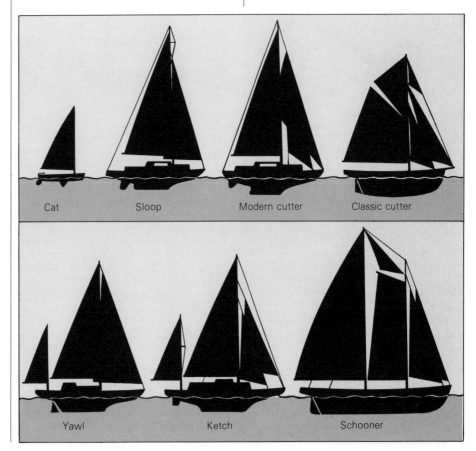

Cat   Sloop   Modern cutter   Classic cutter

Yawl   Ketch   Schooner

A yawl (RIGHT)

BOTTOM RIGHT: Ketch with furled mizzen sail

The double spar called a wishbone in a wishbone ketch rig. This type of rig is seen only occasionally nowadays.

special kind of ketch was developed in 1933 and has a variation of the gaff rig with a double spar, called a wishbone. The broadest part of the mainsail, which looks like a jib set upside-down, lies, in this case, about two thirds of the way up the mast, along the wishbone. This rig is not often used nowadays but is being revived.

If the after mast is taller than the foremast, when it is called the mainmast, the rig is described as a schooner rig. The schooner rig, which can also have three masts or more, is seldom seen in modern yachting, because the large mainsail is difficult to handle. Also, though the rig has plenty of sail area, and performs well off the wind, it is not very efficient to windward. The ketch and yawl rigs, on the other hand, are favourites among cruising sailors. So far as performance is concerned a single-mast rig may be better than one with two masts, but the two-masted rig has other disadvantages which must be taken into account.

Breaking down the sail area into more sails makes them easier to handle and the low centre of gravity makes for good stability. Besides, in a freshening breeze, sail area can be shortened quickly and simply by handing the individual sails, as in the ketch with the furled mizzen shown above.

Classes of boat

As distinct from most cruising yachts, which are built without reference to any class rules, racing boats are divided into different classes. There are, basically, two types of classification: one by class rules and the other by recognition either by the national sailing association of the country (national classes) or the International Yacht Racing Union (international classes).

Some class rules are very strict, others are more freely interpreted. Some classes are designed so that skill in sailing plays the most important part in racing by stipulating that none of the specifications for the boat may be altered. An example is the Laser dinghy. In other classes the measurements may be more freely in-terpreted, even to the extent of making the hull shape optional, as in the International 14. The sails, too, within the total permitted sail area, may have any desired shape. Competition here begins with the buyer's pocket, on the drawing board and in the builder's yard. To some extent the crew is of secondary importance.

Classification by class rules

1 One-design classes

The most exciting racing is to be had in one-designs since, all boats being identical, the outcome of events depends almost entirely on the skill of helmsman and crew. All measurements, materials and fittings have to comply exactly with the class

The Laser dinghy is a strict one-design.

rules. At the moment, the strictest one-design class is the Laser, where absolutely everything is rigidly controlled by the rules and nothing may be changed afterwards. There are, however, one-design classes in which a certain amount of tolerance is permitted and there may be differences in the quality of individual boats and, therefore, in their performance. Classes in which this trend may be seen are, among others, Soling, Tempest and 407.

2 Restricted classes

Any similarity with one-design classes is restricted to a general sameness in the size and appearance of the boats. Measurements, minimum weight, hull shape and sail area are generally laid down, sometimes between narrow tolerances, but many other details are left to the discretion of the designer and owner. Naturally some classes are more strictly governed or more restricted than others, but the general effect is to encourage continuous development, a thing not possible in the one-design proper. The kind of things often left optional are the choice of materials, size of cockpit, and position of mast, etc. Among this group can be found the Flying Dut-chman and Star.

Solings are a one-design class. They are also an international class and an Olympic class.

3 Open classes

This kind of class allows a much freer development of design, especially with regard to the hull and rig, and thus encourages experimentation. The boats are not limited by strict measurements and it is possible to vary the length, beam, weight and sail area subject to the class rules. The permissible variations in the measurements are evened out between the boats by a formula. Level-rated boats compete directly with each other and handicap does not enter into the racing.

4 Offshore classes

Up till 1970 the rules for racing off-shore were set down by individual associations like the Royal Ocean Racing Club and the Cruising Club of America. Now the International Offshore Rule is universally accepted. Boats are built to compete within the formulae and designers use their skill to take advantage of various provisions of the rules.

Yachts are divided into eight classes in all. The rating of each yacht (which is, in fact, her handicap) is expressed in feet. The figure, which is worked out on the basis of a complicated formula composed of many individual measurements taken on the hull, has seldom any relation to any actual hull measurement.

Class	IOR Rating Mk III
Class I	33 to 70 ft
Class II	29 to 32.9 ft
Class III	25.5 to 28.9 ft
Class IV	23 to 25.4 ft
Class V	21 to 22.9 ft
Class VI	19.5 to 20.9 ft
Class VII	17.5 to 19.4 ft
Class VIII	16 to 17.4 ft

Within these IOR classes, there are level rating or ton cup classes, the expression having nothing to do with the weight of the yacht. Level rating classes are designed to a prescribed

An American One Tonner.

IOR rating so that those with the same handicap can race directly against each other. This makes them a particularly attractive proposition. At the moment the following level rating classes exist:

Class	Maximum IOR rating
Two Ton	32 ft
One Ton	27.5 ft
Three-quarter Ton	24.5 ft
Half Ton	22.0 ft
Quarter Ton	18.5 ft
Mini Ton	16.5 ft

Classification by recognition

1 National classes

These classes are usually found in one country only, having been recognized by the official sailing associations in the particular country. A number of national classes have spread worldwide but have failed to gain international status generally because the competition for such rating is very high.

Thistles racing on the east coast of the USA. This is a typical US national class, with about 3700 boats

The international OK single-hander.

¾-ton yachts rounding the upwind buoys, showing the broad beam and distinctive stern common in current design

This Sydney Harbour 18-foot skiff is a popular Australian class

2 International classes

These are classes which have satisfied the strict requirements of the IYRU and have been recognized as suitable for international competition. The following have international status at present: A-Cats, Contender, Dragon, Enterprise, Finn, Fireball, Flying Dutchman, Flying Junior, 505, Laser, Moth, OK, Optimist, Soling, Star, Tempest, Tornado catamaran, Vaurien, 470, 420.

3 Olympic classes

These are widely regarded as the top racing classes and are invariably chosen by the IYRU from the international classes. At present (from 1980) we have the following Olympic classes: Finn (single-hander), 470 (2-man dinghy), Flying Dutchman (2-man dinghy), Tornado (2-man catamaran), Star (2-man keelboat), and Soling (3-man keelboat).

It is interesting to note that only one of these boats was designed before 1950, the Star. The enormous progress in yacht design made after the war has made it almost impossible for the older classes to survive. In a sense the Soling is not a true keelboat, being more of a large planing dinghy with a ballasted fin keel. So far, ocean racing has not been chosen as an Olympic discipline, though the idea has many supporters.

4 Local classes

These are classes of boat which have been developed to meet the special conditions and requirements of certain sailing areas and generally have not spread beyond those narrow confines. They are not recognized nationally or internationally. Here are a few examples of what was once a relatively large and important part of the sailing scene; Great Britain: Essex One Design, X Class, Daring, BSC 14; USA: Cape Cod Knockabout, Dough dish H-class; Australia: 18ft Skiff.

Marlinspike seamanship and maintenance

Knots and splices

You will need to know how to tie a number of seamen's knots to keep the end of a line from slipping out through a fairlead, to join two lines, or to make a line fast to an object. The basic requirement of a good knot is that it should hold well but at the same time be easy to undo.

What is the difference between a knot, a bend and a hitch? While 'knot' is a general term for all rope joining and tying, including bends and hitches, a 'bend', to quote Cyrus Day, is 'a knot used to tie the ends of two free lines together' while a 'hitch' is 'a knot used to secure a line to a spar, ring, post or the like'.

There are countless ways of making functional and decorative knots, but a spare-time sailor will find that the relatively small number illustrated and described in the following table will meet all ordinary situations.

The king of them all is the simple bowline, which can be used in many different situations. You can use it, for instance, to make a line fast to a bollard, ring or crossbeam; you can tie a line around your chest with it or make yourself a rope step. You should practise the bowline until you can do it in your sleep because it is one of the most useful knots. Other knots which should be practised are: figure eight, reef knot, rolling hitch, single and double sheet bend, round turn and two half hitches, clove hitch, and slippery hitch. Simple

Name	Appearance	Effect in use	Practical application	Common use
Figure-eight knot		Stops line running out through a fairlead		At the end of a sheet
Reef knot		Joins two ropes of equal thickness		Tying reef points
Single-sheet bend		Joins ropes of different sizes		Making fast a heaving line to a mooring line
Double-sheet bend		Joins ropes of different sizes — used if single-sheet bend looks inadequate		Extending a hawser
Round turn and two half hitches		Making a rope fast to a post or spar		Securing a painter to a stanchion, ring or post

Knot	Description	Use
Half hitch	Often used with other knots for additional security or to make sure the knot does not pull together too tightly	With a round turn or fisherman's bend — usually two are tied
Clove hitch	Used on spars or poles where no sideways strain is to be applied	Mooring dinghy to bollard. Attaching fenders to stanchion or rail
Anchor or fisherman's bend	Making a rope fast to rings, used with two half hitches for additional security	Attaching an anchor line to the ring of an anchor
Single bowline	Making an eye in the end of a rope which cannot come undone	Making a mooring line fast to a post. Fastening a safety line round one's chest
Double bowline	Making an eye in a double thickness of rope; will not pull tightly together like the single bowline	Making an improvised rope ladder. Improvising a bosun's chair
Rolling hitch	Attaching one line to another when force is to be applied to one side of the hitch (contrast clove hitch)	Attaching a painter to a hawser
Slippery hitch	Makes it possible to undo a knot easily with a tug. In its simplest form a half hitch with a loop. Generally used to finish off other knots as it will make them easier to undo	Usually used on second of two half hitches
Jamming turn	Final hitch overturned when belaying a line on a cleat. Apt to jam if not enough turns have been put on to the cleat first	Belaying a halyard. Belaying a mooring warp to a cleat. Not recommended as it can jam if subjected to considerable strain

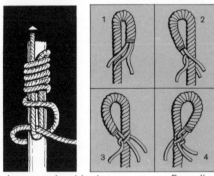

Lazy man's whipping   *Eyesplice*

splicing is also a useful art to master.

The ends of a line must be whipped so that they do not fray. Whipping is very easy to make. All you need is thin twine and a knife. The strongest whipping is made by using a sailmaker's needle and passing the twine through the lay of the rope. The ends of a synthetic line can be fused together by applying a flame but this does not completely avoid the need for a proper whipping.

Two ropes may be joined together by a short or long splice in which the individual strands are interwoven. This is stronger and more permanent than a knot and less obtrusive. A short splice being somewhat bulky tends to prevent the rope from running freely through blocks. In the eye splice the rope is spliced back on to itself to form an eye, possibly with a thimble in it. It is definitely a useful one to know.

Always remember that tying a knot in a line reduces its strength by an amount which varies according to the type of knot used. A reef knot weakens a rope the most (probably up to 40%) and an anchor bend the least (say about 25%). If it is important for a line to retain its maximum strength when made into an eye or joined to another line of equal size, then it should be spliced. This weakens the rope by only 5%.

For the best result a splice should have four tucks and, ideally, five or even six, especially if it is a short splice, joining two lines together.

Handling the tender

A tender is necessary if you have any boat which must be kept some distance from the shore. You can go between the yacht, lying at anchor or to a mooring, and the shore. A tender can also be used for running out warps and anchors. Modern tenders are made of fibreglass or are in-

Stowing a line: first coil it in loops then make several round turns, finally make a loop and slip it over the top.

flatable; the rigid ones have to be as small and as light as possible so that they can be stored aboard large yachts (keel up). Fibreglass or wooden tenders usually have a protective fender around them so as not to scratch the topsides of a yacht when they are lying alongside her. This is generally made of plastic, rubber or rope. Tenders for smaller yachts generally take up to three people and you have to be careful getting into them because they are relatively unstable. You should not stand up unnecessarily. The first part of the boat to be occupied when people are getting into a tender is the centre thwart on which the oarsman will sit. Then passengers should get alternately into the bows and stern of the boat. A pair of oars in oarlocks is used to propel the boat. Rowing should ideally be performed with short strokes and as much of the work as possible done with the back, but this is often impossible in practice owing to lack of space. The oar blades should not dip too deeply into the water or the oars may jump out of the oarlocks.

We consider it unnecessary to feather the oars, a technique used by racing oarsmen, which is sometimes recommended for rowing tenders. It is true, though, that in strong winds it does make the return stroke easier.

The rower can alter course by pulling harder on one oar then the other. The dinghy can even be turned in a circle by pulling with one oar and backing the other. A tender can, in fact, be sculled with one oar only, held in anoarlock or sculling notch at the stern. The oar is moved to and fro with one or both hands twisted through an angle of about 90° between each stroke.

Bring the tender up to a yacht lying at anchor or to a buoy from the stern of the yacht. Come alongside, facing the same way as the yacht. As soon as the tender has been secured alongside, the oars are taken out of the oarlocks and placed inside the boat or put aboard the yacht. The oarlocks themselves are removed, so that they will not scratch the topsides of the yacht. If the tender is to spend any length of time lying by the yacht it is moved aft and secured at the stern of the yacht where it can ride free and will not rub along the yacht's side. A bucket or drogue is often hung over the stern of a tender to make sure it lies to the current and does not ride up with the wind and bump against the yacht.

This tender has a very effective fending rail.

To prevent the yacht's topsides getting scratched the tender is streamed from the stern.

Care, repair and maintenance

All boats, no matter from what materials they are constructed, need attention from time to time to keep them in good order and looking smart. Once a year, generally in the spring, they come in for a complete refit which can be a major job. In between, damage has to be repaired as it occurs and general wear and tear taken care of.

It is still commonly thought that fibreglass yachts need no more attention than an occasional clean down with detergent. The truth is that fibreglass must be looked after very carefully if it is to retain its new look. It is worth bearing in mind that, once the hull of a fibreglass boat has been neglected and become stained, crazed, scuffed and chipped without attention and the gel coat softened, it will be a major undertaking to rejuvenate it. It might even require the services of a boatyard. A wooden boat, on the other hand, can always be returned to its former glory by the application of paint and a good deal of elbow grease.

Much of the effort of fitting-out a wooden boat in the spring can be lightened by a little work when the boat is laid up. Then is the time to remove loose paint and varnish and put a priming coat on to keep the weather out. If the hull is washed down any oil film will be removed and not penetrate the paint during the winter. Some of the small damages suffered during the season can be repaired at once. Often the weather at the end of the season is better than early in the year and you will not be faced with a last-minute rush in order to get afloat.

Tools and materials

There are certain basic tools and materials you need for boat care. As you go along with your own boat you will undoubtedly add to this list, but it is a start.

For cleaning the boat you should use a mild detergent which can be used safely inside and out. If it appears that you have oil on the hull then you will need a solvent like turpentine substitute (needed for thinning paint and cleaning brushes and fingers too). Special cleaners and polishes are made for fibreglass and should form part of your kit. Do not use hard wax polishes as used on cars.

For general care of the surface of fibreglass a tube of gel coat with catalyst (hardener) will come in very handy. Touch up scratches in the gel coat immediately or dirt will soon work its way in and be very difficult to get out.

The surface of the hull of a wooden boat will generally wait till the end of the season for attention but it is still a good idea to have a tube or tin of stopping on board as well as in the fitting-out kit. If the boat has a lot of brightwork or oiled wood then you should have some stopping which will match the colour of the wood. Ideally, stopping should only be applied after a priming coat of paint or varnish. For filling depressions in the hull a synthetic resin-based stopper with catalyst can be recommended.

For the preparation of surfaces for painting after cleaning you need a scraper or two, a putty knife and various grades of abrasive paper. Eighty grade is about as coarse as you need for the hull, with hundred for finishing off, finer for varnish (320-360). For all jobs the finer the better. A sanding block just big enough to fit your hand is a must to make the work lighter. For rounded surfaces the palm of the hand makes an effective sanding block. Among the scrapers you can include two triangular ones, one small, say 1¼ in (3 cm), and one larger, say 1¾ in (4.5 cm), a patent scraper of the Scarsten type with a wide blade, 3-4 in (7.5-10 cm), and some pieces of broken glass. The latter are immensely useful in scraping varnish down, but you do have to watch your fingers! Wire wool is not to be recommended, since small pieces of fine wire get left behind to rust and disfigure your handywork. The putty knife should be a good quality one which is really flexible.

For rubbing down you can use soda or pumice blocks but they are not so pleasant to use, especially since they are used wet. Wet-and-dry abrasive papers used wet are commonly used because they produce an excellent smooth finish and there is no fine dust flying about. The only place where it is essential to use wet-and-dry is the bottom when it has been antifouled. Dust would be most undesirable there since antifouling paints are poisonous. In any case a small face mask or goggles is useful to have while doing any large amount of dry rubbing down.

For any substantial kind of boat it is worth investing in a power sander, which is relatively inexpensive anyway.

The paints you need should be bought fresh as and when you want them. A little of everything in stock, however, will enable you to do touch-up jobs during the season.

For painting bare wood you need a priming paint which is specially designed to penetrate the surface and form a sound base for the next coat. If you propose to paint fibreglass you will need an etching primer which eats into the surface of the gel coat to make a key for the paint. This is usually put on before antifouling paints, though many people think there is no substitute for hard work and abrasive paper to get the same result (or better).

After priming comes the undercoat, a matt paint heavy in pigment, which makes a good key for the topcoat. Always use the undercoat recommended by the manufacturer for the particular topcoat.

Topcoat paint is, generally, specially manufactured for marine conditions. The colour range is usually confined to pigments which last in strong sunlight and salt air and its composition takes these factors into consideration. It is not wise to buy cheaper paints which are not made for use at sea. One-part polyurethene paint is ideal for use on wood while two-part polyurethene, which consists of paint and a catalyst, can be used for painting wood, fibreglass, steel and aluminium.

For brightwork you need varnish. Again this must be marine grade. The old-style yacht varnish is still manufactured and preferred by many. Most used is polyurethene in one or two-pack form. For external use the one-pack varnish is very suitable.

Antifouling paint comes in two forms, hard or soft. They both work on the principle that poisonous chemicals are released in the water to kill the marine growth. During preparation of the bottom for repainting care should be taken not to inhale the dust from these paints and sanding should be done wet-and-dry. On no account burn antifouling paint off; it gives off toxic fumes! Hard antifouling paints are the ones developed most recently and can be given a very smooth finish which makes them ideal for use on racing yachts. They can also be applied a long time before the yacht is launched without losing their effectiveness whilst soft antifouling paint must be immersed in water within twelve hours or it will lose its effectiveness.

At some stage it will be necessary to remove an area of paint or varnish completely and start again. For doing this you will need paint stripper. There are a number of very efficient chemical strippers on the market, some of which can be neutralized, after use with water, which makes them favourite. Be careful to use the correct stripper for removing paint from fibreglass. Anything else is likely to have very serious effects on the gel coat and resin. Although modern paint strippers are very good you should not expect too much of them. Be prepared for a lot of patient work. For removing paint, as opposed to varnish, it is a lot quicker to use a blow torch and burn it off (not on fibreglass hulls, needless to say). There are a number of very good propane blow torches on the market and one of these should be in your tool kit. It can be used for soldering as well.

You need a range of paint brushes, each of which should be earmarked for a specific purpose and, thereafter, used for nothing else. New brushes are not at their best but have to be worn in, gradually getting better as they are used. The hairs wear away to a taper and the brushes become more flexible and easier to use. Naturally the paint surface they produce im proves at the same time. Before using a new brush for the first time it should be soaked in clean, fresh water for several hours to remove the dressing.

Generally speaking, you need large brushes for large surfaces but the largest should not be more than 3 in (7.5 cm) wide. A brush this big, anyway, needs a strong wrist to handle it. With gloss paints, however, it will give a better finish than a small brush. A good average size for big surfaces is a 2½ in (6.25 cm). Two-inch brushes are useful general-purpose ones and you should have several. For the corners and small areas a 1 in (2.5 cm) brush is useful while even a ½ in (1.25 cm) one could come in handy for some tricky jobs. Brushes are an expensive item but it definitely pays to buy the best, since they wear to a better shape, produce a better finish and last longer. Certainly for varnishing you should buy the best natural bristle brushes you can get for that super finish, but for anti fouling, bilge paint or priming cheaper brushes will certainly do. The number you have will depend on the amount of painting and varnishing you do each season; you should have one or two in reserve.

It is important to take care of brushes for two reasons. Firstly, they are expensive to replace. Secondly, they mature with age, especially if they are thoroughly cleaned after use. More paint brushes end up being thrown away because they are caked solid with old paint than get nurtured to a dignified old age. A simple solution to the tiresome business of cleaning brushes is to have a quantity of a chemical brush cleaner (which requires water for rinsing the brushes out), in which you can store brushes when they are not in use. The majority of the paint in the brush is first squeezed out and the brush to be treated is then suspended in a can of the cleaner so that the hairs do not rest on the bottom. When it is wanted, the brush is simply washed out in running water and dried. This way your brushes will remain permanently usable. The brush cleaner can be used again and again.

Rollers can be used for large flat surfaces, where undercoat is being applied, but on the whole their use is not to be recommended for amateurs. They are difficult to clean, too!

Lastly, don't forget to equip yourself with plenty of old rags and a pair of cotton, industrial gloves which will keep your manicure intact, plus a hand cleaner which will remove grease and paint as well as ordinary dirt.

Dinghies drying out at a sailing school after their post-season valet service.

Laying up

In places where the water freezes in the winter it is customary to lay boats up ashore. In any event dinghies which are kept ashore when not sailing will stay that way all winter.

When the boat is removed from the water any underwater growth must be removed before it dries. This should be done with a high-pressure jet rather than the slog of using a stiff scrubbing brush. The mast is then removed. It is customary in these days of alloy spars, stainless steel wire and synthetic ropes to leave all the standing and running rigging in place during the winter storage. It should be sufficient to check everything over for wear and tear so that replacments can be put in hand straight away. If the spars are wooden ones, the rigging should be removed so that the mast can be varnished. As before, check for wear and tear and then carefully coil each separate piece, fastening them with pieces of line and labelling each one with a waterproof tag. In all cases the rigging should be wiped over to remove any dirt or salt.

Galvanized wire rigging should be wiped with boiled linseed oil to prevent rust. Make sure, too, that all the sheaves in the mast are in order and not damaged. It is better to check these things at the end of the season than wait till the spring when there will be a last-minute rush. If the rigging is to remain on the mast secure it in place with lengths of line, bunching the wires together so that they do not hang untidily.

The mast must be stowed horizontally in such a manner that it is supported evenly throughout its length with the groove downwards. If any part is allowed to sag it may suffer irreparable distortion.

The sails are examined for damage and wear and tear and then washed. A mild detergent may be used, if they are especially dirty, otherwise fresh warm water is sufficient. If repairs are necessary they should be put in hand as early as possible to give the sailmaker a chance to fit them into his programme without a mad rush. Otherwise, fold the sails carefully and stow them in a well-ventilated place.

If you are dealing with a dinghy take the centreboard and the floorboards out and remove the rudder. All these items should be stowed where they will not warp as a result of having weights on top of them. There is no harm in varnishing all these things before you put them away, and, of course, check for damage.

The hull should be given a thorough wash over with a mild detergent both inside and out and allowed to dry before being closed up or having the winter cover put in place. If you fail to dry the boat out mildew will almost certainly form and a musty smell will permeate the boat. Wax a fibreglass hull immediately.

A cruising boat will have a great deal of gear and equipment below which should all be taken out, checked and stored carefully. Do not leave gear on board as it will certainly suffer and, since much of it will harbour moisture, will only add to the risk of mildew and decay. It is also a sound idea to lift the cabin sole so that air can circulate through the bilges. To facilitate air circulation you should provide for reasonable ventilation throughout the hull during the winter, and, if possible, open up the boat from time to time while she is laid up.

If your boat is a keelboat do make sure that she is well supported ashore. The ideal solution is to have a special cradle made. Undercover storage is at a premium these days and most boats will have to spend the winter out-of-doors. A canvas or plastic boat cover will protect the boat from the worst of the weather. It should be supported on a ridge pole and framework so that it does not rest directly on the boat, throws off the rain and snow, and air can circulate freely. A transparent cover will enable you to work beneath it in a reasonable amount of light. A very secure lashing is essential to withstand the worst winter gales.

A dinghy can be stored upside down on trestles or boxes which support it evenly along its length. The cover in that case can be draped directly over the bottom and secured by lengths of line which pass underneath.

Fitting out

This is a subject on which whole books have been written and all we can do here is to give some useful hints and tips. Clearly, what is done to put a boat in the best condition to face the new season will depend on what she is built of and in what general condition she is found at the end of the winter. Wooden boats need the most attention and their owners, unless they call upon a boatyard to do the work, tend to treat fitting out as part of the hobby of sailing. As an owner of a wooden boat you will quickly become proficient at all manner of skills from painting to carpentry. In fact, the owner of practically any type and size of boat is likely to acquire a variety of skills connected with keeping it in good condition.

Preparing a fibreglass boat

If the hull and superstructure were not thoroughly cleaned with a fibreglass cleaner before laying up, this should be done at fitting out. This will restore the gloss to the gel coat and special wax can then be applied. Examine the hull for damage and crazing of the gel coat before waxing and treat with gel coat touch-up kit.

A fibreglass hull which is so badly worn as to be in need of painting can be restored to its original shine, but this is a task not lightly to be undertaken. Full instructions are obtainable from the paint manufacturers and here we shall only indicate, in broad outline, what is entailed.

To start with the job is best done in a draught-free building though, at a pinch, it can be done in calm weather out-of-doors. The paint to use is two-pack polyurethene which can be either brushed or sprayed on. On small hulls brush painting is not as difficult as you might imagine providing you work fast and make your brush strokes in a vertical direction.

The most important thing is to ensure that the paint is provided with a first-class key so that it will adhere permanently to the surface. This can be done by applying an etching primer (two coats) which is manufactured for the purpose, or by etching the surface mechanically, quite simply using an electric sander with a medium-fine grit. If this is done, and many people think it is the better way, the hull should be sanded all over until every square inch is matt and the old gel coat has vanished. You now have an excellent surface for the paint. Before this is applied the surface should be thoroughly washed with a degreasing fluid. This applies equally if etching primer has been used and should also be done between coats of paint. It cannot be too strongly emphasized that success in painting fibreglass rests largely on getting good adhesion.

Two coats of paint should be sufficient, the decision to apply more or not resting on whether or not the paint has covered sufficiently well. With some colours the surface might not appear dense enough with two coats. Since two-pack polyurethene paints dry off quickly, the work must proceed smoothly so that there is no risk of the edges of brush strokes drying off and not merging with their neighbours. Painting must also be carried out in the correct air temperature as recommended by the paint manufacturers, ideally not less than 55°F (13°C) unless the manufacturers says so. For anything but a dinghy it is a good idea to recruit a number of helpers so that the work can flow continuously and each side of the boat be painted as one whole at one time.

If you do the work carefully and according to the instructions you will be very pleased with the results. The surface can be touched up as necessary and will have a very good life with high resistance to scratches.

Fibreglass boats need antifouling like any others and this can be applied to the underwater parts after they have been properly prepared, as above. An undercoat paint, specially made for the antifouling, is usually applied first and then two coats of antifouling put on. If a hard racing antifouling is used it can be given a final smoothing with a fine grade sanding paper, applied wet-and-dry.

In common with all boats, the fibreglass boat should be inspected carefully before launching to see that all skin fittings are watertight and the fastenings in good condition. Every so often it is necessary to remove seacocks and other outlets and rebed them. Check the propeller and shaft and, in particular, the stern gland.

Preparing a wooden boat

Ideally the boat should be quite dry before you start work and it must be completely dry before you apply paint or varnish. Varnish is particularly sensitive to moisture and you should only work on your brightwork on a day when the air is dry.

Start on the inside, scraping away loose paint and dirt in the bilges. If you are using bilge paint, which does keep things looking clean, you can paint it on straight after you have removed the loose dirt. Cabin brightwork does not need revarnishing every year and inbetween times you just keep it clean. Look in out-of-the-way corners and in lockers for mildew and spray an anti-mildew preparation all round. Mildew gives rise to musty smell so prevalent in wooden boats. It is no bad idea to paint throughout the inside of the boat behind the furniture and under the floorboards, also inside the cockpit lockers, with a clear wood preservative solution.

Unless the deck is teak laid or has been covered with a non-slip synthetic fabric it will need painting from time to time, but this job can really be left till last and done together with the brightwork. One coat every two years should be sufficient, but as with everything in yachting you really have to be guided by the amount of wear and tear. The external brightwork gets a lot of weathering and wear from the crew. It is essential, therefore, to apply sufficient coats of varnish and to make sure they go on properly. On bare wood you use varnish thinned with the appropriate thinners by about 10-30%. This ensures that it gets into the grain of the wood. Then you need five coats on top of this of unthinned varnish. Each dry coat must be sanded down with fine paper before the next coat is put on. On old, sound varnish you should put at least two coats of unthinned varnish.

If varnish has to be removed, use one of the many excellent chemical paint strippers which can be bought. It is most important to see that the chemicals are neutralized properly before putting fresh varnish on or it will not dry.

Painting the topsides represent the largest amount of work in fitting out a wooden boat. From time to time the paint has to be removed entirely. This is best accomplished by burning it off to the bare wood. The wood is then thoroughly sanded, having been treated first with stopper where necessary. The prepared surface is then degreased and given a coat of priming paint. Then follow two or three coats of undercoat, which forms a key

for the topcoat and, often, provides a background for the colour since undercoat has a lot of pigment. After the undercoat has been rubbed down with fine sandpaper the first topcoat is painted on. When this is thoroughly dry it is rubbed down with fine sandpaper and the final coat put on. The secret of getting a mirror-like finish lies in the degree of preparation, the stillness of the air when the paint is applied, and the smoothness with which the paint flows. Having the right air temperature, the right brush and the correct painting stroke all contribute to this last item.

The underwater part of the hull will be antifouled unless we are talking of a dinghy or other craft which does not live permanently in the water. Never burn old antifouling paint off as it gives off toxic fumes. It has to be removed by the old-fashioned process of scraping and sanding, wet-and-dry. Prime bare spots. Apply antifouling undercoat and then the antifouling paint, two coats.

If the topsides are not to be stripped they are prepared as follows. Remove all loose paint and sand off as much of the old paint as reasonably possible. This will prevent an excessive build-up of old paint over the years. Prime and stop all bare spots and holes, as necessary. Give one coat of undercoat and follow this with one or two coats of topcoat as necessary to give the best finish.

Don't forget to renew the wasting anode if the boat is fitted with one.

Remember always to remove all loose dust before painting or varnishing and to wipe surfaces with a degreasing agent before so doing. If your hand is not steady enough to paint the waterline or boot-topping without help, use masking tape, but be sure you do not put it down on tacky paint or you will not get it off without taking the paint as well.

The tender

This tends to be a much maligned object in yachting circles and, therefore, we feel it should have a special word. It should be painted as regularly as the mother ship. A smart tender does you credit. Pay particular attention to the fender and see that it is properly secured.

Wooden dinghies Most wooden dinghies today are built of plywood and live, for the most part, on land. Consequently they are not subjected to such heavy wear and tear as boats which remain afloat all the time. Complete repainting should not be necessary more often than every third year, though the exact time interval will, naturally, depend on the condition at the time. The important thing is to see that any damage to the paint surface is rapidly repaired so that the weather cannot infiltrate and spread the damage. With the modern glues used in plywood manufacture it is unlikely that bare wood will result in structural damage though it is certainly true that, if the end grain of plywood is exposed, water can get in and delamination occur. Make especially sure, then, if there are exposed lengths of end grain that they are well protected with paint. What is most important to a keen, racing dinghy helmsman is a very smooth finish to the hull. For that reason alone he might think it worth while to apply fresh coats of gloss paint or varnish at the beginning of each season and take a good deal of trouble over the preparation.

Preparing a steel boat

The main problem with steel hulls is in combating corrosion which is aggravated considerably by electrolysis. If no action is taken to protect the surface in sea water the rate at which the steel plate disappears is truly frightening. Therefore, rust patches have to be taken seriously and dealt with promptly.

All traces of rust and scale have to be removed with a wire brush and chipping hammer. A rotary wire brush used with an electric drill is a good tool for the purpose. Every trace of rust must be removed to leave bare, shining metal. If the condition of the hull is bad all over then it may have to be sandblasted which is a job for professionals.

The bare metal is treated with a primer of epoxy-fixed zinc within a few minutes of being cleaned and this forms an anodic protective skin. Fur-

ther coats of paint are then applied according to the manufacturers' instructions. Undercoat and topcoat paints can be applied exactly as for wooden boats but something more durable, like two-pack polyurethene or an epoxy paint is to be preferred. Tar-epoxy paint is also a valuable medium for protecting bare steel.

It is important not to use antifouling paints, which contain copper, on steel hulls. They only encourage electrolytic action.

Mast and spars

The advent of aluminium alloys in spar manuacture has made special care of these items of gear unnecessary. If the spars are properly anodized there should be no corrosion whatever. They can be washed to preserve their clean appearance as far as possible and keep dirt out of the grooves.

Wooden spars are another matter. Unless they are kept well covered with varnish the weather will get into the wood, staining it grey, and they will become unsightly. Therefore, each seaon they should be rubbed down and given at least two coats of varnish, the first of which can be slightly diluted. Bare patches should be treated with a patent wood-stain remover or a solution of oxalic acid crystals in water, which will remove most of the staining that may have occurred. Ideally, they should then be given up to five coats of varnish. Check carefully the screws which attach the tracks to the mast and boom or, if grooves are being used, examine them to see that the edges are smooth. Examine with particular care the fastenings on the mast for the stays and shrouds.

Wooden masts, as we have explained elsewhere, are made up of laminations. It is worth looking at the truck and heel carefully to see that the glue has not given way and the mast sprung. In fact, this could happen anywhere along the length of a laminated spar but is more likely to appear at the ends.

Here are a few reminders about the things to do and not do when you are sanding down and painting.

- Sand down the surface of dry paint or varnish before applying the next coat. Particularly important if the surface is glossy.
- Use a sanding block except where you have a contoured surface when the hand alone will be better since it shapes itself to the contours. Make a sanding block with a concave surface for sanding things like beading.
- Never sand or strip down wood across the grain as this will lift the softer part of the wood.
- Always read the manufacturers' instructions before using paints and glues. This is particularly important in relation to those products which entail the use of catalytic agents.
- It is generally not advisable to apply successive layers or paints of different types or manufacture. Never mix paints of different types.
- Use the correct product to carry out repairs, i.e., marine-grade adhesive should always be used for boat repairs.
- Do not paint a boat in direct sunlight, which will cause the paint to dry too quickly and possibly not adhere properly.
- Do not paint in the rain or even when it is damp or foggy. The paint will not dry properly and will not adhere.
- The best conditions for painting are when it is still and pleasantly warm.
- If you use two-pack paints try to estimate carefully how much you will use since it cannot be kept longer than the drying time specified by the manufacturers.
- Look after brushes and always work with clean ones. Brushes that still have traces of old paint in them leave pieces in the new paintwork.
- Do not use paints containing copper salts on steel boats.
- Apply antifouling paint in the open air, or in a well-ventilated place, because of the poisonous fumes. Wear a mask.
- Never apply polyurethene paint over an oil-based paint. Applying an oil-based paint over polyurethene paint is permissible.
- Do not use wire wool for rubbing down surfaces as the small bits of

wire will be left behind and rust.
- Use the correct polish for fibreglass hulls. Never use a hard silicone polish.

Small repair jobs

Sailors are frequently in the position where they have to do repairs for themselves, simply because there is no shipwright handy, or they need the work done in a great hurry. Here is a suggested list of tools which will enable you to tackle a lot of small jobs.

Tools

Like brushes, tools should be good quality, the best in fact. They always work better and last longer than cheap ones. It is particularly important to buy the best so far as cutting tools are concerned, saws and chisels and drill bits, since good-quality steel holds a sharp edge longer.

Several saws are essential. First you need a general-purpose, crosscut saw, with ten points to the inch. This will enable you to tackle all but the finest joinery work.

Next there is the compass saw with two interchangeable blades, one of which is a keyhole saw. This is essential for working in tight corners. Also, for working with plywood, a fine-toothed frame saw will be useful. For cutting metal you must have a hacksaw with a choice of several grades of blade. Saws must be kept sharp or they leave ragged edges and make hard work. Although amateurs can sharpen saws it is best left to the professional.

If you have a wooden boat you should have one or two caulking irons.

Boring tools are needed frequently. You must have a hand drill with a set of carbon-twist drills. The most useful range of sizes is 1/16-¼in (1.5-6mm). An electric drill with a 5/16in (8mm) chuck is also useful as its speeds work up. Finally there is a

brace with a range of bits. It is difficult to recommend individual ones by size and it would be best to buy a complete set ¼in to 1¼in (6mm to 32m). If you don't want this kind of outlay then purchase them separately as you need them. An expansive bit for boring shallow holes is worth having. So, too, is a rose bit for countersinking screw heads and one or two screwdriver bits.

How many screwdrivers you should have depends entirely on the boat.

If you have an inboard engine then you need screwdrivers suitable for its fastenings. A long and a short electrician's screwdriver, the short one a fine one, are essential, while for woodworking you will need, ideally, four ranging from ¼in to ½in (6mm to 12.5mm) to fit all sizes of screw. It is important to remember that a screwdriver should fit the slot in the head of a screw exactly or it will be damaged.

Two pairs of pliers should be sufficient, a pair of long-nosed pliers for electrical repairs and a pair of bull-nosed pliers for general purposes.

A light hammer, say ½lb (¼ kg) and a heavier one, say 1½lb (¾ kg) will be sufficient. In addition, you should have in the basic kit a 9in (22cm) smoothing place and a couple of chisels, ¼in (6mm) and ¾in (19mm) will do to start. A good sharpening stone of fine texture is essential to keep these latter tools and the plane sharp.

A wood rasp and two files, one half-round and the other flat on both sides, will enable you to deal with most small repair jobs, but a patent tool like a Surform with interchangeable blades which can be renewed and cuts both wood and metal could prove to be one of the most useful tools you acquire.

For working with rope you need a marlinspike and a stainless steel clasp knife, which is always kept sharp, plus a quantity of twine for whipping.

The tool kit can be rounded off by a selection of C cramps without which you cannot make good joints with glue.

Aside from the tools there should be a wide selection of bronze and stainless steel screws, galvanized and copper nails. This is something you

will build up as time goes by so that eventually you have something for nearly every job that comes along. As you use up specific items replace them immediately. Also you need waterproof glue for wood and plastics. Some of these, especially those which require the use of a catalyst, have a limited shelf life and begin to deteriorate quite noticeably even after months. Such glues must either be bought fresh or replaced immediately they have reached the manufacturers' safe working life.

This may seem an awful lot of equipment to have to get, especially if you add it to the recommendations for painting and general maintenance but, if you have a boat of any size, you will find it difficult to do your own handywork without these. You can build up the kit, adding items as they become necessary. In the same way a collection of replacement fittings and shackles can be built up. Add a supply of copper and galvanized wire and a few rolls of insulating tape for good measure.

Here are some hints and tips on various repair procedures which will help you do some of the simpler jobs.

Gluing wood

First of all it is important to see that you use only marine-grade glues, which are completely waterproof, not just water-resistant.

Then, degrease the surfaces to be glued and roughen them so that they provide a good key for the glue. Some timbers need more attention than others as they contain natural oils which make it difficult for the glue to adhere, e.g., teak. Such timbers need especially good keying and degreasing. A few cuts with a sharp knife is a good way to mark the surface.

Mix the glue exactly according to the manufacturers' instructions. This will give you a free-flowing, but firm, glue which will set according to the instructions. If you depart from these very exact instructions you will certainly weaken the glue.

The parts to be glued together will only join well under pressure. This ensures that the glue penetrates the grain of the wood as far as possible.

Tool kit for eye-splicing wire rope (talurit splicing).

The damaged end . . .

. . . is cut off cleanly with bolt croppers.

Use clamps but protect the wood being glued from damage by the jaws of the clamps by placing small offcuts of wood between them and the job.

If you want to ensure that the protective pieces do not accidentally get glued to the job, separate them from the job with pieces of thin polythene sheet.

Resin glues, which harden as a result of a chemical reaction, must be used at the correct temperature. This will be specified by the manufacturer. This is sometimes difficult to ensure, especially outdoors, but the maximum strength depends on the right temperature and this should not be ignored.

Wipe off any excess glue which exudes from a joint before it dries. If you are gluing pieces which are to be varnished afterwards bear in mind that any glue which spreads beyond the joint will prevent the varnish from penetrating the wood and will show up as a light patch on the finished varnish.

Driving screws

A hole must be driven beforehand to take the screw. To do this correctly requires no less than four operations — a pilot hole, a hole for the thread, a hole for the shank of the screw and a countersink for the head. This can, of course, be done with the tools you have in the tool kit but it is easier to

buy a set of patent bits like the Screw Mate, which perform the whole operation in one. Make sure they are suitable for use in an electric drill.

As we have previously remarked the screwdriver must fit the screw head. If you use Philips screws, the heads of which do not burr so easily, you will need special screwdrivers to fit. This type of screw is ideal for use where the head is to be left exposed. Put a small amount of grease on each screw before driving it. It will go in more easily, grip better, water will not penetrate the screw hole and the screw will come out easily if need be.

Take your time putting screws in. Impatience causes breakages and damage to the slots. Bear in mind that you should always be able to remove what you have put in.

Touching up paintwork on wooden hulls

If the paintwork gets scratched so that the wood is exposed it must be touched up. If this is not done water will creep under the surrounding layers of paint and spread the damage. It is also unsightly! Rub down thoroughly an area all round the damage for at least an equal distance. Use fine sandpaper and then degrease. Paint with the same paint as the surrounding area, using primer, undercoat and topcoat. One coat of each should suffice.

Repairing holes in wooden or fibreglass hulls

The quickest way to repair a sizeable hole is to apply a quick-setting filler or trowel cement with a putty knife. This can only be done, though, if a piece of back-up material is fixed to the hull first. This can take the form of a thin piece of marine plywood nailed over the inside of the hole in the case of a wooden boat or applied with a suitable adhesive to a fibreglass hull.

The trowel cement is applied to the hole until it is filled. Chopped fibreglass strands can be added to give the cement extra strength. This will then produce a workmanlike job which will last until you can get to a professional boatbuilder. It is important to ensure that all surfaces are dry before applying the filler.

An amateur can make a very good job of repairing a fibreglass boat himself with the aid of fibreglass matting and polyester resin. Kits are sold widely which contain all the necessary material and detailed instructions, but we will describe the essential work here.

First, clean the damaged area thoroughly and bevel the edge of the hole from the outside, using a coarse file. The hole is then covered from the outside with metal foil and cardboard which is held firmly in place. This is to ensure that the repair will take approximately the shape of the hull. Cu

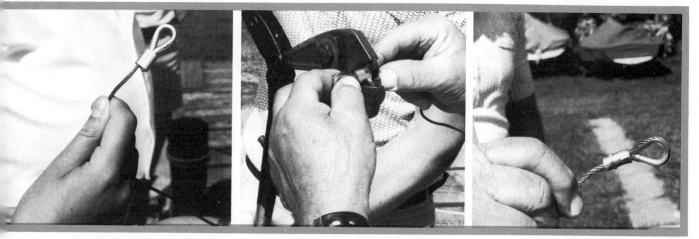

It is threaded through the collar, round the thimble and back into the collar.

The collar is then compressed; considerable pressure is needed.

Nearly finished.

several pieces of fibreglass mat slightly larger than the hole, mix the required amount of polyester resin and, using plenty of resin, laminate the fibreglass mat in place until the hole is full and there is even a bump on the inside of the hull. The mat is the reinforcement and the resin the body of the repair so make sure there is adequate resin in the job. As always with such materials make sure you are working in the right temperature. Press out bubbles from the work (very important!) with a brush or small roller which can be bought specially for the job. Since this is to be a permanent repair expense should not be spared.

Finally the collar is filed smooth.

Leave the resin to harden and then sand down until the hull is smooth and you can see no proud parts. The repair can then be painted.

If the hole is inaccessible from the inside then the repair can be done working from outside. In that case you can place a suitably sized piece of plywood behind the hole, keeping it in place by pulling it hard against the edges of the hole with wire fastened to a screw eye in the centre of the wood. This remains in place until the job is done.

Hair cracks or crazing in the gel coat

The gel coat of fibreglass boats frequently becomes crazed as it becomes older and this is particularly so with thin laminates, as found in dinghies. This does not constitute real damage but water *can* seep through and permeate the body of the resin, which is very undesirable. The simplest answer is to fill the cracks with a proprietary fibreglass filler or touch-up gel coat.

The cracks should be cleaned and then dabbed with gel coat which can be smoothed with a razor blade or a piece of plastic with a straight edge. If filler is used the hull should really be repainted unless the cracks are so small and infrequent as to be unnoticeable. If the results of your work is not particularly smooth you should sand the hull over lightly with a *very* fine abrasive paper, wet-and-dry.

One of the more recent introductions to the market is an aerosol spray for gel coat repairs. This does not dry as hard as the original gel coat but has the same weathering qualities.

Repairing torn-away bolts

If you have to make an emergency repair of such damage you should simply fill the hole with a resin filler and drill a new hole alongside it. Alternatively, you can drive a wooden dowel in the hole together with a waterproof glue. As soon as this is dry you can drill a hole for the replacement bolt in the same place. To be sure the repair is a good one, a piece of ½in (1.25cm) plywood can be placed behind the hole as reinforcement.

On a fibreglass boat the repair is done by filling the hole with mat and resin laminate, allowing this to overlap the hole all round. Make sure you have a good key to this surrounding area by sanding it down well with coarse paper. The area under the hole is reinforced with a plywood disc which can be fixed in place with fibreglass. The new hole is bored on the site of the old one.

It is important when fixing bolts through parts of the hull to ensure that washers are used between the nuts and the boat or they will be impressed in the surface.

Scratches in the topsides

This is one of the more irritating forms of damage which a boat can sustain. It is almost exclusively of a cosmetic nature but proud owners will not hesitate to deal with it at once. On a wooden hull clean the scratch, apply wood primer and fill the scratch with a suitable filler, touching up the paintwork after. With fibreglass clean the scratch and fill with fibreglass filler. Finish off with gel coat. Shallow scratches can be filled with gel coat.

Fitting cleats, winches etc.

Wherever anything is to be fastened to the deck or superstructure which will have to take considerable strain it should only be fastened after the point of attachment has been reinforced. With both wood and fibreglass boats this can take the form of a ½in (1.25cm) plywood board, if possible considerably larger in area than the base of the object to be fastened down. This will then spread the load over a much larger area and prevent a hole being wrenched in the deck in extreme conditions. In both cases the plywood can be glassed in for additional strength. Otherwise, paint it well.

Repairing damage to rub rail

If the rub rail is badly damaged you will need to scarf a new piece or pieces in. A scarf joint is made by cutting the two pieces of wood to be joined so that they overlap. The cut, for maximum strength, should have an angle corresponding to a rise of 1in (2.50cm) in ten. The direction of the cut on the remaining pieces on the hull must be inwards. Holes are bored in the new piece at 4 to 6in (10-15cm) intervals, well countersunk, for screws. If the rub rail is a very heavy one it must be bolted in place. It is not worth applying glue at the scarf joint, the fastenings should pass through it. This is not the easiest of jobs to do on a larger boat, though easy enough on a dinghy. To make a good job of a large scarf you need some skill in carpentry.

You can make the job a little simpler on a dinghy by nailing the rub rail in place with copper nails.

New eye splice in wire rope

Possession of the necessary tools and repair kit (Talurit in the UK) enables the small-boat sailor to make his own on-the-spot repair if an eye splice in a shroud or trapeze wire breaks. The picture sequence above illustrates the procedure.

Some useful hints on repairing your boat

- When you drill start from the smooth side as, when the drill breaks through, it usually leaves a ragged hole and this will matter less on the rough side.
- Be careful not to let the drill tip slip as it may easily do with a power tool. Start the drill in a small depression made with a centre punch.
- When making a saw cut work from the good edge to the less good or damaged edge. As the saw breaks out it usually leaves a ragged edge.

- Apply glue at the correct temperature which means certainly never in the cold.
- Drill holes in most timbers before driving nails. The holes should be roughly half the diameter of the nails and three quarters the depth.
- Be careful using abrasive papers on fibreglass boats as scratches in the gel coat are more permanent than on wooden boats. The best idea is to work with wet-and-dry paper used wet.
- When using fibreglass and resin there is a fire risk. Make sure the ventilation is adequate and do not smoke.
- Fibreglass resin is badly affected by moisture in the uncured state, so do not work on days with a high humidity.
- Mix only the amount of resin and hardener you will need for the job in hand. It sets very quickly and cannot be kept even a matter of hours.
- Resin must be handled with respect. It has a corrosive effect and must not be allowed, in particular, to come into contact with the eyes.
- If you are adding both a catalyst and an accelerator to resin do not add them both at once as there is a risk of an explosion.

There are many things which we have had no space to deal with and, in particular, we have only touched on the skill required in wooden boat construction. There are a number of excellent books on the subject and one that is quite outstanding for its clarity is *Boat Carpentry* by Harvey Garrett Smith. A great deal of skill can be acquired generally by working on your own boat and learning from other people. Always ask if in doubt. You will find most sailors only too keen to help you.

The boat engine

The mechanics of internal combustion engines

The four-stroke gasoline engine

Virtually all internal combustion engines are run on gasoline or diesel oil. Diesel engines are named after their inventor, Rudolf Diesel; gasoline engines were invented by August Otto and are still known in Germany as Otto engines. Both types of engine are piston-driven, a sole exception being the Wankel motor which has a rotor in place of the piston.

In piston engines the vertical up-and-down movement of the piston in the cylinder is converted to rotary motion by linking the piston, through the connecting rod, to a crankshaft. With the four-stroke gasoline engine when the first downstroke of the piston reaches its lowest point of travel (bottom dead centre or bdc), the inlet valve closes; thus, at bdc, the cylinder is filled with the fresh gasoline-air mixture and the induction stroke ends.[1]

The opening and closing of the valves is achieved by a regulating mechanism (camshaft, tappets, pushrods or timing chain, rocker arm) from a gear mounted on the crankshaft. When the piston moves upwards the second stroke begins. Both valves are now closed and the upward movement of the piston compresses the gasoline mixture into a tiny space. Immediately before the piston reaches tdc the spark plug produces a spark which ignites the highly compressed gasoline mixture. Usually the ignition system is also regulated by the crankshaft. Now the third stroke, the power stroke, begins.

1. As a horizontal arrangement of the cylinders is the most common in outboard engines the terms bdc and tdc should, perhaps, be defined: bdc is when the piston changes direction at the point nearest the crankshaft; tdc (top dead centre) when the piston changes direction at the point nearest the spark plug.

With the very high pressure of the compressed and ignited gasoline-air mixture the piston is propelled downwards. On the downstroke temperatures of over 3600°F (2000°C) are reached in the cylinder (see Cooling of outboards, page 75). As the piston travels through the cylinder and reaches bdc again pressure from the burning mixture drops a little. The exhaust valve opens and the fourth stroke begins. The piston, travelling up once more, pushes the burnt gases out of the cylinder through the exhaust valve. At the end of this stroke the exhaust valve closes, the inlet valve opens and the cycle is repeated.

The four-stroke gasoline engine cycle 1 Carburettor. 2 Inlet valve. 3 Exhaust valve. 4 Spark plug. 5 Cylinder. 6 Piston. 7 Connecting rod. 8 Crankshaft. 9 Cooling jacket (water).

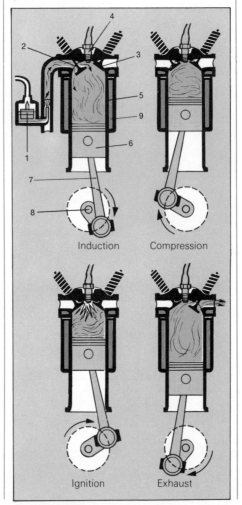

Induction   Compression

Ignition   Exhaust

The four-stroke diesel engine

Diesel engines are driven by diesel oil. Unlike the gasoline used in gasoline engines this fuel cannot be vaporized in a carburettor — it is too heavy. Instead of the carburettor the diesel engine has an injection system whose main parts are a high-pressure pump, a pressure pipe and an injector. On the first downstroke the piston draws clean air — not fuel — into the cylinder. On the following upstroke it compresses the air enormously. Then, at the moment of greatest compression, a small amount of fuel at a pressure of about a hundred atmospheres is injected into the compressed air in a fine spray. A diesel engine has a much higher compression ratio than a gasoline engine. Consequently, the air will have been heated considerably during the upstroke and will have reached a temperature of between 930-1200°F (500-700°C) so that the diesel fuel is ignited on contact with the hot air. This starts the third, or power, stroke.

The diesel engine differs from the gasoline engine in two fundamental aspects. It has no carburettor but an injection system instead and it has no separate ignition system. Ignition is non-electrical and spontaneous.

Some diesels are fitted with glowplugs (not to be confused with spark plugs). The elements of these plugs glow when the starter is switched on and preheat the area around the injector. This means that the fuel will ignite immediately even if some of the heat generated by compression is lost through the walls of a cold cylinder. The purpose of the glowplug is therefore simply to help start a cold engine.

Lubrication of four-stroke engines To reduce friction between the moving parts of an engine to a minimum every component which may be subject to friction must be lubricated by oil. With four-stroke engines, both gasoline and diesel, the oil is held in a sump bolted on to the base of the engine block. A pump draws the oil from the sump and forces it through a number of chan-

nels to the lubrication points. From there the oil returns to the sump.

On its way round the engine, as well as lubricating and cooling, the oil has a third function, cleaning. It picks up the microscopic swarf rubbed off the moving parts and carries them into the sump. Before the oil can be used again on another lubricating cycle, therefore, it has to pass through a filter. This stops the swarf from being returned to the lubrication points and wearing away the surfaces of the metal. In spite of the filtering process, however, the oil loses its lubricant properties in the course of time and should be changed as specified by the engine manufacturers.

The two-stroke gasoline engine

The two-stroke engine is always gasoline-driven. Its name is a little misleading since this engine has a four-action cycle just as the four-stroke engine does: induction, compression, ignition, exhaust. The special design of the two-stroke, however, means that the four-stroke cycle can be achieved in only two movements of the piston and one turn of the crankshaft. Thus it becomes possible to make the crankcase airtight and use it as a sort of induction and injection pump for the gasoline-air mixture blended in the carburettor (see Lubrication of two-stroke engines for details about the addition of oil). The fresh gasoline-air mixture passes through the crankcase and the transfer port into the cylinder.[1]

Whereas with a four-stroke the regulation of the fuel mixture is achieved through inlet and exhaust valves, in a two-stroke the piston performs this function. On its way to bdc it passes the different ports, inlet, exhaust and transfer. At the appropriate moment the piston opens or closes the ports, its walls uncovering or covering the apertures. In order to understand how the two-stroke

works we must look at what is going on in *two* chambers as the piston moves up and down (see diagram).

When the spent gas has been driven out of the cylinder by the fresh gas there is a brief moment of contact between spent and fresh gas. This means that a proportion of the fresh gas will be expelled with the spent, causing increased fuel consumption. At the same time it is possible that not all of the spent gas will be evacuated, which will lead to the cylinder being underfilled with gasoline-air mixture. When the two-stroke idles its uneven running is due to these two facts. Although the various two-stroke engines available

are being constantly improved in terms of gas exchange, the mixture of new and spent gas remains a problem and explains why they are rather less efficient than four-strokes.

Lubrication of two-stroke engines

The special design and operation of the two-stroke demands another sort of lubrication than the pressure-fed system used in four-strokes. On its way through the engine the gasoline-air mixture blended in the carburettor flows past all the moving parts of the motor. In other words it flows past all the parts requiring lubrication. If you introduce a certain amount of oil into the fuel tank the oil is drawn up

This is what happens in the cylinder	The piston moves upwards. The new gas is compressed as the exhaust port is closed off by the piston	Near top dead centre the spark plug has ignited the compressed gasoline-air mixture. The expanding gases push the piston powerfully downwards. The exhaust port is still closed off by the cylinder	The piston reverses direction at bottom dead centre. The exhaust port is cleared by the piston and the burnt gases can escape
This is what happens in the crankcase at the same time	The piston travelling upwards causes a partial vacuum. This draws the gasoline-air mixture through the inlet port into the crankcase as soon as the skirt of the piston clears the opening. The transfer port is blocked by the piston	The inlet port is closed by the piston and the fresh gas just drawn in is compressed to about 1.5 atmospheres	The piston has cleared the transfer port. The compressed gasoline-air mixture can flow out of the crankcase through the transfer port and the piston window, into the cylinder, thus expelling all the burnt gas through the exhaust port

Two-stroke motor:
1 Crankcase
2 Crankshaft
3 Connecting rod
4 Piston
5 Spark plug
6 Inlet port
7 Exhaust port
8 Transfer port
9 Piston window

1: The transfer port connects the crankcase and the cylinder. Many modern two-stroke engines have several such ports in each cylinder which facilitate the passage of the gasoline-air mixture.

through the carburettor with the gasoline mixture and results in a gasoline-air-oil mixture which is then carried to all the lubrication points. With the correct amount of a suitable two-stroke motor oil (preferably that specified by the manufacturers) the ideal lubrication can be ensured. This system of lubrication is simple and reliable but certainly not pollution-free as some of the oil in the unburnt mixture is expelled through the exhaust (see The predominance of two-stroke engines in outboards).

The principle of the carburettor

Although the carburettor of a modern gasoline engine is a fairly complex unit its principal function can be simply explained. The down-draft of the piston causes a vacuum which sucks air into the venturi. At the narrowest point in the venturi the speed of the air is at its greatest and its pressure therefore reduced to a partial vacuum (Bernoulli's principle). At this point you have, in effect, a narrow tube with a partial vacuum whose other end is immersed in gasoline under atmospheric pressure. The unequal pressure causes the gasoline to be pushed up through the tube into the flow of air. The gasoline mixes with the air to form a fine mist which is the explosive gasoline-air mixture required.

Basic principle of the carburettor.

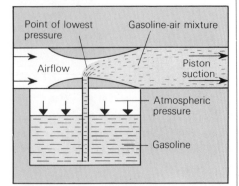

The internal combustion engine in boats

All the engines described in the previous section can be used as boat engines. It therefore depends on the intended use of the motor as to whether an outboard or an inboard installation is more suitable.

The outboard motor

By outboard motor we mean an engine mounted on the transom of a boat in such a fashion that the whole drive unit is outside the boat. An outboard has its engine, transmission and propeller, all its component parts, assembled in one single unit which is then attached to the transom by means of two screw clamps.

The predominance of two-stroke engines in outboards

Neither the diesel nor the four-stroke gasoline engine has yet succeeded in making inroads into the two-stroke's virtual monopoly of the outboard market. This is chiefly because the motor used for outboards must have a power output per unit of weight as high as possible since these engines are used on small, fast speedboats or as auxiliaries for sailing boats. A heavy motor would also make the craft stern heavy. The calculation

$$\frac{\text{Weight of motor (in kg)}}{\text{Power of motor (in hp)}}$$

is called the power-to-weight ratio. From this point of view the two-stroke comes out best because it has neither valves or valve mechanism. With the diesel engine the disadvantage becomes even more evident as the high compression in a diesel

engine demands a heavy construction. With increased compression ratios in four-stroke gasoline engines and lighter construction of diesels as a result of the use of new materials, the gap between the power-to-weight ratios has now narrowed slightly. Modern two-strokes achieve a ratio of about 3lb (1.3kg) per hp while a similar four-stroke would weigh around 4lb (1.9kg) per hp and a diesel outboard something like 7lb (3kg). Apart from the question of transom weight, too heavy an engine makes transport of the motor for over-wintering or servicing rather difficult.

The official international standard unit for measuring power is now the kilowatt (kW). The horsepower rating used hitherto is gradually disappearing (1hp = 72kg/sec), although most brochures and specifications still quote two power outputs, one in horsepower and the other in kilowatts.

3hp	= 2.20 kW	27hp	= 19.85 kW
4hp	= 2.94 kW	28hp	= 20.59 kW
5hp	= 3.67 kW	29hp	= 21.32 kW
6hp	= 4.41 kW	30hp	= 22.06 kW
7hp	= 5.14 kW	35hp	= 25.74 kW
8hp	= 5.88 kW	40hp	= 29.42 kW
9hp	= 6.61 kW	45hp	= 33.09 kW
10hp	= 7.35 kW	50hp	= 36.77 kW
11hp	= 8.09 kW	55hp	= 40.45 kW
12hp	= 8.82 kW	60hp	= 44.13 kW
13hp	= 9.56 kW	65hp	= 47.80 kW
14hp	= 10.29 kW	70hp	= 51.48 kW
15hp	= 11.03 kW	75hp	= 55.16 kW
16hp	= 11.76 kW	80hp	= 58.84 kW
17hp	= 12.50 kW	85hp	= 62.51 kW
18hp	= 13.23 kW	90hp	= 66.19 kW
19hp	= 13.97 kW	95hp	= 69.87 kW
20hp	= 14.71 kW	100hp	= 73.55 kW
21hp	= 15.44 kW	105hp	= 77.22 kW
22hp	= 16.18 kW	110hp	= 80.90 kW
23hp	= 16.91 kW	115hp	= 84.58 kW
24hp	= 17.65 kW	120hp	= 88.26 kW
25hp	= 18.38 kW	125hp	= 91.93 kW
26hp	= 19.12 kW	130hp	= 95.61 kW

A further advantage of the two-stroke is its simplicity and reliability, a result of its elementary mechanics. Except for the pistons, connecting rods and crankshaft and their connecting components, the two-stroke has no moving parts which, especially in the presence of water from condensation and spray, could cause a breakdown. A two-stroke with correctly set ignition and the right fuel mixture is an exceptionally reliable motor. The disadvantage of a higher fuel consumption than that of the

four-stroke can be disregarded as the advantages are overwhelming: low weight, strength and simplicity. The outboard dominates the market, auxiliary engines for sailing cruisers excepted, up to a power output of about 95hp; at this point the inboard takes the lead as the more powerful outboards weigh so much that the inboard, with its lower fuel consumption (despite the previously mentioned advantages of outboards) gains the edge.

With the growing concern for the protection of the environment several governments are at present drafting legislation which could severely restrict the outboard market. In the future two-stroke outboards will only be allowed if the oil content of the gasoline is not more than two per cent — in other words, not exceeding one part in fifty. Although earlier outboards required one in 20 to one in 25 modern designs can achieve the ratio of one in fifty without harming the motor. A reduction in the power output of outboards is also being considered. In order to exonerate the outboard motor from accusations of polluting the environment the manufacturers concerned are heavily engaged in research. As well as improvement of oil mixture ratios high,power oils have been developed which produce only a very limited amount of smoke when burnt and are biodegradable. Despite this, the laws under consideration in some countries at the moment could lead to a growth in popularity for the four-stroke outboard which emits no oil on combustion.

Outboard transmissions

As the engine itself has to be raised well clear of the waterline and the propeller has to be immersed, a transmission shaft protected by a casing must be included to link the engine drive to the propeller. The turning moment of the engine is thus converted into propulsion. The interrelationship of engine, drive shaft and propeller means that the cylinders have to be horizontal. The orientation of crankshaft and transmission shaft is thus the same and therefore only one connection is necessary. This connection is between the lower end

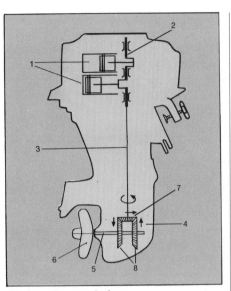

Outboard transmission:
1 Two-cylinder engine with horizontal cylinders. 2 Crankshaft. 3 Drive shaft. 4 Gearbox. 5 Propeller shaft. 6 Propeller. 7 Drive shaft bevel. 8 Bevel gears for forward or reverse gear.

of the vertical drive shaft and the horizontal prop shaft. A system of intermeshing bevel gears forms the gearbox of the outboard. Depending on which bevel gear is brought into contact with the drive shaft bevel, the

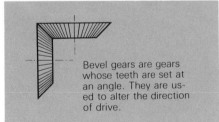

Bevel gears are gears whose teeth are set at an angle. They are used to alter the direction of drive.

prop shaft turns clockwise or counterclockwise. This gives forward or reverse gear and the selection is controlled by a gear lever and clutch. The gearwheels are kept lubricated by a special outboard gear oil which should be that recommended by the manufacturer and changed in accordance with his instructions.

Cooling of outboards

Every internal combustion engine builds up temperatures in the region of 3600°F (2000°C) immediately after ignition. These temperatures would cause most materials used in the construction of engines to glow red hot or even melt within a very short time. Cooling removes enough heat for the engine to maintain an operating temperature of about 175°F (80°C). This is an engine's optimum working temperature, when wear and tear is at its lowest. So that the superfluous heat can be extracted, the parts in the vicinity of the combustion must be constantly in contact with a relatively colder medium — water or air.

Water cooling

Water is a convenient choice of coolant for boat engines. A pump, driven by the transmission shaft and located in the underwater part of the motor near the gearbox, draws in water and forces it through passages up to the cylinders and cylinder head. There the cold liquid circulates round the hot parts of the engine, creating a sort of water jacket. The water immediately heats up while, at the same time, the engine is cooled. The heated water leaves the engine block again and is carried out through an under water exhaust pipe into the wake. To show that the system is operating correctly a small control

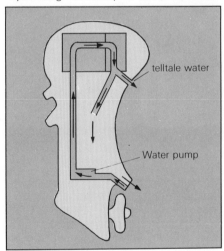

telltale water

Water pump

outlet called a telltale is fitted to the casing which diverts some of the water and indicates that the coolant circulation has not stopped for any reason while the engine is running.

Every cooling system is designed to maintain the engine temperature at

about 175°F (80°C) which, as was explained before, is the most economical operating temperature when wear and tear, fuel and oil consumption are at their lowest. Bearing this in mind, it is obvious that the sooner 175°F (80°C) is reached the better, i.e., the gap between cold start and running temperature should be bridged as quickly as possible. For this reason most manufacturers nowadays recommend that their motors be run under load immediately after starting. Allowing an engine to idle in neutral, as used to be customary, leaves it that much longer at the uneconomic temperature. Another way of building up the temperature quickly is to install a thermostat. Most engines are now fitted with one. A thermostat is a temperature-operated valve which shuts off the flow of coolant in a cold engine until the water around the cylinder and head has reached the operating temperature of the motor. If the temperature of the water drops or rises the valve opens or closes again. When the circulation is shut off by the thermostat a stream of water is still passed out through the telltale. With the thermostat-regulated system, however, the stream may be rather reduced until such time as operating temperature is attained.

A more elementary form of water cooling is the unpressurized system. With this the forward movement of the boat alone is relied upon to force the water — without the need for a pump — all the way up to the cylinder. There the usual heat exchange takes place and the water is carried out of the motor through the exhaust and control outlet. As the necessary pressure is caused by forward travel this system of cooling can only be used with motors that have no neutral or reverse gears.

Air cooling

Air-cooled engines have a constant stream of cold air flowing past the outside of the cylinders and cylinder head so that the air is heated while the engine is correspondingly cooled.

Circuit diagram of a battery ignition (single cylinder):
1 Battery. 2 Ignition switch and key. 3 Contact breaker cam. 4 Contact breaker points. 5 Condenser. 6 Coil — primary winding (few turns, heavy-gauge). 7 Coil — secondary winding (many turns, fine-gauge). 8 Coil — soft iron core. 9 High-tension lead. 10 Spark plug.

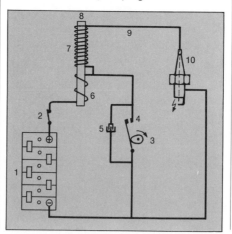

The typical motor for small yachts like these is the outboard.

In order to improve the heat exchange between motor and air the surface area of the cylinders and the head is increased by the addition of cooling fins. If the design of the motor or of the vehicle is such that the airstream cannot flow unhindered and at a sufficiently high speed past the cylinders a fan, driven by the motor, is fitted to ensure the required airflow.

Air cooling is not often used for boat engines. It is fairly obvious that air-cooled engines will be noisier than water-cooled ones as they have no noise-damping water jacket. Anyway, water, that excellent coolant, is ready at hand for boat engines. One or two smaller outboards have combined air-and-water cooling systems. While cooling fins ensure that the cylinders and head are air-cooled, unpressurized water cooling takes care of the exhaust and the lower casing.

The ignition system

The ignition system causes a current to pass through the spark plug at the right moment and this ignites the gasoline-air mixture. The source of the current may be either a battery or a magneto run off the engine itself. Whereas car engines are invariably fitted with battery ignition in boats this is confined mostly to inboard motors which are often built as commercial engines and converted to marine use. These engines are started with a self-starter and a battery is therefore required. With outboard motors the overwhelming majority are fitted with magneto ignition. This system has an advantage in that it has no external source of power — which can suddenly be dead when you need it! These motors use a recoil start. Here a firm pull on the starter cord gets the crankshaft turning relatively fast and this causes a high potential difference in the magneto which in turn creates the voltage necessary for a spark at the spark plug.

With the steady improvement of outboards in terms of convenience of operation the industry is tending to fit electric starters to motors with magneto ignition as well, even to those whose low horsepower means that they can be easily turned over by hand. The convenience of the electric start is combined with the assurance that the motor can be started by hand if a dead battery makes this necessary. If an engine is fitted with an electric starter, an alternator or generator has to be included which will keep the battery topped up while the motor is running.

Battery ignition

So that, at the moment of ignition, a spark can bridge the gap between the two electrodes of the spark plug the low voltage of the battery (about 12 volts) has to be converted into a high potential difference of around 15,000 volts. This is achieved through two separate coil windings. With the ignition switched on and the contact breaker points closed, a current flows through the primary winding; the primary circuit is made (positive terminal of the battery – primary winding – contact breaker – negative terminal of the battery). This induces a strong magnetic field in the soft iron core of the coil. As soon as the points open again the primary circuit is broken and the magnetic field dissolves. The collapse of the field is perpendicular to the direction of the thousands of turns in the secondary winding of the coil and this induces a high-tension current in the secondary circuit (about 15,000 volts). The voltage is so great that, at the moment when the primary circuit is broken, a spark arcs across the electrode gap of the plug which ignites the compressed gasoline-air mixture. In order to ensure that spark build-up time can be kept as short as possible when the primary circuit is broken, a condenser is fitted in parallel with the contact breaker. This swallows the greater part of the current. Eventually the surface of the contact breaker points becomes pitted, however, and burnt to the detriment of the ignition system. They should be cleaned, adjusted and renewed in accordance with the manufacturer's instructions. In motors with more than one cylinder the high-tension current

flows to a distributor. A rotating cam, the rotor arm, sends the current to whichever cylinder is on the point of ignition.

It is only a fraction of a second before all the ignited fuel has been burnt. So that the combustion can take place with maximum force at the exact moment when the piston is at top dead centre the point of ignition must be slightly before tdc. In order that the interval of time between ignition and full combustion shall always remain the same ignition must be advanced as the engine runs faster. The adjustment of the advance for high or low revolutions takes place automatically, either mechanically or by means of a vacuum pipe to the carburettor.

To switch the engine off the ignition key is turned to the off position, the primary circuit is broken and the motor comes to a halt. The advantage of a battery ignition system thus lies in the fact that, despite a low-rpm start, a strong spark can be induced.

Magneto ignition

As the magneto ignition system does not use a battery a current must be induced in the primary winding. To achieve this a permanent magnet is

Circuit diagram of a magneto ignition:
1 Permanent magnet with north and south poles turns round with the flywheel. 2 Flywheel. 3 Primary winding of the coil. 4 Secondary winding of the coil. 5 Soft iron core of the coil. 6 Contact breaker points. 7 Contact breaker cam. 8 Condenser. 9 High-tension lead. 10 Spark plug. 11 Short circuit switch

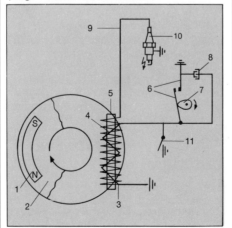

fitted to a rotating flywheel. When the flywheel is turned by means of the recoil starter the magnet mounted on it and its magnetic field passes across the heavy-gauge windings of the primary coil. This induces a current in the primary coil and the soft iron core builds up its own magnetic field. As soon as the revolving contact breaker cam breaks the primary circuit by opening the points the magnetic field breaks down. As it breaks down it induces a high-voltage current in the thin-gauge winding of the secondary coil and this is carried by a high-tension lead to the spark plug where it arcs across the electrode gap. What in the battery ignition system has been said about the condenser, moment of ignition and its setting goes for magneto systems as well. To stop the motor the primary circuit is shorted to earth[1] using a short-circuit switch.

Although the points are still opened and closed by the contact breaker cam no further ht current passes down the lead as, despite the opened contacts, a circuit is completed through the short-circuit switch to earth.

Capacitor discharge ignition

Conventional ignition systems (magneto and battery-type) are very reliable but in certain circumstances they have their limitations:

1 In very high rpm engines the contact breaker is unable to open and close fast enough.
2 Despite the use of very sophisticated alloys for the two contact breaker points these will start to show signs of burning after a number of hours, running. The contact surfaces are no longer clean and flat. The ignition is affected. This burning appears sooner with higher rpm engines.
3 While the 15,000-volt current induced in the coil is enough to cause a spark to arc across the electrode gap of the spark plug under certain conditions (cold, wet or when the engine has stood idle

1. Earth: this is the negative terminal of the battery. All earthed components are thus connected directly to the negative terminal.

for some time, etc.) the spark is insufficient to ignite the gasoline-air mixture. This results in oiled-up plugs, dirty hands and irritation.

These problems with the standard ignition system used to be most apparent in racing speedboats which were fitted with very high-rpm engines until a new, improved ignition system was introduced. This is the high-voltage condenser type, or capacitor discharge ignition (CDI for short). The various manufacturers use different terms to describe this, such as electronic ignition, transistorized ignition, etc. They all work without a contact breaker — effectively without parts that are liable to wear out. In a shorter time than it takes the conventional ignition to work a CDI can build up a voltage of between 25,000 and 35,000 volts. With the higher voltage there are virtually no problems on starting even when conditions are less than ideal.

Also, with CDI, there are almost no limits to the speed at which the engine can run. CDI-fitted motors should use only those spark plugs specified by the manufacturer, which differ considerably from the standard type. The wrong plugs could damage the ignition system which then — and this is the disadvantage of the CDI — would mean that the whole expensive

unit would have to be replaced. While conventional ignition systems can be adjusted and serviced by enthusiastic amateurs the CDIs demand the services of the manufacturer's mechanics who have special tools for the repair of electronic systems. The use of ordinary electrical meters and instruments will wreck the CDI. Apart from the question of expensive damage caused by amateur repair work the high voltage (and current) produced by the CDI could endanger someone's life.

The portable fuel tank

Sometimes included in the purchase price of an outboard motor is a portable fuel tank with a capacity of between one and six gallons (five and twenty-seven litres). These tanks are mostly used on board smaller sports boats and are located at the stern near the motor. Considerations of safety make it essential that portable tanks be firmly secured, to prevent them sliding around, on some kind of mat or in a drained locker. When siting the tank it is important to ensure that the fuel pipe between tank and engine, connected at one or both ends by a clip or bayonet coupling, is not pulled or nipped by steering movements of the motor. Tank ventilation is either automatic upon connecting the fuel pipe to the tank or via a small ventilation screw (e.g., on the cap), which must be loosened. The carburettor has to be primed before starting the engine by squeezing a bulb-shaped rubber hand pump. When the engine is running the fuel pump fitted to the motor takes over the job of drawing the fuel from the tank. A look at the indicator fitted to the tank will show how much fuel is left. Depending on where and how the motor is being used, on the construction of the boat and, not least, on the question of trim, a larger, or two smaller, built-in tanks may be chosen in place of a portable one.

Manoeuvring with the outboard

The outboard motor can be turned through both its vertical and its horizontal axes. By turning it through its horizontal axis it can be set at

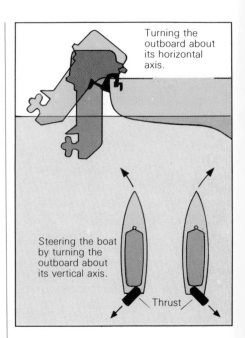

Turning the outboard about its horizontal axis.

Steering the boat by turning the outboard about its vertical axis.

Thrust

various angles of tilt. This influences the boat's trim and also means that in very shallow water and on the mooring the motor can be tilted up so that the prop is clear of the water. By turning the motor through its vertical axis the boat can be steered. With sailing craft under outboard motor the motor is fixed and the boat's rudder is used for steering as usual.

Outboard motors often have tillers fitted by which they are steered. Mostly the free end of the tiller will be fitted with a throttle twist grip. Alternatively, the boat can be fitted with a steering wheel. In this case there will be a steering cable running over several sheaves to the motor, which is linked to the wheel in such a way that the direction of turn corresponds to the direction in which the wheel is turned. With wheel steering there will naturally be remote controls for throttle and gears (forward, reverse and neutral). Very small engines with built-in fuel tanks have enough clearance from the transom to allow them to turn through a full circle in the vertical axis. A reverse gear is unnecessary with these motors. The whole unit is simply turned through 180°.

Motor manufacturers are now tending to build safety features into their starters. Where these are fitted the engine can only be started when the

Portable fuel tank as used on outboards.

gear lever is set to neutral. This stops the boat moving off immediately as it would do if the engine were started in gear. Something that has happened only too often is that a driver has been thrown overboard by the unexpected movement of the boat, especially when he is standing in the stern using the recoil starter. A collision with another boat or a dock possibly follows. But these are minor accidents compared to what *could* happen. Driverless boats can be lethal if there are swimmers about. As well as the starter lock some of the faster motorboats are fitted with a special switch tied by a lanyard to the hand or foot of the driver. If the driver goes overboard while manoeuvring, the lanyard operates the switch. This opens or closes a circuit, depending on the type of ignition fitted, and the motor immediately cuts out.

When outboards are fitted with remote control the dashboard should have a tachometer and a temperature gauge so that the engine temperature can be checked.

Practical hints on the use of outboards

1 Don't forget the maintenance! Outboards today are so refined that they will do their job simply and reliably for a long time. If you don't look after them, though, their reliability diminishes. They retain their qualities only so long as the manufacturers' recommendations for servicing and cleaning are observed. You will get more pleasure out of your outboard if you are familiar with how it works and how it should be serviced. The first and most important step is to study the service manual and owner's instructions supplied with the motor when you buy it. You would also be well advised to get hold of any further information that will explain more of what goes on inside the engine. This does not necessarily mean that you should become your own mechanic. In the maintenance instructions you will find information about minor repairs. Everything else should be left to the mechanic who services the engine.

2 The gasoline-oil mixture When you mix the gasoline and oil make sure it's clean. Small pieces of dirt can block the carburettor jet, preventing the flow of fuel. Mix the oil recommended by the manufacturer with the gasoline in the correct ratio. Mix it in the open and, if you have a portable tank, as far as possible from the boat where no naked flames, lighted cigarettes or electrical sparks can ignite the gasoline vapour. Fuel mixture spilt on board increases the risk of someone slipping. Always use fresh gasoline. If gasoline is left in the tank throughout the winter it gives rise to deposits which can lead to fuel blockages or ignition failures.

3 Take care when starting! First pull the starter cord slowly until the follower catches and only then pull it firmly. Then let the cord re-coil itself automatically. Make sure that when you start the engine there is no one standing directly behind you. The strong jerk you give with the arm when you turn the engine over can result in your crew being knocked out. Close the choke when the engine is being started from cold and open it again when the engine fires. If you have an electric start use it for no longer than twenty seconds at the most. The starter current is like a short circuit and puts a great load on the starter and the battery. Give the starter a rest of about two minutes after every unsuccessful attempt. If the engine fails to start after repeated attempts look for a repair shop as it is unlikely that the engine will take so long to fire unless something is amiss. Finally, when you leave the boat, make sure that nothing is hanging over the side that might foul the propeller (mooring lines, etc.).

4 Checking the cooling system As soon as the engine fires check the telltale to see whether water (or, depending on the model of outboard, steam from the auxiliary exhaust) is coming out. Repeat this check every ten minutes while the motor is running. If the stream of water is not there see whether the water intake is blocked. Often the inlet is choked with weeds or other rubbish. In most cases this will be the cause of the problem. If this is not so the motor will

have to be taken to a repair shop. If the motor is used for even a short time with a defective cooling system more extensive and very costly damage can occur to the water pump and engine.

5 About changing gear When changing gear from forward to reverse or vice versa, or when selecting gear, make sure that the motor is idling. An emergency can sometimes make it essential to change gear at considerably higher rpms, but doing this too often can result in damage to the gearbox.

6 Stopping the engine When you want to stop the engine it is enough simply to use the short-circuit switch or the ignition switch. The motor will then cut out. It is a good idea, however, to get into the habit of cutting off the fuel supply some time before stopping the engine and allowing it to idle until it stops itself as the fuel in the carburettor runs out. When you have sufficient experience you will be able to cut off the fuel at just the right time so that the last drop of fuel will take you into the berth. But take care! Don't try to be clever if there is the slightest risk of getting yourself or others into a fix if you have underestimated the distance and the engine stops too soon.

There are several reasons for allowing the carburettor to run dry:
1 When there is virtually no gasoline left in the carburettor you can tilt the motor without pouring fuel all over the place. If you are unlucky the whole tank can drain itself through the carburettor.
2 When the motor is unused for a long time the heavier constituents of the mixture can stick to the small valves and jets of the carburettor. While the fuel will evaporate in the course of time part of the lubricating oil remains behind. When the engine is started again there will be an excess of oil in the mixture which will make starting difficult.

7 Working on the propeller When you do any work on the propeller make sure there is no risk of being injured if the engine is accidentally started. For example, you can stick a piece of wood between the prop and the cavitation plate. Better still, you can remove the spark plug leads before you begin work.

8 Carrying the motor If the motor has to be carried or transported to the workshop or for winterizing, put it down in an upright position before transporting it and allow the water to run out. The starter cord should be pulled a couple of times as well. Pull off the spark plug leads first, so that the motor cannot start. If the water has run out you can rest assured that none is going to find its way up the exhaust pipe into the cylinder when you finally put the motor in the boot or trunk of your car. You should also make sure, though, that the engine itself is not lower than the gearbox when it is laid down.

9 Winterizing Most manufacturers recommend that an engine be given a yearly inspection at the end of the season. The water jacket is flushed out with fresh water, the outside of the engine cleaned and checked, and small troubles put right. Parts to be lubricated are oiled or greased in accordance with a schedule. After a final test run the motor is put to bed for the winter. A special inhibiting oil is squirted into the carburettor for this run. This flows through the crankcase, transfer port, cylinder and exhaust together with the gasoline-air mixture, leaving a protective film throughout the inside of the engine. The motor should spend the winter mounted, vertically if possible, on a

Gearbox

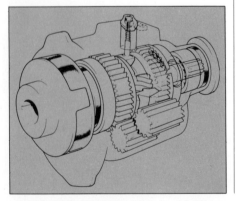

board or trestle in a warmish room. If you really want to put your mind at ease turn the engine over every two or three weeks throughout the winter. This will ensure that any condensation inside the machine does not remain in the same place all the time. If it can be arranged, motors that have been run for a long time in salt water should be operated for a while in fresh water before being laid up. Don't forget the battery altogether during the winter months. Batteries left without being used for a long time lose their charge and dead batteries can be ruined by frost. It is therefore advisable to clean the outside of the battery before winterizing and put it on charge. Make sure the battery is not given a quick charge — it shortens its life. After greasing the terminals with terminal grease leave the battery in a cool, dry place. Every six to eight weeks during its 'hibernation' it should be recharged.

The inboard motor

Inboard engines are those mounted inside the hull of the boat together with their gearboxes. While the two-stroke easily dominates the outboard market, most inboards are four-stroke gasoline or diesel engines. Both these engines have exact, valve-operated regulation of the gas exchange. This results in a rather higher engine weight but greater efficiency as compared to the two-stroke. (Efficiency is the ratio of the power output of the engine to the potential energy put in.) Even with the greater efficiency the internal combustion engine is actually a very extravagant machine. This is because we can use only a small part of the very great heat energy created by combustion. Not only do we get rid of part of the heat by radiation and by ejecting it through the exhaust, we also have to use some of the valuable power of the engine to drive a cooling system to get rid of the superfluous heat, i.e., to dissipate it to the air.

Inboards have, for the most part, a water-cooling system working on the same principle as the outboard

system. With inboards that are usually driven in salt water you will often find nowadays a dual system of cooling. The inner system is a closed circuit filled with fresh water and kept circulating by a pump. Around this inner circuit is a second water jacket which has sea water driven by a second pump constantly passing through it; the sea water takes away enough heat from the inner system to keep the motor at its ideal temperature of about 175°F (80°C).

With the single cooling system using sea water there are certain disadvantages, as sea water heated above 150°F (65°C) leaves deposits of salt and calcium. In time this constricts or blocks the cooling system.

Olympic classes

TOP: The Tempest two-man keelboat, an Olympic class since 1972; length 25ft 10in (6.70m), beam 6ft 6in (1.98m), draft max. 3ft 7in (1.10m), weight 1034 lb (470 kg), sail area 248 sq ft (23 sq m).

CENTRE: The Tornado catamaran, recognized as an Olympic class since 1976; length 20ft (6.09m), beam 10ft (3.04m), draft max. 2ft 6in (0.78m), weight 308lb (140 kg), sail area 235 sq ft (21.83 sq m).

BOTTOM: The Soling three-man keelboat, the largest of the Olympic class boats; length 26ft 8in (8.15m), beam 6ft 3in (1.90m), draft 4ft 3in (1.30m), weight 2200lb (1000kg), sail area 298 sq ft (27.70 sq m).

Inboard transmission

So that the drive of the engine can be carried to the propeller the hull of the boat must be drilled through. The prop shaft is led through a tube, the stern tube, which is fixed in this hole. A stuffing box stops water from leaking into the boat. Every time the motor is stopped the greaser should be operated — usually done by turning a screw cap — to make sure the packing is always well soaked in grease. If water does leak in through the stern gland the packing must be adjusted to press firmly against the shaft. When adjustment is no longer possible the whole packing should be renewed.

Between the drive shaft of the engine and the propeller shaft is located the gearbox for driving the boat ahead or astern. It also serves to convert the fairly high revolutions of the engine into the lower revs of the propeller. This reduction in speed gives the propeller a stronger turning movement. If the box is kept topped up with oil which is regularly changed and if the gear is only changed at low revs, virtually no harm can come to the gearbox.

Depending on the location of the engine there are various ways of taking the power through the gearbox to the propeller. In sailing boats the layout is usually the conventional one where the crankshaft of the engine, the gearbox and the propeller shaft are in line. Alternatively there is the V-drive, where the motor-drive shaft and the propeller shaft make an acute angle. As well as these types of drive the S-drive, also known as the stern-drive or outdrive, as well as by a number of trade names, is becoming more and more popular for motor-boats. Here the propeller shaft is set at right angles to the engine-drive shaft. These units combine aspects of the inboard engine with those of the outboard engine. The engine is installed inboard but the drive unit is outside the boat on the transom and free to move round a vertical and a horizontal axis. Turning through the vertical axis is achieved through the steering wheel. The steering of a sterndrive is thus exactly the same as with an outboard, effected by changing the direction of the propeller in relation to the fore-and-aft line of the boat. By turning the drive about its horizontal axis — usually by pressing a button — you can raise or lower the propeller. This means that the trim can be altered and that, to a limited

Conventional drive layout as fitted to most sailing yachts.

V-drive, less often used on sailing craft.

S-drive or outdrive

Saildrive

Note the simplicity of the saildrive. Weight and space are saved and the modest increase in drag is a relatively small drawback.

extent, the boat can run in shallower water. With the drive raised as high as it will go the boat can be beached or launched without damaging the drive unit.

A method of inboard engine installation which is becoming increasingly popular is the saildrive. In this, the engine is mounted atop, or direct-

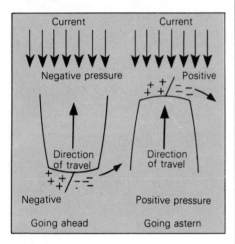

ly adjacent to, the gearbox and driveshaft unit which projects through a watertight flange in the bottom of the boat near the stern. The unit bears resemblance to an outdrive but is rather more compact since it can be made shorter overall. The modern type of hull with a flat after section is ideal for this type of installation. There is a considerable saving in installation costs, plus a lower overall initial cost, making the saildrive an attractive proposition. Homebuilders also find them relatively easy to cope with.

Stern swing according to the direction in which the propeller turns.

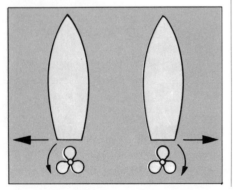

The turning effect of the inboard

Boats that have rudder steering are fitted with saildrive, conventional drive or V-drive. The propeller in these cases is located in front of the rudder so that the propeller thrust streams past the rudder. If the rudder is turned to one side or the other by means of the tiller or the helm this sets up a positive pressure on one side and a negative pressure on the other. The stern of the boat is thus pushed to one side and the boat begins to turn.

The thrust of the propeller can be broken into two components because of the shape and turning direction of the propeller. One component gives the forward movement required, while the second tries to push the transom of the boat to one side. This is the transverse thrust. The direction in which the propeller tries to turn the boat depends on the direction of rotation of the propeller. So a boat with a right-handed propeller (turning clockwise when going ahead, seen from aft) acts as though the propeller was touching the ground and, like the wheel of a car, was trying to turn the stern. In this case the transverse thrust would be to starboard.

Transverse thrust is particularly noticeable when the boat is beginning to move astern. The forward component is directed from the stern towards the bow and the propeller no longer pushes the water past the rudder. Once the boat is moving the rudder begins to work again as it has water from the boat's passage streaming past it. Transverse thrust also occurs with stern drives and outboards although it is hardly noticed as these boats are steered by the propeller rather than the rudder. Adjusting the angle of the drive will cancel out the sideways component.

The fuel system of the inboard engine

The fuel system of a boat is fundamentally the same as that of a car. Fuel is supplied from a built-in tank to the engine by means of a pump and fuel pipe. Depending on the size and construction of the boat one large or

two small tanks may be fitted. Faultless operation of the fuel system is even more important in boats than it is in cars. If for example, the fuel pipe of a car comes undone, the gasoline will, in most cases, drop straight on to the road, whereas in a boat in the same circumstances it will fall into the bilges. There it will form a highly explosive gasoline-air mixture which can be ignited simply by a cigarette or a spark.

The fuel tank

To reduce the risk of fire or explosion on board as far as possible a trouble-free tank installation is necessary. The following things have to be borne in mind:

Tanks for diesel: diesel tanks should not be made of copper, copper alloy or galvanized steel sheet. Diesel oil in copper tanks forms a rubbery precipitate which can cause blockages, especially in the fuel filter. Diesel tanks should ideally be of ordinary unpainted mild steel or self-extinguishing fibreglass.

Tanks for gasoline: these tanks should ideally be made of galvanized steel, copper alloy (Monel, for example, which is an alloy of nickel and copper) or stainless steel (not all types of which are suitable). A good choice would be stainless steel with the designation X5 CrNiMo (a chrome-nickel-molybdenum type). Copper plate should be at least 1/16in 1.5mm thick, steel plate at least 1/14in 2mm.

All larger tanks, including diesel tanks, should be fitted with baffles (plates dividing the tank into several interconnecting compartments), so that the fuel cannot surge when the boat is at sea. This will otherwise make the motion of the boat even more pronounced.

The filler hole should be sited on deck, not under a hatch or on the cockpit sole, where any spilt fuel cannot run down into the boat.

The filler pipe must be secured to the filler opening itself with a jubilee clip so that no gasoline or gasoline vapour can escape at the joint and get into the boat. The filler pipe must lead down into the fuel tank to within a short distance of the bottom and be completely leak-proof.

A breather pipe, gastight as well, should be led from the tank to the outside of the boat. This breather should be left permanently open and should be protected on the outside with a flame trap. The pipe also acts as an overflow tube.

Fuel pipes and ventilation

The fuel feed pipe should be led from the top of the tank and a stopcock fitted to the tank at this point. Where the exit of the fuel pipe has to be below the highest fuel level a non-return valve should be fitted to stop the tank from emptying itself through siphon action.

As a certain amount of dirt and condensation collects on the bottom of the tank in the course of time the fuel pipe to the engine should start just above the bottom of the tank. This will make it less likely that dirt willbe sucked up. With diesel engines especially, the tank should never be allowed to get so low that air is drawn into the fuel pipe. If air does get in it is carried to the motor in the form of air bubbles in the fuel. It then passes through the injector pipe (the pipe between the injection pump and the injector itself) and creates a small cushion of air there. The injector works on the principle that diesel oil cannot be compressed. Unlike air it retains its volume under pressure. When the injector pump exerts a certain pressure a needle in the injector moves to allow a passage and diesel fuel is injected into the combustion chamber. But with an air lock in the pipe the pressure necessary to force the fuel through the injector cannot be built up and the engine will stop. The whole fuel system will have to be bled by hand. This work can be done by amateurs as described in the owner's manual but bleeding always takes a lot of time and the involuntary mechanic will stink of diesel for some time afterwards — not a good way of keeping the other crew members happy. Apart from these inconvenient, but harmless, consequences, it can also be dangerous if the motor

cuts at the exact moment when you need it for an urgent manoeuvre. So always top up the tank with diesel in good time to avoid this particular risk. With a gasoline engine an air lock is of far less consequence, but it is still a good idea to fill the tank in plenty of time, for obvious reasons.

Safety precautions

To reduce to a minimum the risks inherent in fuel — especially gasoline — and electricity in close proximity, a number of safety precautions should be very closely observed. Some of the most important ones are as follows.

Be extremely careful when refuelling!
- Put out all flames.
- Put out cigarettes, cigars and pipes.
- Shut all hatches and ports so that the fuel vapour in the tank does not make its way into the interior of the boat.
- During the refuelling operation you should avoid stepping from the boat to the land or to the bunkering barge. A metal contact should be made between the refuelling pipe and the filler. The reason for this is that static electricity already present or generated during refuelling can lead to an electric discharge, and this could produce a spark if there is a gap for the current to jump. This could, naturally, cause an explosion of the gasoline-air mixture.
- If there is a blower on board that is driven by an explosion-protected electric motor this should be run during refuelling so that dangerous vapours can be sucked out. Such blowers are compulsory in the USA. After refuelling open all hatches and ports wide and ventilate the engine space well.

General safety precautions
- The fitting of a unit which will indicate the presence of a dangerous build-up of gases (known as a gas

detector) is recommended for inboard gasoline engines. Care must be taken, however, to see that no spark is emitted when switching the equipment on and off, as this alone can ignite the gasoline-air mixture which builds up prior to setting off the alarm.
- The fuel supply pipe between the tank and the engine should be checked frequently for leaks.
- Before the engine is started the engine compartment should be well ventilated. Gasoline vapour which may have collected deep in the bilge must be sucked out with a blower.
- The exhaust system should be regularly checked for leakage.
- No loose parts should be left lying around the engine compartment.
- Don't leave oily rags lying around in the engine space, stern lockers or drawers. They should be kept in bins with lids reserved for that purpose.
- An adequate number of fire extinguishers should be carried and always kept readily accessible. The most effective ones are the universal dry powder extinguishers, which are suitable for putting out all types of fire, whereas the traditional foam extinguisher may not be used on electrical fires.

While on the subject of safety precautions the many amateur builders of sailing and motor boats should be firmly discouraged from carrying out the installation of electrical systems or inboard engines and drive units for themselves. The dangers of converting car engines to marine use must also be given special mention. Automobile engines can only be used for marine purposes when they are of a manufacturer's series in which the special safety considerations necessary are taken into account. The electrical system must be insulated in such a way as to preclude the risk of a spark causing an explosion. The official requirements for fuel systems (installation of pipes, material specifications, safety valves, etc.) laid down by various governments must be met. The exhaust system on a boat deserves a great deal more attention than that of a car.

Whereas a leak in the exhaust pipe of a car does not, for the most part, put the owners at risk, since the pipe is outside the passenger compartment, a leaking exhaust pipe in the interior of a boat can be lethal. As the gases (odourless and heavier than air) remain inboard, the dangerous carbon monoxide is breathed in by the crew. This slows down or stops the oxygen supply to the brain. Carbon monoxide poisoning can lead to death in a very short time. The exhaust pipe of a boat engine must also be cooled — unlike that of a car — as overheating could cause a fire. Cooling is commonly achieved by water injection and the installation should only be undertaken by an expert.

Choosing a boat motor

Inboard or outboard? Gasoline or diesel? Four-stroke or two-stroke? To find the right answers to these questions you must ask yourself what the motor is to be used for.

Inboard versus outboard

There are a number of advantages in having an outboard: easy installation, a compact drive unit, a comparatively high degree of reliability, easy manoeuvrability even in shallow water.

Here are the main arguments against the outboard motor. It is protected by its housing from spray but, if a wave breaks over it, the water is bound to find its way into the ignition, whereupon the motor will stop and not start again. If an outboard is used in a heavy sea, with the boat rolling and pitching, it is possible for the propeller to keep coming out of the water. The propeller races and the engine immediately begins to overrev which strains the bearings. If this goes on it can damage the transmission. Long-shaft outboards make this less likely, but the possibility of the propeller coming out of the water is still higher than it is with conventional or V-drive inboards, where the propeller is sited underneath the boat.

Depending on the style of rudder fitted many outboards on sailing boats have to be mounted to one side of the transom. If the yacht is motor-sailed in strong winds at a considerable angle of heel it will be found that she can only be sailed on the tack which makes her heel to the side on which the outboard is mounted, as on the other tack the propeller will be out of the water for most of the time.

There are various arguments for and against this or that type of engine and it really depends on the use to which the boat is to be put. A seagoing sailing yacht will have to be fitted with an inboard motor which can be relied on under even the most ex-

treme conditions. If a motor is used purely to get a sailing boat to a near-by mooring in calm weather, an outboard will be the ideal installation. In many cases boats have to have outboard motors, since as a rule only craft of over, say, 22ft (7m) in length have space for an inboard engine and transmission. Anyone who installs a very small, underpowered unit in his yacht must understand that it will only be of use in calm weather. Anything which changes these conditions — it need only be a current or the tide — will be too much for such a motor. If you want a motor on which you can rely in bad weather or strong tides you need an auxiliary with an output of about 4-5hp (2.94-3.67kw) per ton of displacement. Outboards were designed for a specific purpose, as drive units of small, fast speed-boats, and for this purpose they are ideal. They are not ideal as auxiliaries for sailing yachts.

Gasoline versus diesel

With inboards one has to choose between gasoline and diesel motors. If safety is the main consideration diesel is the more suitable. In contrast to gasoline diesel is not affected by temperature and will not give off an explosive vapour. The danger of explosion is further reduced with diesels as they function without electricity. The diesel engine is also therefore unaffected by water.

The disadvantages of diesel engines do not affect their inherent safety. They are, for example, noisier than gasoline motors and their power-weight ratio is not as good.

Gasoline engines are exactly the opposite. They are usually easy to start (under normal conditions), quieter-running, powerful and relatively light in weight. These are good qualities but they must take second place to the possible dangers of a gasoline engine. There is the risk of fire or explosion due to the combination of volatized gasoline and sparks from the electrics (ignition, electrical fittings) or careless handling of a naked flame (stove, cigarettes). The electric ignition system is adversely affected by water.

Yachts leaving harbour under power.

Sailing theory and sail tuning

The theory of sail power

The driving force necessary to move a sailing boat hull through the water against the resistance of the water and the air in contact with hull, sails and spars is generated by the airflow over the sails. The way in which the energy of the moving air is converted into driving power by the sails is too complicated to explain fully here. It is only necessary for the practical sailor to know that the sail behaves like an aerofoil, much the same as an aeroplane wing, and that, due to its shape and the angle at which the wind strikes it, it is capable of converting the airflow into aerodynamic force. On the windward side of the sail this is due to high pressure, on the leeward side of the sail to low pressure, caused by the acceleration of the airflow.

The total aerodynamic force, also referred to as resultant force, is, in fact, made up of two parts: lift and drag, but this is a purely academic notion which only applies to a sail in isolation and need not concern us. The important thing is that the resultant force, which can be imagined as being concentrated in the centre of effort (CE) of the sail area and which has a definite magnitude and direction, is converted by the reaction of the hull in the water into forward drive and side force (causing heeling and leeway).

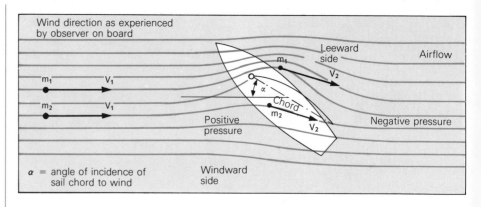

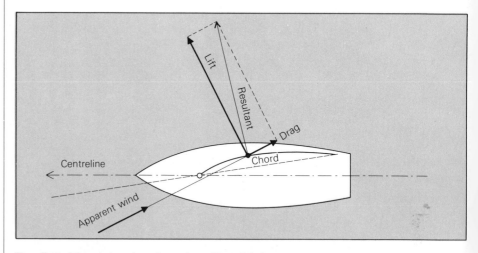

The effect of the wind on the sails produces lift and drag

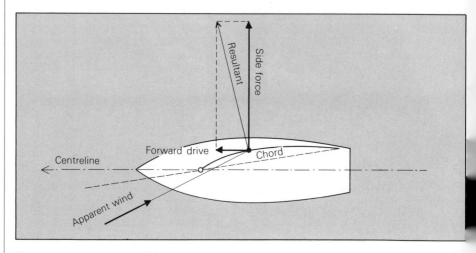

The reaction of the hull splits the resultant up into forward drive and side force.

True wind and apparent wind

In the sections that follow we shall be speaking a good deal about *apparent wind*. This is the wind experienced, both in force and direction, by the observer moving along in the boat and it is the wind really used in sailing. The *true wind*, on the other hand, is experienced only by a stationary observer, either on land or on a boat lying at anchor or at moorings. What it amounts to is that the apparent wind is a combination of the true wind and the self-induced wind experienced by a moving object, in this case a boat, as a result of its own movement. It can be determined graphically with the help of a parallelogram of forces.

The following rules apply to the apparent wind:

- Apparent wind and true wind can never be the same while the boat is under way.
- The strength and direction of the true wind cannot be determined accurately while the boat is moving.
- The apparent wind always comes from further forward than the true wind. Only on a downwind course do their directions coincide.
- To a boat sailing close to the wind the apparent wind is noticeably stronger than the true wind.
- To a boat sailing close to the wind the apparent wind is a disadvantage because it comes from further ahead than the true wind. The greater the speed of the boat the more the apparent wind draws ahead.
- On a downwind course the apparent wind is a disadvantage, too, because its speed decreases the faster the boat sails. The induced wind, in this case, is exactly opposed to the true wind and has to be subtracted from it.

minimize resistance, both from air and water, and to reduce leeway. It is important to bear in mind, especially when racing, that anything which increases resistance will seriously diminish an already small resource of power. Every sailor should try his hardest to increase the amount of driving force generated by the sails and it is for this purpose that we must look briefly at the factors which will result in the best performance being obtained from the sails.

A great deal of interesting scientific research has been done in the field of sailing theory. Any sailor who would like to know more about the mathematics of the subject should turn to *Sailing Theory and Practice* by C.A. Marchaj which is an outstanding book on the subject.

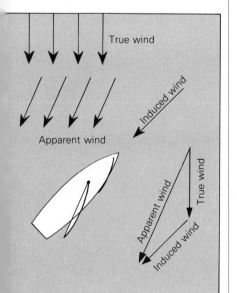

Forward drive and side force

In determining the performance of a sailing yacht, we first consider the resultant force of the wind, which has already been defined. The diagram (right) shows how it is converted by the yacht into forward drive and side force. The parallelogram of forces reveals that the force we need most in sailing, namely forward drive, is the smaller of the two, while the side force, which produces heeling and leeway and which we want least, is the greater.

In fact, it is remarkable that the sailing yacht can convert this relatively small amount of drive force into the high speeds which, for example, planing dinghies can attain. The explanation is to be found in the efforts which yacht designers make to

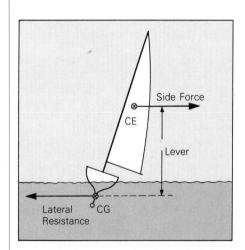

Side force is visualized as being concentrated at CE, th centre of effort of the sail area.

Sail camber and angle of incidence

The shape of a sail in cross-section is what determines how well it performs. Quite simply there is a degree of curvature or *camber* which, combined with the correct angle of incidence (of the wind), results in the sail producing the optimum driving power.

Wind tunnel tests (see diagram right) have shown that:

1 The lift produced by a curved profile with a camber ratio of 1:10 is considerably greater at all angles of incidence (i.e., all points of sailing) than that produced by a flat plate.
2 At an angle of incidence (α) of 15° the curved profile produces its maximum lift.
3 At an angle of incidence of 15° the resultant force produced by the curved profile is directed further ahead than that produced by the flat plate.

The conclusion to be drawn from these tests, in which a number of different camber ratios were tested is that, to put it very simply, a full sail is superior to a flat one.

So far as the angle of incidence is concerned (which is the angle between the chord of the sail camber and the direction of the apparent wind), it has been determined that the optimum angle is $\alpha = 15°$. At larger angles of incidence the airflow detaches itself (see diagram right) and the resultant driving force is correspondingly less.

There are a number of important conclusions that we should consider in trying to get the best performance from a sail.

1 The leading edge of the sail should present the same angle of attack to the wind (αA) over its entire length, and αA should be quite small, between 0° and 4°.
2 The sail should be cambered over its entire width, since flat areas of sail, because they do not divert the airflow, produce very little lift.

3 The sail should not 'close up', i.e., present a negative angle to the boat's centreline, anywhere along its camber, since this would result in an increase in side force and a decrease in forward drive.
4 The maximum camber of the sail should be approximately in the middle of the sail or, if there is no turbulence from the mast, slightly forward of the middle. See diagram at top of facing page.
5 For maximum resultant wind force the sail must be very full (e.g., spinnaker). For very close-hauled work, on the other hand, the sail must not have too much camber in order to fulfil conditions 1 and 3 above.
6 Air should not be allowed to escape from the windward, or high pressure, side of the sail to the leeward, or low pressure, side.

One shape of sail is not enough to fulfil all requirements of a sail in all conditions and point four, above, can be enlarged upon:

a. In all-round sails the maximum draft built in should be around the centre or just forward of it.
b. For sailing before the wind the maximum draft should be aft of centre.
c. Storm sails and sails for sailing close to the wind should have the maximum draft just forward of centre.

It would be unrealistic to be constantly changing sails and in round-the-buoys racing this is not allowed. The answer is an all-round sail which can be adjusted to suit conditions a. to c.

The problem of what degree of camber the sail should have becomes apparent if you consider the case of a fast racing yacht, for example a Soling. Sailing efficiently to windward she can get so close that she needs a fairly flat sail with a camber ratio of 1:20 while off the wind, in the same conditions, a sail with a camber ratio of 1:6 would be much superior.

The: are various ways of getting

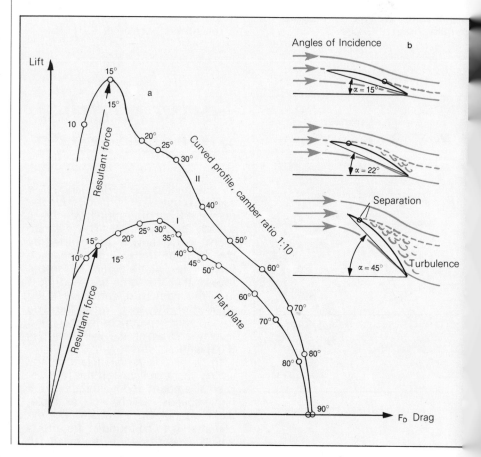

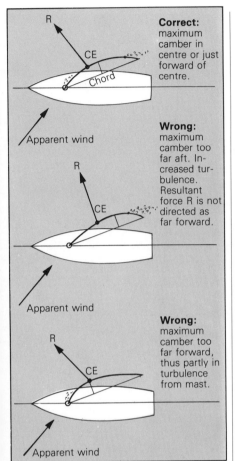

Correct: maximum camber in centre or just forward of centre.

Wrong: maximum camber too far aft. Increased turbulence. Resultant force R is not directed as far forward.

Wrong: maximum camber too far forward, thus partly in turbulence from mast.

round the problem. Changing sails is the simplest, when allowed, but is difficult to do quickly. Ways of adjusting the sail, such as with the Cunningham hole, or by deliberately bending the mast or boom, are simpler to apply. But first let us look at some other factors which affect performance.

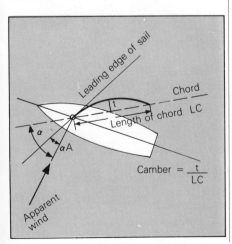

Resistance of a sailing boat

The forces produced by the sail are used to overcome the resistance of the yacht.

This resistance is made up of several components which are more or less easy to reduce.
- Resistance due to friction on the underwater parts of the boat (skin friction).
- Resistance due to the shape of the hull (form resistance).
- Resistance due to the heeling of the boat.
- Resistance induced by leeway (induced drag).
- Wind resistance of the hull and the rigging.
- Resistance caused by rough water (waves).

All these forms of resistance have one thing in common: each form of resistance increases automatically with the speed of the boat.

Skin friction

Friction of the underwater parts of the boat is not a direct friction between the water and the sides of the boat, such as would be the case with a wooden block sliding over a table top, but is the internal friction of individual layers of water against each other near the skin of the boat. In other words, right up against the boat's side there is a very thin layer of water which is going at the same speed as the boat, and this boundary layer rubs against successive layers of water, moving less rapidly because they are further away from the boat. Thus the speed of the layers of water around the hull of the boat decreases the further the water is from the hull. While the boundary layer has the same speed as the boat, layers of water outside a transitional zone which is between millimetres and centimetres thick, do not move at all. What can be done to reduce this resistance, caused by friction, which

increases in direct proportion to the speed of the boat?

The most obvious method would be to decrease friction between the layers of liquid which could, for instance, be done by the addition of polymers to the water. Some time, no doubt, industry will develop paints which leak such polymers into the water, naturally only for a limited period, and thus make the transitional area smaller, which would achieve a decrease in friction. Purely theoretically, friction resistance could thus be reduced by 50% but regulations forbid such a method being used for racing boats.

The second possibility of keeping friction to a minimum is to keep the wetted surface as small as possible without inducing other drawbacks at the same time. Running before the wind, where leeway is not a factor to consider, you can raise the centreboard. And in light winds, when the main resistance is that caused by friction, you can heel the boat slightly, or trim her down by the bow, which in many boats, especially dinghies, has the effect of reducing the amount of wetted surface. It is also essential for the surface of the boat to be absolutely smooth. You should rub it down with fine, not coarse sandpaper, as the latter creates tiny grooves that are, however, like gullies compared to the molecular layers of water. If coarse sandpaper is used, gloss paint or polishing will not make up for it.

Form resistance

Form resistance of the hull (also called dynamic resistance) is mainly caused by the formation of waves on the surface as the hull moves through the water. It also includes resistance caused by turbulence at the bow, stern, keel and rudder, since these underwater parts are not of a perfectly streamlined shape.

Form resistance depends largely on the underwater shape of a sailing boat, which is almost wholly decided by the designer before building and afterwards can only be changed in small particulars, such as giving the centreboard and rudder aerodynamic profiles or adjusting hull trim. On the other hand, form resistance decreases in direct proportion to the weight of the boat so that in all graphic representations the so-called specific form resistance is used, i.e., the form resistance per pound or kilogram of displacement. The most interesting fact, however, is that form resistance of displacement boats, once a certain speed has been reached, increases so steeply that it stops the boat from accelerating any further. This critical point occurs when the boat has reached its maximum inherent speed which is a function of the root of the waterline length and the maximum speed/length ratio. The maximum speed/length ratio for displacement boats is R = 1.35 so that maximum inherent speed is $V = 1.35\sqrt{LWL}$. With planing hulls, on the other hand, the curve of resistance after the critical phase at which the boat starts to plane has quite a different appearance. Resistance stops increasing to any great degree after this critical point. This can be explained by the fact that once planing speed has been attained the boat rises up on its bow wave and the stern wave is left behind.

Once the boat is built there is little the owner himself can do about form resistance. There are three ways in which he can try:

1 Make sure the centreboard and rudder are correctly profiled and when possible raise the centreboard.
2 Trim the boat correctly fore and aft, the most important and most frequent mistake being to allow it to be down by the stern. Especially at speeds below planing the stern should be far enough out of the water for the water to be smooth behind the boat with no turbulence.
3 Have as little weight as possible on board.

Boat speed also depends on correct hull trim.

Heeling resistance

The boat's heeling resistance is really part of form resistance, i.e., it is the increase of form resistance as the boat heels. The following diagram shows how large this increase is.

Here we can see that yachts which heel between 15° and 20° increase their form resistance noticeably, while in dinghies a comparable angle of heel means a quite considerable loss of speed. Hence, dinghies should be sailed absolutely upright, yachts as upright as possible.

Resistance induced by leeway

If your boat is making leeway, you will notice a build-up of waves and eddies as form resistance increases with leeway. The following diagram shows how it increases.

Naturally, leeway cannot be entire-

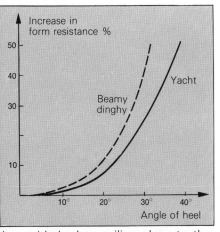

ly avoided when sailing close to the wind, but you should do your best to keep it to a minimum. Never sail to windward with too little centreboard or too much sail!

Wind resistance of hull and rigging

The two forms of resistance described earlier are mainly noticed when you are sailing close to the wind. It is precisely then that wind resistance is at its most important, too. You can see how big a part it plays if you lower the sails and let the boat drift. It

will drift backwards quite fast. Under sail, the speed of the boat, and thus the wind resistance, increases. There

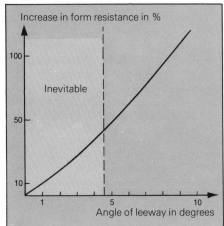

are ways, though, of keeping wind resistance to a minimum.
● All running and standing rigging above deck should be as thin as possible.
● Halyards, shrouds, etc., should run inside the mast if possible.
● The deck should be flat with no superstructure or other projections which could offer resistance to the wind or water.
● The crew should sit as close together as possible and in dinghies the man on the trapeze should not wear clothing which flaps about.

Resistance caused by rough water

Every sailor knows that his boat sails faster in calm water than rough water. This kind of resistance can, naturally, only be decreased by indirect means. It is important to:
● Learn to steer through the waves. The helmsman must find the correct rhythm for doing this and this can be a decisive factor in winning a race.
● Look for calmer water, which is often found closer inshore.

Summary of factors producing resistance

The six different forms of resistance usually occur together but naturally the relationship of the forms of

resistance depends on many factors, such as:
● Speed of the boat.
● Wind, direction and course.
● Type of water (calm or rough) and wind (squally or steady).

Altogether one can say that heeling resistance and resistance induced by leeway, wind resistance of hull and rigging, and resistance caused by rough water, are insignificant when off the wind, but on courses close to the wind account for nearly 50% of the total resistance.

It may be interesting to see, in the diagram, how the various types of resistance relate to boat speed while close-hauled. A noticeable feature as the boat speed increases is the considerable increase of form resistance and the corresponding decrease of skin friction which is very important at low speeds.

NB. Many small adjustments and minor alterations may be needed to reduce resistance to a minimum. If you can do this you will sail much faster than otherwise with the same sails.

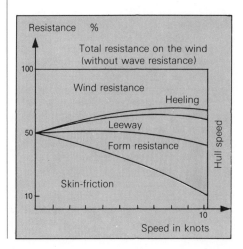

Investigation into heeling

Every boat, whether a yacht or a dinghy, should be sailed in a near-upright position. This is because the hull presents the most favourable shape to the water when it is in this position. Most craft present their best shape when heeled a little. You must experiment to find where the most favourable angle of heel lies. In beamy boats such as the Tempest and Star it will be below 25°, in narrow boats like the Dragon with a good deal of ballast it will be somewhere above 25°. In dinghies it will be around 10°-15° and in catamarans when one hull lifts clear of the water. Heeling simply results in an increase in lateral resistance, thus an increase in leeway, At the same time the sail offers a lower surface area to the wind and thereby generates less driving force. Altogether, then, the boat is much better off when kept at its optimum angle of heel.

Heeling moment is at its greatest on courses close to the wind, progressively decreasing as the boat bears away (heads off) until it has largely disappeared when the boat is dead before the wind.

The angle of heel is controlled as far as possible by a number of factors. Firstly, there is the shape of the hull. A hull with a high beam in relation to length will have high initial stability, the hull shape resisting the tendency for the boat to heel until the heeling moment becomes very high. Secondly, ballast in the form of heavy weights either inside the boat or attached to the keel exert a righting moment through a lever. A deep-keeled boat with a high ballast ratio (ballast weight related to total weight) will have considerable resistance to heeling. She is said to be stiff. A shallow-hulled boat with internal ballast, or shallow keel with relatively little weight on it, may be

said to be tender. The terms stiff and tender are applied in a relative sense as much as an absolute one and are used to compare one boat with another, even when they are of the same class.

Basically, the stability of a yacht depends on the relationship between the centre of gravity CG and the centre of buoyacny CB. Gravity, which is imagined as being concentrated in the CG, is the weight of the hull, ballast, gear and crew and is a force directed downwards. Buoyancy, which is imagined as being concentrated in the CB, is what makes the boat float and is a force directed upwards.

While the boat is on an even keel, the CG and CB lie on the centreline, one above the other. In light centreboard dinghies the CG lies above the CB, in ballasted keelboats it lies considerably below the CB, because the ballast is low down. As the boat begins to heel, the CB shifts to leeward and a horizontal distance opens up between the CG and the CB. This is the righting lever, which determines the boat's resistance to heeling.

To start with, the righting lever increases in length the further the boat heels, especially in dinghies, where the CG shifts to windward as the helmsman and crew (possibly on the trapeze) shift their weight to windward. In our example (see diagrams

below), at an identical angle of heel of 30°, the righting lever of the dinghy with the crew on the trapeze is greater than that of the keelboat. However, as the dinghy heels further, the CG, because it is higher than the CB, will gradually shift over the top of the CB, and as the horizontal distance between the two closes up, the righting lever will eventually disappear, at which point a capsize will occur.

In a keelboat the situation is different. The CG always remains lower than the CB, and since the righting arm lengthens steadily as the boat heels further, her resistance to heeling actually increases all the time and she can never capsize. With an open keelboat there may come a point, of course, where she fills up, because water comes over the side, and she may sink for that reason.

It can be seen that ballast in the form of crew weight plays an absolutely vital part in the case of a centreboard dinghy or catamaran, because it is the only ballast the boat has. In a keelboat it is not nearly so important, although in racing it is usual to shift the crew to the weather side to keep the boat sailing at a smaller angle of heel than she otherwise would, and this is beneficial to speed. Until the rules prevented it, it was not uncommon for racing yachts to carry sacks of sand, which were shifted from one side to the other

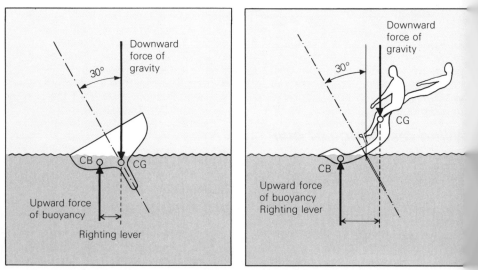

Profile of centreboard, keel and rudder

Three factors are particularly important in connection with any profile:
1 The radius of the leading edge.
2 The ratio of length (l) to maximum thickness (t).
3 The position of maximum thickness of profile (stated as percentage of profile length from the leading edge).

Aerodynamic research institutes, mainly as a result of the work they do for the aircraft and model-aircraft industries, can provide data on all kinds of profiles with different characteristics. It would seem that when it comes to rudders and centreplates the sailing man only has to

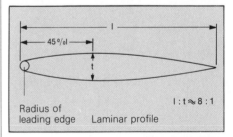

Radius of leading edge   Laminar profile   l : t ≈ 8 : 1

every time the boat tacked. In the Dragon and Star classes the crew used to lie along the weather gunwale (see photograph page 120), and in some 12-Metres the crew could be seen hanging rom the weather gunwale with their feet nearly in the water. Nowadays it is usual for ocean-racing crews to sit on the weather deck with their legs dangling over the side (see photograph page 100), while in open keelboats like the Soling, for example, they hike out with their feet in hiking straps, as is usual in many dinghy classes, too.

In some dinghy classes the crewman sits on a sliding seat, which enables him to project his weight further out than he could by simply leaning over the side.

Sliding seats have largely disappeared, though, because of their weight and clumsiness, and been replaced by the trapeze which naturally requires some degree of athletic skill to be fully effective. It has the great advantage that the crewman can easily adjust the position of his weight. In some classes, where racing is particularly keen, the crew will ballast his clothing by soaking it in water before hiking out. Class rules may not allow this though it is very hard to control in practice. The main limiting factor is the endurance of the crew who needs to have great physical stamina.

In dinghies it usually helps to raise the centreboard a little, so long as the

speed is high enough to keep leeway to a minimum.

To find the right balance takes a good feel for sailing which, for most people, takes a long time to acquire. This is how the superiority of the good sailor shows up in heavy winds when experience counts and differences in skill become most apparent.

Capsizing

Above a certain angle of heel the righting moment in dinghies will not increase any more but will decrease quite dramatically until it equals the heeling moment. This is the point at which the boat will capsize since its centre of gravity is too high for it to recover.

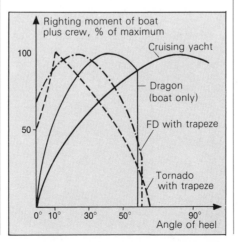

make a choice. This choice is not so easy, however, because the theoreticians' calculations are not always easy to understand. Here are the most important points you need to know.

The optimum ratio of length to maximum thickness (l:t) is basically dependent on speed. For sailing boats sailing between three and seven knots a ratio of between 5:1 and 8:1 has proved most effective. Class rules, however, often stand in the way of the optimum being achieved.

So far as the radius of the leading edge and the position of maximum thickness are concerned we must distinguish between centreboard and rudder because these two considerations depend largely upon the angle at which the profile is set to the flow of water. For a small angle of attack, such as occurs with a centreboard or keel, a laminar flow profile, with its greatest thickness at about 50% and a relatively small leading edge radius, (about $\frac{1}{6}$t), is the best. It produces the least resistance and gives good lift. For an angle of attack of 5-15°, which is fairly normal with rudders because of the many steering corrections that have to be made, the best results are produced by a profile with a larger leading edge radius (about $\frac{1}{5}$t) and the maximum thickness at about 35% from the leading edge. This gives more lift and less resistance for such angles than the laminar profile.

In both profiles the leading section should be parabolic. The trailing edge shape is less important as it is in the area of turbulence. A sharp trailing edge, such as is often thought important, has little effect in practice.

The centreboard and rudder should be as narrow as possible — and, a point seldom taken into account, should not form a right-angle with the bottom of the boat. It has been proved that at an angle of 60-75° between the bottom of the boat and the leading edge of the centreboard the resistance is considerably less than at an angle of 90°. It is a good idea, therefore, to raise the centreboard slightly.

Trimming the sails

The mainsail

A mainsail is inseparable from its mast, and therefore the mast, and the shape it takes, is the chief means of adjusting the mainsail. With a good sail and a bendy mast you can alter the camber and the position of maximum draft, either jointly or separately, for the upper and lower sail areas. The angle of attack can also be altered and the sail opened or closed at the leech.

Mast bend

The actual camber of the sail is put in by the sailmaker (see p. 31). Here are some things which affect it.

With a straight mast the sail will have its greatest draft and the deepest part will lie just behind the mast. By bending the mast aft you can flatten this part of the sail and at the same time transfer the point of maximum draft aft (i.e. more towards the centre of the sail). The tools you use for bending the mast are:

- The backstay, possibly combined with a baby stay.
- The spreaders.
- Tension of the shrouds, especially the upper and lower shrouds.
- The forestay and mast ram.
- The boom vang (kicking strap) and the mainsheet traveller.
- The pressure of the wind.

We must distinguish between two kinds of mast bend. Fore- and aft-bend flattens the entire sail area and shifts the point of maximum draft aft. A lateral bend in the mast means that

Starboard view of a modern racing sailboat showing leech Cunningham in use on mainsail, providing a flat sail for windward performance.

the upper rather than the lower part of the sail will be flattened. You must be sure that the top of the mast bends to leeward and not to windward. Lateral mast bend is achieved by the angle and length of the spreaders, as well as the degree of tension of the upper and lower shrouds. Other gadgets are used to regulate the bend of the mast in a fore-and-aft direction. There are so many different classes of boat, however, that it is impossible for us to give advice here which will hold good for all of them, especially since some devices are not present on all boats. When you get a new boat you should try out all the possibilities, preferably in action (say before a race), and see what effect they have on the mast.

Tension of luff and foot

The Cunningham hole is used to tighten the luff. A second eyelet is fitted to the mainsail above the tack and a tackle runs through it. By this device the tension on the luff can be increased. This flattens the whole sail and brings the camber further forward. Increasing tension on the foot of the sail, on the other hand, has the effect of flattening the sail in its lower part only.

Tensioning and slackening the leech

A mainsail may be fitted with a leech line, but you should not use this to apply leech tension in the present context. To apply the kind of leech tension which is required to flatten the sail the boom end has to be pulled down. This can either be done by altering the pull of the mainsheet by adjusting the traveller or by using the boom vang if it is in the right place.

If the leech is very tight you will generally get a bag in the after part of the sail. Unfortunately this will usually be accompanied by the camber moving aft as well. You can avoid this problem by a correct choice of battens for the sail.

Close-up of leech Cunningham, showing it taking some weight. Below it is the outhaul wire, which is attached to the clew of the sail.

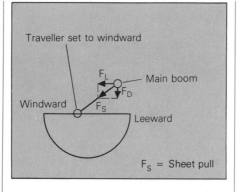

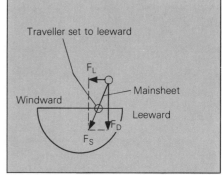

The jib

The jib is generally even more important than the mainsail because the possible ways to trim it are more limited. Therefore, the cut of the sail is all-important and you might just as well discard a bad foresail. Apart from tightening the luff with a Cunningham hole you can change the position of the three corners (head, tack and clew), above all the position of the clew which is influenced by the position of the sheet lead and the degree to which the sheet is pulled in or let out.

In principle, however, the forestay should not be left too slack except when sailing well off the wind. Our diagram gives an idea of the way to find the correct angle for the sheet. Apart from this you should observe this rule of thumb: when you turn the boat very slowly into the wind the jib should begin to lift simultaneously along the whole of the luff.

The spinnaker

The spinnaker is one of the most difficult sails to handle because it calls for utmost concentration — but the theory behind it is very simple.

The points to watch are:

1 The leeward edge of the spinnaker should be as far away as possible from the other sails.
2 The luff is always trimmed so that it is on the point of collapsing one third of the way from the top.
3 The guy and sheet should be at about the same height.
4 The pole should neither rise nor fall; it should be horizontal.

Shape of the sail

The sail must be trimmed for optimum performance on every course and in every strength of wind. In the previous section we show how you can alter the shape of the sail. Now we will explain very shortly *where* it should be altered and *when*. The most important points have already been described in the section Sail, camber and angle of incidence, page 90.

The leading edge of the sail should have the same angle of attack along its entire length. You can see that this is so by coming up slowly into the wind when the full length of the luff should ideally lift ˙at the same moment.

- The maximum camber should lie roughly in the centre of the sail. It is only in a strong wind or very rough seas that it is better to have a sail profile with maximum camber at 35% (see Profile of centreboard, keel and rudder, page 13). In this case the pitching movement of the boat causes the apparent wind direction to change constantly.
- The sail should not curve back, i.e., to weather, at any point. Check the direction of the battens compared to that of the boom.
- If the wind is so strong that the weight of the crew cannot counteract heeling, the upper part of the sail must be flattened first. The diagram below shows how the sail should look:
  - In light winds.
  - In strong winds.

It is not so easy to put these theories into practice since the wind, trying to push the camber of the sail aft, may upset your calculations.

The interaction of the sails

A great deal has been written on the interaction of sails, especially on the subject of slot effects. The one certain thing is that, if the sails are correctly trimmed in relation to each other, the effect of their interaction will be to increase their effectiveness. The few pieces of knowledge we have on the subject may be summarized as follows:

1 The slot between mainsail and jib should be regular all the way down (see also photograph page 36). It should be narrower in light winds (less turbulent airflow) and wider in strong winds.
2 The jib should not be too full in the overlap area. This is the exception to the rule, a case where a sail should be rather flat.
3 The jib should be trimmed first and then the mainsail should be trimmed by the jib.

(see Profile of centreboard, keel and rudder, page 13)

(see also photograph page 36)

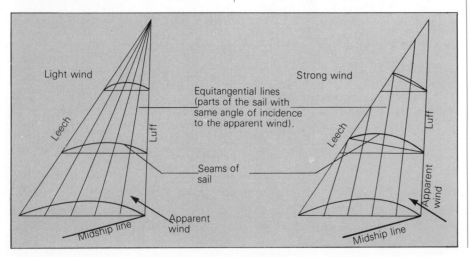

TOP: *When racing in fresh winds a good crew will hardly ever be sitting in the boat but will hang out over the side.*

BELOW: *Demonstration of a typical hiking-out position adopted by the helmsman of a Finn dinghy. His feet are hooked under the toe strap which is adjusted high, while he is sitting well out over the side, is back rounded. Notice the correct grip on the tiller extension, visible also in the picture above.*

TOP LEFT: *Typical hiking-out position on a modern ocean-racing yacht. The crew's legs are dangling over the side.*

TOP RIGHT: *Hiking-out in a Soling three-man keelboat. The helmsman is Erich Hirt, German champion in 1975.*

BOTTOM LEFT: *Hiking out in an FD. Again, notice the correct grasp of the tiller extension.*

BOTTOM RIGHT: *There are several things wrong here.*
1 The toe straps are not high enough so the helmsman cannot hike-out far enough but must compensate for this by stretching backwards uncomfortably. 2 The helmsman is grasping the tiller extension from above and thus his arm is cramped. 3 The trapeze wire is too short so the crew must try to compensate for this by leaning backwards in an impracticable and uncomfortable position.

Oscillation

According to the movement of the waves on the one hand, and the irregularity of the wind on the other, every boat is subject to oscillations, in particular rolling or yawing. These movements mostly have the effect of reducing the boat's speed, especially when the movement is not rhythmically linked with the movement of the waves. The effect is shown with particular intensity when the opposing movements result in violent slamming or pitching. How can one reduce these oscillating movements to bearable proportions?

The simplest way, of course, would be skilful steering! There are other possibilities, however.

● As much weight as possible should be concentrated around the boat's centre of gravity so that the moment of inertia,[1] which is particularly conducive to these oscillations, may be reduced.

● The mast should not be too rigid otherwise it may act as a long lever to reinforce the oscillation. A more flexible mast will not use nearly so much energy. Therefore, the rigging must not be over-tightened in heavy seas.

● The main boom should be held down by the boom vang so that constant alteration of the camber of the sail does not bring about a rolling movement.

● As an excessively full bow and stern encourage a boat to move in sympathy with the waves the designer of the boat's hull has considerable influence on the boat's behaviour.

Oscillation is a phenomenon which has been carefully studied by naval architects. There is an excellent description of it and its causes, effects and possible cures in *Sailing Theory and Practice* by C.A. Marchaj. We recommend all keen sailors to read this account.

[1] Moment of inertia: the mass of a body multiplied by its distance from the centre of gravity.

Preparing for racing

If you want to win you will only do so by preparing thoroughly. In yacht racing this preparation is not limited (as, for instance, in athletics) to physical training but also includes thorough preparation of the equipment.

Preparation has three stages which cannot, however, be sharply separated from one another, though we can draw a rough distinction.

1 Choice of boat, mast, sails and fittings, and ensuring they are in the best possible condition.
2 Getting to know the boat on the water, getting acquainted with the basic adjustments and how to trim her.
3 Tuning and perfecting your technique.

After these three stages of preparation you can confidently race if you have also got yourself into condition and are sure of your sailing tactics. But let us take a closer look at the individual stages.

Stage 1

The choice of boat, sail or mast is a decisive one, and one which can never be solved to the satisfaction of everyone. There are so many factors involved, not all of them to do with the actual sailing, that it is understandable that most novices turn to the equipment used by the experts. Preparation does not just mean buying new sails, etc. It is a matter of getting existing gear into the best possible condition.

Here are a few basic points:

● The surface of the boat must be absolutely smooth and fair.

● Centreboard and rudder must have the correct profile.

● All devices and fittings for trimming the boat must be easily accessible and in good working order and, at the same time, as simple and light as possible.

- Fittings should be chosen to offer the least possible resistance to the wind.
- The boat should have the minimum weight permitted by the class rules.

The principal purpose of this first stage is to ensure that you will not have to improvise during the race and that you know there are no weaknesses in the boat. When you go in for a race you must do so with the comforting knowledge that all your gear is in good order.

Stage 2

Most people pay too little attention to this stage although it is precisely the one which can give you the necessary sense of security which you need if you are to come in among the leaders.

The main aspect of this stage is that you should know the capabilities of your boat down to the smallest detail.

- You should know precisely on what courses and in what wind strength to set the spinnaker or other auxiliary sails to get the best out of them.
- You should know exactly which angle to the apparent wind will bring you the greatest advantage on the beat in the prevailing wind and sea conditions.
- Similarly, you should be able to trim the boat for any change of course or wind quickly and easily so that she will sail her fastest.
- And you should know whether changing course away from the obvious one might increase your speed sufficiently to bring you home faster than if you had taken the direct way.

This is not intended to be a comprehensive survey, only to offer a few examples. These days a feel for sailing is not enough to fulfil all these requirements. You must know as much as possible about how to trim a boat and have the devices for doing this situated so that they can be used with maximum ease and efficiency.

You will find that trimming marks on the appropriate fittings are very useful, but they must be easy to read. One idea is for all data that you can obtain through measurements of

boat speed in varying wind and water conditions to be put on paper as graphs. We recommend the polar diagram method where the angle of the course to the true wind is shown as the polar angle and the speed of the boat as the polar value (see diagrams on right). The advantage of a polar diagram is explained by two typical examples which give you a clear idea of how the information can be used to tactical advantage.

Polar diagram showing speed and course (planing dinghy in calm and rough water respectively.)
We can see that with uniform wind strength the boat sailing on the wind in calm water starts to plane at a relatively small angle to the true wind. The diagram shows the best speed and course made good at a planing speed of V_2 and an angle α_2. In rough water, on the other hand, the resistance of the waves on a close-hauled course stops real planing. Therefore, the best speed and course made good occur at a considerably smaller angle to the wind (α_1). V_1 is not a planing speed and it is considerably smaller than V_2. This theoretical example can help in practice as we shall show in the following illustration.

On the occasion of the European championships in Kiel in 1974 the wind conditions were as shown in the diagrams. The water was choppy and the sea was running at 30° to the wind direction. Thus, on the port tack, the conditions were those of calm water (at right angles to the waves) while on the starboard tack the boat was heading straight into the seas, making it impossible to plane. The successful tactic proved to be that of letting the boat run a little free on the port tack, without trying to point too close, and on the starboard tack to head up over every wave, and squeezing up to windward by all possible means. By the time the other competitors saw the logic of these tactics they hadn't got a hope!

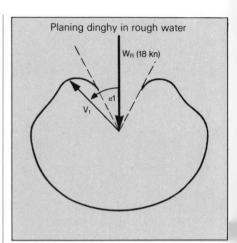
Planing dinghy in rough water — W_R (18 kn), α_1, V_1

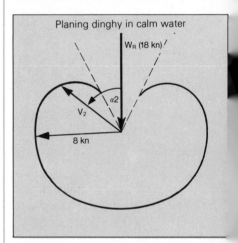
Planing dinghy in calm water — W_R (18 kn), α_2, V_2, 8 kn

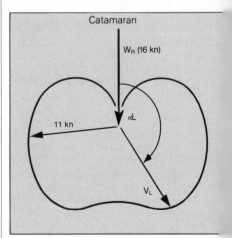
Catamaran — W_R (16 kn), α_L, 11 kn, V_L

Why catamarans tack downwind
The diagram (left) shows at a glance that the increase in speed of a catamaran deviating from a course directly downwind is so great that you actually reach the leeward mark sooner than by sailing dead before the wind. The point here is to realize that the increase in speed will more than compensate for the extra distance sailed. But there is a crucial angle and going a little too close to the wind or a little too far off will nullify the advantage.

No doubt some keen racer or other will say that all this is theory and in practice you must trust to your instinct. But this is not true. On the one hand, the most direct course is not always the quickest one and, on the other, the fastest possible speed is not always the factor that brings success either. You need a precise knowledge of every factor and practically all top helmsmen keep written records on what to do to get the very best out of their boats. Again, many people have so much knowledge of one particular type of boat that they know all the data by heart.

How are these data collected? On large yachts this would seem a ludicrous question for speedometers, anemometers, compasses, etc., are used as a matter of routine. On small boats, however, people usually have to make do with something to show the direction of the apparent wind, in the form of a fly or pennant at the masthead. To get really accurate data, however, you should make use of the instruments mentioned above.

You will find out if you have been getting the right results when you come to the third stage.

Stage 3

This is where the real work begins at the start of the season. After suitable sail training (see chapter on racing), adjusting your fine tuning is important. You need a reliable partner who will sail the same course with you, without altering his trim, until you have experimented sufficiently with your boat to make it faster than his. Then you should act as trial horse for him, and so on in turn, until both boats have reached their optimum speed on the course in question. It is

important to keep a written record of all the adjustments you have made so that you can discuss possible means of improving performance with your coach or your partner on shore, and subsequently try them out.

This stage, of course, is never quite finished and it is a good idea to keep your records in a notebook which can be laid out like the following example:

Suggested layout of log

Coarse adjustments
Mast heel (in (mm) inches: from front edge of mast heel track). Mast rake (suspend a plumb line from the mast top and, with the boat on an even keel, measure the distance of the lead from the mast at boom level, in inches (mm).

Shroud adjustment (distance in inches (mm) from marks).
NB. A difference of 1 mm in the length of the shrouds can cause a lateral displacement of 1-2 in (2-4 cm) at the masthead!

Adjustment of centreboard.

Material used
Jib, spinnaker, mainsail, mainboom, etc.

External conditions
Wind strength, nature of wind, (squally, steady), state of sea, course in relation to wind.

Fine adjustments
Jib sheet leads (fore-and-aft and lateral measurements)
Position of mainsheet
Adjustment of traveller
Adjustment of backstay, clew, Cunningham hole, forestay, etc.
Sail battens.

Speed
a. impression
b. measured

Special remarks
Any tendency to carry weather helm?
Any creases in the sail?
Unusual behaviour of the boat?
Where can improvements be made?

Suggested form for a trimming report

Occasion: _____
Date: _____

Wind
Speed: _____
Direction: _____
Squally or steady: _____
Sea: _____

Trim data
Mast rake: _____
Centreboard: _____
Shroud tension: _____
Special points: _____

Foresail
Creases: _____
Luffing point: _____
Sheet lead: _____
Leech: _____
Special points: _____

Mainsail
Creases: _____
Luffing point: _____
Cunningham: _____
Foot: _____
Traveller: _____
Mast adjustment: _____
Battens: _____
Camber: _____
Special points: _____

Spinnaker
Creases: _____
Characteristics on a reach: _____
Characteristics downwind: _____
Trim of spinnaker pole: _____
Special points: _____

Speed
Pointing: _____
Weather helm: _____
Place in race: _____
Possible improvements: _____
Special points: _____

Sailing practice

The boat at her moorings

Lines and making fast

A boat is made fast to her moorings by means of rodes. They consist of bow and stern lines, together with springs and, sometimes, breast-ropes. In certain situations, you may have to use the anchor gear. Fenders are essential with certain types of moorings. Often a large eyesplice is made in the end of a mooring line so that it can simply be thrown over a bollard. If there is no such eye a knot is used for making fast. With small boats, like dinghies, a round turn and two half hitches on a pile or bollard is usual. Lines of larger boats are made fast to such piles or bollards with a bowline. If there are rings to which you can make fast a bowline is the knot to use or alternatively a round turn and two half hitches.

Here is a good tip. If lines from other boats are already in place over a bollard the courteous way to make fast your own boat is to put your spliced eye, or an eye made by a bowline, up through the eyes of the other lines from below and then place it over the bollard. Each line can then be undone without disturbing the others.

Bow line	Line leading forward from the bow
Stern line	Line leading aft from the stern
Spring line	Line used in conjunction with the bow and stern lines, its pull working in the opposite direction
Forespring	The spring line pulling aft from the bow
After spring	The spring line pulling forward from the stern
Breast rope	Line which, in contrast to bow and stern lines and springs, is placed almost at right angles to a pier or neighbouring boat.
Putting out	Taking a line to a certain place, e.g. a bollard
Taking out	Taking out a line when you need to use a tender to do it
Hauling in	Hauling a line back on board. You haul hand over hand, or, on large boats, by walking along the deck. Sometimes a winch may be needed.
Heaving a line	Throwing a line somewhere, e.g. ashore. A heaving line or messenger is a light line which is attached to a heavier rope (with a heaving line knot). It is then heaved ashore, for example, and the heavier rope pulled after.
Making fast	Securing a line to a cleat, bollard or ring
Slackening off	Slackening, easing or letting out a line
Casting off	Freeing a line completely
Tending warps	Altering the tension of the warps to suit new circumstances, e.g. in tidal waters
Taking up the slack	Re-adjusting a line which has become too slack to fulfil its function
Bend together	Join two lines together, e.g. a warp to a heaving line
Slip rope	A rope fastened on board is taken to a bollard or through a ring ashore and then back to the boat. It can then be slackened or hauled in from the boat.

Methods of mooring

Mooring to a buoy

Keelboats are often moored to a buoy, especially in rivers. They are usually made fast to a permanent strop attached to the buoy or sometimes by a bow line from the yacht made fast to the buoy. When they are only to be moored for a short time a slip rope is a good idea. Smaller buoys are usually brought on board and their chain secured to the samson post or mooring cleat.

On dry land

Modern planing dinghies (such as Finns, FDs, Corsairs, 470s, 420s, Lasers), and often small keelboats like the Star, are brought ashore after use. A slip or crane is used. These dinghies are in the water only while in use.

A short-term parking method can be used if conditions allow. A dinghy is moored to a jetty with such a short painter that her bows are lifted a few inches out of the water. This keeps the dinghy steady; her stern will not swing round, nor will her bows push under the jetty.

Mooring to a float

Many boats have permanent moorings at a float in a marina where piles are provided so that the boat can be secured with her bow close to the float, while her stern is held in position by lines from her quarters to two piles or buoys astern. You can also moor a boat the other way round, stern to float, but this means risking damage to the rudder if the stern should come too close to the float. The two stern lines leading to the piles (or, if the boat is moored the other way around, the two bow lines) should be of the same length so as to hold the boat central. With large boats two bow lines should be taken to the float, the second one being made fast at least a yard from the first.

Do not tighten the bow lines, but leave a little slack so that the boat has some freedom of movement.

Mooring the boat's bow or stern to a pier

This form of mooring is often used when cruising, especially in areas of little or no tidal rise and fall. Often buoys are not provided to hold the boat in position. In that case you

Yachts moored fore and aft to dock.

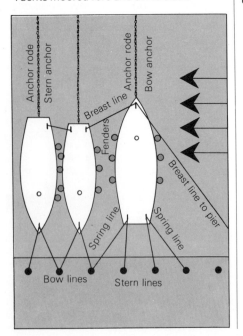

must use the anchor. If the boat is to be moored bow on, the anchor must be made ready at the stern in good time. If the boat is to be moored stern on, the heavier and more reliable bow anchor is used. As with marina mooring, the boat is made fast (but not too tightly) with two lines to the pier. In some circumstances you may also need to use a spring line and, in addition, in bad weather and with a beam wind, a breast line. Do not forget fenders and make sure the boat is lying so that her mast will not tangle with the masts of other boats if she rolls.

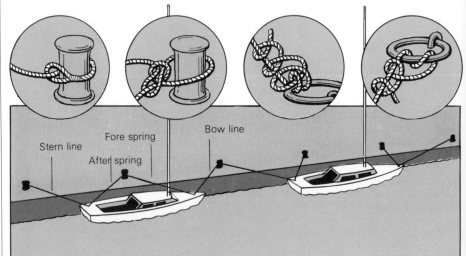

Mooring alongside a pier

Mooring alongside a pier or jetty is common in certain areas. It is best to lie in the lee of a pier, but lying alongside on the windward side is perfectly possible so long as enough fenders are put out. If the pressure on the fenders is too great, as a result of wind and waves, something must be done to keep the boat away from the pier. If there are no buoys or piles to which you can take lines, anchors must be laid out to windward from the bow and stern. If the conditions are too bad you should leave the berth. When lying alongside making the boat fast with bow and stern lines alone is never sufficient since, without other lines, she will surge along the side of the pier. In this case spring lines must also be used to hold the boat steady.

Mooring alongside in trots; rafting

In areas where it is usual to lie alongside at moorings reasons of space often make it necessary for boats to lie moored in trots. This is called rafting in North America. This entails a number of boats lying alongside each other but so arranged that the masts will not touch. The point to remember is that larger boats should lie inside while smaller ones lie outside. If possible, bow and stern lines are fastened to a bollard or pile

When lying alongside it is not enough to make fast with bow and stern lines alone. You also need to put out additional lines called spring lines.

If a yacht is not held at her moorings with springs she will swing to and fro as shown.

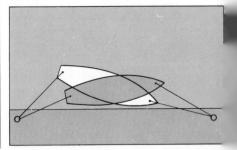

LEFT: Boats rafted. Land lines are clearly visible.

BELOW: How to furl a mainsail and cover it with a sail cover.
BOTTOM: the crew of the well-known Admiral's Cup yacht Rubin *has furled the mainsail very neatly in this picture.*

as well as to the boat lying alongside on the inside. Spring lines are always used in these circumstances. If there is a crosswind the outer boat at least must have a line to the shore or to the float. Fenders must be put out on the shore side by each boat. Other fenders are hung out if possible on the other side too. Rafting between posts in a river is also common. Here each boat must be attached by a line to the posts ahead and astern as well as mooring to the boat alongside.

It is often necessary for a yacht to moor alongside you. You will probably have to cross over other boats to get ashore. Ask permission, if anyone is on deck, before setting foot

Points to remember when moored

In tidal waters you must check the mooring lines frequently and adjust them when necessary. After making fast the mainsail is neatly furled (sometimes taken off) and covered with a sail cover. The jib is stowed away in its bag. As a basic principle the centreboard of a dinghy is always completely raised. A fixed rudder is left shipped but a lifting one is raised and the tiller secured amidships. Put the cover on if the boat is to be left for some time.

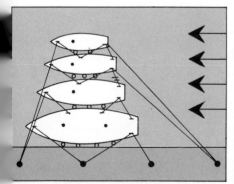

When rafting it is important for lines to be taken ashore from the outer boat, especially in the upwind direction. (But beware of overnight wind shifts!)

on someone else's boat. You should move quietly and you should always cross by way of the foredeck as far as possible from the cockpit and main saloon. Of course, wear clean shoes.

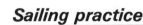
Getting under way

Before getting under way you should make sure that everything on board is ready for use, especially the halyards and sheets. On no account forget to lower the centreboard of a dinghy and the same goes for the rudder blade, if you have a lifting rudder. The way in which you get under way depends on the type of boat you have, her mooring, the direction of the wind, and the amount of sea room. According to the circumstances there are various possibilities (see page 166).

Setting and handing sail

Modern yachts and dinghies generally have Bermuda mainsails. The luff, reinforced with a boltrope, is either fitted into a groove in the mast or is fitted with slides which run up a track on the mast. The foot usually runs in a groove on the main boom. On yachts the main boom is generally supported with a topping lift, a halyard which leads from the end of the boom to the masthead. This takes the weight of the boom while the sail

is being set or reefed. On dinghies with no topping lift a boom crutch can be used or the boom can be held up by hand. The boat should generally be lying head to wind when the sail is reefed. If the yacht is not lying head to wind but is in harbour on the windward side of a jetty, for example, then you have the following possibilities for setting the mainsail:

● Shift the boat round to the leeward side.
● Paddle up to a buoy or sail to one with the jib set.
● Paddle out into clear water (or sail out under jib alone, and then head up into the wind and set the mainsail.
● If you have a motor use it to get you into open water.

A jib which is not set in a groove, but is hanked on to the forestay, can be set and handed on any point of sailing. Other factors come into consideration, however, when the luff of

the jib is hoisted in a Headfoil, as has become customary on modern offshore racing yachts, and may soon be seen more commonly on cruising yachts. After the mainsail or jib is set the halyard concerned is made fast on a cleat. On big yachts the halyards usually run over halyard winches. On racing dinghies the halyard is made fast on a cleat and tensioned the required amount by a lever. Sometimes the sail is held by means of a modern halyard lock at the masthead.

Before any sail is set, it must be prepared.
● Slide the foot of the mainsail into the groove on the boom.
● Make fast the clew and tack.
● Shackle the head to the main halyard.
● Make sure the mainsheet is free.
● Shackle the tack and head of the jib.

A foresail being set in a Headfoil.

The hanks of the jib are clearly visible on this Dragon. Such boats as Dragons and Solings, and most cruising yachts, still use hanks. It can only be a question of time, however, before these boats, too, are equipped with Headfoils.

- Check that the halyards are not twisted and are running free.
- Do not forget to put the battens in.

After it is taken down the jib is stowed away in a bag (providing it is not wet). The mainsail is furled and covered with a special sail cover. If the boat is not going to be used again for some time, the mainsail is taken off and stowed away in a bag.

Hints

1 Fasten the tack and clew securely when setting a mainsail, first the tack then the clew.
2 Setting the mainsail on small boats without a topping lift, the helmsman holds the boom up to support it.

3 Before hoisting the sail the luff must be pulled well forward so that it will enter the groove more easily.

4 On small boats a jib can be set more tautly by pulling the forestay aft while the sail is being hoisted.

5 Coil up the fall of each halyard and wedge it behind the standing part of the halyard above the cleat. If

you make a neat package, as shown here, and hang it on the cleat there is a risk that it will be lost if you have to haul the sail down in a hurry.

6 When lowering the sails the helmsman takes hold of the main boom, if there is no topping lift, and places it in a boom crutch.
7 The mainsail should be pulled down by the luff, not just any part of the sail.
8 After the mainsail has been removed, and if the main boom is fitted with roller reefing, the boom is turned over so that the groove faces downwards. No rain water can then collect in it.

Basic sail trim

The mainsail must be trimmed to have the amount of camber appropriate to the wind conditions. To flatten the sail (in strong winds and when sailing closehauled) the luff and foot must be tightened. In light winds, and especially when sailing with the wind on the quarter or from astern, the luff and foot are kept slacker so that the sail can fill more. If the leech of the jib flutters then the position of the sheet must be moved further forward. If the foot flutters the lead must be moved aft. If the lead is not adjustable similar effects can be achieved by raising and lowering the tack of the jib.

More about sail trim can be read in the previous chapter.

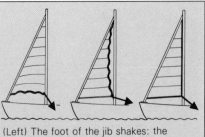

(Left) The foot of the jib shakes: the sheet lead must be moved aft.
(Centre) The leech of the jib shakes: the sheet lead must be moved forward.
(Right) If neither foot nor leech shake then the sheet lead is in the correct place

Different points of sailing

The main points of sailing are close to the wind, with the wind on a beam, and with the wind from astern. If one is sailing as close as possible into the wind, the boat is said to be closehauled while, if the boat is turned even further into the wind so that the bows are directly into it, we say she is head to wind.

The point of sailing between closehauled and with the wind on the quarter, where the true wind comes from abeam, is called a beam reach. Closer to the wind than this is a close reach, further off is a broad reach. When closehauled, a modern sailing boat can, on average, achieve an angle of 45° to the true wind but the latest racing yachts and dinghies achieve a smaller angle, the most efficient getting as close as 35°.

When sailing with the wind astern the boat is said to be running.

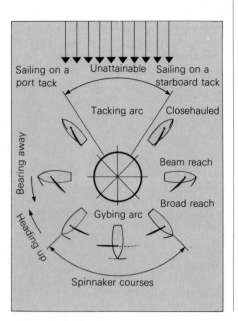

Terms and manoeuvres

Starboard tack		The wind comes over the starboard side, the sails are set on the port side.
Port tack		The wind comes over the port side, the sails are set on the starboard side.
Leeward and windward sides		The side of a boat from which the wind is coming is the windward or weather side. The side on which the sails are set is the leeward side. As a rule the helmsman sits facing the mainsail, i.e. on the windward or weather side.
Head up (UK luff up)		Turn the boat nearer the wind, e.g. when changing from a broad reach to a close-hauled course.
Bear away		Turn the boat away from the wind, e.g. a change of course from closehauled to a broad reach.
Free sheets		Ease the sheets off. When bearing away, the sheets are freed as the boat does so.
Harden up		The opposite of free; haul the sheets in.
Lifting (UK freeing)		A change in wind direction favourable to the boat's course; coming from further aft. The boat can be luffed up, or if the same course is to be held, the sheets must be eased.
Heading		The wind comes from further ahead. To maintain the same point of sailing it will be necessary to bear away.
Tacking		The action of turning the boat through the wind from one tack to another.
Gybing		Manoeuvre performed when running. The stern is turned through the wind and the sail is taken over to the other side. In strong winds this manoeuvre must be carried out with great care.

Three different points of sailing: left, running; centre, reaching; right, closehauled.

Trimming the sails

In sailing one should always try to trim the sails for maximum efficiency. The sails are sheeted well in when closehauled and eased as the boat bears away. As a general rule-of-thumb as to how the sails should be trimmed, we can say that the position of the boom on all courses (except for courses with the wind astern) should roughly bisect the angle between the centreline of the boat and the direction of the apparent wind.

When running with the wind from dead astern you should ease the sheets as far as the rig will allow without, however, letting the main boom touch the shrouds. On all other headings the sheets should be eased until the sails are on the verge of shaking and the luff is on the point of lifting. It is also important for the mainsail and the foresail to be sheeted in by roughly the same amount so that the airflow past the mainsail is not disturbed and can pass smoothly over the windward and leeward sides.

For each course the crew trims the sails in a different way. On the wind the sheets are hardened in and the helmsman's skill is used to steer so that the sails remain full. On a reach, however, the helmsman holds his course and the sails are trimmed to make best use of the wind. On a run the sails are eased right off and the helmsman steers so that the sails draw properly and it is relatively unimportant whether the sails are set on one tack or the other. If the jib is

blanketed by the mainsail it cannot be effective and if no spinnaker is set it is better to swing the jib out on the opposite side to the mainsail and sail goosewinged. To do this you will need a whisker pole to hold the jib out. Spinnakers (see section on spinnakers, page 156) can be set with the wind anywhere from abeam to dead

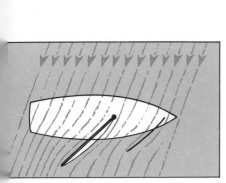

Mainsail and foresail trimmed correctly in relation to each other.

Wrong. The jib is sheeted in too tight in relation to the mainsail. The airflow from the jib is backwinding the mainsail. The airflow over the leeward side of the jib is breaking away and causing turbulence.

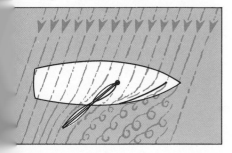

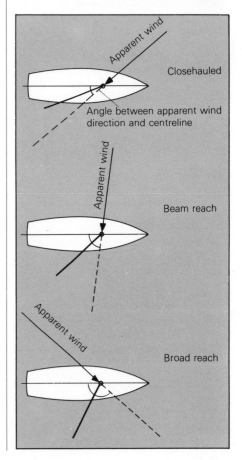

Closehauled

Apparent wind

Angle between apparent wind direction and centreline

Apparent wind

Beam reach

Apparent wind

Broad reach

Pirat dinghies running wing and wing with their jibs held out on the opposite side to their mainsails by whisker poles.

astern. If you are sailing a dinghy, the centreboard is raised more and more the further you bear away from a closehauled course.

Hints

Closehauled

1 It is important to use the mainsheet traveller properly. The basic principle is to push the traveller to leeward in a strong wind and keep it more amidships or even to weather in a light wind.
2 Keep the boom vang tight in a strong wind.
3 If a heavy squall comes and the boat heels a lot the simplest thing to do is to ease sheets in a controlled manner. In a lighter squall head up to gain distance to windward but do not forget to bear away again in good time when the squall eases. In a very strong wind raising the centreboard of a dinghy slightly will make the work easier.

Reaching

1 In a dinghy raise the centreboard about half-way.
2 If the wind is not very strong more fullness in the mainsail, achieved by slackening the luff and foot, will give you more speed.

3 You should try to start planing or surfing in suitable wind conditions. It is exciting and results in a substantial increase in speed.

Planing on a reach: a Laser dinghy. Note the centreboard, more than half raised.

Running Careful attention should be paid to steering and holding the boat steady on course. You risk an involuntary gybe if the boat bears away too much. In strong winds this can damage the rigging and a dinghy might capsize and there may even be a risk of a member of the crew drowning. It is better to avoid an unintentional gybe in strong winds and high seas by choosing not to sail

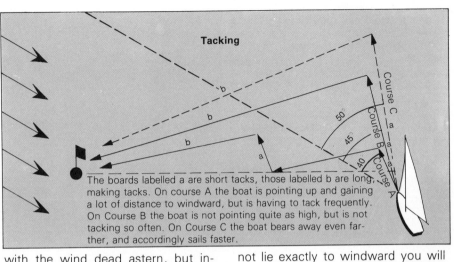

The boards labelled a are short tacks, those labelled b are long, making tacks. On course A the boat is pointing up and gaining a lot of distance to windward, but is having to tack frequently. On Course B the boat is not pointing quite as high, but is not tacking so often. On Course C the boat bears away even farther, and accordingly sails faster.

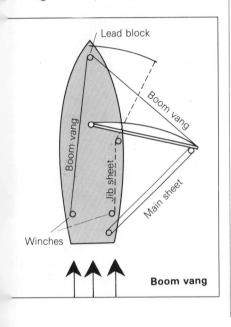
Boom vang

with the wind dead astern, but instead to sail a broad reach with the wind on the quarter and now and then make a controlled gybe, so that you tack down wind. On a larger boat you may use a vang to hold the boom in place, led from the end of the boom to the bow.

Tacking If your destination is in the direction from which the wind is coming, you will have to tack back and forth to get there. This means sailing closehauled, in turn on port and starboard tacks, along a zigzag course which is described as a beat to windward. When your destination does

not lie exactly to windward you will find that the boat points more nearly towards it on one tack than on the other. The tack which takes you closest to your destination is called the *making* tack.

It depends on conditions and on the type of boat whether you will reach your goal quickest by sailing as close to the wind as you can or by easing off a few degrees, not pointing so close to the wind, but sailing faster. Here are a few general hints. A great many short tacks may mean loss of speed because of the frequency of turning, something which is naturally of more significance in large

Racing yachts beating to windward. Four yachts are sailing on the starboard tack, G15 is on the port tack.

yachts than in light dinghies. Long tacks, on the other hand, can be disadvantageous if the wind shifts and is not in your favour. Racing helmsmen generally prefer short tacking (this is the rule in dinghy sailing) unless they are gambling on the possibility of a favourable wind shift on a long tack. If the wind shifts the wrong way, you may lose out completely with this gamble. It may be possible to reach your destination quicker by easing off a little to a close fetch. Though you will sail further your speed through the water will certainly be higher and in rough conditions the boat will travel more smoothly.

Planing and surfing

A boat normally displaces the water to either side as she moves forward through it. In suitably fresh winds, however, a lightly built boat with a flat hull section (especially towards the stern) can sail faster than her own bow wave, climb on top of the wave and plane. Heavy boats with ballast keels can seldom if ever plane and thus must always displace the water as they move. Many light modern dinghies, however, are designed expressly to plane. Among them are Flying Dutchmen, Corsairs, 470s and Finns. They can generally plane in winds from Force 3 onwards and the Laser can do so even in lighter airs. Conventional, heavier dinghies such as GP14s, and light keelboats such as Stars, can plane, but only in a very strong wind.

Two planing dinghies at full speed. The crew on the trapeze tries to keep the boat upright; ABOVE: a 470; BELOW: an FD.

The normal points of sailing for planing are reaching and broad reaching. Some modern dinghies, however, can plane even on a course fairly close to the wind, i.e., on a close reach. This is called semiplaning. In planing the hull is lifted by hydrodynamic force and thus offers much less resistance since less of it is in the water.

It is not very difficult to plane. Here is what you do:
1 Make sure that the centreboard of a dinghy is about two thirds raised.
2 See that the boom vang is hardened well down so that the sail does not twist.
3 See that the crew sit aft, to increase the tendency of the bow to lift.
4 Do not let the bow dip into a wave.
5 Keep the boat as upright as possible.

It is best to start planing in a gust. You bear away slightly, adjusting the

Conventional speed

Planing

sail correspondingly and, as soon as the gust eases, you head up slightly, carefully hauling in the sheets to prolong the plane. To plane for a considerable distance, therefore, you must work the sheets. In steady planing winds the sheets must be hauled in after the first acceleration as the apparent wind moves forward because of the higher speed. Surfing has a certain similarity to planing.

Surfing is riding the existing waves and is not confined to dinghies. It is possible when either reaching or running. It is done by sailing down the faces of the waves from crest to trough. The boat accelerates as a result of the surface flow of the water. The additional speed is dependent on wave height and steepness and the course and speed of the boat in relation to the wave. At the bottom of the wave the boat meets a reversed surface flow which will tend to slow it down again. When surfing on a run you need to start by steering so that the boat's stern is sitting on the crest of a wave rising aft. The crew now moves aft, heads up, hauling in the sheets, and you sail at an oblique angle down the accelerating front of the wave. Once this wave has passed

you try again, bearing away first. When surfing with the wind on the beam you start on top of the wave, bear away slightly down the wave, and head up again to the top of the next wave.

Helmsman and crew

In small keelboats, and especially in dinghies, the helmsman handles the mainsheet as well as the tiller. The sheet does not always, as used to be the case, have to be held in the hand, but nowadays can sometimes be secured in a jam cleat. Fine adjustments, if necessary, are made with the slide of the traveller.

Tiller and wheel steering

Many of today's modern ocean-going yachts are fitted with wheel steering.

The most important crew terms:

Helmsman	The person at the tiller or wheel steering the boat.
Skipper	Whoever is responsible for the boat.
Crew	In two- or three-man boats, whoever is not steering. The member(s) of the crew handling the jib sheets, seeing to the spinnaker, and going out on the trapeze if necessary.
Crew	Collective noun for all persons on board other than the skipper.
Navigator	Member of the crew responsible for navigation.
Watch	On long voyages the members of the crew are usually divided into watches, each watch led by one person, and being on duty to see to the ship for a predetermined period. Often referred to as the starboard watch and the port watch. Whichever members of the crew are not on duty are described as the off watch.
Bo'sun	Crewman responsible for maintenance and repair work of all sorts on board.

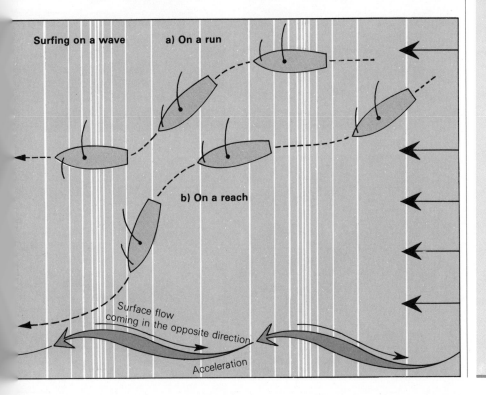

Surfing on a wave
a) On a run
b) On a reach
Surface flow coming in the opposite direction
Acceleration

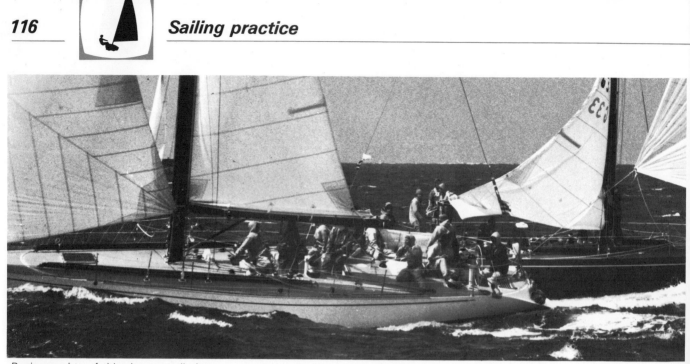

Racing yachts of this size normally have wheel steering.

The rudder is not turned by a tiller but by a wheel whose action is transmitted by means of a mechanical linkage like a worm drive or by a hydraulic system to the rudder. There are three kinds of steering wheel:

1 Spoked wheel with or without safety rim.
2 Smooth-rimmed wheel.
3 Fastnet wheel with spokes radiating from the hub at an angle, so that the rim is set back and you can get a greater distance between it and the steering pedestal.

The advantage of wheel steering is that the helmsman can sit more comfortably, is protected, and can get the best possible view of the compass.

1 *Dinghy with yoke tiller, not often seen today.* 2 *Tiller without tiller extension. With such a tiller the helmsman cannot hike out.*
3 *Tiller extension, an essential for sailing performance in dinghies.*
4 *You use a very long tiller extension on single handers which are sailed with the aid of a trapeze. The illustration shows an A-class catamaran.*

Smooth-rimmed wheel

Fastnet-type wheel

Spoked wheel

Cable steering
linkage

Pedestal

Protective rim

Hydraulic steering
mechanism

Wheel steering

ted to the tiller. Good hiking-out techniques are only possible with such an extension. The old-fashioned yoke tillers are hardly ever seen any more. They have been made superfluous by tiller extensions.

Hints

The use of a tiller extension involves a special technique. It is best to put your hand on the extension from below, holding it around the middle in a light wind, and closer to the end when the wind is stronger and you are hiking farther out. Inexperienced helmsmen are always seen holding it from the top, a thing racing helmsmen very seldom do. It is an acceptable practice in a light wind but proves impractical as soon as you hike out. Your arm gets cramped because of the unnatural position in which you are holding the extension. The extension should be held as close to your body as possible, but not in front of your stomach.

Main faults in sailing with a tiller extension:
- Failing to use the extension at all.
- Holding the extension in line with the tiller.
- When bearing away putting the extension over to the other side, away from you, and pulling the tiller towards you instead of simply using the extension to pull the tiller up to windward.
- Pushing the extension downwards with the risk of damaging the swivel joint between tiller and extension.

Good sailors always hold the tiller extension from below (left and centre).

RIGHT: You can see the cramped position of the arm caused by grasping the tiller extension from above.

The disadvantages with wheel steering are that there is a greater chance of damage or failure than with tiller steering and that it is more complicated to repair if it gets broken.

Other advantages or disadvantages vary from boat to boat and are regarded in a different light by different skippers. Although wheel steering is now found even on small yachts they are still usually equipped with alternative tiller steering. All well-equipped dinghies and small keelboats (such as Tempests or Solings) have a swivelling extension fitted

The finer points of helming

The first question is whether the rudder should be held still or moved slightly, or even a lot, as the boat sails through the water. A good answer is given by a German expert, Willy Kuhweide, who says that in the normal way you should move the rudder as little as possible. The rudder certainly steers the boat, but every steering movement has a braking effect. If you are constantly moving the rudder you are slowing yourself down. Naturally you must move the rudder at times, since you want to steer a determined course, and thus you have to put a certain pressure on. But this pressure should never be greater than necessary. Most helmsmen move their tillers too much. Steering does not mean keeping the rudder completely still, however. It consists of making an imperceptible, but continuous, movement which synchronizes with the waves. This action, however, serves to neutralize the various movements of the water caused by the waves and affecting the boat. If you were to hold the rudder still while sailing through a wave, there would also be a steering effect since it makes very little basic difference whether you are doing something to the water or the water is doing something to you. And if there is a wave about then the water is doing something to you so it must be neutralized by a counter movement of the helm.

FROM TOP TO BOTTOM:
a. Correct: A good sailor uses the tiller extension even in a light wind. It forms an angle with the tiller and is held close to the body.
b. Incorrect: sailing without a tiller extension and sitting too far aft.
c. Incorrect: holding the extension in line with the tiller.
d. Correct: when bearing away pull your arm back.
e. Incorrect: when bearing away, putting the extension over to the other side of the boat and pulling the tiller towards you.

Sitting position

The correct position of helmsman and crew in a sailing boat plays a part which should not be underrated in determining the boat's speed. First, though, we accept that the helmsman normally sits opposite the mainsail, on the weather side, the exception being with wheel steering where the helmsman can sit amidships, looking forward. The rest of the crew sits in such a way that the boat is correctly trimmed, both fore-and-aft and athwartship, according to course and wind conditions.

Fore-and-aft and athwartship trimming

The difference between the helmsman and crew sitting forward or aft in the boat has a considerable effect upon the fore-and-aft trim of the boat, and hence upon her speed. Here is a point to look out for. If the stern sinks into the water because the crew is sitting too far aft, the water flow will be disturbed, eddies will be created and they will act as a braking force. This is particularly true of dinghies and keelboats with a stern similar to that of a dinghy. Therefore the crew should move further forward, the helmsman should move away from the tiller and make use of the tiller extension if there is one. Conversely, the crew must move further aft if there is any risk of the bow diving into a wave when broad reaching or running. When planing and surfing, too, as described earlier, the weight of the crew should be shifted aft.

Fore-and-aft trim also has an influence on the steadiness of the boat's course. When sailing closehauled, for instance, you can head up or bear away by shifting the weight of the crew forward or aft. Shifting weight aft makes the boat bear away; shifting it forward makes the boat head up. The positions of helmsman and crew also have a considerable influence on the lateral trim of the boat, i.e., how much she heels. In strong winds heeling has an unfavourable effect on the airflow past the sail, causing an unwanted

TOP: Bad fore-and-aft trim. The helmsman is sitting much too far aft.

CENTRE: here the helmsman has moved his weight from the stern and the boat is now correctly trimmed.

In light winds the crew should sit right forward. This picture of a 470 dinghy clearly shows the transom completely clear of the water.

luffing moment and increasing leeway. Exaggerated heeling also means loss of speed and diminished windward performance. The result is that in a strong wind the crew must be placed on the weather side in such a way that the boat sails as nearly upright as practicable. Naturally, hiking-out plays a considerably more important part in sailing dinghies and light keelboats than in large sailing yachts which already carry a considerable weight in the ballast keel.

In very light winds a slight angle of heel is generally a good thing as it causes the sails to hold their aerofoil shape better. Heeling is achieved by sitting in the right place. The helmsman and crew no longer hike-out on the weather side but sit in the boat herself, or in a very light wind, even down to leeward.

Ways of hiking-out

Placing oneself right out on the weather side of the boat is called sitting-out or hiking. According to the type of boat concerned various methods can be used.

There is the usual hiking position employed in dinghies and light keelboats (such as Tempests and Dyas) in particular by the helmsman, the extreme dinghy hiking-out position, as used by the crew in a Star, or the crew in a Soling, and the technique used in offshore racing yachts where the crew sit on the weather side looking outward with their legs hanging over the side of the boat. The technique of lying prone along the gunwale, which used to be especially widespread years ago, for instance in Dragons and Stars, is not usual today now that toe straps are permitted. If there is a trapeze, an extreme hiking-out position is unnecessary for the crew, or the helmsman in singlehanded trapeze boats such as Contender dinghies or A-Class catamarans, since he can use his weight to much better effect.

Hiking-out on dinghies

The most extreme hiking-out position is to be seen in singlehanders, such as Finns, Lasers or OK dinghies since, in the absence of support from a crew, the helmsman has to rely exclusively on using his own weight to the greatest possible effect. The prerequisites of a good technique are:
1 Toe straps of the right length.
2 A tiller extension of adequate length.

The straps under which the feet are hooked must be long enough to enable the helmsman to sit well outboard. He rounds his back at the same time in order not to place too

Laser dinghy in light wind. The helmsman is no longer hiking-out but prefers to make the dinghy heel slightly to leeward.

Often the angle of heel you want can only be achieved in a light wind if the helmsman sits to leeward.

much strain on the stomach muscles. The upper part of the body should only be stretched back for a short time as, for example, when weathering a strong squall. A good racing sailor must be able quickly to get into a hiking-out position both in winds which demand it and after going about. He must also be able to get back into the boat just as quickly in a sudden lull or when starting to come about.

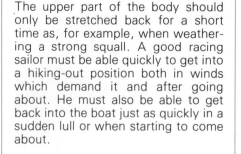

The crew is sitting to leeward in this 470 to keep the heeling angle correct and the helmsman is no longer sitting on the side but in the boat.

The technique of hiking-out in a prone position. No longer as common as it used to be but still to be seen in Dragons.

Common mistakes

● Sitting so near the tiller that it can only be moved away from you.
● Sitting too far aft when sailing closehauled.
● Sitting too far forward when trying to plane.
● Incorrect adjustment of the toe straps.

Going about

Going about, or coming about as it is known in North America, is the manoeuvre used in tacking when the bow of the boat is turned through the wind so that the wind blows on the other side. A boat sailing on port tack will be on starboard tack after coming about. Coming about is always performed from a closehauled position with the sails set accordingly. If you are broad reaching and want to put the boat about you first head up, sheeting in harder. If the sails are not sheeted in the result will be loss of way and there may be difficulties in going through the wind. Coming about is a simple manoeuvre but good technique is important — although there are fewer problems on slower boats, such as heavy dinghies and displacement yachts.

The faster a boat is, the greater the difficulties can be since the faster a boat sails, the further forward the apparent wind moves and the greater is the quadrant of opposing wind through which the boat must pass when coming about. A slow boat can come closer to the true wind so the angle to be described when tacking is not so great. In the normal course of events the manoeuvre does not entail any problems. In a fast planing dinghy the angle is already greater so if you make a mistake there is a greater danger of missing stays. Catamarans, being very fast boats, do not point very close and must thus describe a large arc when tacking. They are correspondingly slow to tack and they may come to a complete standstill.

How to do it

The helmsman gives the signal for the manoeuvre. The crew gets the leeward jib sheet free. The helmsman then puts the helm down. The boat comes up and turns through the wind on to the new tack. Meanwhile the crew lets the jibsheet fly in good time so that he can sheet it in again on the new tack.

Usually the mainsail remains sheeted in and on larger boats the sheet is made fast to a cleat. On large yachts with a large jib sheeting in the sail must be started as the yacht is turning through the wind. If you leave it too late the sail will fill and be difficult to sheet in. If running backstays are fitted you must take care to free the windward one as the helm is put down and haul in the other one on the new tack. The crew changes sides as the boat's bow passes through the eye of the wind.

Technique

In all dinghies and light keelboats, which are all normally equipped with a tiller extension, you should use a well-defined coming-about technique in fresh winds.
1 The helmsman puts his back foot on the leeward side, pushes the tiller away and ducks under the main boom as it swings across the boat. If the boat has a very low boom, as in a Finn dinghy, you can get more room to manoeuvre by slackening the mainsheet a little.
2 As soon as the boom has gone across the helmsman stands up, raising the tiller extension. In a standing position he makes a half turn, facing forward. The hand

which was holding the sheet grasps the tiller extension behind his back together with the sheet. The free hand now takes the sheet. At the same time the helmsman hikes-out in his new position.
3 The crew will generally change sides facing aft since in this way he is less likely to become entangled with the boom vang.

The time taken for this manoeuvre can be comparatively long in light winds with a marked hesitation after the main boom has swung over. In strong or very strong winds places must be changed very quickly when coming about and the helmsman should stand up only very briefly. In sensitive dinghies, such as the Laser, he probably won't stand up at all. He must never let go of the tiller.

This light centreboard day-cruiser is heeling too much in the prevailing wind. The helmsman should use the tiller extension and place more weight outboard.

Wrong. sitting so far aft and so near the tiller that it can be moved only to one side.

This dinghy is heeling too much and sailing badly because the helmsman is not using a tiller extension and is sitting too far inboard (right).

Tacking

The diagrams on this page show, firstly, how there is a correct angle at which the sailboat sets off on the new tack. For the best performance the boat must be neither too close to the wind nor too far off the wind. Next there is the simple manoeuvre performed by the crew in changing sides as the sailboat goes through stays and finally, at the bottom, we show the turning-angle of three different kinds of craft, where speed affects things very much,

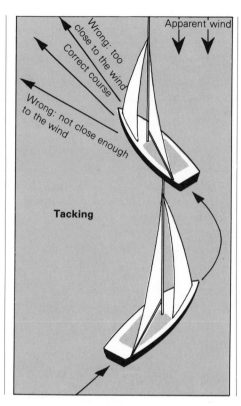

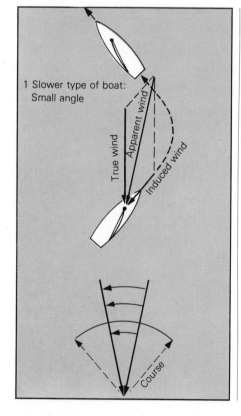

1 Slower type of boat: Small angle

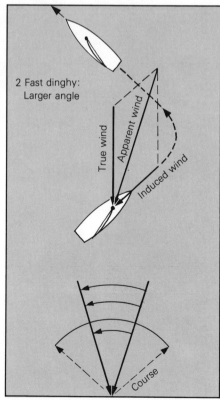

2 Fast dinghy: Larger angle

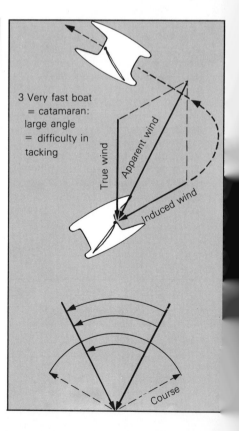

3 Very fast boat = catamaran: large angle = difficulty in tacking

Coming about in a racing yacht. The pictures show the admiral's Cup yacht Christine *racing off Heligoland, photographed in a force 7 (hence the reefed mainsail).*

Technique of coming about in a Pirat dinghy (from top to bottom): the helmsman is heading up, coming into the wind . . .

. . . ducking under the boom and standing up, raising the tiller extension.

Standing, he makes the necessary turn, while his sheet hand grasps the tiller extension behind his back.

His free right hand has now taken the sheet and the helmsman will sit down again and if need be hike-out.

Putting a Laser dinghy about. In a sensitive display such as this, if the helmsman were to stand up after the main boom has swung over, there could be unwanted heeling on the new tack. The helmsman must either be very quick in standing up or remain in a stooping position.

Hints

1 Do not come about until the boat has plenty of way on.

2 Do not put the tiller over too violently. This causes the rudder to exert a braking effect.

3 A good moment to start coming about is when the boat is heading up and wants to tack of her own accord.

4 A boat heads up of her own accord when heeling to leeward. You can deliberately cause the boat to heel by sitting less far out just before coming about. The boat will then head up without pressure from the rudder and the manoeuvre can be completed with the help of the rudder.

5 If you find yourself in difficulties in choppy water, especially in a heavy type of boat, and cannot come about, then back the jib to reinforce the turning movement. If

the boat starts a drift astern, reverse the rudder.

6 In a heavy boat, sail a little on the new tack to start with so that the boat can gather way.

7 German yachtsman Willy Kuhweide comments that it is a bad thing in coming about to be extreme about any of your actions. Each type of boat has its right speed of tacking and this varies with every strength of wind. You must neither come about very fast or you will be left without way on, nor turn too slowly when, despite a certain gain to windward, you will lose way. Thus, in tacking, you should take as little way off the boat as possible. This is particularly true of heavier boats, such as Solings or Dragons. This is how

Willy Kuhweide comes about. 'First I ensure that I have enough way on to come about. On the new tack I do not sail my normal windward course at once but bear away slightly with a slackened traveller so as to gather speed. As soon as I am settled on the new tack, that is as soon as I have reached my previous speed again, I come up into my normal position, adjusting the traveller to sail at the optimum speed and angle to the wind.'

Common mistakes

1 The boat does not turn properly through the wind and the sails shake too long.
2 The boat's bow falls off too far after going about, thus losing valuable distance to windward.
3 The jib sheet is let fly too soon and the sail shakes without producing any drive.
4 The jib is held aback by not freeing the sheet properly or too late.
5 The jib shakes too long on the new tack.
6 The helm is put down too hard with a consequent braking effect from the rudder.
7 The helmsman and crew take up their new positions clumsily.
8 The helmsman tries to put the boat about when she has little way on, and has to push the helm hard down, thus reducing the speed even further.

Gybing

Gybing is a manoeuvre performed when running. The stern is turned through the wind, so that the mainsail is swung over, to set on the opposite side of the boat. The difficulty of gybing lies in the fact that the manoeuvre is normally performed at full speed, so that the mainsail swings across fast and unbalances the boat. As a rule gybing is described in sailing literature as a difficult manoeuvre and even the famous helmsman, Paul Elvström, wrote in his book *Expert Dinghy and Keelboat Racing* that gybing in a strong wind is the most difficult manoeuvre for a dinghy. The faster a boat is sailing, the easier it is to gybe since, at high speed on course, dead before the wind, there is hardly any apparent wind. Bringing the sail across is not so difficult. It is easier to gybe in a light, planing dinghy than a heavier displacement one, or a slower keelboat. This, however, is only true if the gybe is correctly performed. Gybing usually involves a change of course, bearing away with wind astern and heading up again with the sail on the other side. In races over triangular courses the gybe comes at the leeward mark. For gybing with a spinnaker see section on Sailing with a spinnaker, page 160.

Here is a typical mistake when coming about. This boat has little way on yet the helmsman still wants to come about and is pushing the helm hard over. The result is that the boat will only go sideways and will not go through the stays. The correct thing to do here is to wait until the boat has more way on before starting to tack.

How to do it

The helmsman warns the crew to stand by to gybe. The crew gets ready. On the order to gybe the boom is pulled in amidships. The helmsman puts the tiller over far enough for the boom to swing over to the other side as the wind comes behind the sail. As the boom passes the midships position the sheet is run out quickly. This is the real danger point in gybing. The boat has a tendency to head up on the new tack and broach to. There will be a strong heeling moment if the sails are not eased off quickly enough. In a dinghy this will result in a capsize if the wind is strong.

You can prevent the tendency to turn and the danger of capsizing, however, by using the rudder at the critical phase to help the boat keep on a course with the wind from dead astern until the danger is past. Only then does one head up to the new course required. Explicit orders are

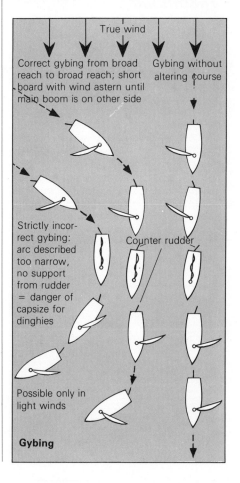

True wind

Correct gybing from broad reach to broad reach; short board with wind astern until main boom is on other side

Gybing without altering course

Strictly incorrect gybing: arc described too narrow, no support from rudder = danger of capsize for dinghies

Counter rudder

Possible only in light winds

Gybing

necessary when sailing yachts in which the helmsman does not work the sheets himself. In dinghy sailing, however, where the helmsman normally looks after the main sheet as well as the tiller, abbreviated orders are sufficient.

Technique

In gybing the mainsheet is hauled in as fast as possible and then eased off rapidly but under control. This process can also be described as controlled gybing. In boats with a mainsail that is not too large (all dinghies) it is usual, at least in racing, for the helmsman to grasp the entire tackle of the sheet in a bunch and throw the boom and sail over with one movement. This kind of gybing in a dinghy calls for a precise technique.

1 The helmsman stands in the dinghy with legs apart, or kneels on one knee.

Gybing correctly: maintain a course dead before the wind and put the helm up once the boom has swung over.

2 The hand nearer the boom grasps the sheet (the right hand on the starboard tack) and brings the boom over. Do not forget to use the rudder to hold the boat on course. The advantage of this way of handling the sheet is that the body is in a natural position, without being twisted or being placed on one side. After gybing

Correct attitude during the gybe: the helmsman stands up or kneels while the hand nearest the sail grabs the sheet to pull the boom across. In the illustration on the right he does it incorrectly. He uses the wrong hand and by leaning across makes the boat heel.

the helmsman has the tiller and the mainsheet ready in the correct hand as he starts off on the new tack.

NB. The jib presents no problems in gybing. The only thing you have to look out for is that it does not hang uselessly for too long, blanketed by the mainsail.

Hints

1 In a dinghy, raise the centreboard by about two thirds. This means that, if the gybe is incorrectly performed in a strong wind, the boat will slip sideways, and the heeling moment be decreased, thus diminishing the risk of a capsize.
2 In a strong wind, gybe only when the boat is running at her best speed. This ensures that the apparent wind is reduced to a minimum.
3 Do not gybe in a squall, or when the boat has been slowed down by a wave. In these circumstances the apparent wind will be stronger.
4 Harden in the boom vang so that the sail does not twist.

Common mistakes

1 Trying to haul the mainsail in before the boat is dead before the wind. This increases the tendency for the boat to broach.
2 Failing to apply rudder correction as the stern goes across, or intentionally heading up. The boat will have a tendency to pivot and heel a lot.
3 Heading up while the mainsail is not completely freed off results in pronounced heel and a risk of capsizing.
Before you try gybing, a manoeuvre which is not really difficult if properly performed and is quite safe in a light wind, you must

master the technique of holding a course downwind. Sail a long distance with the wind astern, gybing as often as possible. Since you are practising racing performance, the correct position must be taken up before each gybe. Once you have mastered the art of gybing, try it round a buoy for the first time.

Tacking instead of gybing

If conditions are too rough for a safe gybe to be done the helmsman may 'do a granny' as the Australians call it. Coming from a run he gradually brings the boat round to the closehauled position from which he tacks and with the wind on the other side, bears away again to a run. This is not always as easy as it sounds since, as the boat rounds up, it can heel excessively and broach to. Secondly, there is a risk of the boat losing way and thus being stopped by the waves. This would leave the boat very vulnerable to the wind and waves.

The manoeuvre is chiefly used in man-overboard drills. Dinghy sailors seldom use it because it takes as much time to perform as righting the dinghy in the event of a capsize but some racing helmsmen do recommend it in very strong winds.

Sailing stern first or making a sternboard

If you want to be a complete master of sailing techniques you must also learn how to sail stern first in certain situations. Such situations can arise when you leave moorings on the leeward side of a landing stage of dock. You find you have to manoeuvre yourself stern first out of a narrow space. In a larger boat you would use the engine or be towed out, but a good helmsman can sail smaller boats out stern first. Racing sailors often use the technique before the start of a race in order to keep on the starting line by falling astern and then sailing ahead again. Occasionally they pull themselves out of a bunch of boats before the start by making a sternboard.

How to do it

Correct positioning of the rudder is the decisive factor in making a sternboard (which is often a matter of just drifting astern).

Typical dinghy gybe demonstrated on a 470 with helmsman kneeling (from bottom to top).

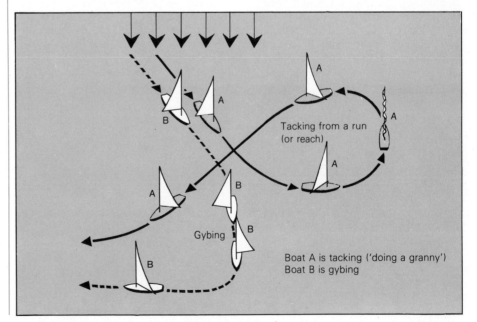

Tacking from a run (or reach)

Gybing

Boat A is tacking ('doing a granny')
Boat B is gybing

NB. The stern will turn whichever way the rudder blade is pointing.

This principle, however, is effective only if the boat has way on astern. Sternway can be increased by:
1 Backing the jib with the clew well forward.
2 Backwinding the mainsail.
3 Pulling the topping lift to cause the mainsail to pump out air, which is usually less effective.

Naturally the boat must always be head to wind. Part of the technique of sailing backwards is the ability to turn the boat at once (bear away) if you want to sail ahead. This is done by having the rudder at the correct angle. If, for instance, you want to turn the stern to starboard you put the helm to port. The jib can be backwinded to help, in the normal way, but on the correct side (in our example the starboard side). You should haul in the mainsheet as the boat pays off so that she will be quick to stop turning and then gather way forwards.

Hints

1 Have the rudder amidships before the boat gathers way astern.
2 When backwinding the jib, do not do this by pulling on the sheet but use your hand to hold it by the clew.
3 Pushing the mainsail aback is a job that the helmsman can do himself

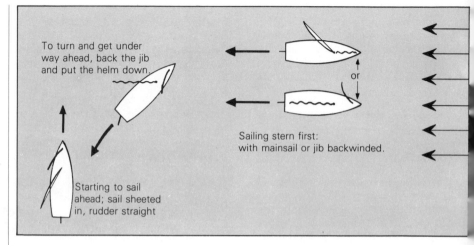

To turn and get under way ahead, back the jib and put the helm down.

Starting to sail ahead; sail sheeted in, rudder straight

or

Sailing stern first: with mainsail or jib backwinded.

in a dinghy by standing up, pushing on the boom and steering with the tiller extension.
4 So that the boat can gather way ahead as quickly as possible sheet in the mainsail as she pays off.
5 With wheel steering turn the wheel exactly as you would do when reversing a car.

Common mistakes

1 The boat is already drifting or sailing stern first but the helmsman uses the rudder as if he were still going ahead.
2 During the reversing movement the rudder is moved too much.
3 The jib is not held far enough forward so that the bow is pushed sideways instead of backwards.

4 The mainsail is backwinded although the boat is not lying head to wind.
5 While paying off to go ahead the helmsman positions the rudder for going ahead although the boat is still actually moving astern.

Practice

1 The best thing to do to get the feel for the right position of the rudder in sailing stern first is to practise on a dinghy, starting without a sail, and having someone on the foredeck to paddle the boat astern.
2 Start by a dock with plenty of clear water to leeward, then have the boat pushed hard astern and sail as many boat's lengths as you can by backing the jib or mainsail. At the same time practise paying off, with the bow pointing out to sea, of course!
3 Practise as in 2 but without being pushed away from the dock first.
4 Start in open water. Keep the boat ahead to wind as long as possible with sails shaking. Try sailing astern as soon as the boat stops or begins to drift astern.
5 In a dinghy drift sternwards towards an obstacle. Just before you reach it pay off quickly towards clear water and sail away.

Sailing stern first with backed mainsail.

Sailing stern first with backed jib.

Heaving to, lying to

If a boat under sail is to be brought to a stop, and is then to remain close to the place where she has stopped, lying relatively stationary, she must be hove to. The boat then lies with the wind coming rather more from ahead than on the beam. According to the force of the wind and the underwater profile of the hull, the boat, lying to, will drift at between 1.5 and 3.5 knots to leeward (these figures are for gale conditions) and, according to the set of the mainsail, there will be minimum forward movement. Should there be heavy breaking seas their effect will be minimized by a zone of eddies on the weather side, which is why heaving to can also serve as a means of riding out a storm. Heaving to and lying to mean very much the same. Strictly speaking, heaving to is the manoeuvre itself while lying to describes what the vessel does after. Sailing boats behave in various different ways when lying to, according to the nature of their lateral plane. In general one can say that yachts which have a large lateral plane (i.e., with a long keel) can be made to lie to very well. The manoeuvre must be mastered by every good sailor, as it has many uses. It can, for instance, be used:

- To ride out a storm.
- To allow you to do repairs on board in peace.
- To allow you to reef sails in peace.
- To allow you to wait for other boats to come alongside.
- To stop while picking up a man overboard.
- To stay near the starting line before a race.

How to do it

The manoeuvre is simple to perform. Backwind the jib and, according to the type of boat, pay off the mainsail a moderate amount, and lash the helm hard down. There will be differences of adjustment according to the purpose for which the manoeuvre

This 470 is hove to.

is being carried out (such as to ride out a storm or simply to enable one to do a repair), and what type of boat is involved, keelboat or dinghy.

Dinghies

There is not much point in expecting a dinghy to lie to and ride out a storm. When heaving to for the other reasons the jib is backed and the mainsail eased off. To keep the mainsail from flogging and possibly being damaged, however, it should be hauled in a little. According to the amount of drift you want, the centreboard can be raised a certain amount. Singlehanders without a jib can be hove to as well. In this case the mainsail only has to be eased off and the rudder, as before, set to weather. Dinghies with a large jib, such as FDs or Corsairs, should be treated like singlehanders when heaving to. Do not backwind the jib but roll it up, since in some winds to backwind a large jib can result in a capsize.

Yachts

Heaving to in yachts in light winds (for instance, to make a repair), you can follow the dinghy procedure. In strong winds or storms, however, this is what you do.

1 A storm jib must be hoisted and backwinded.
2 The mainsail must be reefed or replaced by a trysail. The sail is then sheeted in fairly hard.

3 Storm jibs too are backed on ketches or yawls but sometimes the mainsail is furled and a reefed mizzen is set.
4 The helm is always lashed hard down.

Hints

Heaving to is easily done as the conclusion to tacking. You tack in the normal way, but:

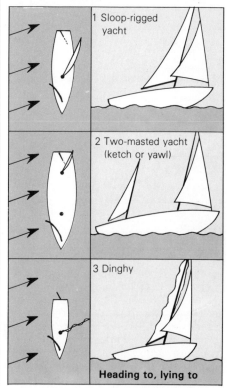

1 Sloop-rigged yacht

2 Two-masted yacht (ketch or yawl)

3 Dinghy

Heading to, lying to

a. Leave the jib sheet fast.
b. Ease the mainsheet.
c. Pay off more than you would for a closehauled course.
d. Put the helm down only when the boat has lost most of her way.

Common mistakes

1 Putting the helm down too soon when heaving to from going about, as the boat will come up into the wind.
2 Failing to put the helm down far enough when lying to.
3 Backwinding the jib wrongly by trying to hold it with your hand instead of using the weather sheet.
4 Mainsheet not eased enough (in dinghies).

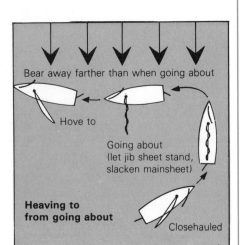

Heaving to from going about

Bear away farther than when going about
Hove to
Going about (let jib sheet stand, slacken mainsheet)
Closehauled

Man overboard

A person or an object might fall overboard and must be rescued as quickly as possible. For this there is a special manoeuvre so that you can pull the person out of the water quickly and safely. You should do this unless you are first heaving to for an emergency (see p. 129) To practise the manoeuvre use a floating object like a buoy or a lifebelt which you throw overboard. Do not describe the object as a man when practising. Keep the word for a genuine emergency.

We will only describe the manoeuvre itself at this stage. The procedure to be followed in an emergency, and how you can bring a person on board, is described in detail in the chapter on safety.

The basic principle of the manoeuvre is to turn round by tacking or gybing, then round up into the wind and let the sheets fly. The boat should then lose way and stop by the object in the water.

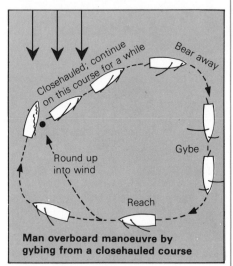

Man overboard manoeuvre by gybing from a closehauled course

Closehauled; continue on this course for a while
Bear away
Gybe
Reach
Round up into wind

Gybing

Start from a closehauled course in order to perform the manoeuvre in the fastest and most practical way, providing gybing seems safe in the prevailing wind conditions. Throw the buoy overboard, sail some three boat's lengths further on your course, then bear away before the wind, gybe and head up until you are in a position to let the sheets fly and stop by the buoy.

Tacking

● Starting from a closehauled or reaching course:
As soon as the buoy has been thrown overboard bear away on to a reach or broad reach and, after a few lengths, you will be able to head up and tack. Then bear away again far enough to be able to sail to the spot where you can round

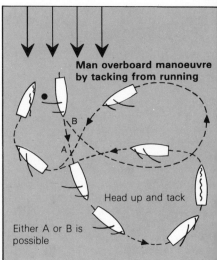

Man overboard manoeuvre by tacking from running

B
A
Head up and tack
Either A or B is possible

up into the wind and again stop by the buoy.
● Starting from a broad reach or run: head up slowly and tack, then bear away again and finally round up to stop by the buoy.

Rounding up

You should not come directly head to wind when picking up a man overboard, as you would when you are mooring, but stop *almost* head to wind. You do not head for the man from a point exactly downwind from him. Start from an imaginary position one or two boat's lengths either side of this line. The sails, flapping, are no longer amidships but rather to one side, and you can control the boat's speed by either letting them flap or hauling them in a little.

Advantages:
1 The boat's speed can be easily controlled by hauling in or easing the sheets, combined with careful steering. In particular, you can get under way again easily, if the boat has stopped too soon, by hauling in the mainsheet. In a heavy yacht with a sea running, however, this may not always be possible.
2 You can steer so that the man is either on the weather or the leeward side (see diagram p.13 bottom). The danger of hitting the man and injuring him is lessened
3 If you want to heave to whil

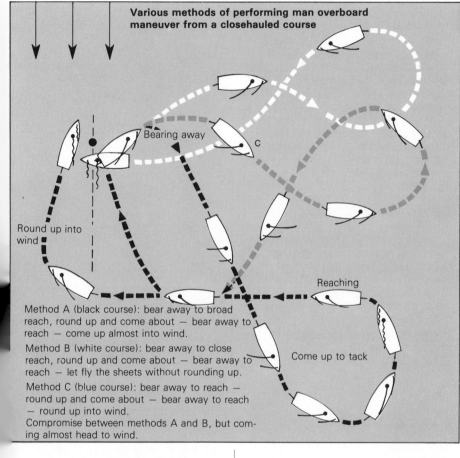

Various methods of performing man overboard maneuver from a closehauled course

Bearing away

C

Round up into wind

Reaching

Come up to tack

Method A (black course): bear away to broad reach, round up and come about — bear away to reach — come up almost into wind.

Method B (white course): bear away to close reach, round up and come about — bear away to reach — let fly the sheets without rounding up.

Method C (blue course): bear away to reach — round up and come about — bear away to reach — round up into wind.

Compromise between methods A and B, but coming almost head to wind.

ward side to the leeward where it is easier to recover him. The freeboard on that side is often reduced because the boat is heeled that way.

Disadvantages:
- In a heavy sea there may be a risk of the boat driving too hard toward the man who may be unconscious. In severe weather he may even be sucked under the turn of the bilge and disappear altogether.
- It is not possible to pull someone on board or for him or to climb aboard over the leeward gunwale of a dinghy so he must first be taken round to the stern or even the weather side.

2 Man to windward

Advantages:
- The man can climb aboard or be pulled aboard a dinghy at once.
- There is no danger of the boat driving towards the person with the risk of injury.

Disadvantages:
- There is considerable risk of the boat drifting away from the person to be picked up.
- It is seldom possible to climb in, or be pulled in, over the high side of a yacht. So the person to be rescued will probably have to be towed round to the leeward side.

After weighing the various advantages and disadvantages it looks as though there is some justification, under different conditions, for preferring either the windward or the leeward side. Everybody should, ideally, practise both alternatives so that in an emergency you can decide which side will be best according to circumstances and the type of boat. It is of doubtful value, however, to have this choice of possibilities. In an emergency it would be better to use just *one* way, the way you have practised and now know thoroughly, and avoid any risk of making mistakes. In the search for one and only one correct way, either windward or leeward, the author carried out a series of experiments which gave the following result.

recovering the man this can be done quickly by backing the jib and putting the helm down.

Windward or leeward?

You should steer towards the man to be picked up in such a way that the boat stops alongside him. The man should not be ahead or astern of the boat. The question is, do you want the man on the leeward side or the windward side of the boat? There is some controversy over the answer to this question, so instead of giving a definite answer, we will list the advantages and disadvantages of both alternatives.

1 Man to leeward

Advantages:
- You are usually sure of reaching the man since you are not being

driven away but drifting towards him.
- You can heave to and will not be driven away from, but towards, the man.
- On a yacht you can get a man on board at once without first having to tow him round from the wind-

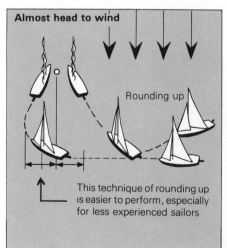

Almost head to wind

Rounding up

This technique of rounding up is easier to perform, especially for less experienced sailors

The manoeuvre almost always succeeds if the object is brought to lie to leeward. Usually the drift of the boat is useful (for it is going in the right direction) and it is only in extreme cases and with large yachts that there may be any danger and even then only if there are not enough hands on board to help pick the man up. With the man to windward, on the other hand, there need only be a small error in boat handling and you will be driven away from the man and be unable to reach him, which would be a serious matter in a real emergency.

Hints

1 Dinghy sailors should practise the manoeuvre singlehanded as well as with a crew. Dinghies are often handled by only two sailors and if one of these should fall overboard, the other will have to pick him up singlehanded.

2 When sailing dinghies you can, on occasion, spare yourself the whole manoeuvre as just described and use a quicker method if your reactions are good enough. You can round up by letting the sheets fly and stop. The distance to the man overboard will then only be a few yards and he can easily swim back to the boat.
3 It is a good idea, when recovering a man who has fallen overboard, to heave to so that the boat is stopped.

Common mistakes

1 Sailing too large an arc in performing the manoeuvre, with consequent loss of time.
2 Bearing away too fast when carrying out the manoeuvre using the gybing method. This takes you too far to leeward and you may have to beat back to windward again.

Solings racing, with spinnakers set and the wind on the quarter, on the way to the first mark.

The following pages turn attention to the question of moorings, and of coming into a berth at a marina such as this one.

Coming about in a Laser. The helmsman would really do better to have the sheet leading from below rather than from above.

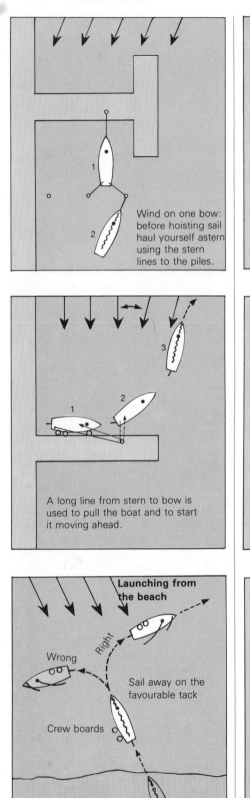

Wind on one bow: before hoisting sail haul yourself astern using the stern lines to the piles.

A long line from stern to bow is used to pull the boat and to start it moving ahead.

Launching from the beach

Wrong

Right

Sail away on the favourable tack

Crew boards

Boat on beach, head to wind

Leaving a dock from the leeward side: drop back out of the berth.

A slip line aft keeps a large yacht from moving about in a confined space.

Hoist mainsail

Turn and hoist jib

Turn head to wind

Warp boat astern

Leaving from the windward side of dock, bow to

Undocking and docking

Getting a sailboat underway from or back to a mooring or dock is something which is very largely a matter of experience. Almost every occasion on which it is done is different from all the previous ones. The wind may be stronger or lighter than last time, the current may be setting differently, you may even have different sails set. Also local conditions vary to a considerable extent from one place to another. Therefore the advice we can give is bound to be general in nature and it is up to you to adapt it to match the circumstances, and to learn as you go along.

Leaving a mooring

This is a simple manoeuvre. After hoisting sail you let the buoy go (on the windward side so that you do not sail over it), put the helm up, and sail off closehauled. If the wind is blowing onshore, however, you should not cast off from the buoy until you have got your bow turned so that the wind can take you off immediately you drop the mooring. If you don't do this you will drift inshore. Back the jib and walk the mooring aft to give you some forward movement and, therefore, steerage way.

Leaving a berth on the leeward side of a dock

In this case the sails can be set. If the boat is lying alongside on the leeward

Leaving a berth on the leeward side in a dinghy. *(Read from right to left)*
a *The crew lets go the painter. b The crew pushes the boat astern while the helmsman keeps the helm amidships and tells the crew to back the jib. c The jib is backed and the helm put up while the* *boat drops astern. Then the boat bears away to port. d The mainsheet is hauled in as the boat bears away, the jib sheets are hauled in on the leeward side and the boat sails off on the port tack.*

side, however, the spring lines and stern line must be freed first so that the boat is head to wind as you hoist the sails and is secured only by her bow line.

If the boat is lying at the end of a dock, with plenty of clear water round about, then it is simple to turn the bow away from the dock, haul in the sheets and sail comfortably away. If you do not have much room, for instance if there is a boat moored next to you, or there are mooring posts in the water, you must first move out stern first. This can either be done by sailing stern first as described earlier (p.127), or you can haul yourself off with the stern lines.

If the boat is lying with stern lines to mooring piles from each quarter, and the wind is blowing rather more from one quarter, then you can pull yourself out stern first before hoisting the sails and make the boat fast to a pile with a bow line. The boat can then lie head to wind as you hoist the sails. If the space is very limited, and your boat is a large yacht, you can prevent her from moving about by means of a stern line leading to the dock.

Leaving a bow-on berth on the windward side

From a berth on the windward side, and the bow towards the pile or dock, you haul yourself out stern first with the help of stern lines. Naturally you set no sails. Once you have enough room the helm is put over so that the

boat turns towards open water and, at the same time, the jib is hoisted. You then sail out into open water under the jib alone, using paddles if necessary and, as soon as you have enough room, you come up into the wind to set the mainsail. When you round up into the wind ease the jib sheet or the boat will be difficult to steer. In a large yacht you can use the engine.

Leaving a berth alongside with an onshore wind

If you have no engine on your boat she must be moved out from the berth, where she has been lying alongside, far enough to have sufficient room for the sails to be hoisted. This is done as follows. A line is taken from the stern, which is brought well forward along the dock to a bollard or ring, then led back to the bow. If you pull on this line (running aft along the deck) the yacht will move forward. The mooring lines are released in good time in the following order: the fore spring, after spring, stern line, then bow line.

Take care:
a. That the hauling line has eased away in good time after the boat has started to gather way so that the movement is not braked again.
b. When turning the rudder, because of the danger of the stern hitting the dock. Protect the quarter with fenders.

When getting under way like this with a very strong onshore wind

blowing you may have to make use of a kedge anchor. Row the anchor out to at least five boat's lengths from the pier. After the anchor has been recovered it should be kept ready for use until the yacht is safely under way as it may be needed again in a hurry.

Getting under way with the help of the engine when lying alongside

When getting under way from a dock an auxiliary engine is usually essential

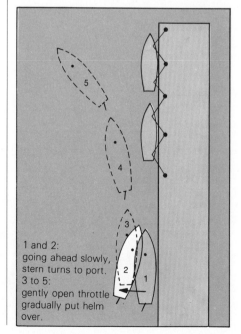

1 and 2:
going ahead slowly,
stern turns to port.
3 to 5:
gently open throttle
gradually put helm
over.

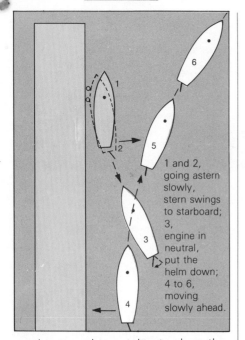

1 and 2, going astern slowly, stern swings to starboard; 3, engine in neutral, put the helm down; 4 to 6, moving slowly ahead.

on large yachts, at least when the wind is blowing onshore. You must be careful not to put the helm over too hard or the stern will hit the dock. The yacht must be got far enough away from the dock for it to turn clear of the dock. Leaving when the wind is blowing off the berth is no problem since the wind will blow the boat off. When the wind is not blowing off the berth, or there is a calm, you can make use of the paddlewheel effect of your propeller when you are getting under way. This is why you should know which way the propeller turns, left or right.

The paddlewheel effect comes about because every propeller has a secondary effect in that it causes a sideways movement of the stern. The stern is moved as if the propeller were a wheel running on the ground. If the propeller is turned to the left when the boat is going ahead, the stern will be moved to port, while with a propeller which is turned to the right the stern will be moved to starboard.

Using the paddlewheel effect to get under way will then look like this with a screw turning to the left (the other way around with one turning to the right):

Example 1: screw turning left, dock to starboard
1 The engine is started, the lines are cast off, the fenders are made ready, the crew uses boathooks to push the yacht some way off the dock.
2 The engine starts to move the boat slowly forward. At the same time fenders are held in readiness at the bows. The paddlewheel effect now moves the stern away from the dock.
3 If the yacht is now far enough away from the dock, you open the throttle gently and move ahead. As you do so you must not put the helm over hard or you will turn too sharply with the risk of the stern hitting the dock.

Getting under way from the beach.

Example 2: screw turning left, dock to port
1 Start the engine, cast off the lines, and push the yacht a little way out with boathooks.
2 With a lefthanded screw, as the boat goes astern, the stern will move to starboard. The boat is put into slow astern and the rudder turned slightly to starboard. At the same time fenders are held ready at the bow since, as the stern moves away from the dock, the bow will swing in towards it.
3 After two or three boat's lengths you stop the engine and turn the rudder the other way to stop further movement. Move slowly ahead and turn the rudder carefully to starboard again so that you move away from the dock.

Getting under way from the beach

In many coastal areas with sandy beaches and no docks, it is usual for dinghies to be launched directly from the beach. This manoeuvre is very simple.
1 The dinghy, standing on the beach, is turned so that her bow points into the wind for hoisting sail. If the boat has a lifting rudder this is shipped, but the rudder blade is drawn right up.

Heaving a line ashore for making fast. This is not as easy as one might think!

2 With the bow pointing into the wind (offshore wind = bow pointing inland, onshore wind = bow pointing seaward) the boat is launched. The crew gets wet feet in the process. Boots or shoes are put in the boat first.

3 Get in, pushing the boat off as hard as possible. The helmsman immediately lets the rudder blade down a suitable amount or ships the rudder if it is a fixed one. If the water is not deep enough the crew should go far enough forward to lift the stern so that the rudder can be shipped.

4 There is no problem in sailing off if the wind is offshore. If the wind is onshore push the boat off as strongly as possible when you get in and make sure that you choose the more favourable tack to sail off. The centreboard must be lowered as far as possible at once (be careful that it does not touch bottom, especially if the conditions are choppy).

Berthing

The basic point of any berthing manoeuvre is that the lines should be used quickly and correctly. You should note the following points:

1 Lines for making fast must be prepared in good time and sent ashore at the right moment.

2 A member of the crew should jump ashore to make the lines fast. If you are in a large yacht and this is impossible then someone will have to land in the tender unless there is someone on the dock already.

3 The ends of lines are made fast ashore, to bollards or piles, and the slack is then taken in and adjusted on board.

Coming in on the leeward side of a dock. Sail in with wind on the beam, turn head to wind. A good sailor will bring his boat to a standstill an inch away from the landing stage.

4 A boat can be stopped only by means of a line working against the direction of the boat's movement. For example, forward movement can be stopped only by a stern line. If you try to use a bow-line instead, there will be too strong a turning moment towards the pier and the bow can be damaged.

When berthing there are two basic approaches according to the direction of the wind:

a. Coming in on the leeward side and rounding up into the wind.

b. Coming in on the windward side, letting the boat run in under bare poles.

Berthing on the lee side of a dock

The basic principle is to approach head to wind. The boat is headed up into the wind so that she loses way, sails flapping, and comes to a standstill in her allotted berth. You look for a suitable spot outside the moorings in which to round up into the wind. Observe the direction of the wind from the flags or burgees of moored boats and head straight up into it. The distance over which the boat will carry her way depends on the type of boat and her displacement and on the wind and the waves.

Here is a useful tip for dinghy sailors coming in on the leeward side. Leave the centreboard down, or at least down as far as possible in shallow water. The lefthand pictures show a boat coming head to wind with her centreboard raised. You can see clearly how the boat drifts sideways as she rounds up, comes close to the posts and thus does not reach her berth. In the righthand pictures the dinghy is sailing with centreboard down. The leeway is clearly reduced and the dinghy easily gets to her berth.

A heavy sailing boat will carry her way longer so plan to round up sooner. A light planing dinghy will come to a standstill almost at once so you need only round up at the last moment. The stronger the wind and the bigger the waves, the greater the braking power they exert. The boat will bring up in a shorter distance. The lighter the wind and the smoother the water the longer the boat will carry its way so you will need a longer approach.

Generally, if you observe these rules and gradually get a little experience you will manage in most circumstances. There are a few dodges you can use to help you. If you have miscalculated the distance and the boat has too much way on, you can quickly put the helm down and let the boat head up. On the other hand, if you have allowed too long an approach you can hold the tiller very still to encourage the boat to go a little further. During the heading-up manoeuvre you can slow the boat down by scandalizing the mainsail or by backing it. If you have lost way too quickly you might save the situation by bearing away a little and briefly hauling in the mainsheet. This will be easier to do if you have made the approach on a reach.

Ideally you sail to the spot at which you will come up into the wind, with the wind on the beam, since this point of sailing offers the best chance of making corrections. With the wind abeam you can head up or fall off as needed. To perform the berthing manoeuvre on the leeward side correctly in a large yacht you hand the jib before starting your approach. The sail will not be damaged by unnecessary flogging, and there will be no risk of injury to the crew working up forward or of the jib being fouled and caught aback. Visibility will be improved and you will have more space to work with bow lines on the foredeck.

In smaller yachts, and in all dinghies, the jib is usually left up. The reason is that the points just mentioned do not apply so much in the case of a smaller jib and, if you should miss your berth or mooring, then sailing away with the help of the jib is easier.

The simplest form of leeward approach is that used to pick up a buoy.

These boats are running into harbour under jib alone.

Getting caught up under sail on the weather side of a dock is not very seamanlike.

A dinghy coming in correctly on the weather side of a dock.

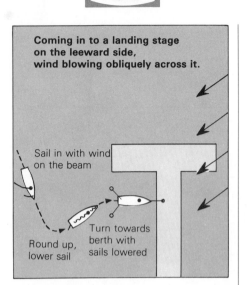

Coming in to a landing stage on the leeward side, wind blowing obliquely across it.

Sail in with wind on the beam

Round up, lower sail

Turn towards berth with sails lowered

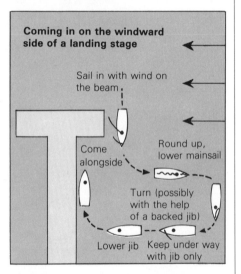

Coming in on the windward side of a landing stage

Sail in with wind on the beam

Come alongside

Round up, lower mainsail

Turn (possibly with the help of a backed jib)

Lower jib   Keep under way with jib only

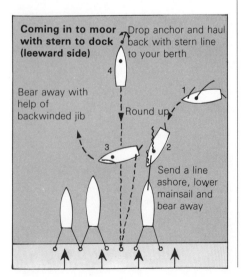

Coming in to moor with stern to dock (leeward side)

Drop anchor and haul back with stern line to your berth

Bear away with help of backwinded jib

Round up

Send a line ashore, lower mainsail and bear away

Do not grab the buoy if you are still going fast or you may describe an ungainly somersault or wrench your arm. If you are sailing a yacht with a lot of freeboard you must remember to have a boathook ready to pick up the buoy. When coming in to a landing stage or dock you should not always approach bow on. With large yachts it is often less risky, providing you have enough space, to drop all sail as you approach and then come alongside under bare poles, thus avoiding any damage to the bow. The mooring lines are used to stop you.

Berthing on the weather side

The main point here is that the sails are handed before you come in, and the boat approaches the dock or the landing stage under bare poles.

How to do it

1 Reach in till near the dock. The main halyard is cleared and, in a dinghy, the crew gets ready to raise the centreboard if the water is shallow.
2 The approach must be made just in front and a little way back from the berth in such a way that the boat can drift in with the following wind.
3 As soon as the boat has come up into the wind the mainsail is dropped and the helmsman now grasps the boom and stows it.
4 As soon as the mainsail is lowered the helmsman uses what way remains to turn the boat. The jib can be used to push the bow round.
5 With the jib sheets eased the boat now moves in the direction of the dock.
6 The moment at which the jib is lowered depends on the strength of the wind. The stronger the wind the sooner the jib comes down and vice versa.
7 Bow and stern lines must be made ready.
8 If there are piles on the dock stern lines are run out. If there are no piles a stern anchor may be used, otherwise you go alongside the pier or dock and put out fenders.

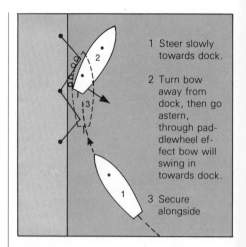

1 Steer slowly towards dock.
2 Turn bow away from dock, then go astern, through paddlewheel effect bow will swing in towards dock.
3 Secure alongside

If the yacht is to lie with her stern to the dock, the bower anchor is let go as soon as she comes to a standstill. With the anchor rope paid out the boat then drifts sternwards into her berth.

Beachings

In coastal areas with sandy beaches and no docks you have to bring the boat ashore. Naturally this is only possible for dinghies. Landing is very easy in light winds under full sail.

Here are the basic actions. Retract

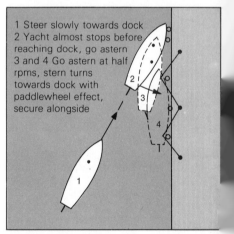

1 Steer slowly towards dock
2 Yacht almost stops before reaching dock, go astern
3 and 4 Go astern at half rpms, stern turns towards dock with paddlewheel effect, secure alongside

the centreboard partly or wholly, as soon as the water gets really shallow, and lift the rudder blade. Then round up into the wind (with an onshore wind, bow pointing seawards; with an offshore wind, bow pointing towards the shore). The crew gets out. If the dinghy has a fixed rudder it is removed. Now the dinghy is pulled up the beach, bow to wind, and the sails lowered.

The boat should on no account be left on land, with the sails hoisted and flogging in the wind, for any length of time. This can do a lot of damage to both the sail and the hull.

Berthing alongside under power

In a large yacht one very often comes in without sails, under power. Normally this does not entail any special problem. You have only to watch for the paddlewheel effect of the propeller (see p. 138) or, indeed, make use of it. As with leaving a dock there are two main ways of using the paddlewheel effect when coming in.

Lefthand screw, dock on the port side

1 The mooring lines and the fenders are made ready on the port side.
2 Steer at very low speed towards the dock at an angle of about 30°, turning parallel to it in good time.
3 When the boat is close to the dock she should, ideally, be almost stationary, bow towards the dock. If she still has too much way on, steer so that she has the bow away from the dock after running parallel to it for a short distance. Now go astern with half rmps (rudder to starboard) and shortly afterwards, if need be, put the engine into neutral. The stern is thereby turned away from the dock and the bow turned towards it. During the manoeuvre a paddlewheel effect to starboard has been created.

Lefthand screw, dock on the starboard side

1 Clear lines for making fast and fenders on the starboard side.
2 Going as slowly as possible steer at about an angle of 30°, putting the engine into neutral in good time.
3 If the bow is near the dock the yacht should almost have stopped. Now go astern at half rmps so that the paddlewheel effect causes the stern to turn to starboard and the boat to lie parallel to the dock.
4 Fenders are rigged on the starboard side in the following order: bow, stern, amidships.

Anchoring

Anchoring does not play much part in dinghy sailing though most class associations make it a rule that a small anchor should be carried when racing. Moreover, if you do need to drop anchor from a dinghy it is very easy.

Anchoring is particularly important if you go cruising, however.

The composition of the seabed is important in relation to the holding power of the anchor. Sand, ooze, mud and clay are good holding grounds. Weedy, stony and slimy bottoms are poor. Rock and coral often give a good grip but you may have great difficulty breaking out the anchor or even lose it entirely. Good anchorages are often marked on charts by an anchor symbol though these may be suitable mainly for large commercial vessels and uncomfortably rough or even dangerous for yachts.

Some points to consider

In addition to the composition of the seabed there are a few points you should consider before anchoring:
● Check that there is enough water under the keel. On the other hand, it should not be too deep. A good depth is about 12-22ft (4-7m).
● The anchorage must be well sheltered from wind and waves.
● Avoid anchoring on a lee shore, i.e., with an onshore wind.
● If there are several boats nearby drop anchor in such a position that your rode will not foul that of another yacht.
● The distance from other yachts at anchor must be sufficient to allow all boats to swing freely in a circle around their own anchors.

How to drop anchor

1 First the jib is rolled up or lowered, then the foredeck is cleared in preparation for the work. Take soundings.
2 The anchor rode is flaked out on deck (laid in bights) and made fast at the required length. If a rope is used instead of a chain cable there should be 2 to 5 fathoms of chain shackled in place between anchor and line. A line is adequate for a dinghy. The anchor is made ready and its fastening to the rode checked.
3 The anchor is now held overboard or laid with its shank in the bow fairlead.
4 Meanwhile, the helmsman rounds

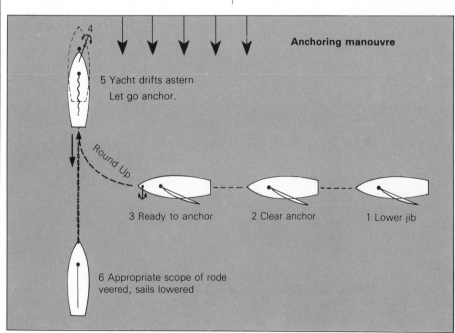

Anchoring manouvre

5 Yacht drifts astern
Let go anchor.

Round Up

3 Ready to anchor   2 Clear anchor   1 Lower jib

6 Appropriate scope of rode veered, sails lowered

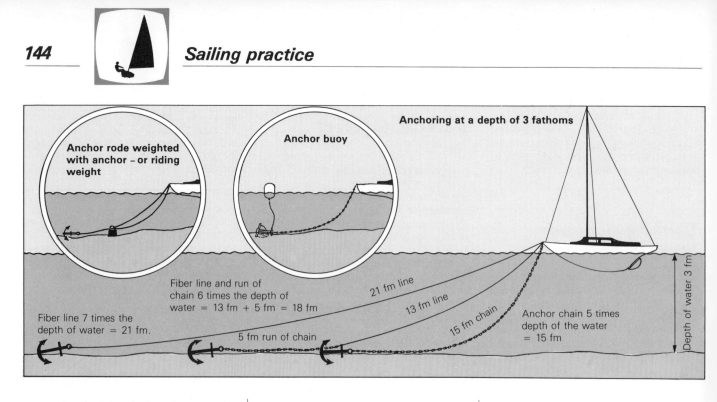

Anchoring at a depth of 3 fathoms

Anchor rode weighted with anchor – or riding weight

Anchor buoy

Depth of water 3 fm

Fiber line and run of chain 6 times the depth of water = 13 fm + 5 fm = 18 fm

21 fm line

13 fm line

Fiber line 7 times the depth of water = 21 fm.

15 fm chain

Anchor chain 5 times depth of the water = 15 fm

5 fm run of chain

up to the intended anchorage. As soon as the yacht has stopped and has started to make sternway the anchor is lowered slowly by its rode to the bottom. Do not let the rode rush out or simply throw it overboard. Never drop the anchor while the boat is stopped. The chain could foul the anchor and stop it digging in. Slight way ahead is preferable to being stationary but is generally less preferred than some sternway. By going astern under power you can put pressure on the rode and help the anchor dig in.

5 According to conditions of wind and sea, and distance from the shore, the rode is now veered to a scope of at least three times the expected depth at high water. Secure the rode to a cleat or samson post on the foredeck.

6 Now lower the mainsail and clear the boat up.

Hints

1 First lead the end of the rode to be attached to the anchor through the pulpit and then bring it over and back on deck. If you don't the rode will end up running over the pulpit and you will have problems.

2 Before dropping anchor the rode must, of course, be made fast. First calculate a length of about three times the depth of water you expect.

3 If you only have a fibre line at your disposal for anchoring you can improve the holding power to some extent and reduce snubbing by using an anchor weight, called a riding weight, which will help keep the angle between anchor line and the bottom small. A piece of lead or iron is suitable for a riding weight. Using a sliding shackle and a mooring line it is lowered down the line. It pulls the line down towards the bottom. Of course, you can also use a riding weight with a chain rode but it is necessary only in heavy weather.

Lying at anchor

If the anchor is holding, sufficient rode for the conditions must be veered, between three and ten times the expected depth of the water at high tide. On average, and in normal circumstances, you will choose five times the depth of water for chain and at least seven times the depth using fibre rope. If you are using a length of chain attached to rope, or an anchor weight, a middle value between the appropriate lengths of chain and fibre rope should be chosen. As soon as you have veered the correct scope you hoist the anchor ball, or in darkness the anchor light (a white all round light), on the forestay. By taking soundings and bearings you can also check if the

anchor is dragging. An anchor watch is set, according to conditions, to take further soundings at intervals and to watch the weather. If a yacht starts dragging her anchor this can sometimes be stopped by veering more rode. If this does not work it is best to reanchor. Sometimes a second anchor must be dropped.

Weighing anchor

Points to consider:
- Do you have neighbouring boats to consider?
- Is there enough room to enable

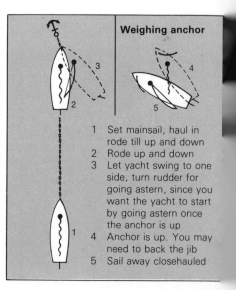

Weighing anchor

1 Set mainsail, haul in rode till up and down
2 Rode up and down
3 Let yacht swing to one side, turn rudder for going astern, since you want the yacht to start by going astern once the anchor is up
4 Anchor is up. You may need to back the jib
5 Sail away closehauled

you to go ahead at once after a short drift astern?
- Is there a strong wind blowing on-shore so that you need to take special precautions?

How to do it

Set the sails but roll the jib up.
The rode is hauled in so that it is almost up and down (vertical) in the water but with the anchor still fast in the bottom.
If there are unfavourable winds the helmsman must now wait, using the rudder to help him, for the boat to swing to one side or the other so that he can get under way at once. If the yacht is not yet lying in such a way that she can sail away you backwind the mainsail so that you start to move astern and then turn the rudder in such a direction that you can start to move ahead.
- As soon as the anchor is off the bottom the jib is unrolled or hoisted and on some occasions backwinded so that you can get underway as fast as possible — as when leaving a mooring.
- Once the anchor is up on deck you clean it (taking care, of course, not to mark the boat) and stow it away with its rode or lash it down.

Hints

If yours is not a large yacht, equip-ped with a windlass for bringing in the anchor rode, breaking out and hauling in the anchor can be hard work. In order to avoid back strain, or even a slipped disc, you should be careful not to haul with your up-per body bent, using the muscles of your back. It is better to keep the upper part of your body upright. Bend your legs instead and use your leg muscles.
If breaking out the anchor presents problems the following procedure often helps. The whole crew assembles forward and the cable or hawser is hauled in as far as possible and belayed. The crew now goes aft. This may break out the anchor.

3 An anchor may get fouled up on some obstacle, so that it cannot be broken out. In this case a tripline with an anchor buoy may help, the line being already fastened to the anchor. A mooring line long enough for the maximum depth of water is fastened to the crown of the anchor. A small buoy on the surface of the water indicates its position. By pulling on the tripline in a different direction to the angle of the rode or hawser you can usually break out a fouled anchor.

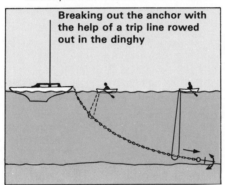
Breaking out the anchor with the help of a trip line rowed out in the dinghy

4 If the anchor has got caught under someone else's rode, and has no tripline on it, then it might be possible to raise the other rode a little with the aid of a small kedge anchor. You can also try bringing your own anchor, with the other rode, as near the surface as possi-ble and passing a line under the other rode. Then make both ends of the line fast on board so that the rode is lying in the bight. By slackening your own anchor rode you may be able to free your an-chor.
5 A fouled anchor without a tripline may also be recovered in the following way. Row out from the bow of the yacht in the tender towards the anchor, pulling a line made into a bight around the rode after you, and try to get this under the anchor. Then give a strong pull to break out the anchor.

Anchoring in tides and strong winds

If you anchor in tides, or in strong winds and steep seas, you may have difficulty in making your anchor hold, especially if the seabed is not ideal where you wish to anchor. If one an-

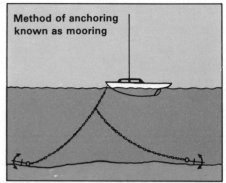
Method of anchoring known as mooring

chor does not hold you may need to use two. Try one anchor upstream and another downstream, one behind the other, or one beside another.

Mooring In tidal waters, if you moor a boat with anchors both upstream and downstream, rodes of both run to the bow of the boat. Better still, you can attach one rode to the other at a depth low enough to be below the keel. When you anchor you can drop the upstream anchor first then let yourself drift a few boat's lengths downstream and drop the second one. You then centre the boat bet-ween them by hauling on the upstream anchor rode. In a weaker current you can lie between a bow and a stern anchor, but then remember to lash the tiller or wheel amidships.

Anchors in line

In an offshore wind, or when there is poor holding ground, you can in-crease the holding power of your an-chor by putting a second anchor on the same rode. You attach a second, usually smaller, anchor and rode to the crown of the first anchor and let the smaller anchor go first. The distance between the two should be more than the depth of the water.

Dropping a second anchor beside the first

If the anchor does not hold, or you are afraid it may not hold, you can drop a second anchor so that the load is divided between the two. The an-chors should be positioned so that they and the bow of the boat form a triangle. The second anchor is either taken out in the tender or let go when the yacht sheers well out to one side.

A summary of the basic manoeuvres discussed

Manoeuvre	Basic principle	Technique	Hints	Common mistakes	When used
Coming about (tacking)	Turning the boat's head through the wind from close-hauled on one tack to close-hauled on the other.	Mainsail sheeted in, crew changes from side to side. In dinghies, tiller extension raised helmsman usually changes places while standing	Don't put the helm down too hard. Go about only with plenty of way on. Do not let sails shake too much.	Bearing away too far after going about. Boat stops be-cause of lack of way and misses stays. Main-sheet too slack.	When going through the eye of the wind.
Gybing	Turning the stern through the wind on a run, so that the main boom swings over to the other side.	We distinguish between con-trolled gybing (large boats) and gybing all-standing (dinghies and small keel-boats). Stay on course with wind from astern till boom swings over, steer slightly above course until settled and then bear away (see p. 126)	Do not gybe in a squall or gust. Raise the centreboard of a dinghy by about two thirds. Gybe when sail-ing fast, with apparent wind at a minimum.	Describing too narrow an arc. i.e. heading up before the boom swinging over is squared off. Failure to counter with the rudder early enough after the boom crosses.	On a broad reach or run, changing from one tack to the other, wind from astern. Rounding down-wind mark in racing.
Sailing stern first	Position the rudder correctly when sailing astern; the stern will go in the same direction as the rudder blade.	Back jib or back mainsail.	Keep tiller amid-ships at start of sternboard. Haul in mainsheet when ready to go ahead again.	Incorrect pos-ition of rudder, too much rudder move-ment.	Sailing stern first away from a mooring. Be-fore the start of a race: moving ahead and astern on the starting line.
Heaving to	Boat remains lying relatively still with wind on the bow.	Mainsail slack, jib backed, helm down.	Easy manouvre to perform from going about; tack, let jib stand, slacken mainsheet and put helm down late in man-ouvre. (Haul very gently on mainsheet so that sail does not flog too much.)	Helm not hard enough down, jib not backed enough, main-sheet of a dinghy not slack-ened enough.	When riding out a storm, when reefing in heavy weather, to make repairs, to rescue man over-board, before the start of a race.

Manoeuvre	Basic principle	Technique	Hints	Common mistakes	When used
Man over-board manoeuvre	Turning round to approach object by tacking and close reaching.	Head off at once to a reach or broad reach, luff up after a few boat's lengths and tack. Head off again and then round up letting the sheets fly.	When boat comes to a standstill near object, heave to.	Describing too large an arc, taking too long. Not rounding up properly.	When a person or object falls overboard. It is better to perform this manouvre than to gybe in a strong wind.
Man over-board manoeuvre gybing from a close reach	Turn by gybing and then come head to wind when near the man.	Sail on about three more boat's lengths, then bear away onto a run, gybe, head up to a reach and then round up. All one continuous movement.			
Coming in on leeward side of a dock	Round up head to wind.	Sail up on reach if possible, round up head to wind. Let fly sheets (usually before heading up into the wind).	Use topping lift or push out main boom if too much way still on. If not enough way on, bear away and haul mainsheet in.	Misjudging distance (generally by underestimating way). Bumping into dock.	When coming in to moor on leeward side of a dock or picking up moorings in a harbour.
Coming in on windward side	Lower sails first and drift in to moorings under bare poles.	Round up into the wind, lower mainsail, turn in direction of moorings with jib only set; hand jib and then come in.	If there are no piles for stern lines, go alongside. Raise centreboard of a dinghy before turning to go alongside so that the boat can drift towards the dock.	Main halyard not clear when boat is head to wind; mainsail lowered though boat is not head to wind; jib not lowered in time.	When the berth is on windward side.

Manoeuvre	Basic principle	Technique	Hints	Common mistakes	When used
Leaving from leeward side of dock or moorings	Hoist sail and push boat off or drop astern out of moorings.	Sail stern first out of small space: adjust rudder and back jib so that the bow is pointing towards open water.	Keep rudder amidships at first, until boat is out of berth. Haul in mainsheet when turning.	Letting bow line go at wrong moment; boat turns too soon and fouls next-door boat; boat turns wrong way, i.e. land-wards.	Sailing away from moorings on leeward side.
Leaving from windward side of dock or moorings	Getting away from moorings without sail.	Move away from moorings with no sails or with jib only. Look for berth on leeward side or a mooring. Or turn head to wind, if there is enough space and sail.	If you round up to set sail wait to hoist until the boat is drifting astern: you can keep head to wind better that way. Hoist the mainsail first.	Boat is not kept head to wind when sail is hoisted.	Sailing away from a weather side berth.
Anchoring	Round up, drop anchor.	Get anchor ready, flake rode down; lower jib; round up; drop anchor — when boat drifts astern, veer rode; lower sails.	Pass rode under pulpit outwards first. Check to see if rode is secure before dropping anchor. If using line use anchor weight too.	Anchor let go while boat is stopped and rode fouls anchor.	When there is no berth at a dock. On cruise to wait for tide. To avoid being swept back by currents in calm weather.
Weighing anchor	Haul in anchor and sail away.	Hoist sails but keep jib furled; haul anchor rode up and down; break out anchor and get under way at same time; set jib.	Do not haul in anchor with back bent. Trip-line helps break out anchor. Crew can shift from fore to aft.	Breaking out the anchor too soon	When leaving an anchorage.

Towing and being towed

If you want to tow another boat with a sailing boat you sail closehauled across the bow of the boat to be towed, taking the towrope as you go. Then you bear away and stay on the same tack. Motorboats take a tow coming from a stern or from the leeward side but should then pass on the weather side and stop ahead of the damaged vessel.

If a boat is to be towed the sails should be lowered. In the case of a dinghy the centreboard should be pulled up. A towrope can either be made fast to a painter with a rolling hitch or to a cleat in the bow if there is a good strong one available. It is better to secure the towrope to the mast, however, using a round turn and two half hitches. If possible you should use your own towrope. Get it ready to throw by coiling it in small bights and then dividing them between both hands.

Steer so that you stay in the wake of the towing boat. As you get under way do not let the towrope take up with a snatch but take up the slack gradually. Normally a long line is used but, if the boat is full of water, it mus

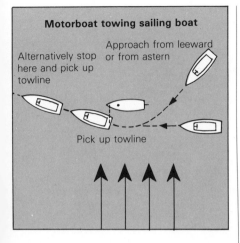

Motorboat towing sailing boat

Alternatively stop here and pick up towline

Approach from leeward or from astern

Pick up towline

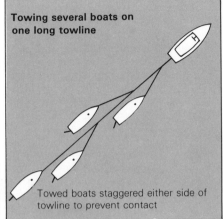

Towing several boats on one long towline

Towed boats staggered either side of towline to prevent contact

be shortened so that the bow is fairly high. The weight of the crew should be kept aft. If boats are towed at sea the towrope should be long enough for both tug and towed boat to be in the trough of successive waves or be on their crests at the same moment. In really bad weather the towrope can be attached to the anchor rode and enough rode veered for there to be a deep catenary between the boats. If you are offered a tow by a boat you do not know, you should get the question of a towing fee settled first or you may find you are suddenly facing unexpected and unwelcome expenses, even a salvage claim.

What to do in locks

Locks come in all shapes and sizes. Also local conditions can vary widely so that it is impossible to lay down a series of hard-and-fast rules for going through locks. Here is some general information however.

● When you see a red light it is forbidden to enter or leave a lock. Wait for the green light. If you see green lights together it means exit or entry will soon be possible.

● Go slowly where there are locks. Don't trail anchors, cables or hawsers. Naturally you must not anchor in such places.
● When entering a lock make sure there is nothing (except the fenders) hanging overboard; clear lines for making fast and have fenders ready.
● Manoeuvre slowly into locks (preferably without any sail and using the engine, or under jib alone) steering first for the middle of the lock and then looking for a place to make fast.
● Use your fenders, get bow and stern lines ashore (or on to the boat you are going to lie alongside).
● While in a lock, unless there is a pontoon which rises and falls with the water, the lines must be adjusted as the water level changes and the fenders adjusted as necessary.

Hints

1 Get information about the locks, through which you are going to pass, in good time from a pilot book (the times at which they are open, the fees, signals and regulations, etc.)
2 Broad fenders are usually more effective than long sausage-shaped ones.
3 Locks collect dirt so a second set of old (but sound) lines for making fast is a good idea, sparing your normal mooring lines.
4 Unless you have to give way to commercial traffic the first boat should go as far into the lock as possible in order not to block the entrance for other boats.
5 Keep boathooks at the ready.
6 Make fast with a slipline. There must be no knots in the line or it will jam as it is pulled through. At the very worst the boat might even get hung up as the water level subsides. Make sure lines are long enough to cope with any fall in the water level. You look silly if they run out halfway down!
7 Make sure your engine is running before you cast off to leave the lock.

A dinghy, an FD, under tow.

Using a trapeze

The trapeze is an important aid to keeping a boat upright when sailing in fresh to strong winds. Thus it helps those equipped with it to attain their maximum speed. The Flying Dutchman, designed in 1951, was the first standard dinghy to be equipped with a trapeze. Today, it is a matter of course to find one on all modern two-man planing dinghies (like the 470, 420, Corsair, Jeton, 505), and a trapeze is also fitted to small keelboats like the Tempest and Dyas. Trapezes are even used on some singlehanders like the Contender and A-class catamaran.

Parts of the trapeze

A trapeze consists of the following parts:
1 A trapeze wire attached to the upper mast fittings on both sides of

the boat. There is a comfortable handgrip attached to the lower end of the wire and the trapeze rings, made of plastic or stainless steel, is below that. A piece of shock cord pulls the trapeze wire back into place after use.
2 A trapeze harness which fits firmly, but as comfortably as possible, because it must take the whole weight of the crew over quite a long period. Up-to-date trapeze harnesses are all equipped with adjustable braces for supporting the back and shoulders. The trapeze hook is mounted on a plate on the

By holding one arm the man on the trapeze can put some of his weight further outboard.

LEFT: *The trapeze ring should be adjusted at this height.* RIGHT: *Up-to-date trapeze harness.*

Incorrect gybing can cause a dinghy to capsize.

TOP LEFT: *Up to this point all is well. The boat is sailing with the wind from astern, the helmsman is oversteering a little . . .*

BELOW LEFT: *. . . now the boom begins to swing over but the boat goes on turning because there is no counteraction from the rudder.*

TOP RIGHT: *The mainsail is not eased off enough yet on the other side and the boat, without rudder correction, is heading up . . .*

BOTTOM RIGHT: *. . . and in a strong wind this is the result.*

ABOVE: Gybing around the second mark during a race. The Corsair, G 1388, has performed the gybe correctly and has no problems. The helmsman of the other dinghy, however, is gybing badly. He is not applying rudder correction so there is pronounced heeling. You can also see how much sideways drift there is from the big wave along the starboard side.

BELOW: This gybe led to a capsize and a ducking for the crew. The accident happened because the helmsman did not apply sufficient rudder correction. The heading up was uncontrolled. It, too, happened during a race, at the second mark.

harness and must be adjusted so that the trapeze wire can be unhooked easily but will not come unhooked by itself.

3 A suitable surface on the gunwale on which to stand. This surface must be made as non-slip as possible for the trapezist, by means of ridges, or some non-slip material so that the feet can get a good hold.

The latest thing is the so-called endless trapeze which can be seen especially on FDs. The crew using this system no longer needs to unhook and hook himself on again when going about. The system consists of two pieces of tube about 1ft (0.3 m) long, each bent into a hook at one end, hanging on the trapeze wire. They are joined together by an elastic strop about the thickness of a finger. A reel runs over the tubes and sling and the fitting for adjusting the trapeze is fastened to this with a ring which is attached to the trapeze belt. Once this is hung in place the crew remains connected to the trapeze by the reel the whole time. As the boat goes about, the reel slides from one hook, over the sling, to the other hook.

Hints for adjusting trapeze height

Normally on a reach, because of the low heeling moment, it is sufficient to hook the trapeze to the upper ring.

Endless trapeze on an FD. If the crew was standing further out the helmsman would be sailing the boat more upright.

When planing, however, the trapeze must be hooked to the bottom one so that the trapezist can place himself farther aft. When tacking the trapeze is hooked higher or lower according to how far the hook is from the trapeze belt. If the belt is a good fit, with the hook close to the body, the lower ring is usually the better choice.

Technique of trapezing out

● The crew slips well out overboard and brings the trapeze into play by letting himself hang there.

● His front foot is placed on the gunwale (people who are not very strong push the foot against the shroud plate), his forward hand holds the trapeze grip, his after hand the jib sheet.

● By straightening his front leg, and sometimes pushing with his hands too, the trapezist swings himself out and places his other foot on the gunwale too, a little way from the first foot.

● He then proceeds to stretch out, or move in, according to the need to keep the boat upright.

The forward leg is under particular compression strain. Thus the forward foot must always be placed on the gunwale a little ahead of the perpendicular body and mast to counter the tendency for the trapezist to fall forward and get entangled in the shroud.

Method used by expert racing sailors The trapezist bends both legs and goes into a crouch. The trapeze wire remains taut. Now he pulls up both feet and lets his legs slide into the cockpit. His forward hand holds the grip or pulls at it. Sliding back by this method is very quick and is possible without transferring one's weight aft.

Method used by the less experienced The trapezist swings back around his slightly bent forward leg, takes the other foot off the gunwale, and tries to get a foot hold under either the mainsheet traveller, or the top of the centreboard case, or under the toe straps. This method has certain disadvantages. The trapezist may get too close to the helmsman as he swings back and thus may get in his way. Moreover, the movement of weight aft which is entailed has a bad effect on the fore and aft trim of the boat which means a loss of speed.

ABOVE: *Sliding back, racing technique.*

BELOW: *The man on the trapeze is flexing his knees to absorb the shock of hitting waves.*

Technique of sailing with a trapeze

A good trapezist needs to be physically fit and to have good feel for the action. He has to move in such a way that the optimum trim of the boat is not altered and to do this he needs good technique and quick reactions.

Here are the hallmarks of a good technique:

get the boat back to its normal trim.

6 His extended body should be at an angle of about 85°-90° to the mast.

7 When the wind eases or a squall has passed the trapeze hand should abandon his extended position in good time and bring his weight close to the boat by getting into a sitting or crouching position.

Common mistakes

1 Trapeze wire too short, making it impossible to get into the best position.

2 Trapeze belt too slack or with the hook too far above the navel.

3 The trapezist does not stretch out

The upper part of the body is much too upright.

ABOVE: Sailing on the trapeze can be a wet experience.

RIGHT: A good trapeze technique calls for the ability to crouch in good time to keep the boat correctly trimmed.

1 The trapeze wire must be hooked on close to the centre of gravity of the body, or just above it. The ring of the trapeze wire should, therefore, be somewhere around the navel.

2 The trapezist should be relaxed and light on his feet as he stands out on the trapeze, not exerting a lot of force being tensed up.

3 He should not stand with the entire soles of his feet on the gunwale but use the balls of his feet or his toes.

4 If necessary his body should extend straight out, without a hollow back. He must flex his knees and ankles to every wave, however. The legs should be relaxed with no stiff knee joints.

5 If there is a heavy gust in which he cannot stretch out in the normal way he can put one arm back behind his head to increase the weight outboard and do so until the helmsman has headed up to

enough when climbing out or getting back and uses his arms too much.

4 The upper part of his body is too upright as he climbs out or slides back and keeps him from hanging in the correct position.

5 He keeps his back too hollow for too long. This is tiring and can cause backache.

6 His knees are too stiff especially when the boat is crossing waves.

7 He does not stand on the balls of his feet or his toes enough.

8 Trapezing barefooted.

9 He slides back into the boat too late as a gust moderates, thus getting an impromptu bath, slowing the boat down, and possibly causing her to capsize to windward.

The main things to remember about spinnaker handling are that you must have good drills for hoisting and lowering the sail and you must keep it filled and pulling when set. A spinnaker which goes out of control, especially in fresh winds, can cause a lot of trouble including a broach to or even result in a blown out sail. Since spinnakers are very expensive this is something to be avoided at all costs. Start off in moderate winds and get your crew well versed in the correct drill so that they can do it every time without mistake. If you feel that the wind is getting too strong for comfort then get the sail down sooner rather than later and never leave yourself too little time to take it down if it has to be done, for example, before rounding a racing mark. A well controlled spinnaker is an excellent sail for getting that little bit extra out of your boat whether you are racing or simply cruising.

The trapezist is not hanging out enough and so is in difficulties.

Here the man on the trapeze has come in too late.

Spinnaker handling

These days sailing with a spinnaker has become a standard part of sailing technique. Spinnakers are used as the most important extra sail for all courses except those close to the wind, not just in racing boats but on cruising yachts, too. They make it possible to go quite a bit faster, especially in offshore racing yachts, which can set a variety of other extra sails as well. Many sailors are rather timid where spinnakers are concerned, but using them is not very difficult and, once you have mastered the technique, is great fun.

RIGHT: Double spinnaker sheets have bee. common for some time in racing yachts c this type in the USA. They make it muc. easier to gybe the spinnaker.

Setting a spinnaker

There are various ways of setting a spinnaker according to the type and size of boat. In general, however, the spinnaker sheets must be outside all the standing and running rigging and the spinnaker itself must be stowed in the boat, often in a special container called a spinnaker turtle, in such a way that it cannot twist. When a turtle is used both corners of the spinnaker stick out, one each side, with the head in the middle. The sail is hoisted by the halyard, while you control the sail with the sheets. The spinnaker boom is attached first to the guy and then to the mast and the lift and downhaul attached.

It is easiest to set the spinnaker when you are sailing directly before the wind when the sail can most easily be passed under the jib and set in its lee. If you set the spinnaker to weather it must be passed outside the forestay. Setting a spinnaker on a reach can be done to leeward only and must be done quickly and ac-

Lowering the spinnaker

It is easiest to lower a spinnaker when sailing directly before the wind. The sail can be pulled under the jib to leeward and through into the cockpit. If the sail is to windward it can be pulled in and gathered up by the mast before being pulled through into the cockpit. If you are sailing with the wind more on the beam, lowering the sail to leeward is the only practicable thing to do. Before the halyard is eased off the wind must be taken out of the sail by slackening the sheet. In two-man boats the crew gives the sheets to the helmsman who also looks after the halyard. The crew detaches the boom and stows the sail.

Sailing with a spinnaker

General points to note:
- In two-man boats the helmsman sits to leeward and the crew to windward when the boat is on a run. With the wind on the quarter or beam they both sit to windward. In boats with a trapeze the crew can operate the spinnaker from the trapeze.

curately since there will, anyway, be a strong tendency for the boat to heel. This can increase considerably if the wind fills the sail before you have got it properly under control. In two-man boats the helmsman controls the halyard and sheets while the crew attaches the spinnaker pole to the spinnaker guy and the boom to the mast fitting.

A comparison of spinnaker handling between two world-class crews at the first mark. Above, the Englishman Keith Musto and Peter Sweetman; below, the German double medallists Ulli Libor and Peter Naumann. The helmsman controls

the spinnaker halyard in each case, and then the spinnaker sheets, while the crew looks after the spinnaker boom. You can see clearly how much earlier the English pair have the spinnaker set and drawing.

- The spinnaker is trimmed by adjusting the sheet and guy so that the spinnaker boom is roughly at a right angle to the apparent wind. More precisely, you should adjust the guy so that the luff of the sail is on the point of collapsing but not quite.
- Tack and clew should be at the same height.
- The spinnaker is continuously trimmed by the sheet. The guy can be held in a jam cleat.
- The spinnaker boom should be

kept as near to horizontal as possible (no higher than about 80° to the mast). If the boom goes round till it nearly touches the forestay you have to ask yourself if the spinnaker is still pulling properly.
- When heading up you haul in the sheet and slacken the guy. Reverse the process when falling off.
- A jib has no effect, and may even have an adverse effect, before the wind. It can either be left set or, even better if possible, furled.

Naturally, with the wind on the beam you let the jib fill too. Modern offshore racing yachts sometimes set special additional sails with the spinnaker (see chapter on sails.
- In a squall you first ease the spinnaker sheet slightly, spilling some wind, then haul it in again until it is again slightly eased as the boat loses way. In very heavy squalls you can, if necessary, ease the sheet so much that the spinnaker collapses.

From left to right in each row: Gybing the spinnaker.

Gybing the spinnaker

If the boat is gybing, for instance, around a mark in a race, the spinnaker must be gybed too. The spinnaker boom must be taken across to the other side. It is possible with practice to gybe without allowing the spinnaker to collapse. The best method for small boats is for the crew to detach the spinnaker pole from the mast and attach it to the former clew which now becomes the tack. Then he removes the other end of the pole from the former tack, now the clew and attaches it to the mast.

Hints

1 In a light wind tack and clew will tend to sag so you should sail with the boom rather lower than usual. In a stronger wind the tack and clew will rise and in this case you can let the boom go some way with them.
2 In winds of about Force 2-3 it is generally not worth while hoisting the spinnaker all the way to the block at the masthead (the distance of the head from the mast can be between 11-12in (28-30cm) in dinghies, and up to 6ft (1.8m) in large yachts). The effects of turbulence will be lessened. In a very light wind, however, you should take the head of the sail to the top or the sail will drop too low.
3 In the normal way spinnaker sheets run right back to the transom so that the downward pull on both sides of the sail is kept to a minimum. In a strong wind, however, it is better to have the sheet leads further forward. The spinnaker will be less inclined to swing from side to side and will be easier to control.
4 On a broad reach it is best to have the spinnaker sheeted as far aft and as far outboard as posible, so that the leech of the sail is clear of the mainsail and can open out. If the leech is closed the yacht will heel more and will be backwinded too much.
5 Spinnaker sheets should be as light as possible and for this reason they are usually so thin, especially in small boats, that they are rather uncomfortable to handle in strong winds. Then it is a good idea to wear gloves.
6 Spinnaker sheets can be marked so that you can cleat them at the right length before gybing. Many sailors use an endless sheet and thus avoid having to search around for the ends all the time.
7 If the mainsail has to be sheeted in very close because it is being backwinded by the spinnaker it is time to lower the spinnaker.
8 To make full use of the spinnaker you must constantly work the sheet and guy and make sure that the luff does not collapse.

Spinnaker gear

The following table summarizes what you need in the way of equipment, along with the most important technical expressions:

Spinnaker halyard	Is used to set the spinnaker. Runs over the spinnaker halyard block on a swivel above the forestay. There may be a second block at the foot of the mast which leads the halyard either to the cockpit or to a cleat on the mast.
Spinnaker sheet and guy	Used to work the spinnaker. The leeward control line is called the sheet, the windward one the guy. These descriptions are exchanged when the spinnaker is gybed.
Spinnaker boom	A spinnaker boom is necessry to keep the spinnaker set and is always carried on the windward side i.e. the opposite side from the main boom. It is usually made of wood or aluminium and has fittings at both ends for attaching it to the mast and sail. The boom of smaller boats also has a fitting in the centre for the lift and downhaul.
Mast fitting for the spinnaker boom	On the forward side of the mast there is a special fitting to which the boom is attached. In its simplest form it is just an eyelet, but you can find adjustable systems of all kinds on big racing yachts.
Lift and downhaul	In light winds, the weight of the spinnaker boom presses the spinnaker tack down. To prevent this a lift is fitted which runs from the end of the spinnaker boom to about three-quarters of the way up the mast. On the other hand, in strong winds the spinnaker boom is pulled up by the lift and held down by a downhaul. On smaller boats the lift and downhaul may be combined, the spinnaker boom being attached in the centre.
Head, tack, clew	The three corners of a spinnaker are given the same names as those of a mainsail. However, a spinnaker always has the tack on the windward side, attached to the spinnaker boom, and the clew on the leeward side. Thus the names of the corners change when the sail is gybed.
Luff, leech, foot	The three sides of the sail are given the same names as those of a mainsail. However, the luff and leech change places according to which gybe the boat is on, the luff always being on the weather side.
Spinnaker chute	Found on many small boats this is a plastic tube set in the foredeck of the boat, where the spinnaker is stowed when lowered. To make this possible a light line is fastened to the centre of the sail, outside, and this runs through the chute into the cockpit. There it is used to draw the sail in.

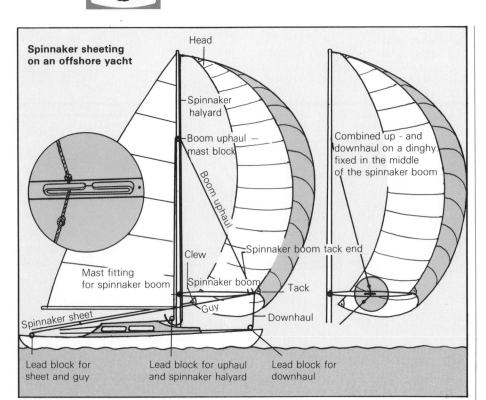

Spinnaker sheeting on an offshore yacht

Head
Spinnaker halyard
Boom uphaul — mast block
Boom uphaul
Combined up - and downhaul on a dinghy, fixed in the middle of the spinnaker boom
Clew
Spinnaker boom tack end
Mast fitting for spinnaker boom
Spinnaker boom
Tack
Guy
Spinnaker sheet
Downhaul
Lead block for sheet and guy
Lead block for uphaul and spinnaker halyard
Lead block for downhaul

Capsizing and righting

Nowadays, it is only in older types of dinghies with little buoyancy, which tend to fill with water, that capsizing is considered a serious accident. In modern planing dinghies capsizing and righting the boat again is considered a part of normal sailing technique. The only question is how fast the boat can be righted. It is fairly easy to right most types of planing dinghy after they have capsized. You should practise the technique in a calm or a very light wind. You will find it is fun and you will be more confident when it happens in an emergency.

A dinghy may capsize either to windward or to leeward, usually in a fairly strong wind.

Main causes of capsizing to leeward:
- The boat broaches to when the spinnaker is set on a broad reach.
- Uncontrolled gybing.
- Wrong correction with the rudder, or rudder correction is applied too late, when meeting a squall from the beam or quarter.
- Heading up too far while clawing your way to windward in a strong wind, resulting in the boat losing way and thus stability.

Main causes of capsizing to windward:
- Squall catching the boat aback while closehauled, the crew failing to react quickly enough.
- Heavy rolling downwind.
- Crew does not get in quickly enough at the end of a gust after hiking out or being out on a trapeze.
- The crew is out on the trapeze and the sheet breaks or is let fly suddenly and out of control.

Capsizing to windward is comparatively rare, but is more uncomfortable since the crew is usually thrown into the water and there is a chance that someone will get caught under the mainsail.

Righting technique

If the boat is to be righted quickly, even in difficult conditions, the crew must react fast. There are three methods, according to circumstances and the type of dinghy concerned.

Sequence showing Laser capsizing and being righted.

Starting position for centreboard method of righting.

Centreboard method

This is without doubt the most common method and is employed in all dinghies with a high degree of buoyancy. Immediately the boat has capsized one man (or two) climbs out on the centreboard. Holding the gunwale he then tries to pull the boat upright by throwing his weight backward. As soon as the sail comes up out of the water and the boat begins to come upright the crew must climb back in. There is no problem normally over climbing back into dinghies. If there are two people standing on the centreboard, however, it is a good idea if one of them goes round to the other side to hold the boat level while the other climbs in over the opposite side.

Mast method

This method is better for dinghies with low buoyancy which lie so far down in the water that if anyone stands on the centreboard they ship too much water. The method is also to be recommended for capsizes to windward if the crew is thrown out near the mast. The crew does not climb on to the centreboard but swims to the upper third of the mast and pushes it up. If the boat is lying head to wind, the wind will get under the sail and help the work. If the sail is pointing into the wind (as is roughly the case in a capsize to windward) the boat will come up so violently after the mast is raised that she may capsize on the other side. The crew must be hardened to this!

Climb in from the windward side or over the stern.

Combined method

A combination of the two methods may be successful for many two-man dinghies and in very rough weather. One man climbs out on the centreboard, the other raises the mast.

Dinghies with good buoyancy at the sides such as the 470, or with good buoyancy and small cockpits (such as the Laser) will be almost empty after being righted. Boats which ship a certain amount of water, according to the speed with which they are righted and the technique used, must be sailed until empty which means opening all self-bailers. Sometimes a bucket can be used to bail out if you have one available.

Righting a boat which has turned over

Dinghies with a lot of buoyancy are inclined to turn right over because, by virtue of the buoyancy, they float so

Righting a boat by the mast method. This would have been a better method for the crew shown below, too, who are pushing the hull too far into the water.

Righting a trailer sailer which has turned upside down requires a motor boat.

high that the mast is already slightly inclined downwards. The 470 is an example. The dinghy can turn right over too, if the crew reacts too slowly after a boat has capsized and one of them holds on to the centreboard case or tries climbing on to it.

Righting a boat which is upside down may be done as follows:

1 The crew stands near the gunwale and pulls at the centreboard until the boat gradually comes up and rolls on her side. If this is skilfully done at least one person can keep dry.
2 If the centreboard is not far enough out of its case, or pulling at it does not work, then you need an additional lever. You can use a line, like a jib sheet, fastened to the gunwale on the side away from you and then pull towards you. You will sometimes succeed if you

pull on the mainsheet but, due to the fact that the mainsail is still hoisted, there will be considerable resistance as you try to move this through the water.
3 As soon as the boat is on her side, the centreboard having been pulled right out for the purpose, you proceed as for a normal capsize.

Hints

1 Act as fast as possible so that there is the minimum of water in the boat.
2 The best way to empty a boat with self-bailers is on a reach because you sail faster.
3 If there is a lot of water in the cockpit you should concentrate more weight in the stern until the boat is empty so that the bows will not plough into the waves.
4 It is difficult to right a boat with a spinnaker set so you take the spinnaker down first.

5 Free the sheets before righting the boat, or at least directly afterwards, or she may capsize again.
6 If you are not standing on the centreboard, but have fallen or jumped into the water, it is a sound idea to attach yourself to the dinghy by a line or, once righted, the boat may drift away from you.
7 If you get caught underneath the mainsail when the boat capsizes you should surface at the leech of the sail.
8 When righting a boat which has turned upside down you can pull on the jib sheet in either direction. It will only go so far because the figure-of-eight knot at the end will jam at the fairlead.

Multihulls

Multihulls

Multihulls can boast a long history, originating in the Pacific islands. Multihulls did not achieve popularity among yachtsmen until the second half of this century. Modern building methods, new materials and a rapidly growing market for yachts brought them to their present state of development. The results were not always successful, so even today these craft are often regarded with suspicion.

To build a boat and then load it with a lot of lead so that it can remain upright and sail does not appear to be a very sensible notion. This principle, however, is used on all keel boats to achieve the necessary stability under sail. In yachts the ballast accounts for between 30% and 60% of the total weight. Multihulls, on the other hand, achieve their stability from their shape. By having two or three hulls which, of course, have correspondingly more buoyancy, more weight and greater form stability (the latter

being a result of the greater beam) than a single hull the multihull produces a sufficiently large righting moment to counteract the heeling force of the wind. In contrast to a keel boat, a multihull achieves its greatest righting moment at a relatively low angle of heel — about 5° — from which point the righting moment rapidly decreases. Keel boats achieve their greatest stability at the maximum angle of heel, as it is at this point that the weight in the keel is raised to its highest point and exerts the greatest downward force.

There are three types of multihull:
1 Proa
2 Catamaran
3 Trimaran

Catamarans and trimarans form the largest groups. In Europe there are very few proas.

The Proa

A proa consists of a main hull and an outrigger with another smaller hull. This smaller hull must always remain to windward, as the righting moment is dependent on the lever effect of the outrigger and the weight attached to it. The outrigger hull is not built to give buoyancy by displacing water as

it would if fitted to the leeward side, and it is therefore very small. When close-hauled, the sail has to be kept on the same side, so that the outrigger remains to windward. To do this, the boat is built without a specific bow or stern; these change with each tack. The English-built proa *Crossbow* was designed to break speed records. This boat can only sail in one direction (without changing its bow) as it has no means for the position of the sail to be altered after making a tack. At present *Crossbow* holds the speed record for sailing boats at over 31 knots.

The Catamaran

Catamarans are twin-hulled boats with identical hulls connected by a bridge deck consisting of either a trampoline or a solid platform. The leeward hull must be capable of providing enough buoyancy to support the whole craft. In light racing cats the windward hull often lifts clear of the water. In seagoing cats this is avoided, for reasons of safety, by having the sail area correspondingly reduced. Cruising cats with cabins offer a considerable amount of space

B-class Tornado catamaran

The proa Crossbow, *which holds the world sailing speed record at 31 knots.*

and living accommodation together with a relatively high speed potential. Examples of racing cats are the Olympic Tornado or the A-class cats (single-handed catamarans), which have been adopted for their all-round ability. *British Oxygen* (renamed *Kriter III*) is an example of a extreme type, built like *Crossbow* purely for racing. Catamarans are divided into four large class groups — A, B, C and D — which lay down maximum length, beam and sail area. The A-class consists of cats with a maximum sail area of 150 sq ft (14 sq m). B-class boats, which include the Tornado, can carry up to 235 sq ft (21.8 sq m) sail area. C-class cats carry up to 300 sq ft (28 sq m). The so-called Little America's Cup, sailed in C-class cats, has produced a great deal of useful experience. It was in this competition that revolving aerofoil masts and the una rig were first used in catamarans.

The Little America's Cup

This is a challenge race for C-class cats, which are regarded as the fastest and most exciting boats in the world. The first series of this annually held race took place in September 1961 in Long Island Sound off Sea Cliff, New York. On that occasion the British catamaran *Hellcat II* (24 ft, 7.30 m) beat the smaller *Wildcat* from California, and the race was nicknamed the Little America's Cup after the large America's Cup for 12 Metre boats. England then defended the cup annually, alternately against the U.S.A. and Australia, till 1969, when the Danish catamaran *Opus III* won.

The Trimaran

A trimaran consists of a main hull and two other smaller hulls, of which the leeward one gives the boat, when sailing, stability through its buoyancy. The trimaran does not offer as much living space as the cat, as the two outer hulls are usually small and can at most be used for storage. Living accommodation is confined to the main hull.

Sigma, an interesting trimaran, was built and developed in Germany by Prof. Dr. F. Wortmann, the director of the Institute for Aerodynamics at Stuttgart University. The prototype came on to the market in 1972. This type can have the outriggers retracted in harbour to reduce the beam. A specially developed sail plan avoids the risk of overloading, reducing the danger of a capsize.

Multihulls can be built lighter and with less draft than keelboats, as they have no ballast. Their behaviour in heavy seas normally presents fewer problems, as they float higher in the water than keelboats. Problems mostly arise from the high windage and the small underwater profile, which can cause problems when manoeuvring at low speed. The high initial stability, the low water resistance and large sail area allow multihulls to attain speeds far higher than the normal length ratio speed.

Catamarans on different points of sailing

Sheets and sheet control

It is often thought that the arrangement of the sheets in a cat is different from that in a monohull. This is wrong, and on the whole the positioning of the sheets corresponds to that in a monohull. The only peculiarity is the wider traveller demanded by the greater beam. As a rough guide for the use of the traveller, here are a few tips.

1 In contrast to sailing monohulls, you do not constantly adjust the traveller; you set it according to the conditions.
2 At high speeds the traveller is set close to the centre line.
3 When sailing off the wind, you set the traveller well to leeward.

The Sigma class trimaran has outriggers that can be retracted in harbour.

By holding back one arm the man on the trapeze can put some of his weight further outboard.

Here you can see the very wide traveller track, which results from the considerable beam.

4 On a beam reach and board reach in smooth water and with a steady wind, you need as straight a leach as possible, and the traveller is pushed farther to leeward.
5 In rough water and with a variable wind a full sail is better, and the traveller should be centred.

Close-hauled

Among the most up-to-the-minute developments in sailing are today's multihulls with rotating aerodynamic masts and full-battened sails. In theory they are capable of sailing as close to the wind as and, at the same time, faster than monohulls. Because of the higher speeds, though, the apparent wind moves ahead so that for the most part the highest possible point of sailing is not reached. Instead the multihull sails a rather freer course due to the higher speeds it attains. The average is between 40° and 50° off the true wind.

The faster a multihull sails, the stronger the apparent wind becomes and the farther forward it moves. Therefore, the faster the boat sails, the farther it moves away from the true wind.

In high seas attaining the maximum possible speed depends mostly on the length of the hull being sufficient to bridge the wave troughs. With the Tornado, for example, it is possible in heavy weather to shoot over wave-crests, but then fall with considerable force into the troughs. At this stage

Fully battened mainsail of a Tornado cat. This sail belongs to world champions Spengler and Schmall.

you are no longer concerned with maximum speeds, but with the robustness of the construction. Indeed, on *British Oxygen* helmets are worn as protection against spray! The strain imposed on the crew as well as the whole craft under such conditions is, of course, considerable.

Steering correctly through waves is extremely important in racing. The technique is as follows. The helmsman, making good use of the high initial stability, heads up slightly as the boat climbs a wave and bears away on the crest fairly hard, thus accelerating the boat. In calmer waters multihulls give very good directional stability because of their long narrow floats.

With a fully battened sail it is hard to see if you have chosen the correct angle of incidence to the wind as, unlike a normal sail, it does not begin to shake if you start to pinch. It is also hard to tell if you are sailing too free, as the angle of heel is very slight due to the high initial stability. Good helmsmen have, as a result, a highly developed feeling for optimum speed, which they can judge by observing the lee hull to see how deep it is in the water.

TOP: Excellent trapeze technique: extended position, legs relaxed, the balls of the feet on the gunwale.

TOP LEFT: Endless trapeze, a device frequently used on Flying Dutchmen.

TOP CENTRE: Another excellent trapeze position using the balls of the feet.

TOP RIGHT: It is important to move in your weight in good time to keep the trim of the boat correct.

BOTTOM LEFT: This position is often adopted to keep the boat upright.

BOTTOM CENTRE: Using a trapeze on a Tornado catamaran.

BOTTOM RIGHT: On an A-class catamaran the helmsman himself uses the trapeze.

1

2

3

4

5

Yarn tufts attached to the sail and known as telltales or streamers can give information about the air-flow. Most Tornado sailors, for instance, have about five tufts in the mainsail and three in the jib. The number of tufts varies according to the preference of the sailor, with the result that many helmsmen fasten up to 10 tufts on each side of the sail. A tuft which is in a good air-flow points horizontally aft. If its stable state changes to an unstable one, it collapses, i.e. it flutters, points downwards, upwards or forwards. It is a mistake, though, to expect the tufts to point exactly as they should in theory. The air-flow on the windward size of the sail is very hard to describe; you can only learn by observation. It is best to trim the sails in company with another boat. When the optimum course and speed have been attained, pick one tuft that is on the point of collapse and use this as

1 and 2 Weight distribution, going to windward. The helmsman is sitting by the shroud and the crew is standing one body-width forward of him. If there is a lot of wind and a rough sea, the crew places himself behind the helmsman to concentrate weight and reduce the pitching to a minimum. The weather hull has already lifted clear of the water so that the cat has maximum stability with minimum form resistance.

3 The Tornado can have the windward hull this far clear of the water without loss of speed. The mast angle is about 60° from the vertical, and the sail has a slight twist camber to reduce pressure at the masthead. The helmsman should be sitting farther forward to give the stern of the leeward hull a cleaner run through the water.

4 The weight of the crew is too far forward. The leeward hull is digging into the water and throwing up a lot of spray. This is slowing the boat down so that the wind is becoming freer, and the boat quickly starts to heel . If this happens, the jib must be eased alarmingly to take the pressure of first the leeward bow and the mainsail second.

5 Good trim on Tornado seen from bow.

the indicator from then on. On sea-going cats electric measuring instruments are used to give wind strength and direction.

Weight distribution is not very different from that practised in a dinghy. A smooth flow of water at the stern is very important. The bows should not be submerged in strong gusts, as this will slow the boat down too suddenly.

In strong winds it is sometimes advisable to ride out gusts by bearing away. This advice cannot always be taken because in multihulls you run the risk, by altering course in this way, of forcing the lee hull under, which causes an abrupt loss of speed and also causes the apparent wind to move farther aft. Both situations are to be avoided. Controlled heading up, and, in an emergency, freeing the sail are exactly the same when close-hauled as in a conventional boat, and the best way to keep the boat under control. In contrast to monohulls, the high initial stability of multihulls enables them to absorb a strong heeling moment without lying over too far. Hull resistance does not change appreciably. It is therefore possible to sail at a very small angle of heel at which the sail produces maximum lift and consequently maximum drive. The danger lies in the air-flow breaking off. If this happens the sail has to be freed to restore the air-flow and get the boat moving again properly. Multihulls have, for this reason, a wider optimum angle in which they can successfully sail close-hauled. The increase of the apparent wind with increasing boat speed is important in this connection.

Catamarans reach their maximum stability at the moment when the weather hull has lost all buoyancy and is working simply as counterweight. This happens as the hull is just lifting from the water. At this moment the entire water resistance of the weather hull disappears. As the boat heels further, not only does the righting moment diminish but the sail area presented to the wind decreases. This is why multihulls are often considered unsafe. Whereas in monohull keel boats the righting moment increases the further they heel, in multihulls it actually decreases.

Reaching

On a broad reach, multihulls show their superiority in speed over dinghies or keelboats. Dinghies can, however, reach similar speeds when planing.

Catamarans do not plane, unlike dinghies, in which the whole fore part of the hull lifts out of the water and sits on the bow wave. The long narrow floats remain in the water, so the catamaran does not alternate between two completely different hull states, but continuously reaches its maximum speed, which it can maintain for long periods. Dinghies, on the other hand, can only remain on the plane for relatively short periods.

Multihulls are not without their dangers on a reach because of the impressive speeds attained. The strong wind force driving the boat forward, combined with a partly freed sail, exerts a powerful force on the fore part of the lee hull. This force is capable of pressing the lee hull under water. This in turn causes a sharp loss of speed, so that the heeling force increases disproportionately and makes the boat capsize over its lee hull. It either rolls over or pitchpoles. The crew can prevent this danger by correctly positioning their weight and by trimming the sails properly. The weight of the crew and helmsman should be placed as far aft as possible, with the crew standing in his trapeze right at the after end of the hull. The pull of the jib sheet and the trapeze wire, combined with sudden loss of speed when the hull submerges, can make this a highly dangerous position for the crewman. He can easily be flung forward, possibly resulting in the boat's capsizing.

Hiking straps have been developed for the crewman to put his feet into, and these will give him a better foothold on the reach. Further aids are special lines fastened to the stern. They have hooks or loops which the crewman attaches to his trapeze

From TOP *to* BOTTOM*: Tornados racing, beating to the first mark . . ., rounding it (centre) . . . and bearing away on a reach*

harness or puts over his arm, and which give him a purchase. These attachments are not popular, however, as they prevent the crewman from freeing himself quickly in the event of a capsize.

The risk of submarining can be diminished by freeing the jib and then the main at the right time. Sudden sheeting-in should also be avoided, as otherwise the lee hull will be overloaded.

On a reach strong gusts can be weathered as in a monohull. The boat is not allowed to luff but the helm is pulled up, and at the same time the traveller is set to leeward.

On a reach, requirements are for a full forward section to the hull, but this contradicts the requirements when close-hauled, when a fine bow is an advantage. The Tornado was a successful design from this point of view, and revolutionized B-class boats within a year. The Tornado is well-mannered, although it is definitely a sensitive racing-boat. The dreaded submarining does not normally lead to a capsize in the Tornado, only a drenching for the crew. With the Tornado you can literally sail

Hiking strap on a Tornado

with both hulls under water. The fully enclosed hulls, and the trampoline that allows the water to run through, allow the boat to clear itself rapidly of water.

Weight distribution on a reach. Helmsman and crew are right aft, one behind the other, to reduce pressure on the leeward bow.

ABOVE:
A very fast reach executed by ex-world champions Jessenig and Polaschegg. Both centreboards are retracted to let the boat make leeway in the gusts. The traveller remains in the middle to give the sail a full camber. Helmsman and crew are right aft and one behind the other.

Incorrect weight distribution on a reach. From the leeward hull you can see that the helmsman should be farther aft (far left).

company with other boats. In gusts a significant increase in speed can be achieved by briefly heading up and then bearing away a corresponding amount. Of course, in very strong winds, in which the boat is already making its maximum speed in relation to the wave formation, it is advisable to forget about such manoeuvres, since they can easily end in a capsize. In the Tornado World Championship in Australia in 1976, for instance, it was blowing Force 8 during one race. Added to this there was a short steep sea. The only way to survive was to slow the boat down as much as possible by sailing dead before the wind with the jib goose-winged.

Wind force and wave height influence the correct course. When close-hauled, an angle of 45° to the wind has proved successful. The weight of the crew should be so disposed as to prevent the stern dragging on the one hand and the hulls being pushed under on the other.

1975 World Champions Spengler and Schmall sailing fast and with perfect trim

Downwind

Most cruising multihulls are equipped with spinnakers, as their sail plan is kept fairly small for the sake of safety. The spinnaker handling technique is the same as for monohulls. At critical moments, i.e. when the lee hull is going under water, it must be possible to let the spinnaker fly at once.

The situation is different with racing catamarans sailing without a spinnaker. Revolving masts and fully battened sails with an effective profile produce greater forward thrust when the sails are set to give a correct aerodynamic air-flow and are not merely being pushed by the wind from behind. This correct air-flow can only be achieved if you do not sail directly before the wind, but tack downwind. The longer distance sailed to reach the destination is normally compensated for by the significantly higher speeds attained when broad reaching. Finding the right course is a matter of practice, requiring experience, and preferably practised in

Manoeuvring

In all manoeuvres it should be remembered that multihulls are lightly built, have high windage, small lateral surfaces and small rudders.

Tacking

A tack should begin with a large turning circle which gets smaller as speed decreases. The jib should remain sheeted in till it lifts. Excessive use of the rudder only acts as a brake and causes the boat to lose speed and fail to come through the wind. Instead, it stops and drifts astern. If this happens, the boat can, of course, be brought on to the new tack by putting the rudder the right way, but this is hardly a good technique. Well-executed tacking is really no more difficult than it is in a dinghy. Slightly freeing the mainsail on going about helps the bow round and allows the helmsman to set straight off on the new tack as he sheets in.

With a fully battened mainsail, as used on multihulls, the camber of the sail will not come across by itself when the boat is tacked in light winds. It is therefore necessary to reverse the camber manually. With the mainsheet free, the boom is first pulled down and to windward. The leech is then suddenly slackened by the boom's being lifted and pushed to leeward. At the same time the boom is given a determined jerk which makes the camber flip to leeward. The crewman who performs this manoeuvre has to throw the whole weight of his upper body into it.

The crew themselves should remain on the inner (weather) hull for as long as possible in order not to slow the boat down.

Gybing

Gybing presents no special difficulty. Multihulls, because of their wide beam, don't roll, so that this manoeuvre can be carried out without any danger of a capsize. The technique for gybing is exactly like that used in a monohull, i.e. to run before the wind, put the mainsail on to the other side and at the same time pull the helm up to weather to prevent an involuntary luff.

A fleet of fast-moving Tornados can make quite a fuss on a reach

Multihulls are no different from other boats — each type is different in the way it handles from another. So the helmsman must learn how his own craft behaves, what its special characteristics are and what vices, if any, it has. A simple example of the type of difference to be met may be quoted. Some catamarans have centreboards and some do not, but are still shallow draft, lightweight boats. Those with centreboards will handle quite differently to those without, especially in manoeuvres like tacking and sailing to windward. There are even catamarans with semi-displacement hulls, which have certain characteristics similar to those of displacement monohulls. The trimaran is something different again and the proa needs a great deal of skill to sail. For an account of sailing one of these exciting craft the reader should refer to *Project Cheers,* where Tom Follett tells of his experiences crossing the Atlantic and taking part in the OSTAR in a specially designed proa.

1976 World Champions Reg White and John Osborne tacking. These pictures show a sequence of movements of helmsman and crew which works well in medium to strong winds

Docking and departing

Docking and departing in a multihull follows precisely the same lines as those explained in the chapter on boat handling. There are some special points, however, which you might note.

When docking in and departing from harbours where there is little open water you should bear in mind the large turning-circle. Bearing away from a close-hauled course always results in a significant increase in speed, which is especially noticeable on a wide turning-circle. If you are lying head to wind at a dock and have to leave the harbour with the wind astern, you should ease the boat round on a stern line with the sails freed right off, only letting go when the turn is completed. This can sometimes be the only way to manoeuvre in a confined space.

Shooting up to a berth on the lee side of a dock should be accomplished in the same way as in a planing dinghy. That is to say, it should be a relatively short manoeuvre, since a multihull stops very quickly.

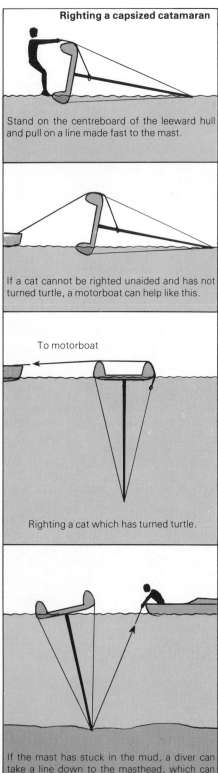

Righting a capsized catamaran

Stand on the centreboard of the leeward hull and pull on a line made fast to the mast.

If a cat cannot be righted unaided and has not turned turtle, a motorboat can help like this.

To motorboat

Righting a cat which has turned turtle.

If the mast has stuck in the mud, a diver can take a line down to the masthead, which can then be pulled up.

Capsizing

Action to be taken after a capsize, which is a less common occurrence in multihulls than in monohull dingies, depends very much on the type of boat.

When a multihull capsizes, because of its great beam the mast points diagonally downwards and it has a tendency to turtle. A watertight or foam-filled mast helps to prevent turtling, as does a float attached to the masthead. These masthead floats are not popular with multihull sailors because of their wind resistance. On cruising catamarans and trimarans capsizing can be avoided altogether by using, for example, an automatic sheet release, which operates at a pre-determined angle of heel.

Light racing catamarans can often be righted by their crew. This is also true of the A-class Wing cat, which because of its wing mast has sufficient buoyancy. The B-class Tornado cat can only occasionally be righted with the help of big waves and the wind under the trampoline. Several crews practised this in the pre-Olympic races in Kingston in 1975. To right the boat after a capsize, the crew stands on the lee float and assists the righting moment by pulling on the trampoline and the cross members. To aid the pull you take a line from the mast over the weather hull. If you can turn the boat so that the wind helps by getting under the trampoline, the work is made easier. A rescue boat can pull up on the masthead and right the boat with the help of the crew. The crew of a boat which has turtled should fasten a line to the masthead, take it over both hulls and pass it to a motoboat. The craft can be righted by a pull on this line. Boats which are on their sides can drift at up to 4 knots before the wind. It is therefore absolutely essential that the crew should hold on to the boat or to a line fastened to it, as it is quite impossible to swim after it.

Tornado cat being towed.

Windsurfing

Windsurfing

Windsurfing is sailing in its most elementary form, surfing both with and without waves, competing in fact with wind and sea.

This new sport began in California in 1969. In an area where thousands of surfboards were in use among the huge Pacific waves, Hoyle Schweitzer and Jim Drake invented the Windsurfer. Instead of using the waves as its primary force, as the ordinary surfboard does, it uses the wind.

Especially in Europe, where there is little surf and therefore little opportunity for genuine surfing, windsurfing caught on tremendously. There are now many versions of the original Windsurfer, and these are known generically as sailboards. Many countries in Europe and elsewhere hold national championships and the brightly coloured, distinctive triangular sails have now become an established feature of the watersports scene.

Sailboarding is particularly suitable in areas where there are crowded waters and a dearth of moorings and waterside storage facilities; the equipment used needs no harbour or berth, and can simply be carried home under one arm. Sailboarding has for thousands of enthusiasts become their main outdoor sport, whether racing, surfing or just sailing around.

The sport is especially suitable for the landlubber who decides it is time he took up an activity that puts him on the water. On many of the larger lakes of Europe, on the coastal stretches and in several southern holiday resorts, windsurfing schools have sprung up to introduce enthusiasts to the new sport.

The equipment

A whole range of boards is now available. They all work on the Windsurfer principle and vary merely in shape, construction and material. While the Windsurfer and some other boards are made in polyethylene, fibreglass and ABS plastic are also popular.

The basic boards

The Windsurfer. The one that gave the sport its name is now the world's most widely used sailboard. It has been in production since 1969 and there are builders in the USA, Holland, Japan and Australia. The hull is of foam-filled polyethylene, which gives it a very high strength-weight ratio: at 19kg it is one of the lighter boards, and its main advantage is that the polyethylene is the most resilient material when it comes to withstanding knocks on the beach. Being a simple flat surfboard shape, the Windsurfer is one of the best boards for sailing in strong winds and rough seas. Also, being the largest one-design board in the world, it is ideal for racing.

The Windglider. This board, made by the firm of Fred Ostermann, is fibreglass, and therefore not as strong as the Windsurfer. However, being longer, it has more directional stability and is considerably easier to sail. The rig is also easier to handle, with a fibreglass mast and alloy wishbone - though the Windsurfer is now also following in this direction. The Windglider claims to be the second most popular board in the world, and has been chosen as the board for the Olympic Games in 1984.

Other boards. Manufacturing and selling sailboards has become a highly competitive and cut-throat business, with a marked similarity to the commercial business of skiing. In 1980 over 100,000 boards were sold in France and Germany - to date the biggest markets in the world. Broadly speaking there are a handful of major manufacturers producing boards by the thousand, and a great many smaller concerns producing them by the dozen or hundred - often flat-out racing boards or ones specially designed for jumping.

For the moment the position is further complicated by the Windsurfer patent which is held by Hoyle

Schweitzer. At present this holds good in a number of countries, where only boards that he has licensed can be sold. The majority of boards worldwide are of course unlicensed, and this has led to litigation in a great many countries, including Britain.

The major manufacturers. In Europe the largest manufacturers are Ten Cate who produce the Windsurfer in Holland, Windglider in Germany, Mistral in Switzerland, and Dufour in France. Others of note are Sailboard, Hi Fly, Sainval and the British Flying Panthers and Sea Panthers. Buying a board for the first time can be a complicated decision. We would advise you to go to a reputable dealer and only to buy a board which is reasonably well known and has a good chance of resale. Cheap offers on unknown makes of board should be treated with suspicion.

The sport of sailboarding is growing fast throughout the sailing world, particularly in those countries with warm climates and water. A new international industry has grown up almost overnight to produce the wide variety of boards demanded.

It is to be regretted that in this section we cannot provide any more than a brief list of some of the better-known sailboards. Many national sailboard associations have been set up and can give further guidance on the selection of boards; where there is no such association, industry federations will usually be pleased to help.

Clothing and accessories

Sailing and skiing both require the participant to wear warm, practical clothing. The same goes for sailboarding, where special gear should be used. In northern latitudes especially, it is advisable, at least for the beginner, to wear a neoprene wet suit. This gear has a number of good points: for one, its acts to a small extent as a buoyancy aid, and for another it keeps the wearer warm and makes it possible to go windsurfing even when the water and the air temperatures are very low. In any case, the suit should include anti-slip boots like those worn by divers. Even better grip, especially on the very slippery polyester boards, can be obtained with sneakers, preferably those with soft rubber soles.

Whether to wear a wet suit or not is up to the individual, though wet suits do have a certain amount of residual buoyancy and, if you stay with it, the board will never sink. The last main accessory you are likely to need is a harness for hooking onto the boom to take the weight off your arms. No sailor should try one until he can sail confidently in winds of force four.

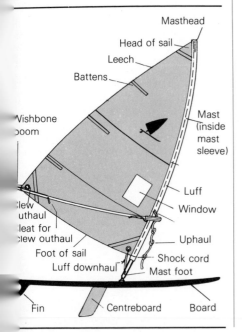

Masthead
Head of sail
Leech
Battens
Wishbone boom
Mast (inside mast sleeve)
Luff
Window
Clew outhaul
Cleat for clew outhaul
Uphaul
Foot of sail
Shock cord
Luff downhaul
Mast foot
Fin
Centreboard
Board

Basic principles of the sailboard

As in sailing, in windsurfing the sail acts as the motor that drives the board forward with the help of the wind. The main difference between the two sports is that the sailboard has no rudder: it is steered with the sail.

The mast of a sailboard is mounted on a universal joint. It is controlled by holding the boom in the hands and can be inclined forward, aft or sideways to steer and to trim the sail.

Steering works on the same principle as trimming the sails on a sailing-boat, i.e. by adjusting the centre of effort of the sail and the centre of lateral resistance. The farther forward the mast is inclined on the sailboard, the farther off the wind the board turns. Conversely it heads up when the centre of effort is brought aft of the centre of lateral resistance by inclining the mast towards the stern.

Sailboards are among the most manoeuvrable of water craft. While a sailing-boat has to be turned head to wind to stop, a sailboard can be turned on the spot by using a technique called the stop gybe, can be manoeuvred in a very short space and, if necessary, can be brought to a halt immediately with the sail itself acting as an anchor.

A sailboard has virtually no displacement. Its low weight (about 18 kg, 40 lb) gives it a draft of only a couple of inches so that it is very quick to start planing. In surf-sailing it becomes twice as enjoyable, as you can ride a breaker, the power of the wind in your hands. The sport is thus a successful combination of sailing and surfing. The sailboard, by the way, can also be used for water-skiing (see Boat surfing).

Tips

The best way to learn sailboarding is to go to one of the numerous windsurfing schools. Within a group and under the instruction of experienced teachers you will very quickly learn to balance on the rather wobbly board. In any case, in a school you will be able to see what windsurfing is all about and have at least one lesson, under supervision, on dry land.

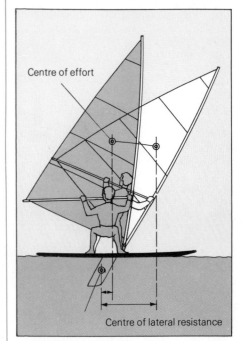

Centre of effort

Centre of lateral resistance

The simulator

In most surfing schools simulators are available on which you can learn the most important aspects of grip and steering. However, the most valuable lesson taught by a simulator is the effect of the wind on the sail. If you want to learn windsurfing quickly and safely, the best way is to train on sail and board separately, finding out how to handle the sail on land, then how to balance and steer the board in the water.

The wind

If no simulator is available, you can practise with just the rig — mast, boom and sail. First determine the direction of the wind. You will have to do this every time you practise, whether on land or in the water. The universally jointed mast should only be raised with your back to the wind so that the sail is to leeward. To give you an idea of the strength of the wind, hold the sail up against the breeze.

Now take the knotted uphaul in your hands and allow the sail to swing freely — this will show you the direction of the wind. Grasp the boom with your mast hand (the hand that holds the end of the boom nearest the mast; which one you use will depend on which tack you are sailing on). With your other hand, the 'sail hand', haul the sail in and lean into the wind. The power of the wind supporting you now will later be used to push the board through the water, at the same time holding up the rig. In advanced manoeuvres on the unsteady board you will find that the boom gives you a good hold.

Coming about can also be practised on land. From a close-hauled position, grasp the uphaul with the sail hand, then let go of the boom with the mast hand. The sail will swing freely to leeward. With both hands on the uphaul, walk around the mast, taking very small steps. Grasp the boom with the *new* mast hand, then with the new sail hand. For this exercise the mast foot should be stepped, either in a sailboard or in a hole in the ground.

Exercises on land should also include easing off the sail. The sail hand simply allows the pressure of the wind to take the sail, and you stretch your arm until you are once again in control and can manage the wind with the reduced surface area of the sail.

With a simulator you can learn the most important techniques while still ashore.

Balance exercises

The first practice afloat will be getting to know the narrow board. After putting the centreboard down in sufficiently deep water, you first try kneeling on the wobbly contraption. Then, near the centreboard slot — where the sailboard is most stable — slowly stand up. With your legs straight and arms stretched, try rocking the board. If there are waves to contend with, use your legs to absorb the movement, as you would if you were waterskiing. The ultimate test of balance is to turn a full circle in both directions.

Sail and board in the water

When you can stand confidently on the board, insert the rig. With your back to the wind, pull on the uphaul so that the sail comes free of the water, as shown by the girl in the photograph. One or two small holes — for example, made with a cigarette — in the mast sleeve of the sail about a foot from the top of the mast will make raising the sail considerably easier. The holes will allow the water that will have collected in the mast sleeve to drain out.

Practising on land with just the rig.

It is very important to have your feet in the right position when you raise the sail. One foot should be placed in front of the mast, the other on the centreboard slot. The mast should lie at right-angles to the board. You have to crouch down a bit to get hold of the uphaul. With arms bent and legs straight, lift the sail out of the water, using the whole weight of your body to do so. To begin with, lift the rig slowly until the water has run off the sail — this saves a lot of effort. Hold the uphaul at arm's length just below the boom. The sail will turn in the wind. Now turn the sail to the left and the right with the uphaul, and the board will automatically yaw in the opposite direction. With small steps, make your way around the mast. Do this several times in both directions, and the board will describe a circle of 9 to 18 m (10 to 20 yd) in diameter.

The start

Starting off on a sailboard can only be successful once you have mastered the exercises given above and follow this procedure:
1 The board should lie at right-angles to the sail and therefore to the wind.
2 Hold the uphaul with both hands at arms' length just below the boom.
3 First take hold of the boom with the mast hand and pull it towards the bow and slightly to windward until the mast hand is near your shoulder. Now grasp the boom with the sail hand about 18 to 20 in (46 to 51 cm) aft of the mast hand.
4 Keep your back straight. Under no circumstances bend forward to get your sail hand on the boom. If the boom is too far away to reach, bring it nearer with the mast hand.
5 Harden the sail using your sail hand. Be careful, though; usually the board will tend to head up without your noticing it. You can counteract this tendency by inclining the mast towards the bow, which will make the board bear away again.

Steering

As already explained, the sailboard is steered by inclining the mast fore and aft. The power of the wind is transmitted to the board through your arms and legs. By shifting your weight, you can transfer more of this power to the foremost or aft most foot, thus assisting the steering.

To head up: incline the sail aft towards the stern, putting your weight on the rear foot.
To bear away: incline the sail towards the bow, putting your weight on the forward foot.

Now you are almost ready to learn the two important techniques of coming about and gybing.

Coming about

This is achieved by inclining the sail aft until the end of the boom is in the

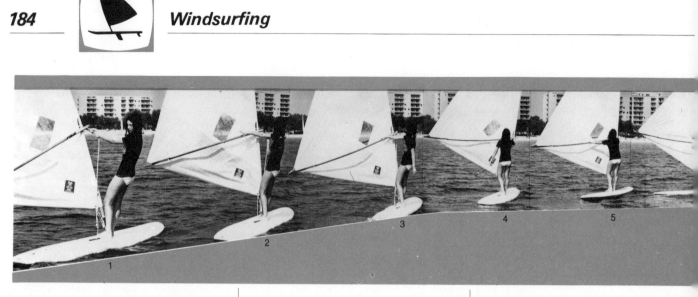

1 *The sail is held at right-angles to the board with your arms extended and grasping the uphaul.* 2 *The mast hand reaches over the sail hand and takes hold* of the boom. 3 *The sail hand releases the uphaul.* 4 *The body is turned towards the direction in which the board is heading, the mast hand inclines the sail forward* and slightly to windward. 5 *Now the sa. hand takes hold of the boom about 20 i (50cm) aft of the mast hand. The body re mains upright.* 6 *By lightly sheeting i with the sail hand you get under way.*

water. Hold on to the boom with the sail hand and the board will turn into the wind. As soon as the pressure on the sail eases off, move to the other side of the board, stepping around the front of the mast as you learned in the first exercises. While you are doing this, keep hold of the sail by gripping the uphaul. As soon as the sail and the board are at right-angles once again, you can start off again.

Gybing

Bring the board on to a run so that the wind is blowing from astern. When the pressure on the sail drops, take hold of the uphaul with both hands and let the sail swing out over the bow from one side to the other. Grasp the other side of the boom, first with the mast hand, then with the sail hand, and haul it in. At the same time head up.

The different points of sailing

At the beginning it will be easiest to sail on a close reach. You should then try the more difficult points, such as broad reaching and running. At first, bearing away will be particularly difficult, so it is worth learning to start off with the wind abaft the beam. The starting procedure remains the same, but the right-angle between sail and board changes so that the sail lies over the bow, while the bow points almost directly away from the direction of the wind.

Real enjoyment, though, comes from broad reaching. Lean right back, keeping both the sail and your body bent into the wind. You will find yourself surfing up and over waves at an angle, with the board sometimes climbing as far as the centreboard

slot out of the water. When sailing o this point, if there is a strong wind you should raise the centreboard hal way out of its slot as soon as you pic up speed. This will prevent the sort c crash capsize where the sailboar overturns in a flash.

1 *From a close-hauled position . . . 2 th sail is inclined aft . . . 3 the sail hand take the uphaul, you round the mast with sm steps . . . 4 and with both arms extende and holding the uphaul turn the board s it is at a right-angle to the sail . . . 5 th mast hand takes hold of the boom and . . . 6 you are off again*

The best way to master running is with the sail tilted aft. With your feet firmly planted on either side of the centreboard slot and your legs straight, try keeping your balance as the sailboard rises and falls to the movement of the waves. You can also kneel if you want to on this point of sailing, with one leg beside the slot and the other farther aft. This brings the centre of gravity lower, which will make you less likely to be thrown in the water by a sudden gust or squall.

1 The mast is inclined forward and to windward. 2 With both feet aft of the mast, hold the sail ahead of you and run downwind. 3 The sail hand releases the boom and the sail swings round. 4 The sail hand becomes the new mast hand and grasps the other side of the wishbone boom. 5 Now the new sail hand does the same, the feet take up a position to one side of the mast and . . . 6 the sail is slowly hauled in

1 From a close-hauled position . . . 2 abruptly back the sail so that it presses against the wind. 3 Turn the board under the sail . . . 4 Change the position of the feet and slowly sheet in

Position of feet for different points of sailing

	Wind direction	Light air (1-2 Beaufort)	Moderate air (2-4 Beaufort)	Fresh breeze (4-5 Beaufort)
Close-hauled				
Reaching				
Broad reaching				
Running				

Key:

Mast foot Centreboard	Foot: Full weight	Half weight	Light weight	Persons weighing over 150 lb

Position of the feet

The close relationship you have with the sail makes it vital that you have a firm footing. This should be altered for every manoeuvre carried out. The board is most stable if you don't leave the area of the mast and centreboard. The table above shows the correct position for your feet. You will notice that the stronger the wind, the more weight should be put on the forward foot and the farther apart the two feet should be. The exact posi-tion will depend to some extent on your own weight. Lightweight sailors may be able to stand at the edge of the sailboard, whereas heavier ones should keep to the centreline, if possible with their forward foot abaft the mast so that the bow of the board will not nosedive into each wave.

Running: you can kneel with one leg by the centreboard slot

This picture gives a good impression of the sheer excitement and physical involvement of wind surfing

Start of head dip

ABOVE: *Windsurfing is also fun in a group.*

BELOW: *A fast broad reach with a body dip*

Catapult fall

Surfing in strong winds

The best part about windsurfing is sailing in strong winds and high waves. This is the reason for the boom in the sport's popularity on windswept stretches of the coast. Here as well you will find the experts training for a new game, the surf race. These competitions are races that take place on a traditional Olympic course laid out in surf water.

Strong winds allow the sailboarder to give a performance close to acrobatics, as the fresher the wind, the more you have to load the boom with your body weight.

Head dip and body dip

With the sail pulled well to windward, arms extended and the upper part of your body leaning right back, you will be surfing inches over the waves on a broad reach. If the wind is steady enough, you can dip your head or your body in the water. Hauling in with the sail hand will present enough surface area to the wind for the sail to pull you up again. The important thing to remember when sailing in strong winds is to incline the rig well to windward, which reduces the sail surface area and creates enough pressure on the sail to counterbalance the weight of the sailboarder hanging from the boom.

The catapult fall

If you bear away while suspended over the water, be sure to ease off the sail as soon as the board starts to turn. In other words, bring the rig round to the position for running. If you have the sail in too hard while bearing away, you will suddenly find yourself going for an unexpected swim as you perform what is known as a 'catapult fall'. The rig suddenly turns into a catapult which hurls the sailboarder several yards through the air into the water. This catapult fall is often done on purpose for fun.

Windsurfing in surf

If you are fortunate enough to have high waves as well as a strong wind, the power of your sailboard will be multiplied considerably since the speed produced by the wind will be increased by an extra burst as you surf down the face of a wave. You should not, however, venture into surf until you are competent in long swells.

With wind waves, it is best to keep to a broad reach. On the crest, haul in the sail a little and shift your weight aft a bit so that the board climbs high and doesn't risk being overtaken by the wave. Then surf down, your body bent right back, into the trough.

Breakers are more difficult to master, as the waves have a tendency to suddenly build up and break. When sailing from the shore it is best to hit the wave bow-on and at full speed. The board will rear up. Then, like a rider taking a fence on a horse, you should immediately get ready to absorb the shock of the fall with your legs as the board goes over the crest and dives into the trough. As soon as you are over, haul in, pick up speed and head for the next wave.

Once past the surf, take a rest, have a look at the waves and steer on a broad reach between two breakers which are a safe distance apart. Keep your speed adjusted with the sail hand so that the wave astern slowly overhauls you and begins to lift the stern of the sailboard.

This is where the double-speed bit starts. The speed you attain on the waves is often so great that the sail begins to shake and can no longer be used to control the board. It is a real test of balance. With the sail loose and your weight concentrated aft, surf along the face of the wave. Take an oblique course, never straight downwards. The sailboard is too long for this and would immediately bury its nose in the water and capsize. This type of fall can be rather dangerous.

Storm sail and centreboard

The technical construction of a sailboard is very basic. There are no fittings or extras such as reefing points, for example. For sailing on the coast, where the winds are likely to be stronger, it is worth having a heavy weather sail and centreboard – both smaller than the standard ones and, as indicated by their names, designed for use in strong winds. With the heavy weather sail (about two-thirds of the size of the normal one) you can windsurf in winds of force 7 or 8.

Sailboard racing

The sailboard lends itself naturally to racing, especially because of the highly technical nature of its development. The sole deciding factor in a race is the ability of the sailboarder. In most countries where the sport has gained a foothold there are national championships, and the IYRU has now classified the Windglider as the next Olympic board, and also given the Windsurfer and Mistral Competition international status.

Courses and rules

Sailboarders are expected to conform to IYRU rules when they are racing. A two-day event normally consists of four to six races, national championships taking longer. The traditional Olympic course is used, except that the distance between buoys is reduced.

The requirements for entry in a race or regatta are the same as in normal racing – see Racing, page 217. Anyone hoping to race a sailboard should first of all make sure he is in absolute control of his machine. The slightest error in grip or a miscalculation of wind or wave can result in an involuntary dip which will cost him or her the race. Getting all the manoeuvres correct is largely a matter of good balance. Simple exercises designed to get the stance right are the best way of improving stability. Try sailing around a couple of buoys.

Racing tack

A sailboard is a very light craft. The normal sailing tactics where you try to tack as little as possible do not apply when windsurfing. Quite the opposite, in fact. The narrow board, with its minimal draft, can use every minute change in the direction of the wind. But to do this you need to learn a more advanced form of tacking. Whereas in light winds you use the ordinary method, in which you sheet in and keep the board moving smoothly as you turn it through the wind, in strong winds you use a fast technique called the jump tack.

The basic tack is carried out by inclining the sail aft into the water and sheeting in the rig with your sail hand. The board will describe a circle of at least three yards and change tack without actually stopping. You round the mast with small steps, remembering to keep the board turning steadily by steering with the sail.

With the jump tack, you don't gain as much to windward as you pass through the wind. You round the mast with a jump and immediately carry on on the other tack. This technique is best used in a choppy sea and with a strong wind blowing. Both methods should be practised around a buoy, trying to clear it by inches. This is how to learn accurate steering.

The racing gybe

n cruising you can go how you like round buoys. In racing, however, here is usually at least one buoy round which you will have to gybe s closely as possible. Gybing a ailboard is considerably more difcult than tacking; not because it is nore dangerous than gybing a boat, vhere the boom will swing across, ometimes with great force, but ecause the sail, which is used for teering, is rather hard to manhandle

and the board is at its least stable during this manoeuvre.

To practise gybing, steer for a buoy on a broad reach or a run. Begin the gybe slightly upwind of the buoy. You can also do this if you can't avoid a turning-circle of several yards. During the exercise, try to take into account the distance you are going to lose and begin the manoeuvre earlier each time, so that eventually you can round the buoy with the sail already on the opposite tack. If the wind is strong enough, the mast hand can hold the rig to windward and flat over the water; the wind will then take it around over the bow automatically. If you take hold of it again on the other side and haul in smoothly, the gybe will become an elegant, fast manoeuvre that will win you precious seconds in races.

Class racing

Sailboarding lends itself particularly aptly to the one-design type of racing: the boards themselves are essentially simple - far more so than sailing dinghies - they are easily transported to wherever a race is being held and the extraordinary growth in the popularity of the sport has meant that all the major classes can put on well-attended events. Under one-design rules only standard boards of a specific make may be entered for a race, and with the Windsurfer class you may only use the standard size of sail.

Open racing too is flourishing throughout the sailboarding world, especially where there are numerous different models in common local use. Again because of the simplicity of the equipment the Open Class boards are measured within fairly simple parameters of length, weight, and sail area and end up with similar performances.

TOP TO BOTTOM: 1 Incline the mast aft . . . 2 so that the boom touches the water. 3 Pull the sail across the middle of the board . . . 4 Jump up with both legs . . . 5 land on the new weather side and . . . 6 start again with the mast hand

Boat surfing

The sailboard can be used as a water-ski behind a boat. Anyone who has ever used a monoski will want to try this kind of surfing. Stand on the board near the centreboard slot — the sail and the centreboard are not needed and can be removed — with the boat a safe distance away. The basic technique is the same as in waterskiing except that the start is much easier as the board begins to move as soon as the slack has been taken up on the towline. You steer by moving your weight from side to side. Even at a fairly slow speed the bow rises some three feet out of the water. This can be prevented by moving farther forward.

Heavy powerboats with a high wash make it possible to surf. Riding the wash should not be tried, though, until you have grasped the technique of steering the board while standing. You use the towline to pull you up near the boat and in front of the wake, then let go of the line. As soon as the wash lifts the board, move your weight forward and you will surf along at the same speed as the boat.

Safety

Since the sailboard is so esaily transported and launched from the shore into the water, there is obviously a great temptation to go exploring, especially in unfrequented waters, perhaps far from any other people. It is therefore as well to bear in mind that you will not be able to call on anyone for help if you get into difficulties. Be sure, anyway, that you tell somebody where you are going and when you expect to be back and be sure not to go out in winds which could prove to be excessive. Even if you can stay afloat on the sailboard there always remains the risk of suffering from exposure.

By all means go exploring, but try to do it in company and always take all the precautions which any sailboat skipper would observe. This means taking note of things like tides and the time of day, so that you are not overtaken by darkness, and not sailing so far down wind that you cannot sail back into the wind to your point of departure or perhaps not even reach the shore at all. These are all fairly obvious points, but in an ex-citing sport like this you can easily forget them. There are miniature distress flares (see Safety Chapter) which you can carry in a waterproof pouch and which the lone sailor could well carry.

Race organisers now insist that a boardsailor competing should also leash the mast foot to his board, and carry a length of towing rope with a suitable towing eye provided in the board.

Boat surfing is very much like waterskiing

This is the easiest way of carrying the rig

This way several sailboards can be towed behind one motor boat (right)

If becalmed you can use the mast to paddle home

Tandem surfing

If you like sailing in a team and want to get the most enjoyment out of windsurfing, you should try tandem surfing. This variation of sailboarding was invented in Germany in 1973. Fred Ostermann tried several ideas for using two sails before settling on a 7 m (23 ft) sailboard with two three-cornered sails. The tandem is stable and difficult to capsize. It is also easier to stand on than a normal sailboard.

The interesting thing about this fast board is its steering. Both sailboarders steer in unison. The relative positions of the centres of lateral resistance and effort are once again all-important. The board therefore heads up when the aft sail is sheeted in and the forward sail eased. Reversing the procedure makes it bear away. Tandems can reach high speeds.

When racing, the team must be really in tune with one another. The slipstream from the forward sail or from others makes it particularly difficult, as finding yourself in someone's wind shadow will show. Lose pressure on the sail and you will instantly fall overboard.

A sailboarder gives a tow to a fellow enthusiast in distress

Safety

Sailing is a hazardous sport. Wind and water are elements that are by no means always benign, and the risk of having an accident cannot be altogether ignored. However, most of the accidents of which we hear every year could have been avoided. Accidents are often caused by insufficient experience, an inadequate boat, lack of essential gear or safety equipment, or through sheer carelessness. The first rule of safety is to be adequately equipped for the job by being knowledgeable on all aspects of sailing, knowing all the rules, and having a sound, well-equipped boat. The second rule is to be alert at all times, to keep an eye open for other boats, for shipping, for hazards marked on the chart, and especially for the weather. Good sailors develop a respect for the sea which makes them ever watchful and ready to act. That is not to say you should be fearful, because that would impair your judgement, and the results could be the same as if you were negligent.

Sailors who cruise offshore have to be particularly careful and well equipped, since rescue, if an accident were to happen, may be a long time coming even if they make their plight known. Sailing is a sport that develops self-reliance to a high degree. We will outline here some of the most important things which have to be taken into account and suggest some ways in which to tackle situations. In many cases you will develop your own ideas with ex-

perience. Sadly, many of the lessons can only be learned this way, but you should at least equip yourself with the necessary knowledge of what must be done before it happens. The very best book on the subject of bad weather is *Heavy Weather Sailing* by Adlard Coles, which should be compulsory reading for all who venture offshore.

This crew is following the correct safety procedure. As the wind freshens, they reef down and put on safety harnesses. A lifebuoy is hanging on the pushpit ready for immediate use.

Clothing and lifejackets

Let's start with clothing. This topic is far from being out of place in a chapter on safety. Suitable sailing-wear is one of the most important pre-requisites for health and accident prevention. If you put on oilskins or a sailing-suit in time when the weather worsens or the wind gets up, and if you change your sailing-shoes for boots, you will reduce the chance of

catching a chill. If you never sail barefoot, even in warm summer weather, but wear sailing, tennis or gym shoes with grip soles, you will reduce the chance of slipping and injuring your back or the back of your head and also avoid injury to your toes when you trip over that deck block for the umpteenth time. If you wear a pair of tough jeans instead of swimming trunks, you will avoid grazing your legs on the gunwales or centreboard casing. And if you keep the upper part of your body covered

With a singlehander like the Laser, which has a fairly rough deck surface, sailing in a swimsuit is not recommended even if it is nice for the onlookers. You could hurt yourself.

rather than baring it, you will not get sunburned, catch cold or scratch yourself when you're being thrown about.

If you want to sail properly, you have to be prepared to dress properly. The clothing industry now supplies everything you need for sailing. The essentials are:

- Long, hardwearing trousers with a suitable sports shirt and a warm sweater.
- Sailing shoes.
- Oilskins or a sailing-suit and sailing-boots for bad weather or windy days.
- A wetsuit for dinghy sailing in cold weather.
- When it is cold, it is worth wearing quilted underwear under your oilskins.
- In hot weather, bermuda shorts and a T-shirt are most suitable. Bermudas because they are short and cool, but still protect your thighs. If you are hiking out you will find it a great help to have a layer of cloth between you and the deck, as anyone who has tried racing will tell you.

A lifejacket is as important an item of sailing gear as the boat itself. No one should go on board without a lifejacket, or rather it should be the other way round, as there should be a lifejacket on board for every member of the crew. Obviously it must be immediately accessible at all times.

In the shops and in chandlers you will find a wide variety of lifejackets. There are those with automatic inflation, others for hand or mouth inflation, those with hard and soft buoyancy fillings, and jackets with or without collars. The types incorporated in a full-length waterproof coat are often referred to as 'safety jackets'. Inflatable jackets allow freedom of movement, but they can let you down if they are damaged. They should be treated with care and inspected regularly. A non-inflatable lifejacket does tend to restrict the wearer because it is bulky, but if it is properly made it is very reliable. A sailing-coat that incorporates a lifejacket can be both functional and smart but will not necessarily be safe if the wearer is knocked unconscious.

The most important function of a lifejacket is to support an un-

conscious wearer in safety. Whether you are going ocean racing or merely cruising, you should have one that will do this. Its main buoyancy should be concentrated on the chest in such a way that the jacket will quickly turn the wearer on to his back, where he will float safely even if unconscious. The head should be supported by a collar, so that the face is held clear of the water and so that it is impossible for the head to flop over to one side. The jacket should also have a crutch-piece to stop it slipping up and off the body.

What we have just described is a lifejacket. There are also so-called buoyancy aids without a collar but these will not ensure that the wearer will float face upwards if he is unconscious.

Automatically inflatable lifejackets should not be worn if you are sailing in a dinghy. In a capsize, where you can usually right the boat and climb back aboard quite quickly, the jacket may inflate itself against your wishes. Nor do dinghy sailors in general go for the full lifejacket, which restricts their freedom of movement, preferring instead a buoyancy aid.

Lifejackets for use in coastal waters and on the open sea should have a two-tone whistle attached — two-tone so that it cannot be mistaken for the cry of a seagull.

Lifesaving equipment

The various items of equipment listed below belong on an offshore yacht. They need to be taken along on every trip.

Lifebuoys

A bit dated now, but still widely used, are the well-known circular lifebuoys made of polythene or cork with a cloth or canvas covering and a line around the circumference. It is better to have the modern horseshoe-shaped lifebuoy made of plastic foam

(polyvinyl chloride). At least one should be carried on board in a position where it is always within easy reach of the cockpit. The helmsman should be able to remove it from its holder and throw it overboard without preparation. If you are really safety-conscious you can attach to it the following items: a small sea-anchor to stop the buoy drifting downwind too fast, a flashing light with an automatic switch, a two-tone whistle, a dye container which releases a dye to stain the sea and help search aircraft, and a marker buoy. This marker buoy consists of a three-metre-long fibreglass rod or alloy tube with a float and counterweight and a yellow or orange flag. It could also have another flashing light fixed on top so that you can see it at night. This type of marker buoy makes it easier to spot a man who goes overboard in a heavy sea. It is helpful to have about ten fathoms of buoyant line attached to the lifebuoy, but the line must not, of course, be belated on board! If you really want to go to town on safety you can include at a price another device, an automatic transmitter that will start sending a radio distress signal as soon as it is afloat. The signal is picked up by the radio receiver on board and used to home in on the position of the man overboard. This is a worthwhile addition on a yacht which is fitted with the necessary receiver.

A lifebuoy like this is decorative (especially as a picture-frame) but is outmoded and should be replaced by one of the more modern types available.

Boarding a liferaft

You can see the rescue marker buoy on the backstay of this yacht. Nearby on the pushpit are two lifebuoys

Liferafts

These rafts are no longer a rare sight on yachts as they are the most useful piece of rescue apparatus to have if there is a total loss. The raft, a sort of inflatable boat with a protective canopy, is packed in a portable valise or a fibreglass container. In an emergency you give a tug on a line to trigger the inflation mechanism and the raft is ready for use in seconds. Rafts for yachts will hold four, six, eight or sometimes ten persons and are practically uncapsizable. They are also fitted with double floors for safety and insulation and have other features such as double buoyancy compartments, a sea-anchor, boarding ladder and so forth. Most of them are also equipped with emergency gear like a sponge, penknife, torch, bailer, pump, paddle and, of course, emergency rations and distress flares. Liferafts should never be stowed below deck and should be inspected by the manufacturer or his agent at least once every two years.

Safety harness

Every offshore cruiser or racer must carry on board a safety harness for each member of the crew. This is as important as carrying lifejackets. At the skipper's discretion every crew member wears a harness when on deck and attaches himself to a strongpoint, wherever he is working, by means of a line (9 ft, 2.7 m, approximately) and carbine hook. This will minimize the risk of someone falling overboard. Good attachment points are the shrouds, stays, grabrail, pulpit and pushpit. It is probably true to say that a safety harness is even more important than a lifejacket.

This is how the safety line is made fast to the harness

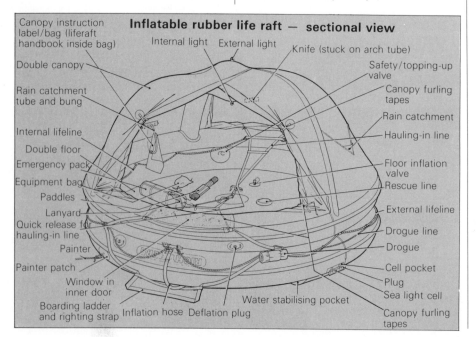

Inflatable rubber life raft — sectional view

Canopy instruction label/bag (liferaft handbook inside bag)
Double canopy
Rain catchment tube and bung
Internal lifeline
Double floor
Emergency pack
Equipment bag
Paddles
Lanyard
Quick release for hauling-in line
Painter
Painter patch
Window in inner door
Boarding ladder and righting strap
Inflation hose
Deflation plug
Water stabilising pocket
Internal light
External light
Knife (stuck on arch tube)
Safety/topping-up valve
Canopy furling tapes
Rain catchment
Hauling-in line
Floor inflation valve
Rescue line
External lifeline
Drogue line
Drogue
Cell pocket
Plug
Sea light cell
Canopy furling tapes

Pyrotechnics

Distress signals are an invaluable aid to the sailor when trying to attract attention in an emergency. There are various types for use in different situations, marketed under various trade-names. The most important are:

Parachute flare

A red, hand-launched parachute-suspended flare that rises to approximately 1000 ft (304 m) and is visible by night for 20 to 25 miles (30 to 40 km). It should be used at distances in excess of 7 miles (10 km) from land to attract initial attention.

Two-star and five-star flare

A hand-held signal that emits two or five red stars respectively, one after the other, which rise to a height of between 50 and 150 ft (15 and 46 m) according to make and can be seen between 5 and 10 miles (8 and 16 km) away. It is used in coastal waters within a reasonable distance from land, and when low cloud is likely to obscure a high-rising parachute flare.

Very pistol

This is certainly one of the most reliable methods of signalling, but it has the disadvantage that in certain countries it can only be purchased by the holder of a firearms licence. Different types of cartridge can be used with it.

Pen-type projector

This is a very small projector that can easily be carried by a dinghy sailor in the pocket of his oilskins. Different coloured cartridges can be used, which are projected to a height of 200 ft (61 m) and burn for about 5 seconds. It is suitable for inland waters. A firearms licence may be required.

Red hand-flare

A hand-held red signal, very bright and visible for about 5 miles (8 km), day or night. It is used in inshore waters to attract initial attention but also in offshore waters to guide rescuers in at night once they are within visual range.

Orange smoke

Orange smoke is for daytime use only. It can be bought as a hand-held signal or a float which is thrown overboard and emits large quantities of bright orange smoke for 3 to 5 minutes. It is visible for 1 to 2 miles (1.5 to 3 km) and is used inshore to raise the alarm and also offshore to guide rescuers by day.

White hand-flare

Contrary to the red hand-flare, this is not a distress signal but is used at night to attract attention and warn off shipping if there appears some risk of collision. It should be kept separate from other flares to avoid confusion.

Numbers and types to carry

It is recommended that the following should be carried by sailboats:
Inshore (up to 3 miles: 5 km from land): 2 red hand-flares, 2 hand-held orange smoke, 2 white hand-flares.
Coastal (up to 7 miles: 11 km from land): 4 red two-star, 4 red hand-flares, 2 hand-held orange smoke, 4 white hand-flares.
Offshore (over 7 miles: 11 km from land): 4 red parachute rockets, 4 red hand-flares, 2 buoyant orange smoke, 4 white hand-flares.

A few tips

- Flares and smoke-signals should be kept in an easily accessible place on board and be stored in a waterproof container.
- Be sure that every person on board knows where distress signals are kept and how they are used so that no time is lost in an emergency.
- Watch the expiry date. Out-of-date signals are unreliable and may cost you your life.
- When you actually are in distress, don't use your signals thoughtlessly and thus waste them. There is no point in shooting everything off at once and then sitting in the dark with nobody able to find you. It is best to fire the first two signals at an interval of about 2 minutes. When within view of potential helpers, use red hand-flares, or orange smoke by day.
- Always discharge flares downwind.

- Use red signals *only* when you are genuinely in distress. When wanting to draw attention to your position, use white hand-flares. When needing assistance but not in distress, signal V in Morse code or hoist the code flag V.

Other safety equipment you should carry

To improve the safety of the boat the following things are vital: guardrails, pulpit, pushpit, fire extinguishers, bilge pumps, a torch, foghorn, radar reflector, emergency tiller, tools and, obviously, a first aid kit.

Safety equipment in dinghies

It stands to reason that a dinghy need not carry the extensive safety equipment required by a yacht setting out to sea. If you are racing or just going for a day's sail, you should have with you the following gear:

- Fixed buoyancy which is not prone to damage and which will keep the dinghy afloat, its gunwales and centreboard casing above water even if swamped.
- A buoyancy aid for everyone on board.
- A bailer, which should be carried even if the boat is fitted with self-bailers. The bailer should be attached by a length of line.
- One or two paddles.
- A small anchor with at least ten fathoms of rode.
- A mooring line which can be the same as the anchor rode.
- Two red signal flares.
- Fenders.

International distress signals

There are certain internationally recognized signals which should be used in the case of distress. This list is as set out in the International Regulations for Preventing Collisions at Sea.

The following signals, used or exhibited either together or separately, indicate distress and need of assistance:

a) a gun or other explosive signal fired at intervals of about a minute;

b) a continuous sounding with any fog-signalling apparatus;

c) rockets or shells, throwing red stars fired one at a time at short intervals;

d) a signal made by radiotelegraphy or by any other signalling method consisting of the group ...---... (SOS) in Morse code;

e) a signal sent by radiotelegraphy consisting of the spoken word 'Mayday';

f) the International Code Signal of distress indicated by N.C.;

g) a signal consisting of a square flag having above or below it a ball or anything resembling a ball;

h) flames on the vessel (as from a burning tar barrel, oil barrel, etc);

i) a rocket parachute flare or a hand-flare showing a red light;

j) a smoke signal giving off orange-coloured smoke;

k) slowly and repeatedly raising and lowering arms outstretched to each side;

l) the radiotelegraph alarm signal;

m) the radiotelephone alarm signal;

n) signals transmitted by emergency position-indicating radio beacons.

Damage

Damage may occur to the boat or its equipment as a result of storms, collision or gear failure through lack of maintenance or simple neglect. Most damage occurs in bad weather. The best way of guarding against this kind of mishap is good maintenance. Check all gear before every trip, paying particular attention to the condition of the standing and running rigging.

Damage to a boat can put the crew's lives in danger. It is up to the crew to master the situation and prevent accidents or even tragedy occurring at sea. The skipper must decide

whether the position is critical and whether the safety of the crew is in jeopardy. There is one thing you should always bear in mind. A yacht will take a lot more punishment than you might think, so do not abandon ship hastily. A boat that is still afloat is the best piece of rescue equipment there is.

In general, you will find yourself faced with minor breakages that can be repaired simply with the aid of the boat's tool-kit. But there may be more critical damage which you will also have to deal with yourself. In particular you should know what to do in case of the following types of accident.

Damage to standing rigging

Shrouds and stays can work themselves loose or come undone as a result of lost screws and bolts, or they can break as a result of metal fatigue, corrosion, or an incorrect or a badly executed gybe. If the mast is kept up by the remaining stays and doesn't actually break, you should without delay put the boat on the other tack so that there is no tension on the side with the broken stay and so that the damaged part can be removed.

If a weather shroud parts you should immediately come about. In a small boat with only one shroud on each side of the mast, it is advisable to ease the main sheet before tacking, so that pressure on the mast is reduced more quickly. If the forestay fails, you should bear away on to a run, leaving the jib hoisted. Its luff will take the strain in place of the stay. In the case of a broken backstay, which usually happens on a run, you should head up into the wind and hand the jib and, most important, the spinnaker. It is when carrying a spinnaker in a strong wind that the mast is most at risk.

Broken wire rigging cannot be replaced at sea, of course, but as a temporary repair you should try and resecure it with a line, or better still a tackle, made fast to the broken end. If you have a pair of clamps in the boat's tool-kit you can make an eye in

the end of the shroud to take the line or tackle. As an alternative, a simpler repair can be effected by making the jib halyard fast to the chainplates.

Broken boom

Remove the foot of the mainsail from its track and carry on sailing with the sheet made fast directly to the clew of the sail. With ingenuity it may be possible to use the spinnaker pole in place of the boom if it is long enough.

Broken mast

With modern alloy masts and improved rigging, mast breakage is a much less common event now than it used to be. If a mast collapses as a result of rigging damage, it will usually be the top third that goes. The part hanging down should be lashed so that it doesn't get in the way and any bits of mast or rigging that have trailed into the water should be cut free or taken inboard so as to avoid damaging the hull. Standing and running rigging should be removed from the broken section, if necessary by cutting them. A jury-rig can be constructed by using the section of mast still standing together with the main boom or spinnaker boom and staying it as best you can. Every ocean-going yacht should carry a pair of bolt-cutters for this type of emergency.

This yacht has been jury-rigged with the aid of two spinnaker booms after losing her mast

Steering gear failure

If the tiller breaks and cannot be lashed to the rudder stock, a paddle, boathook or other suitable piece of gear may be used as a replacement. With wheel steering, a broken cable or wheel can often be bypassed by using an emergency tiller fixed to the rudder stock.

If the rudder itself breaks or is lost, the only thing you can do is to rig an emergency rudder using a paddle with a board screwed or nailed on to it to increase the effective surface area of the makeshift blade.

It may be that the crew will be left with no alternative but to steer with the sails. To head up you harden in the mainsail and ease off the jib; to bear away, ease off the mainsail and harden in the jib.

Incidentally, international and most national safety recommendations suggest that you should have an emergency steering system either fitted or available on board for long voyages. In offshore racing under IOR each yacht may be checked to see that there is a spare tiller on board.

Leaks

Minor leaks which only let in a little water, are not dangerous and are more a matter of maintenance (see that section). Bigger leaks caused by collision, grounding or heavy seas can put the whole boat in jeopardy. But before you leap for the liferaft you should make sure that you have tried the various alternatives for saving the boat from a total loss. So keep calm, man the pumps, and establish the exact position of the damage. Then, depending on the circumstances, follow the procedure given below:

1 Plug small leaks with handkerchiefs, sailbags or similar objects.
2 If the leak is not too far below the waterline, try to heel the boat so that the hole is above the waterline.
3 Plug larger leaks from inside with a foam pillow or mattress. This can be wedged in place with a board; a deck board or a locker door would be ideal.
4 One good idea is to push an inflatable lifejacket into the hole and then inflate it with a cylinder of CO_2. This should give a very effective seal, providing the hole is not too jagged.
5 If the leak is in a locker or stowage space, cram the space with anything you can.
6 The external water pressure can be minimized by using a sail to cover the hole. Take a jib right under the boat (from the bow) and make it fast on both sides of the boat so that it is pressed against the leak.

If all attempts to plug the leak fail, you will have to send out distress signals immediately and make the liferaft ready for use. If possible you

should try to get to the nearest shore, or at least shallow water, so that the yacht stands a chance of being recovered. In a dinghy the procedure is the same as for a capsize.

Running aground

There is always a risk of running aground when sailing. On inland waters or in places without dangerous rocks or shoals this is usually less serious and you should be able to get afloat again without too much difficulty.

Grounding in unfavourable circumstances like bad weather, where there is a dangerous sea bottom, on a lee shore or with a falling tide can result in stranding and loss of the boat. The worst combination is when there is an onshore wind blowing and a heavy sea running. Once aground, the boat will be pushed further onshore and become more firmly grounded with each successive wave, eventually breaking up. The only thing to do in this case is to call for assistance.

To avoid a situation like this you should always look at the chart carefully and look out for shallows and dangerous shorelines.

You may be able to float the boat off on your own if you use the following techniques.
- Put out a kedge anchor and try to haul the boat off. Either use the tender or swim. If you have to swim, attach the anchor to some buoyancy, such as a lifejacket, so that it doesn't drag you under.
- Reduce the draft by heeling the boat.
- Reduce the draft by altering the trim, moving weight forward or aft as necessary.
- Reduce the draft by offloading weight.
- Whether you can kedge off or not, put out the anchor to prevent being carried further onshore.
- Leave the sails up if this will help; if not, stow them without delay.
- Using a paddle or boathook and holding the jib aback, try to turn the bow towards deep water.
- Heel the boat and start the motor.

Heeling the boat to reduce the draft can be done in the following ways:
1 Get the crew to hang out from the shrouds. This method is most successful in light-displacement boats. Sheet the sails in at the same time.
2 To increase the angle of heel, sit the crew on the end of the boom, which for this exercise should be swung out and lashed to the shrouds. You can reinforce the topping lift if you attach the main

halyard to the clew end of the boom as well.
3 Fill the tender with water and attach it to the end of the boom with the main sheet. This will hold the boat over.
4 Take the main halyard to the kedge anchor from the masthead and haul down the halyard winch.

Collision

A collision between two boats usually results in a hole or leak of some size which should be dealt with by one of the methods described earlier. If both boats are jammed together, they should not immediately be drawn apart. The best plug for a hole in the side is, initially at least, the bow that made the hole. When the necessary preparations have been made to plug the hole as instructed, you can start to think about separating the boats. After this, both boats should carry on in convoy and help each other until such time as there is clearly no further danger.

It should be remembered that every sailor is obliged under international law to afford assistance to any other seafarer whose life is in danger.

Before the two boats go their separate ways, names, addresses and details of home and registered ports should be exchanged so that insurance claims can be sorted out without too many problems. If you carry a logbook on board, precise details of the collision should be entered while the accident is still fresh in your mind.

Beached! If she isn't refloated before long she stands a risk of breaking up

Fire on board

The best precaution against fire on board is to have a few rules which are rigidly adhered to.
1 Follow the suggestions on fuel and fuel tanks given in the section on boat engines.
2 Carefully check all electrical cables and equipment for short circuits

| Crew in the. shrouds | Crew on the boom. Tender lashed to boom | Anchor rode taken from main halyard | Anchor rode with bridle to the boat |

which can result in sparks.

3 Keep strictly to the advice and instructions for use given by the makers of your stove.

4 Treat oil-lamps with great respect.

5 Avoid the use of gas heaters on board as their strong radiant heat can ignite some materials.

6 Do not smoke in the cabin or engine compartment as it can be dangerous.

If a fire does break out on board, a fire extinguisher is the most efficient piece of firefighting equipment. You should have two of the dry powder type, one accessible from on deck and the other to hand below. Water and foam extinguishers are suitable only for boats in which there are no gas or electrical appliances, whereas dry powder extinguishers can be used on any of the following fire classifications without harm.

Classification of fires

Type A Inflammable solid materials (will burn or smoulder)

Type B Inflammable liquids (will burn)

Type C Inflammable volatile liquids under pressure (will burn)

Type E Fires of types A and B caused by electrical faults

There is a *Type D* classification concerning inflammable light alloys, except alkali ones, but these materials are not used in boat-building.

Another thing you can do to control fires is to close all windows and hatches and shut the ventilators. This will prevent draught fanning the flames and with luck will confine the fire. The extinguisher jet should be aimed at the base of the fire, not at the smoke or the flames.

Don't forget, when you use water to put out a fire, to man the pumps so that the water doesn't remain in the bilges. Don't use water to put out diesel, gasoline or oil fires, as the burning fuel will only float and continue to burn.

You should take great care when opening bulkhead doors. Open them slowly and from a crouching position as flames will emerge at the top. When opening hatches, stand on the

A yacht sailing close-hauled in a squall

Weathering a gust on a broad reach; ease the sheets and counter weather helm by putting the helm up

hinged side. Burning mattresses are difficult to put out and should be dunked overboard.

It is not advisable to squirt an extinguisher at someone who is on fire. The best thing to do is for him to jump overboard quickly while you throw him a lifebuoy or lifejacket. You may find it possible to smother the flames by wrapping the victim in a blanket, preferably wet. To save at least his face from the worst burns, start at the head and work down.

For small, localized fires you can use one of the patent fire-fighting sheets which will smother the flames.

Weathering squalls

A squall is a temporary increase in the force of the wind brought about by unstable weather conditions. Approaching squalls are easily seen by a rapidly moving line of darker water, often with white breakers. If the boat heels in a squall to such an angle that there is a risk of capsize in the case of a dinghy or damage to the rigging in the case of a yacht, you will have to do something about reducing the angle of heel. There are different ways of weathering squalls depending on whether you are running, reaching or close-hauled. Running in squally weather is not recommended owing to the risk of broaching or gybing involuntarily, unless you are well reefed down and have a boom vang rigged.

Dealing with squalls when close-hauled

There are three alternatives:
● Head up
● Ease sheets and spill the wind
● Hike out farther

If you try to weather a squall by heading up, remember that the manoeuvre will have to be instantly successful,' otherwise the angle of heel will increase even more. Experienced sailors use a technique in which they sail 'on the luff' (which means so close to the wind that the luff is just short of lifting) and at the critical moment head up so hard that the boat comes upright and the sails lift slightly. If you ease sheets, don't do it by letting the main sheet fly, or you will lose control altogether. Just ease the sheets gently, holding on to them until the gust dies and you can harden them in again without losing way. Experienced helmsmen will ease the traveller rather than the sheet. It is important to keep way on the boat at all times when you use this technique.

Dinghy sailors should, if possible, raise the centreboard a little if there is a risk of capsizing. This will reduce the heeling moment.

Squalls on a broad reach or run

Easing the sheets and hiking out as far as possible will also prove effective on a broad reach, but it is crucial that you should under all circumstances avoid heading up. With the onset of the squall, pull the helm towards you so that the boat remains on course. Sometimes, on a broad reach, it is even necessary to bear away slightly. So the drill is to hike out, ease sheets and counteract the rudder pressure.

ABOVE: The Admiral's Cup yacht Duva, *carrying modern lifebuoys on the pushpit. Notice the guardrail*

BELOW: A racing-yacht with reefed sails in Force 7. The crew are, of course, wearing safety harnesses

Weathering a squall on different points of sailing

Gust approaches, apparent wind frees

Close-hauled

Head up and hike out or ease sheets and hike out

Broad reach

Helm up and hike out or in some cases bear away, ease sheets and hike out

Running

Pull the helm up to prevent the boat heading up

ABOVE: *The crew is not being very sensible about safety. The girl on the right is using the trapeze barefoot, a bad mistake.*

BELOW: *Sailors wearing life vests on a Hobie 16 cat. Note that both helmsman and crew are using a trapeze.*

Righting the boat after a capsize

Modern dinghies have enough built-in buoyancy for them to be righted without difficulty. You should follow the procedure given in the chapter on sailing practice. Heavy, old-fashioned wooden boats and modern dinghies with damaged buoyancy tanks or under-inflated buoyancy bags will remain swamped after a capsize, however, and will need some assistance. Capsizing in such boats is therefore something that should be avoided, although there are steps you can take if and when it does happen. Before we explain the procedure there are two vitally important things to be mentioned.

● In weather in which there is the remotest chance of a capsize, all the crew should wear lifejackets all the time.

● Boats that cannot be righted after a capsize should not be taken so far out to sea that they cannot be seen if they do go over.

Many dinghy-sailing fatalities occur because the capsized crew are not spotted and die from exposure, exhaustion or drowning.

What to do after a-capsize:

1 Find the other member(s) of the crew.
2 Most important, stay with the boat. An upturned boat will be seen far more easily by would-be rescuers than a small head bobbing about in the water. Swimming away from the boat, even if you are wearing a lifejacket, is always dangerous.
3 It is unlikely that you will end up under the sail. Should this happen, however, you should slide out towards the leech so as not to get tangled in the shrouds. Trying to lift the sail is futile.
4 Prevent the boat from turning turtle by holding on to the centreboard.
5 If it seems that you have not been spotted, make yourself more noticeable. It helps a great deal if you can send up a flare.
6 As long as there are no further problems likely to crop up, you can start to collect all the gear that has floated away, such as paddles, spinnaker boom, etc. But only swim away from the boat once you have attached a line from yourself to the boat and if you are wearing a lifejacket.
7 If you can get someone to give you a tow, drop the sails and try to right the boat.
8 Attach a strong towrope around the mast at deck level with two round turns and two half hitches. When you are under way, the centreboard should be lifted to stop the boat from slaloming across the wake. You should also weight the stern and, if possible, steer the same course as the towing vessel.

Man over-board

The situation and how to prevent it

If someone falls overboard (and this almost invariably happens in heavy weather and correspondingly high seas), you are faced with a dangerous situation which could become fatal.
1 In a heavy sea and bad visibility it is very difficult to keep the man overboard in sight, and it is therefore likely to prove a problem to find him.
2 Cold water induces a rapid loss of body heat, followed by energy drain, which makes it impossible for the man to swim back to the boat or climb aboard and leads to unconsciousness. This makes it difficult to haul the person back aboard.
3 Even after a successful rescue, the victim's body heat loss may have reached a critical point, making immediate first aid essential, which is all too often not possible.

To reduce the risk of anyone going overboard, a responsible skipper will make sure that there is a guardrail right round the deck and that crew members wear their safety harnesses at all times.

What the crew should do

When someone falls over the side, the lifebuoy and its attached equipment (marker buoy, smoke canister, etc.) should be released immediately so that the position of the man overboard is marked and can be found again. At the same time, at least one member of the crew should watch the victim closely and constantly. If those on the boat lose sight of the man in the water for one second they may find it impossible to locate him again. Next comes the man overboard procedure described in the chapter on sailing practice. As an alternative to the procedure given, it may be possible, if the helmsman acts quickly enough, to round up or heave to so that the boat remains in

the immediate vicinity of the accident and upwind of the marker buoy and the victim. It will then be considerably easier to keep sight of the man overboard and you will have time to consider ways of rescuing him. In any case, you should start the engine to be prepared for anything (but don't take the sails down!). You then let the boat drift to the spot where you last saw the man. The man in the water may swim towards the boat once it is close enough, or a line may be thrown out so that he can be hauled in. We assume that he is wearing his lifejacket!

If the above procedure is out of the question, for example because the crew did not react fast enough in heaving to, and the man appears to be getting further and further away, then the standard man overboard procedure should be adopted. If all attempts to rescue the victim fail and you are finding it difficult to keep sight of him, you should radio or signal for help.

Recovery

Once the rescued person is alongside, you will find it difficult to haul him back on board, especially if he cannot actively assist himself. If it proves impossible simply to lift him

Recovering a man with block and tackle and a special sling

up by his arms and legs, you will have to resort to one of the following methods, all of which have proved effective. The techniques should be practised in calm weather so that they can be used with confidence if the need arises. In a yacht with a high freeboard, recovery should be effected from the leeward side, where the freeboard can be reduced by heeling the boat.

Boarding ladder or rope sling
As long as the man overboard is still able to help himself, a boarding ladder is the best way of getting him back on board. Since a ladder is not always available, you can make one out of thick piece of line knotted into several bights. The victim can then use the bights to haul himself up to the stanchions and climb back on deck.

Block and tackle
If there is a tackle with a working ratio of 3:1 or more on board, this is the best way of recovering someone from the water. The procedure involves attaching one block to the jib halyard and hoisting it up to normal working height. The second block is attached to the victim's harness or, if he's not wearing one, to a line around his chest, and he is hoisted back on deck. It may be necessary for another member of the crew to get into the water to make the attachment.

The mainsheet
The main boom is used in this exercise as a kind of derrick. Unshackle the lower mainsheet block and attach it to the victim's harness, swinging the boom out as far as necessary. Hoist the man out of the water using the mainsheet tackle. For this manoeuvre you need to have a strong topping lift and a lower mainsheet block that can be unshackled quickly.

Main boom and topping lift
As long as the topping lift and its block can take the weight, this method is very successful. Let go the mainsheet, then haul on the topping lift to raise the boom as high as possible. Secure the fall of the topping lift to the man in the water and lift him by hauling on the mainsheet. The advantage of this rather contrived manoeuvre is that the fulcrum is at the mast head, so that the person can be hoisted right over the rail.

The jib
Make the jib tack fast to a stanchion forward, outside the guardrail. Haul in on the jibsheet aft so that the foot of the sail is along the guardrail, then put the head of the jib in the water with the halyard still attached, so that it forms a sling in which the man can be hoisted aboard.

You can pull someone into a dinghy from the weather side (picture strip on right), or over the transom if there is no afterdeck in the way

The liferaft

If the recovery presents problems and there is no more time for further attempts before serious body heat loss sets in, you will have to use the liferaft. Launch it, making sure it is made fast to the boat, and give first aid in the raft.

Recovery in dinghies

In dinghy-sailing the situation is rather different. You will certainly never be far out at sea, but on the other hand in a real emergency there is no hoist or tackle which you can use. What is more, you will usually be alone in the boat. Most dinghies are crewed by two people and if one falls overboard the other will have to recover him without assistance. It is surprisingly difficult to drag someone back on board a dinghy, especially if he is unconscious or immobile. The best way to do so is to grasp him from behind under the shoulders. You should do this over either the transom or the windward side of the boat. Push him firmly down into the water, then pull up strongly. This down-up movement allows the victim's buoyancy to propel him out of the water and will be particularly effective if he has legs extended and is wearing a lifejacket.

The problem of exposure

A sailor who falls overboard is in grave danger of suffering from exposure. Even a small drop in body temperature will cause giddiness, followed by unconsciousness and eventually death. As water conducts away heat 25 times as fast as air, loss of body heat in cold water is considerable. The human body does a lot to try and minimize the heat loss either by slowing down the cooling process, which it does by contracting the blood vessels in the surface of the skin, or by increasing the energy flow and thus heat production. To help decrease the cooling effect, therefore, you should try to conserve energy. Here are a few rules.

- Keep all your clothes on under all circumstances. Even wet clothes help prevent heat loss.
- Avoid unnecessary movement and shouting, both of which waste valuable energy. You should wave, however, if there is a chance of your being seen.
- A whistle (there should be one attached to your lifejacket) is much mre effective than shouting and uses less energy.
- Panic costs energy. Keeping calm is well worth while if you can.

Recovering a man overboard does not end with his being brought back on board. There is a critical phase in cases of exposure. First aid treatment must be given in the half-hour immediately after rescue if it is to prove effective in saving life. There are two main objects of the treatment:

1 To warm up the body from the outside.
2 To stop the cooled blood from reaching the middle brain.

To help the warming process, wet clothes should be replaced with a dry woollen garment and the patient wrapped in blankets and tucked in. Arrange hot towels or hot water bottles around the nape of the neck. This will warm the blood supply to the brain.

As an emergency measure, put the survivor in a bunk between two crewmates, who should be undressed in order to make heat transfer easier. As soon as any feeling of faintness or dizziness on the part of the patient has passed, he may be given small quantities of hot drinks. On no account should alcoholic drinks be given after any accident. They cause additional heat loss, because alcohol dilates the blood vessels and also causes an increase in the amount of low-temperature blood being pumped into the inner body.

To prevent blood of subnormal temperature from reaching the middle brain, you should rub and massage the arms and legs and bind a light tourniquet around the upper arm and thigh. This will restrict the quantity of cooled blood returning to the heart.

Resuscitation

If the victim is not breathing, it is imperative that you should clear the air passage and apply artificial respiration correctly and without delay. The most effective way of doing this is to use mouth-to-mouth or mouth-to-nose respiration. For this exercise the patient should be laid on his back and his head tilted as shown in the diagram. The reviver kneels by the patient's head, gripping the hair with one hand and placing the palm of his other under the unconscious man's chin. Depending on whether mouth-to-mouth or mouth-to-nose respiration is to be used, the hand under the

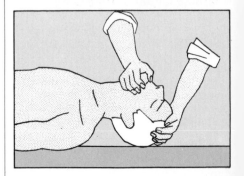

chin should hold either mouth or nose closed. The reviver breathes in deeply, then exhales, blowing the exhaled air into the patient's nose or mouth. While the air is escaping, as it will of its own accord, from the patient's lungs, the reviver breathes normally.

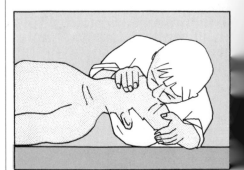

Mouth-to-mouth (or mouth-to-nose) resuscitation. The top picture shows how to position the head properly, while in the bottom picture the reviver is blowing in air

This respiraton should be carried out as if the patient were breathing normally (about 12 breaths a minute) and should be continued without interruption until he revives. Where there is no heartbeat, of course, artificial respiration will be futile, since

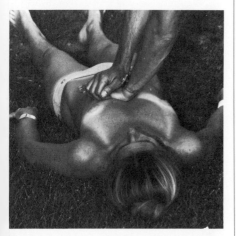

Heart massage. This is how a helper kneels by the patient and puts his hands, one on top of the other, on the lower sternum. Artificial respiration should be continued at the same time

there will be no blood flow to carry the oxygen to the brain. In this case start heart massage without delay. This is best done with a second helper kneeling on the opposite side of the prostrate victim. The second man will put both hands, one on top of the other, on the patient's lower sternum and press down, regularly and firmly, about 60 to 80 times per minute. Artificial respiration should be carried on at the same time.

Weathering a storm

Sailors should ideally ride out a storm in a sheltered harbour. On lakes and reservoirs there is really no reason why you should not be able to get to shelter in time if you watch the changes in the weather and act accordingly. On coastal passages you should also make for shelter if a storm is forecast or appears to be building up. If this is not possible, you should head out to sea and deep water so that you can weather the storm

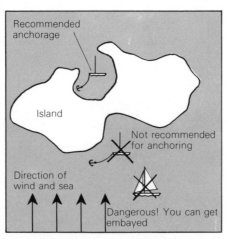

without having to worry about shallows, rocks or breakers.

Then prepare the boat for the storm.
1 Stow and secure all heavy gear on deck such as the anchor.
2 Clear the deck. Gear that cannot be stowed, such as the spinnaker boom, should be lashed down extra hard.
3 Pack away and stow the inflatable dinghy. A tender should be made fast, keel upwards, so that it doesn't fill with water and affect the stability of the yacht.
4 Have all distress signals ready to hand.
5 Close the main and forehatches, so that the cabin will not be swamped by sea coming aboard.

Ocean racing fleet at the start of the Miami-Nassau race sweeping past the start buoy with well-reefed mainsails.

If the wind begins to freshen noticeably, the first thing you should do is reduce sail by removing a sail (in the case of a ketch or schooner) or by reefing. When reefing you should also change the jib for a smaller one, such as a storm jib, but as a rule priority is given to reefing the mainsail.

Reefing

There are two basic methods of reefing the mainsail, with points or using a roller reefing gear. With points reefing, two rows of reefing points are sewn into the sail parallel to the boom. Many modern yachts may have so-called slab reefing, where a single line is used to secure the reef through a row of cringles sewn in at the height of the reef. In roller reefing the mainsail is rolled round the boom. To do this, the boom is turned with a handle attached to a worm gear mounted at the gooseneck. To reef the mainsail, you sail the boat close to the wind and ease the mainsheet off until there is little or no pressure in the sail. The sail is then gradually lowered on the halyard and wound round the boom. Because roller reefing has certain disadvantages when compared to points reefing, the latter is enjoying a return to favour in the form of slab reefing, especially in racing circles.

Disadvantages of roller reefing and advantages of points reefing

1 Too many crew are needed to reef properly. One eases the halyard, one turns the handle, and one or even two may be needed to pull the sail aft to make sure that it is wound round the boom without wrinkles or creases.
2 However hard you try, wrinkles of some sort are almost unavoidable, and the sail is liable to be strained or to lose shape.

Points reefing, on the other hand, is a much faster procedure and demands less manpower. What is more, the sail is not strained at all. Its disadvantage is that the amount you reef depends on the position of the

reef points, which are fixed. In a roller system you can take as many turns round the boom as you feel are warranted.

There is no problem in converting to points reefing. You simply take the mainsail along to the sailmaker, who will put in two rows of reefing points parallel to the foot of the sail. He will also fit luff and leech cringles on the edges of the sail. If reefing pennants are used, these are tied either under the sail itself or round the boom, or secured on small hooks fitted to the boom. If slab reefing is to be used, a small block and cleat is fitted to the boom at the clew end, together with a hook or eyebolt at the tack end, and the reefing line is reeved through these.

The procedure for reefing with the points system is this. You ease the main halyard until the luff cringle is level with the boom hook. The reef-

ed, you will have to stow the mainsail and try some other way of riding out the weather. The following are possible solutions.
1 Heave to.
2 Run before the wind under bare poles.
3 Put out a sea anchor.
4 Hand sails and let the boat lie ahull.
5 Pour oil on the water.

It is impossible to say which of these alternatives is best. It depends to a great extent on the circumstances and even more on the type and characteristics of the yacht. A boat with a long keel will react quite differently from one with a fin keel.

It is up to every skipper to consider the methods we describe below and test them in bad weather so that in an emergency he will know exactly how the boat is going to respond.

With roller reefing, one person operates the main halyard while the other uses the reefing handle to turn the boom

Reefed down. The main is slab-reefed; the jib has been changed for a smaller one

ing line is then threaded through the block on the clew end of the boom and made fast to a cleat. If the sail has fixed reef pennants, these should be tied round the boom. If there are no pennants and only cringles, these can be used to reeve the fall of the reefing line through. It may be necessary to slack off the topping lift and mainsheet to tighten the reefing line. The mainsail can be hoisted, in the case of slab reefing, as soon as luff and leech have been secured to the boom.

If the storm is so violent that it is no longer safe to sail, even with the storm jib set and the main fully reef-

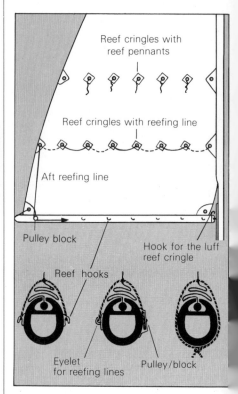

Reef cringles with reef pennants

Reef cringles with reefing line

Aft reefing line

Pulley block

Hook for the luff reef cringle

Reef hooks

Eyelet for reefing lines

Pulley/block

Heaving to

Heaving to is an effective way of riding out a storm, especially for a boat with a long keel. The mainsail should be fully reefed or exchanged for a trysail, and a storm jib set. Although the direction of the waves will be oblique to the heading of the yacht, the fact that you are drifting in the same direction means that eddies are formed immediately to windward of you, which, to some extent, reduce the sea. To this you can add the fact that the sails will tend to steady the yacht and diminish her tendency to roll. As heaving to is a manoeuvre that has other applications besides being a way of riding out a storm, it has already been described in the chapter on sailing practice.

Running under bare poles

If you have a lot of sea room to leeward, you can weather a storm by

wind course, there is in such circumstances a definite risk of broaching and suffering a subsequent knockdown.

To improve directional stability and reduce the tendency for the stern to be lifted and accelerated by the sea, you can use a very simple but practical technique. You trail over the transom, the longest and thickest warp you have, made fast on both quarters so that it forms a bight. Other gear can also be trailed from the stern (fenders, small sea anchors, lifebuoys, etc.) to increase the drag. One problem of trailing warps and gear is that they will chafe and the lines eventually part. This can be reduced by wrapping sailcloth round the lines where they pass through fairleads or over the transom itself. You should not deploy so much line that the yacht can no longer be steered.

in large yachts the anchor has to be fairly big. Recent years have seen the appearance of parachute-like drogue anchors. These are made of comparatively lightweight man-made material and are easily stowed. A small buoy is often attached to the top edge of the forward opening, with a weight directly opposite it on the lower edge. This means the anchor unfolds as soon as it is dropped in the water.

Racing sailors are not over-fond of using sea anchors, although they have one very important use in an emergency, and that is to reduce the speed of a boat drifting on to a lee shore. However, this braking effect also accounts for the main disadvantage of a sea anchor. Not only does it exert a strong pull on itself, so strong that it can break adrift, but it can also strain the boat and the rudder.

The question of whether a sea anchor should be rigged over the bow or over the stern is commonly asked. If it is rigged from the bow, the boat will tend to swing broadside on to the sea.

Juan Baader, in his book *The Sailing Yacht,* recommends that you should rig a steadying sail as far aft as possible to induce a somewhat more stable position. On a two-masted yacht this should take the form of a trisail rigged on the mizzen mast, with the sheet hardened right in. On a sloop-rigged boat, a storm jib can be set on the topping lift or backstay.

It can be more satisfactory to stream a sea anchor from the stern, which will produce an effect similar to, but stronger than, that which is achieved when running under bare poles. Most boats in this case will act in a much less uncontrollable way because the mast will be in the vessel's after third and will have a steadying effect. To reduce the tendency of the boat to broach, you can rig a steadying sail, as suggested by Juan Baader. In this case it may be a storm jib set quite normally on the forestay.

The steadying effect of this sail sounds fine in theory. In practice things are rather different. How many skippers, caught out in a storm and glad at last to have taken in all canvas, relish the idea of having to mess about setting with a sail on the

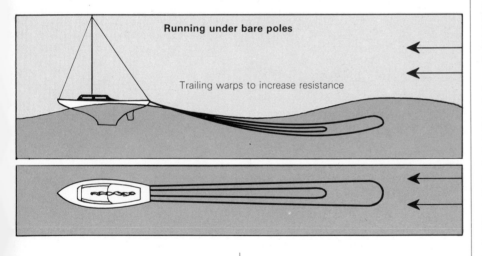

Running under bare poles

Trailing warps to increase resistance

running under bare poles. That is, you can allow yourself to be driven directly downwind without an inch of canvas up, a technique that is somewhat unpredictable in its effects. Running downwind, the yacht will be overtaken by the waves, which can be dangerous. If a wave crest picks up the stern, it will cause that part of the boat to accelerate considerably. If, on the other hand, the bow drives into the trough, where the water particles are moving backwards, this will slow the boat down. Since, in any case, a yacht is always difficult to handle on a down-

Lying to a sea anchor

A conventional sea anchor is a strong tube made of canvas or sailcloth and open at both ends. The forward opening is larger and is reinforced by a steel hoop; it is secured to the rode by a rope bridle. The aft end of the anchor has a smaller opening and an eyelet to which a trip line is attached that can be used when hauling in the anchor.

The problem with this type of sea anchor is that it is unwieldy and difficult to stow, since to be of any use backstay or topping lift?

In conclusion, then, we can say that the sea anchor does not really have much application on a cruising yacht. If you do use one, however, the length of the anchor rode should be equal to the wavelength of the sea, from crest to crest, so that both boat and anchor are at the same point in successive waves.

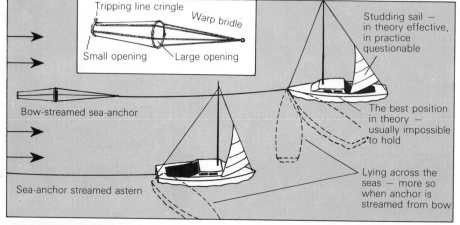

Tripping line cringle
Warp bridle
Small opening   Large opening
Bow-streamed sea-anchor
Sea-anchor streamed astern
Studding sail — in theory effective, in practice questionable
The best position in theory — usually impossible to hold
Lying across the seas — more so when anchor is streamed from bow

Lying ahull

This method of weathering a storm, which means handing the sails and letting the boat find it own natural attitude to the wind and sea, is frequently successful. Without sails or the braking effect of a sea anchor there is little strain imposed on the yacht, which will adopt and maintain the position relative to the wind that suits it best, either broadside on to the waves or at a shallow angle to them. As it drifts to leeward, the yacht will leave eddies to windward which moderate the approaching sea. This does not, of course, prevent waves from breaking over the deck. The tiller should be lashed, and the best thing for the crew to do is to stay below. The irregular, violent motion of the boat will make them very tired.

Unfortunately, how the yacht will react to this technique of riding out a storm, or whether it is suited to it at all, can only be determined when the yacht is put to the test.

Pouring oil on the water

Theoretically at least, it should help to spread oil on the water, as it increases the surface tension, thus making the sea calmer. If you are able to pour a reasonable quantity of oil to windward you will immediately notice the sea becoming calmer. Waves will no longer break as they have been but will break on the edge of the slick.

Release the oil by pumping it overboard through either the head or the sink. It will automatically spread itself to windward because of the boat's drift to leeward. As an alternative, you can trail a small canvas or dacron bag holding 3 to 4 pints (1.5 to 2l) of oil. The bag should be stuffed with oakum for best results and punctured in several places.

This technique should normally be used with another of the procedures we have just described. When hove to, the boat should trail the bag from amidships on the windward side; when running under bare poles, from both sides of the bow; and when riding to a sea anchor, from the anchor itself.

The best oil to use is raw linseed oil, the next best whale oil or lube oil. Diesel is fairly ineffective and gasoline quite useless. In fact, releasing oil is not always reliable as a method. Although the oil will always be effective in creating a surface film, the boat will not necessarily remain in the right position to take advantage of it. It is also possible to have the oil blown back on board in the form of

spray, which will make the deck and cockpit slippery. Apart from its being highly dangerous, since you may lose your footing, the oil will be difficult to clean off afterwards. Besides, few yachtsmen have the right oil or an oilbag on board.

Gale warnings

Gale warnings are issued by all meteorological services. They are broadcast by radio or are available to yachtsmen by phoning the coastguard service or national and local weather stations. This information can also be obtained from the met. centre at any airport. Regular shipping forecasts are available in many areas and these are of particular value, since they invariably describe weather patterns for a day ahead and give the seafarer a good idea of whether conditions will improve or not.

First aid kit

A first aid kit, as we have already mentioned, is one of the most essential items of equipment for a cruising yacht. The size and scope of such a kit depends on the length of the trip, the nature of the area in which you are sailing and the crew you are taking. A kit for a weekend sail would be insufficient for a six-week trip, even in sheltered waters; a kit for a six-week voyage would not be extensive enough for a round-the-world voyage.

An excellent article on shipboard medicine chests was written by the round-the-world sailor and pharmacist Karla Schenk in Bobby Schenk's book *Sailing in Theory and Practice*. The recommended inventory for a medicine chest for a yacht with three to four crew in an area where they would be no more than a couple of days from harbour (Mediterranean, Caribbean, etc.) is given below with the permission of the publisher.

The Medicine Chest

Medicament	Quantity	Application
Oxazepam or Diazepam (Valium/Adumbran)	25 tablets 20 tablets	Nervousness, insomnia
Indomethacin	20 capsules	Inflammation, swelling
Propicillin K	10 tablets	Ear, nose and throat infections, skin air passages, mouth, teeth and gums
Ampicillin 1 g 2 g	20 tablets 5 ampoules	Infection of trachea, urinary tract, or gall bladder, blood poisoning
Bromohexine hydro chloride (Bisolvon)	20	Influenza, fever
Hyoscine	20 tablets 5 ampoules	Gripes, cramps
Codeine and phenyl toloxamine	20 tablets	Bronchitis, coughing
Pethidine	10 tablets 5 ampoules	Very severe pain
Analgesic (Dolviran, etc.)	20 tablets	Severe pain
Ear-drops (Neomycin)	10 g	Inflammation of outer and middle ear
Bisacodyl (Dulcolax)	30 tablets	Constipation
Milk of Magnesia	40 tablets	Stomach acidity, ulcers
Ilonium ointment	10 g	Boils
Ambazon	20 tablets	Mouth abscesses
Charcoal tablets	20	Diarrhoea
Lasonil ointment	40 g	Sprains, buises, bleeding haemorroids
Chloramphenicol eye-drops	10 g	Styes, etc.
Phenylmercuriborate	50 g	Antiseptic for wounds
Halquinol and phanquone	20 tablets	Diarrhoea
Nitroglycerine	15 capsules	Angina pectoris
Norphenephrin hydrochloride	20 g (drops) 5 ampoules	Heart attack
Tincture of opium	10 g	Chronic diarrhoea
Paspertin or other anti-emetic	5 tablets	Severe vomiting
Medozine hydrochloride	2 × 25 tablets	Seasickness
Trifluoporazine hydrochloride	3 ampoules	Severe vomiting
Decongestant spray (Rhinospray)	10 g	Colds
Anti-allergic drug (Sandosten calcium)	20 tablets	Allergies
Methylprednisilone	10 tablets	Allergies, severe (insect bites)
Diazepam (Valium)	5 ampoules	Hysterics, hyperexcitement
Phenylephrin boric acid eyedrops	10 g	Inflammation of the cornea
Burn ointment	30 g	Burns, sunburn, grazes, insect bites

Instruments

1 thermometer
10 disposable gloves, sterile, large
1 pair tweezers
1 scalpel (disposable)
10 wound clamps
1 pair of scissors for dressings
10 5 ml syringes
5 20 ml syringes
20 hypodermic needles, size 1
1 enema tube
1 disposable catheter
100 ml isopropylalcohol 70%, in plastic bottles

Dressings

1 triangular bandage
50 g cotton-wool
3 large packeted wound dressings,
3 medium-sized
10 zinc bandages 60 × 80 cm
3 small zinc bandages
10 assorted adhesive bandages for strapping
40 adhesive bandages for minor wounds
Pressure bandage, 5 m × 2½ cm, 5 m × 5 cm
2 each of 6 cm, 8 cm and 10 cm gauze dressings
1 nasal pack
1 eye-patch
1 finger-stall, size 5 and size 3
4 splints, 10 × 25 cm (preferably those that can be joined to form one long splint)
Safety-pins

You may find it impossible to obtain some of these products without a prescription

Racing

Racing is one of the most exciting aspects of sailing, but anybody approaching racing for the first time must be bewildered by the complicated rules and huge range of types and classes of boat from which to choose. Our advice is quite simple. Start with a boat that has a modest performance and in which you will not have to face up to top competition at once. You can then discover if you like racing and, if so, to what degree. Don't try too hard in the beginning, but go along with the fleet and watch how the others do it. So far as the rules are concerned, you must remember that they are based firstly on the basic rule of the road, which applies to all sailboats, whether racing or not. If you start off with this and gradually add to your knowledge as you go along, the rules will not seem half as difficult. A lot can be learned by example, too, and situations will arise that draw your attention to particular rules. In the very beginning a simple dictum to observe is that a collision must be somebody's fault, so make sure that it is not yours. Take every action to avoid one, even when you are convinced you are in the right. In fact, the rule of the road makes *both* parties responsible for avoiding collisions anyway. When you have graduated to more competitive racing, a sound, even detailed knowledge of the rules will be essential, as it will enable you to plan your tactics properly. At this stage Paul Elvström's book *Paul Elvström Explains the Yacht Racing Rules* will make useful reading.

When it comes to the boat, cost enters into the argument very much. Ocean racers are the most expensive of all racing craft, but even a highly competitive racing dinghy like an FD can cost a great deal of money, consume a great deal of time in tuning, and absorb any amount of spare cash for gear and fittings as you go along. Buy what you can afford to run properly and keep in top condition, because a neglected sailboat not only is a sorry sight but can also be dangerous and will almost certainly diminish your racing chances.

Round-the-buoys racing is probably best if you have a wife and family because you won't be taken from home quite as much as you

would with other types of racing. It is rare to see families race together except in the less ambitious classes. Ocean racing is the real creator of sailing widows, since it takes skippers and crews away from home for considerable periods. However, all forms of regular racing impose a heavy commitment on spare time.

To be able to race you will have to join a sailing club. This does not rigidly apply to the crew, but a crew member who is not a club member is not normally permitted to helm in a race. All racing of any consequence is organized by sailing clubs. Usually, a complete programme is arranged for the season, or the year if you are lucky enough to live where sailing can be enjoyed all the year round. A merit board is kept, so that the winners on points at the end of series are known and rewarded with trophies and cash prizes for their efforts. An entrance fee is charged for each race to provide a contribution to the prize fund. Not uncommonly, successful skippers collect a prize for each race, but they are always very modest sums. Larger clubs frequently support several classes of boat for racing and possibly a handicap class as well. There is never any shortage of advice from the sailing fraternity on how to go about things in the best way, and a visit to a sailing club secretary or race organizer is a good way to tackle matters at the beginning. Clubs enhance an important aspect of sailing generally by providing a meeting-place for kindred spirits. By coming into regular contact with like-minded people you can build up a strong fellowship and an active social life as well.

Handicap or yardstick racing is by no means a bad way to get acquainted with racing, because the competition is less fierce, and close contact with other yachts is reduced. However, many will regard this as very tame, so a start in a local or modest national class is perhaps a better idea. This can be fun without being taxing. Some of these classes of dinghy, although less highly bred than the international classes, are still very good performers in which you will acquire plenty of sailing skill. An advantage, too, of class racing is that you can take part in racing wherever

the class is based and have the benefit of local and national championships. Class loyalty is often strong, and through a class association there can be a very useful exchange of ideas on gear and tactics.

The move to a really hot class with stiff competition, where everything is taken exceedingly seriously, will depend simply on how keen you are on racing and how well you have already done. Do not underestimate the mental and physical demands of a fast, highly competitive machine like a Fireball or an A-class cat. On the whole, this is an area for the younger sailor, since physical fitness and agility play a big role. As you get older, you can graduate to keelboat or ocean racing, but even they call for physical fitness.

All racing is dependent to a large degree on a good basic knowledge of the rules and tactics, so these have been dealt with in some detail in this chapter. Even so, the information given here must only be regarded as a start for the keen racer and must be supplemented by specialized literature on the subject.

Types of Racing

Racing has a following in countries all over the world, even on the lakes in land-locked Switzerland and Austria, and is one of the world's fastest-growing participant sports. There are three groups into which we may divide racing, and these apply everywhere.

Firstly, there is one-design racing which is held over a triangular or Olympic course in boats of exactly the same kind. This is the most widely practised kind of racing and in many classes there are national and international championships, while six classes are represented in the Olympic games.

Secondly, there is handicap and yardstick racing. Here the boats do not compete on a level basis because they are neither one-designs nor restricted classes. Instead, widely differing types of boats, many of them belonging to no particular class at all,

race against each other and have their finishing times adjusted to take account of their differences in speed. Handicaps are often worked out locally as a result of knowledge of the boats' performances. Sometimes they come about as the result of a recognized formula. Yardstick racing is the result of an attempt to give all recognizable classes of boat a number by which they may be compared with each other. These yardstick numbers are then applied with a formula to the elapsed times and the final result is much the same as working out a handicap allowance. Races are held either round Olympic-style courses or simply round courses laid out to suit local conditions and using local buoys. This style of racing enjoys popularity among the less keen and competitive and is regarded as great fun.

Both these kinds of racing are known as round-the-buoys racing.

Ocean racing is vastly different and regarded by many as the very pinnacle of yacht racing (though keen dinghy sailors would not agree). The boats sail long distances, frequently starting in one country and finishing in another, but always finishing in a different place to that from which they start. They sail over large stretches of open water, sometimes for many days at a time. Recently there have been long-distance races that last months. The yachts are rated according to an internationally agreed system, being divided into classes according to ratings. The rules under which they sail are very strict. Ocean racing has become a popular branch of the sport that has quite a big public following. It must be admitted, though, that it is a very expensive hobby.

Rules and points system

Yacht racing is governed by a comprehensive set of rules drawn up and administered by the International Yacht Racing Union (IYRU). Practically all clubs use the rules, which are an efficient way of dealing with all problems arising in the course of a race. It is even possible for a dispute to be referred to the national sailing association, and over the course of the years the IYRU has built up a useful case history which makes it possible to get a decision in more difficult cases. The rules have as their basis the rule of the road, with modifications to take into account the special circumstances of racing. They are up-dated every four years. Organizers of races may incorporate rules of their own which must be set out in the race instructions.

The difference between a regatta and a race is simple, though the two are often confused. A regatta is a meeting at which there is yacht racing and in which several races are competed. Technically, a race is defined as the period between the warning gun (5 minutes before the start) and the moment you have crossed the finishing line or retire. In important events like championships, five to seven races are sailed. Olympic series always consist of seven races, of which one is discounted. In a series of races the overall winner is calculated by awarding points for each race and then totting up the totals at the end. The Olympic points system is as follows.

The winner is the boat with the lowest total of points.

In handicap racing the result has to be calculated by adjusting the elapsed time of each boat by its handicap. The resulting corrected times will give the position of the boats. In offshore racing the rating of the boat is applied to a formula which, related to elapsed time, will give a corrected time.

The course

The usual course is one sailed round three buoys which are so positioned in relation to the wind that the boats have to sail a beat, a reach and a run. This is the Olympic course. Providing there is sufficient space, the three buoys can be laid out to make a suitable course whatever the wind direction.

No. 1 buoy is laid directly to windward of the starting line, where No. 3 buoy is laid. No. 2 buoy is laid either to the right or left so that it forms the point of a triangle with the other two. The course is so designed that over 50% of the sailing by time is done to windward, that being the point of sailing on which most skill can be applied. The finish is in the region of No. 1 buoy.

The upwind leg is 2 miles, though it is reduced to one and a half miles for single-handed dinghies and the minimum recommended distance for championships is one mile. The total length of an Olympic course for dinghies is about 7 miles (longer for keelboats) though this is not the actual distance sailed, which is nearer 12 miles.

The complete race goes like this. Beat from start to No. 1 buoy, reach from 1 to 2 and again from 2 to 3, beat from 3 to 1, run from 1 to 3 and finally beat from 3 to finish. In short, the order is start — 1 — 2 — 3 — 1 — 3 — finish. Where there is insufficient room for the 3 legs to have their full length, they are shortened and instead an additional triangle is sailed, i.e. start — 1 — 2 — 3 — 1 — 3 — 1 — 2 — 3 — finish.

It is usual to lay the marks just before the start so that a last-minute change in wind direction can be allowed for.

While the Olympic course is now regarded as the ideal course for small boat racing, there are plenty of occasions when it is not used. It may be, for example, that a club has to use fixed marks, such as local navigation buoys, and starts its races from the shore. The race officers will then endeavour to set a course that gives a beat, a reach and a run and possibly choose other marks for the second and third circuits to add variety. Naturally, any course can in theory be set, though in practice it may not make for fair competition. The Olympic course has been developed to do just this. It is not used, either, in ocean racing, where other considerations prevail.

Signals

Races are started by the use of visual signals, reinforced by audible ones, flags being used in conjunction with either a gun or horn. It is the visual sign, though, which is the one to take notice of, the audible signal being intended simply to draw the sailors' attention to what is happening. Each class of yacht, including handicap, is allotted its own distinguishing flag which tells the helmsman that his race is the next to start. Ten minutes before the start this flag is flown, warning yachts that they should gather in the start area. At the same time there will be an indication of

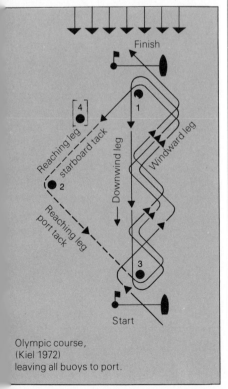

Olympic course,
(Kiel 1972)
leaving all buoys to port.

which way round the course is to be sailed. If marks are to be left to port, a red flag is flown, while if they are to be left to starboard the flag will be green. Sometimes a board is used to give the same information. Five minutes before the start International Code P (Blue Peter) will be flown alongside the class flag and at the start of the race both these flags will be taken down.

There are a number of other signals that can be flown to indicate special requirements. If, for example, the race has to be postponed for any reason the answering pennant is hoisted together with the class flag. It indicates a delay of 15 minutes. Abandonment of the race at any stage is signalled by hoisting Code N (Negative) while shortening the course is done by showing Code S. One or more boats may have made a false start and be over the line before the gun. This will be indicated by Code X. Should the whole fleet be over before the start then the First Substitute (Repeater) will be flown and the race re-started. Code Y means that life vests or buoyancy aids must be worn.

Important definitions

If you are racing for the first time you should acquaint yourself well in advance with all the information you need to start and sail the race according to the rules. You may be disqualified for breaking them.

To start with, there are a few points that you will find useful. The first three are definitions of terms as explained by the IYRU Rules, while the remaining four are aspects of racing tactics.

1 **Proper course.** A proper course is any course which a yacht might sail after the starting signal, in the absence of the other yacht or yachts affected, to finish as quickly as possibly. The course sailed before luffing or bearing away is

presumably, but not necessarily, the yacht's proper course. There is no proper course before the starting signal.

2 **Leeward and windward.** The leeward side of a yacht is that side on which she is carrying her mainsail. The opposite side is the windward side. When neither of two yachts on the same tack is clear astern, the one on the leeward side is the leeward yacht. The other is the windward yacht.

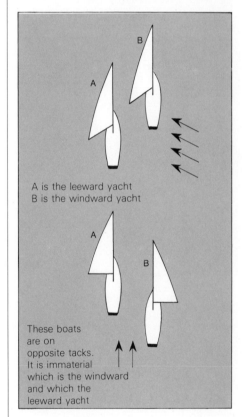

A is the leeward yacht
B is the windward yacht

These boats are on opposite tacks. It is immaterial which is the windward and which the leeward yacht

3 **Clear astern, clear ahead, overlap.** A yacht is clear astern of another when her hull and equipment in normal position are abaft an imaginary line projected abeam from the aftermost point of the other's hull and equipment in normal position. The other yacht is then clear ahead. Yachts overlap when neither is clear astern or if, although one is clear astern of the other, there is an intervening yacht which overlaps both of them.

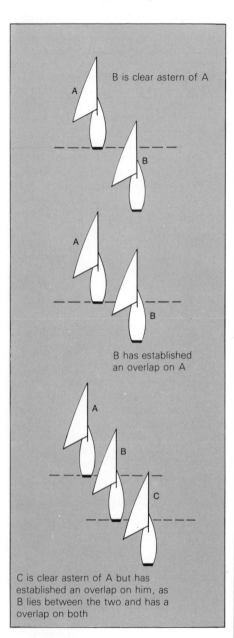

B is clear astern of A

B has established
an overlap on A

C is clear astern of A but has
established an overlap on him, as
B lies between the two and has a
overlap on both

4 **Safe leeward position.** This is an
interesting situation since you
would think that when sailing to
windward, the windward boat of
two would be able to pass the
leeward boat. However, this is not
always so and if the deflected wind
from the leeward boat affects the
sails of the windward one, she will
not be able to get past. In fact, she
may drop back and then try again
unsuccessfully. This situation
arises when the two boats are too
close together and the only solu-

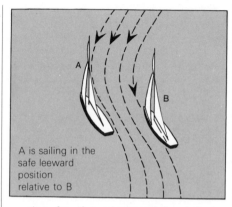

A is sailing in the
safe leeward
position
relative to B

tion for the windward boat is to
tack and break away.

5 **Safe windward position.** This is
a position in which a yacht takes
advantage of the rule that says you
must only tack if you have ample
room to do so properly. If two
boats are sailing close-hauled
together, the leeward boat which
is ahead can only tack when she
can completely clear the windward
boat. Consequently, the windward
boat can hold the leeward boat
where she is until she wants to
tack herself. Thus she occupies
the safe windward position. The
leeward boat can, of course, tack
and go round the stern of the
windward one. The windward boat
is in an even stronger position if
they are both on the starboard
tack, since the leeward boat will be
on the port tack if she tacks and
will therefore have to give way.

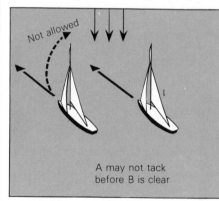

A may not tack
before B is clear

6 **Luffing match.** A yacht being
overtaken to windward may luff as
she pleases to avoid being overtaken but, if the windward boat is
persistent and the helmsman
determined, a point will be reached

when she can probably sail by. As
soon as the helmsman of the windward boat finds himself abeam of
the mast of the leeward boat he
can request the other helmsman to
stop luffing by calling 'mast
abeam'. Then the overtaken boat
can no longer sail above her proper
course and the windward boat can
sail by.

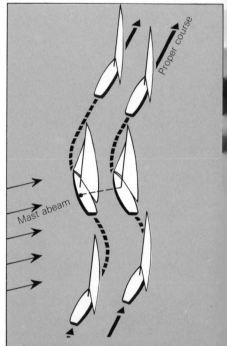

B is being overtaken by A and may luff
until A has reached the mast abeam
position. B will then have to bear
away on to a proper course

7 **Wind shadow and dirty wind.**
On the leeward or downwind side
of every sailboat there is an area of
turbulence known as wind shadow
or dirty wind. There is a similar

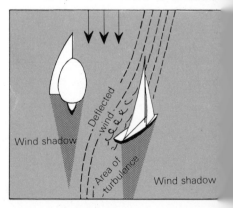

area of disturbance on the wind-ward side and astern as the air is deflected by the sails. It is important not to get into either of these areas, as they will have an adverse effect on the airflow over the sails of your boat. You will no longer have clean wind. When a sailboat casts her wind shadow on another boat she is said to blanket her.

Sailing too close to another boat also brings you into the area of turbulence created by her hull moving through the water, and her bow wave, in particular, can have a detrimental effect on your progress.

The most important rules

A selection of rules is given here which you will find a useful basis for racing, but it must be emphasized thatthese are only a very small number of the total. To be an expert racing helmsman you will need to know the rule book thoroughly.

Right of way rules on all points of sailing

Opposite tacks: basic rule
Rule 36: A port-tack yacht shall keep out of the way of a starboard-tack yacht.

Same tack: basic rules
Rule 37.1: A windward yacht shall keep out of the way of a leeward yacht.
Rule 37.2: A yacht clear astern shall keep clear of a yacht clear ahead.
Rule 37.3: A yacht which establishes an overlap to leeward from clear astern shall allow the windward yacht ample room and opportunity to keep clear; while the overlap exists the leeward yacht shall not sail above her proper course.

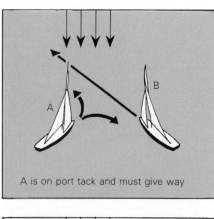

A is on port tack and must give way

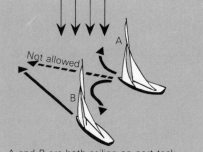

A and B are both sailing on port tack. A is the windward yacht and must keep clear

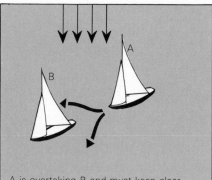

A is overtaking B and must keep clear

Rules at the start

Rule 40: Same tack — luffing before starting
Before a right-of-way yacht has started and cleared the starting line, any luff on her part which causes another yacht to have to alter course in order to avoid a collision shall be carried out slowly and in such a way as to give a windward yacht room and opportunity to keep clear, but the leeward yacht shall not so luff above

a close-hauled course unless the helmsman of the windward yacht (sighting abeam from his normal station) is abaft the mainmast of the leeward yacht. Rules 38.4 (Hailing to stop or prevent a luff), 38.5 (Curtailing a luff) and 38.6 (Luffing two or more yachts) also apply.

Rule 42.4: At a starting mark surrounded by navigable water
When approaching the starting line to start, a leeward yacht shall be under no obligation to give any windward yacht room to pass to leeward of a starting mark surrounded by navigable water, but, after the starting signal, a leeward yacht shall not deprive a windward yacht of room at such a mark by sailing either above the course to the first mark or above close-hauled.

Rule 44.1 (a): Returning to start
After the starting signal is made, a premature starter returning to start, or a yacht working into position from the course side of the starting line or its extensions, shall keep clear of all yachts which have started or are starting correctly until she is wholly on the pre-start side of the starting line or its extensions.

Rules applying to luffing

Rule 38: Same tack — luffing and sailing above a proper course after the start
38.1: Luffing right. After she has started and cleared the starting line, a yacht clear ahead or a leeward yacht may luff as she pleases, subject to the proper course limitations of this rule.
38.2: Proper course limitations. A leeward yacht shall not sail above her proper course while an overlap exists if, when the overlap began or at any time during its existence, the helmsman of the windward yacht (when sighting from his normal position and sailing no higher than the leeward yacht) has been abreast or forward of the mainmast of the leeward yacht.
38.3: Overlap limitations. For the purpose of this rule, an overlap does not exist unless the yachts are clearly within two overall lengths of the

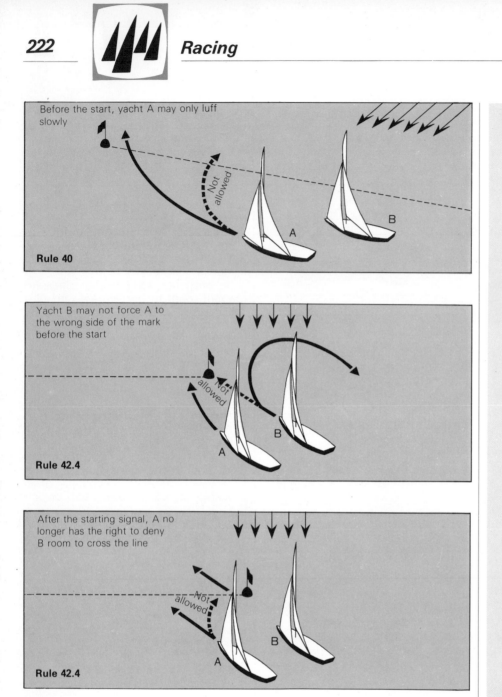

longers of the longer yacht, and an overlap which exists between two yachts when the leading yacht starts, or when one or both of them completes a tack or gybe, shall be regarded as a new overlap beginning at that time.

38.4: Hailing to stop or prevent a luff. When there is doubt, the leeward yacht may assume that she has the right to luff unless the helmsman of the windward yacht has hailed 'Mast abeam', or words to that effect. The leeward yacht shall be governed by such hail, and, when she deems it im-

proper, her only remedy is to protest.
38.5: Curtailing a luff. The windward yacht shall not cause a luff to be curtailed because of her proximity to the leeward yacht unless an obstruction, a third yacht or other object restricts her ability to respond.
38.6 Luffing two or more yachts. A yacht shall not luff unless she has the right to luff all yachts which would be affected by her luff, in which case they shall all respond even when an intervening yacht or yachts would not otherwise have the right to luff.

TOP: Ocean-racing yacht with a radial-cut spinnaker.

CENTRE: Flying Dutchman dinghies on a spinnaker course.

BOTTOM: recognizable a long way off by its star, the starcut spinnaker.

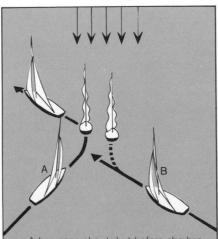

A has gone about, but before she has completed the turn, B is forced to alter course. A has committed an offence

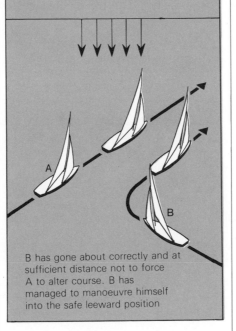

B has gone about correctly and at sufficient distance not to force A to alter course. B has managed to manoeuvre himself into the safe leeward position

Rules for changing tack

Rule 41: Changing tacks — tacking and gybing

41.1: Basic rule. A yacht which is either tacking or gybing shall keep clear of a yacht on a tack.

41.2: Transitional. A yacht shall neither tack nor gybe into a position which will give her right of way unless she does so far enough from a yacht on a tack to enable the yacht to keep clear without having to begin to alter

her course until after the tack or gybe has been completed.

41.3: Onus. A yacht which tacks or gybes has the onus of satisfying the race committee that she completed her tack or gybe in accordance with rule 41.2.

41.4: When simultaneous. When two yachts are both tacking or both gybing at the same time, the one on the other's port side shall keep clear.

Rules which apply at marks and obstructions

Rule 42: Rounding or passing marks and obstructions

42.1: Room at marks and obstructions when overlapped. When yachts are about to round or pass a mark, other than a starting mark surrounded by navigable water, on the same required side or an obstruction on the same side:

a) an outside yacht shall give each yacht overlapping her on the inside room to round or pass the mark or obstruction, except as provided in rules 42.1(c), 42.1(d) and 42.4 (at a starting mark surrounded by navigable water). Room includes room for an overlapping yacht to tack or gybe when either is an integral part of the rounding or passing maneouvre.

b) When an inside yacht of two or more overlapped yachts either on opposite tacks or on the same tack without luffing rights will have to gybe in order most directly to assume a proper course to the next mark, she shall gybe at the first reasonable opportunity.

c) When two yachts on opposite tacks are on a beat or when one of them will have to tack either to round the mark or to avoid obstruction, as between each other, rule 42.1 shall not apply and they are subject to rules 36, (Opposite tacks — basic rule), and 41 (Changing tacks — tacking and gybing).

d) An outside leeward yacht with luffing rights may take an inside yacht to windward or a mark provided that she hails to that effect and begins to luff before she is within two of her overall lengths or the mark, and provided that she also passes to windward of it.

Spinnaker handling during a race.

TOP: *Flying Dutchman sailing towards the second mark. The crews are lowering, not gybing, the spinnaker because they are sailing too close to the wind to make it set.*

CENTRE: *The red boat (1251) is not in as good a position as M14 but has already lowered her spinnaker and can concentrate on rounding the buoy.*

BELOW: *G 1251 has got the better of M 14, while IS 28 has left the spinnaker up too long.*

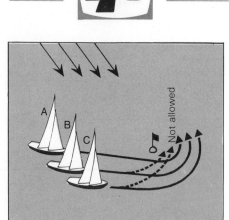

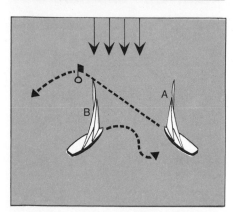

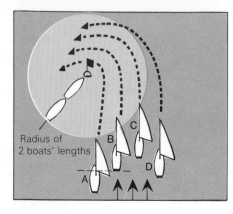

42.2: Clear astern and clear ahead. When yachts are about to round or pass a mark, other than a starting mark surrounded by navigable water, on the same required side or an obstruction on the same side:

a) A yacht clear astern shall keep clear in anticipation of, and during, the rounding or passing manoeuvre when the yacht clear ahead remains on the same tack or gybes.

b) A yacht clear ahead which tacks to round a mark is subject to rule 41 (Changing tacks — tacking and gyb-

ing), but a yacht clear astern shall not luff above close-hauled so as to prevent the yacht clear ahead from tacking.

42.3: Limitations on establishing and maintaining an overlap.

a) A yacht clear astern may establish an inside overlap and be entitled to room under rule 42.1(a) (Room at marks and obstructions) only when the yacht clear ahead is (i) able to give the required room and (ii) is outside two of her overall lengths of the mark or obstruction, except when either yacht has completed a tack within two overall lengths of the mark or obstruction, or when the obstruction is a continuing one as provided in rule 42.3(f).

b) A yacht clear ahead shall be under no obligation to give room to a yacht clear astern before an overlap is established.

c) When an outside yacht is overlapped at the time she comes within two of her overall lengths of a mark or an obstruction, she shall continue to be bound by rule 42.1(a) (Room at marks and obstructions) to give room as required even though the overlap may thereafter be broken.

d) A yacht which claims an inside overlap has the onus of satisfying the race committee that the overlap was established in proper time.

e) An outside yacht which claims to have broken an overlap has the onus of satisfying the race committee that she became clear ahead when she was more than two of her overall lengths from the mark or obstruction.

f) A yacht clear astern may establish an overlap between a yacht clear ahead and a continuing obstruction such as a shoal or the shore or another vessel only when at that time there is room for her to pass between them in safety.

42.4: At a starting mark surrounded by navigable water. When approaching the starting line to start, a leeward yacht shall be under no obligation to give any windward yacht room to pass leeward of a starting mark surrounded by navigable water, but after the starting signal a leeward yacht shall not deprive a windward yacht of room at such a mark by sailing either above the course to the first mark or above close-hauled.

Rule 52: Touching a mark

52.1: A yacht which either
a) touches
  i) a starting mark before starting,
  ii) a mark which begins, bounds or ends the leg of the course on which she is sailing, or
  iii) a finishing mark after finishing
or b) causes a mark or mark vessel to shift to avoid being touched
shall immediately retire, unless either
  i) she alleges that she was wrongfully compelled by another yacht to touch it or cause it to shift, in which case she shall act in accordance with Rule 68.3 (Protests) unless the other yacht exonerates herself by accepting an alternative penalty when so prescribed in the sailing instructions, or
  ii) she exonerates herself in accordance with rule 52.2.

52.2:
a) When a yacht touches a mark surrounded by navigable water, she may exonerate herself by completing one entire rounding of the mark, leaving it on the required side and thereafter rerounding it without touching it, as required to sail the course in accordance with rule 51.2 (Sailing the course) and the sailing instructions.
b) When a yacht touches
  i) a starting mark, she shall carry out the rounding after she has started; or
  ii) a finishing mark, she shall carry out the rounding, and she shall not rank as having finished until she has completed the rounding and again crosses the finishing line in accordance with the definition of finishing.

Alternative penalties for an infringement of a right of way rule

1 720° turns. A yacht which acknowledges infringing a rule of Part IV may exonerate herself by making two full 360° turns (720°), subject to the following provisions:

1.1 When the yacht infringed against intends to protest, she shall notify the infringing yacht at the first reasonabl

opportunity by hail and by displaying a protest flag. (The first reasonable opportunity for a hail is usually immediate.)

1.2 At the first reasonable opportunity after such notification when a yacht realizes she has infringed a rule of Part IV, the yacht acknowledging fault shall make her turns. While doing so, she shall keep clear of all other yachts until she has completed her turns and is on a proper course for the next mark.

1.3 The turns may be made in either direction but both in the same direction, with the second full circle following immediately on the first.

1.4 When the infringement occurs before the starting signal is made, the infringing yacht shall make her turns after the starting signal is made.

1.5 When an infringement occurs at the finishing line, the infringing yacht shall maker her turns on the last leg of the course before being officially finished.

1.6 When neither yacht acknowledges fault, a protest may be lodged in accordance with rule 68 (Protests) and the sailing instructions.

1.7 Failure to observe the above requirements will render a yacht which has infringed a rule of Part IV liable to disqualification or other penalty, but when an infringing yacht's turns do not conform with the above requirements, the yacht infringed against is relieved of further obligations under rule 32.2 (Contact between yachts racing).

1.8 An infringing yacht involved in a collision which results in serious damage to either yacht shall be liable to disqualification.

1.9 The race committee may disqualify a yacht for an infringement of the rules which results in an advantage to the infringing yacht after completing the 720° turns, whether or not serious damage results. The race committee's action shall be governed by rule 73 (Race committee's action against an infringing yacht).

The start of a race

The starting line and procedure

The starting line is marked by buoys at either end or by one such buoy and a mast on the committee boat. With a lot of starters, which will make it necessary to have a very long starting line, the duty boat will often lay a third buoy in the middle so that the contestants can see the line better. The start of a race usually takes place into the wind, so the line is set more or less at right-angles to the direction of the wind. There are four possibilities.

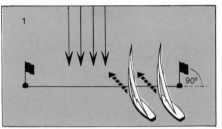

1 The line is at right-angles to the wind. The disadvantage of this arrangement is that the boats to weather on the starboard end of the line, i.e. those on the starboard tack and therefore having right of way, have an advantage over the others.

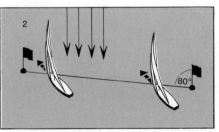

2 The ideal line is one where the port mark is laid slightly ahead of the starboard one, so that the line itself is at an angle of about 80° to the wind rather than 90°. In this case no part of the line has an advantage.

3 The wind has veered and is now coming from farther to starboard. The starboard end of the line is a better starting position.

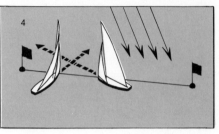

4 The wind has backed. It is better to be on the port end of the line.

Ten minutes before the starting time given in the race programme the signal is hoisted and attention is drawn to it by a gun or horn signal. At the same time the course signal and the class flag are hoisted. Five minutes later comes the preparatory signal (in the USA a red shape, in the UK Code P, the Blue Peter) accompanied by a gun or horn. At the start a red shape is hoisted, or Code P is lowered, respectively, again being marked by a sound signal. If there are several classes due to start in succession, they will usually set off at 10-minute intervals so that the starting signal for the first class is also the warning signal for the following one, and so on. If an individual recall signal is made (Code X), boats that have started too early should turn round and recross the line without getting in the way of other competitors.

If a number of unidentified boats start too early, or there is an error in starting procedure, there will be a general recall and the race will be restarted. The recall is indicated by flying the First Substitute.

To avoid any more false starts, the one-minute rule can be invoked by hoisting Code I. This means that any yacht that crosses the line in the minute before the start will be automatically disqualified unless she returns to the pre-start side of the line across one of its extensions and restarts correctly. This is called the round-the-ends starting rule. The one-minute rule can also be operated as a five- two-minute rule, in which case the sailing instructions will contain a stipulation to this effect.

Starting tactics are very important. Willy Kuhweide, the Olympic medallist who helped with the writing of this chapter, explains how he gets off to a good start. First of all he figures out whether one side of the line has an advantage. If neither side does, he looks for the strongest competition and heads for them. This means that if, say, the wind changes and he unexpectedly finds himself in a bad position, at least he will be near his main opponents. With an unbiased line or one where the advantage is to the starboard end, he always goes to starboard, not right to the limit

A and B have adopted the best starting positions: they are on starboard tack and therefore have right of way as well as enough room to leeward to bear away and increase speed. B would have a special advantage if the wind backs, and if he tacks he becomes the weather boat. C is pinching and has no room to leeward. D is definitely going to have to bear away. E is also pinching but will be unable to bear away because he has no room to do so. Although he is in the second rank, K's start is not a bad one, and he will be able to pass C after crossing the line, then tack and sail off on his own. F and G are doing badly; they are starting on the port tack and will have to give way and lose a lot of distance. H and I are too far from the line

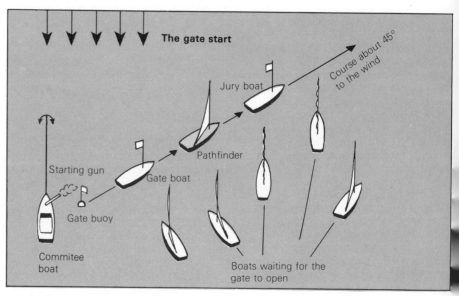

The gate start

mark since everyone will be concentrated there, but just to leeward of this weather group. This way he loses a couple of yards but gains the important advantage of being able to make a clear start. A boat to weather is much easier to handle than one to leeward, which makes it difficult to bear away and get sailing and whose dirty wind will spoil windward performance. If the port end of the line has the advantage, but only slightly, there will not usually be too much congestion there, as many helmsmen will not even notice the small advantage. When this happens, he tries to get right up to the buoy, preferably being the nearest boat to the leeward mark. With a major advantage at the

port end he naturally starts there, on the starboard tack, but with the aim of getting on to port tack as soon as possible. A port-tack start with a port-end advantage, starting right up against the limit mark, is, when successful, the most stylish way to start a race. If you can get off without interference and pass the others you will be leading the field. But the chances of doing this are not very good, and the risks of a port-tack start are rather too great. Incidentally, bluffing plays a major part in starting. Basically you bluff all the time by pretending to make all kinds of moves which you have no intention of completing.

The gate start

For this type of start you need a committee boat, a jury boat, a gate boat and a so-called pathfinder, or rabbit, who will be one of the contestants. First Code G is hoisted to indicate the start area. The warning and preparatory signals are fired as usual 10 and 5 minutes before the start. The competitors gather to leeward of the committee boat and the pathfinder. Three seconds before the starting gun a buoy is thrown overboard from the stern of the gate launch, known as the gate buoy, and the launch begins to open the gate. The gate boat follows the pathfinder and the jury boat precedes both of them. The start line lies between the

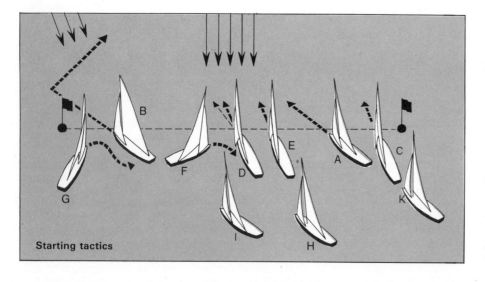

Starting tactics

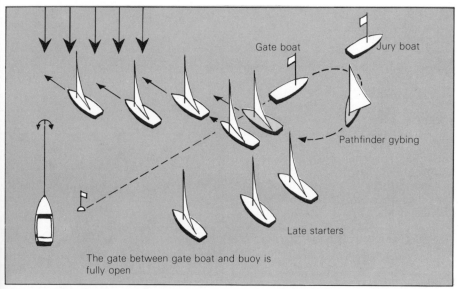

Gate boat

Jury boat

Pathfinder gybing

Late starters

The gate between gate boat and buoy is fully open

buoy and the centre of the transom of the gate launch.

On the starting gun the boats may cross the line behind the gate boat. It is up to each helmsman to decide whether he wishes to start by the gate buoy or whether he wishes to carry on with the pathfinder. After about five minutes the pathfinder is released by the jury boat. Before he joins the race, however, he must gybe across the stern of the gate boat. Gate and jury boat then either stay in the same place or continue on the same course until all competitors have passed through the open gate. The gate is then closed by sounding a signal and lowering Code G, after which no one else may start.

The beat

This is the most important part of a race because this is where the race is usually decided. In a normal Olympic course there are three windward legs and in an extended one, four. Tacking therefore becomes the critical manoeuvre.

Some time before the start you sail towards the first mark to find out which is the long leg and which the short leg. Once you have discovered

A familiar right-of-way situation on the beat: the boat on port tack (in the foreground) has to keep clear

which is which, the decision is simple: always make the long leg first, come about, then make the short leg. In theory, at least, the logical thing to do is to sail one long leg, say, on port, followed by a shorter one on starboard. But it is not always a successful technique. There are two conditions if you use it. You must be among the leaders, if not be the actual leader, otherwise the risk is too great. Secondly, the wind must be steady. If it shifts by more than about 4° or 5°, as it nearly always does on inland waters, you will have to tack. Sometimes ten or twenty tacks will be necessary.

The question of whether you sail as close as possible or bear away a little and get the boat sailing faster is difficult to answer. You have to compromise. First get the boat moving well, then try to find the best point between sailing close and sailing fast. Once you have found the point, you should try to keep it whatever the strength of the wind. But you will always find some (maybe 30% of the field) who sail closer but slower, and some who sail faster but make less to windward.

Anticipated windshifts will make a difference to the length of the boards you make. If, for example, you anticipate that the wind will lift, then you will have to tack at once in order to sail the best course. It is important to time this properly. If you expect the wind to lift, it may still be wrong to make all your boards on the starboard side of the course since the wind may not lift until you are on the reach. The lift may not come until the second or third lap, but when it does you should be on the right side of the course for it.

Clouds and any other visual clues, such as other sailing boats, flags on land, smoke from chimneys, etc., should be watched closely. If you are in the northern hemisphere and there is a front approaching, you will have to reckon that the wind will lift by at least 10°. Scattered storm-clouds

and cumulus indicate a windshift or increase in wind. Always sail towards the darkest (thickest) clouds, as that is where there will be more wind.

Covering tactics are those where you take on one or more of the competitors nearest to you. Normally you should sail the first rounds on your own, making the best time you can over the course. When you get near the finish, however, you may well have to concentrate on a particular rival, especially if his placing in the series will influence your own. Sometimes, though, it is better to let a boat through unhindered rather than let five or more others pass you.

If you are in the lead and are being pressed hard by another boat, you must keep calm. Trying to blanket him could result in a tacking match, which would slow down both boats. If by chance he does tack, you should go about too and cover him, but not blanket him. You should only blanket those competitors who are on the last beat to the finish, and even then only when you are literally in the last few yards.

When an opponent just ahead and to windward cannot be overtaken by bearing away to leeward of him or by tacking, you can try the tacking game. But only do this when it can be safely done in relation to the rest of the field. You tack, the other man tacks. When you have done this a

good many times, the other yacht will either get fed up with tacking or the helmsman will fluff a tack. If this doesn't happen, the pursuer can usually make good half a yard on each tack by performing the manoeuvre better than his opponent. This will give him the chance to get by eventually.

Two techniques used in this type of duel are the false tack and the double tack. If the leading yacht always tacks properly and at the right time, you can try bluffing him with a false tack. If he doesn't fall for it, try a double tack. In between these manoeuvres you could try again to tack to break out to leeward in order to further mislead your opponent.

The double tack. Instead of a false tack, you go about as discreetly as possible in the normal manner. After a moment's caution the opponent will respond with a tack, but will often carry it out in a hurry and lose way. At this point you tack again

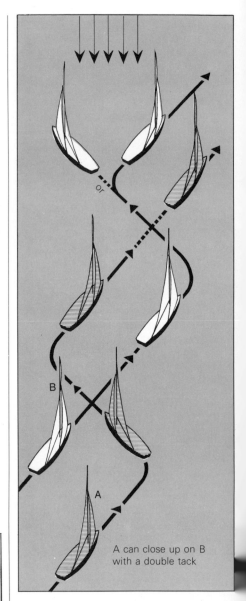

A can close up on B with a double tack

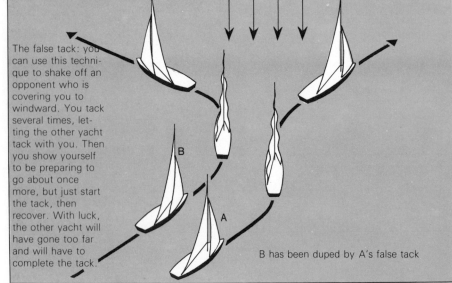

The false tack: you can use this technique to shake off an opponent who is covering you to windward. You tack several times, letting the other yacht tack with you. Then you show yourself to be preparing to go about once more, but just start the tack, then recover. With luck, the other yacht will have gone too far and will have to complete the tack.

B has been duped by A's false tack

Reaching

After the first beat there is a broad reach from the first mark to the second, then another to the third. If all the marks are to be left to starboard, the leg between the first mark and the second will be on the port tack, and after a gybe at the second mark the leg between 2 and 3 will be sailed on the starboard tack.

When marks are left to port, the leg between 1 and 2 will be sailed on the starboard tack and between 2 and 3 on the port tack. If the expanded Olympic course with two triangles is to be sailed, each of these broad reaches will be sailed twice. The yachts will reach their top speed on these, which can be increased by hoisting a spinnaker.

Anyone who can get his dinghy up to maximum speed on to a long plane has a chance of gaining a big lead. In stronger winds there is an increased risk of dinghies capsizing, brought about by the spinnaker which sometimes causes a boat on a broad reach to broach. Expert opinion on the technical considerations to be borne in mind on a reach is that with a steady wind, no swell and no currents, you sail the fastest course by sailing directly, in a straight line, to the next mark. This holds true, however, only as long as you don't indulge in tactics against other boats. If there are waves, you should work the helm so that the boat can ride with them. A gusty wind should be used to increase the speed of the boat along the following lines. When it freshens, head up; when it moderates, bear away a little. If you head up in a freshening wind, your speed will increase disproportionately to the force of the wind. If the wind freshens further, these rules should be applied in reverse. There is a point (in the case of a Soling this occurs at about Force 5) at which you should start bearing away in a gust and head up in a lull in order to have enough room to leeward when the gusts come, as you will not otherwise be able to control the boat.

Carrying a spinnaker in a wind which is coming from ahead is difficult. The first thing to remember is that you hold on to the spinnaker as long as you can. Sometimes this means that you will have to sail downwind of the next mark, heading up for the last bit before the buoy and lowering the spinnaker. If the wind is stronger than between Force 4 to 5, and is coming from too far ahead, then you should take the spinnaker down, then sail higher than the straight line course so that you will be in a position to carry a spinnaker on the approach to the mark. With a very strong wind coming from ahead, the Soling reaches a point where the

Dragons on a broad reach approaching the 2nd mark

spinnaker can no longer be held and is merely bringing trouble and no extra speed.

To try to pass your opponents on the reach you have two possibilities. Firstly, you can sail the first half of the leg up to windward, bearing away for the second half and setting the spinnaker. Secondly you can do precisely the opposite, bearing away for the first half and coming on to the wind for the second half.

With small dinghies or single-handers such as Lasers or Finns which plane, the chance of breaking through to leeward is considerably greater than it would be with a larger boat under spinnaker, as blanketing becomes less important the smaller the boats are. In a Finn, for example, you are as likely to get through to leeward as you are to windward. In Solings, on the other hand, the chances of a break through to leeward are negligible, especially if your opponents are on their toes. In any case, you would have to go down so far to leeward that the length of the diversion would lose you any advantage you might have gained. However, if you can get an unobstructed leeward position from the start, you will be at a definite advantage, because on the second half of the leg, when the boat points

higher, it will be going faster than the boats that are sailing closer on the first half of the leg and now have to bear away. However, this only holds good for light to moderate winds and for stronger winds only in the case of boats without a spinnaker. If you set a spinnaker in a fresh wind and bear away on the first part of the leg, then you will be too close on the second half of the leg to continue to carry the spinnaker to the mark. In this case it would be better to play safe and go to windward first, which leaves you the possibility of bearing away in the gusts.

You must be able to defend yourself when a rival is coming up astern. If he wants to pass you to leeward, you cannot balk him because of Rule 39 (Sailing below a proper course after starting). But you can at least get as close to him as possible to ensure that he has to overtake you through your wind shadow. However, if a boat wants to overtake you to windward, you can stop him by luffing him to the limit. You should only indulge in a luffing match when you can do so without jeopardizing your position relative to the rest of the fleet. If you can't afford the luxury or are in doubt, let him sail past and concentrate on the others.

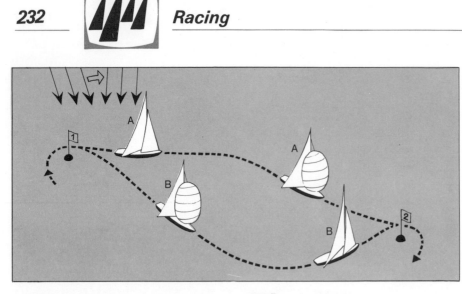

Holding spinnakers in a heading wind. In fresh winds, Willy Kuhweide starts by sailing to windward and without a spinnaker so that he can then bear away and carry one for the last stretch (boat A). With less wind he will carry the spinnaker for as long as possible during the first stretch, even as far as below the mark in some circumstances, then luff up for the last bit before the mark (boat B).

Catching an important rival who is ahead of you requires some special skills. First of all try and sail up directly up his transom. Dodge from one side to the other, so that he is unsure exactly on which side you intend to pass. When your boat is close to his, wait for a favourable moment, and then make a quick, decisive move. Unless your opponent reacts quickly, he gets into your wind shadow and thus loses the opportunity for a successful defence. If he does react well and quickly enough, you have to try and catch him out by altering course to leeward abruptly and try to get alongside to leeward. Later you may be able to get through him to leeward by luffing.

The run

After the second beat comes a run from the first to the third mark. Boats with spinnakers will, under all normal circumstances, be carrying them on this leg.

For most boats the same basic principle holds good: it is better to sail on a very broad reach than dead before the wind. If possible, you should plan to remain on the same tack as you were on when you rounded the first mark. Ideally, if the circumstances don't change, you should keep on this tack at a fixed angle to the wind for the first half of the leg. After gybing, you sail the second half of the leg on the opposite tack, but still keep the same angle to the wind, all the way to the third mark. The extra speed you gain with this system of downwind tacking more than justifies the extra distance you have to travel. But the use of the technique depends on the wind. The stronger the wind, the less important it becomes to tack downwind, as you will eventually reach a speed beyond which it is impossible to go. If there is also a considerable swell, the angle between your course and the wind can be reduced still more, so that it may be possible to sail directly before the wind.

Incidentally, sailors often trim their boats poorly when running. Many position their crew's weight too far aft, causing the stern to sit too deep in the water. In light to moderate winds the transom should be clear of the water, otherwise it will create turbulence that will slow the boat down.

Willy Kuhweide and his crew on the way to the 2nd mark

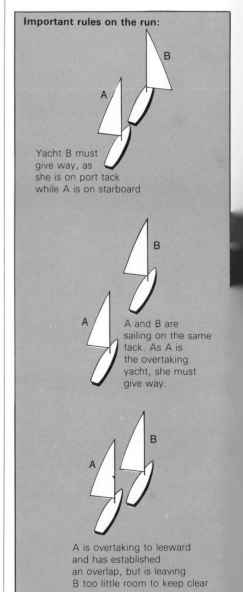

Important rules on the run:

Yacht B must give way, as she is on port tack while A is on starboard

A and B are sailing on the same tack. As A is the overtaking yacht, she must give way.

A is overtaking to leeward and has established an overlap, but is leaving B too little room to keep clear

Rounding the marks

Marks have to be rounded in accordance with the racing rules. You can lose a lot of time by making technical or tactical errors at these marks.

Here are some useful tips about rounding marks.

Everything should be prepared before the mark, so that you are

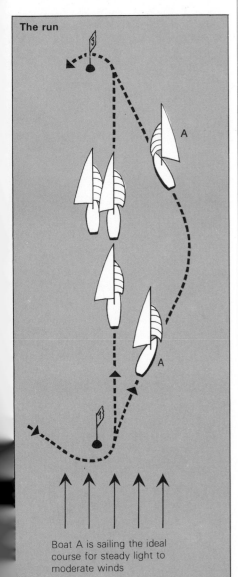

The run

Boat A is sailing the ideal course for steady light to moderate winds

ready for the necessary maneouvre. For example, the gybe at the second mark. If you have to sort yourself out during the manoeuvre, you run a risk of fouling it up.

The arc you describe round the buoy should be as performed by all good car drivers and racing-drivers. In other words, you point the bow at an imaginary point to one side of the buoy and keep to the circumference of a circle of constant radius. Under no circumstances should you head straight for, or too close to, the mark or you will find yourself having to make allowance for the width of your bow at the last minute, a mistake that is particularly expensive when rounding a leeward mark.

After rounding the leeward mark it is advisable not to tack immediately, but to continue on the same tack for a few more lengths (unless *tactical* considerations dictate that you don't). This way you get a chance to get your breath, but you will also not lose way, as you would if you had gone about immediately.

If you are sailing a boat with a spinnaker, it would be wrong to lay a course directly for the next mark immediately after rounding the windward mark (as would generally be the case). The reason for the exception is that during rounding and shortly afterwards there are at least a few seconds before the spinnaker is up and drawing. During this period you should not bear away too far. Keep the boat on a reach and sailing fast until the spinnaker is absolutely ready.

Strictly speaking, the next point comes under the heading of tactics. With a course in which the marks are left to port, you should try to arrange your windward leg so that your last tack before the first mark is made on the starboard tack. To sail up to the buoy on the port tack is asking for trouble, not least because you have no right of way. However, if the port side of the beat is the favoured one and you have been sailing on that side, the question of rounding the buoy on the starboard tack may well be of secondary importance. In any case, the main consideration must be what the wind is doing and which is the quickest way of reaching the buoy. In other words, choose the

tack that is best suited to the conditions, bearing in mind the principle of long tack first, then the short.

With a course in which the marks are left to starboard you can please yourself on which tack you round the mark. If you approach on port tack, you should aim for a spot at least a boat's length above the mark so that starboard-tack yachts, who have right of way, can tack inside you. In fact, it may be better to approach on port tack, so that when you have rounded the mark you only have to bear away and do not need to tack (as the yachts on starboard will have to).

In general, you should try to get an inside position so that you can take advantage of the right of way rules. This is true for all marks but especially the leeward ones.

If a close rival gets round the first mark just ahead of you, you can attack in one of two ways. You can go to either windward or to leeward, depending on the situation or the type of boat you are sailing. With the Soling, Kuhweide would try, whenever he had sufficient room astern, an attack to windward, as it is not always possible, in a mass of boats, to get the spinnaker up and drawing immediately. If the attack to weather was unsuccessful he would bear away for the next mark, so that he would at least get the inside position.

If a close rival is rounding the windward mark fairly close behind you and you want to prevent him from passing you, you wait to hoist your spinnaker until his is up. It would be a serious mistake to put yours up first. As soon as his spinnaker is hoisted, hoist yours as quickly as possible and keep to windward in order to stay clear of him. If he tries luffing without the spinnaker, respond as necessary. If he bears away to hoist his spinnaker, since otherwise other boats may get past, do the same.

A key opponent has rounded the leeward mark immediately before you, and you want to pass him. If the gap between you is so small that your boat is almost touching his transom, the outcome will depend on what your opponent does and you may know his weakness at this point. If he is a helmsman who usually sails freer

than you do, then you should, at the cost of a certain amount of speed, try to get past him to windward. But if you know him to be a helmsman who generally points as high as you do, you can either tack or attempt a breakthrough to leeward. In this case you will certainly have to lose distance to windward.

If your opponent is separated from you by a wider gap than this, then ask yourself whether he is affecting you or not. If he, or rather his wind shadow, is not causing you any problems, sail behind him and consider how you should lay the best course for the mark in pure sailing terms. This way you can determine whether it would not be better to tack away from him altogether.

TOP: Sailing up to the windward mark on the port tack. Rounding the mark, the inside yacht (GO5) . . .

CENTRE: . . . has right of way

BOTTOM: Rounding the 2nd mark. At this point it will be necessary to gybe the mainsail and spinnaker

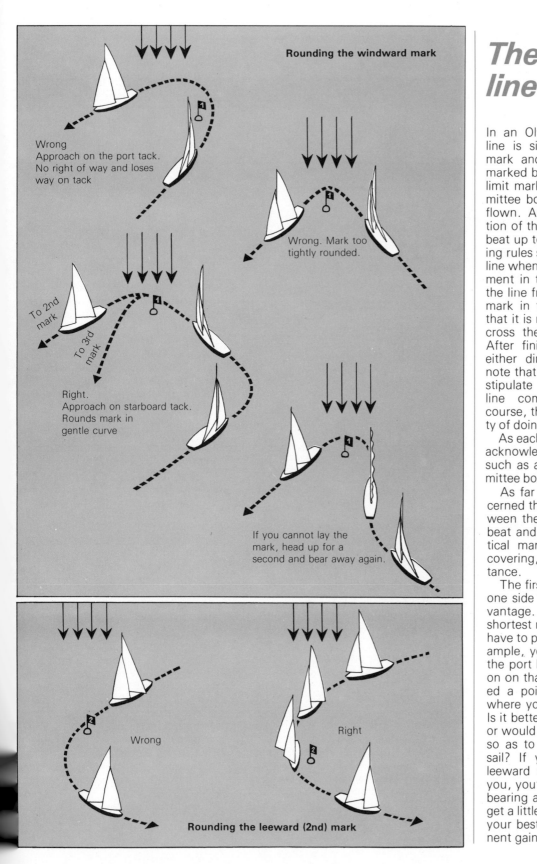

Rounding the windward mark

Wrong
Approach on the port tack. No right of way and loses way on tack

Wrong. Mark too tightly rounded.

To 2nd mark

To 3rd mark

Right.
Approach on starboard tack. Rounds mark in gentle curve

If you cannot lay the mark, head up for a second and bear away again.

Wrong

Right

Rounding the leeward (2nd) mark

The finishing line

In an Olympic course the finishing line is situated near the windward mark and, like the starting line, is marked by two limit marks or by one limit mark and the mast of the committee boat, on which a blue flag is flown. Approaching from the direction of the leeward mark you have to beat up to the finishing line. The racing rules state that a boat crosses the line when any part of its hull or equipment in the normal position crosses the line from the direction of the last mark in the course. Rule 51.5 says that it is not necessary for a yacht to cross the finishing line completely. After finishing she may clear it in either direction. It is important to note that the sailing instructions *may* stipulate that competitors cross the line completely. In practice, of course, there is usually no opportunity of doing anything else.

As each boat crosses the line this is acknowledged by an audible signal, such as a gun or horn, on the committee boat.

As far as sailing technique is concerned there is no real difference between the starting beat, the finishing beat and the beats in between. Tactical manoeuvres, though, such as covering, assume a major importance.

The first thing to do is to find out if one side of the finish line has an advantage. The rule is to choose the shortest route to the line, even if you have to put in an extra tack. If, for example, you think that you can fetch the port limit mark, you should carry on on that tack until you have reached a point close to the finish line, where you have to make a decision. Is it better to sail straight for the line, or would it be worth putting in a tack so as to have a smaller distance to sail? If you have an opponent to leeward and only slightly ahead of you, you can try for an advantage by bearing away a couple of degrees to get a little extra speed. You should do your best to avoid letting that opponent gain the safe leeward position. If

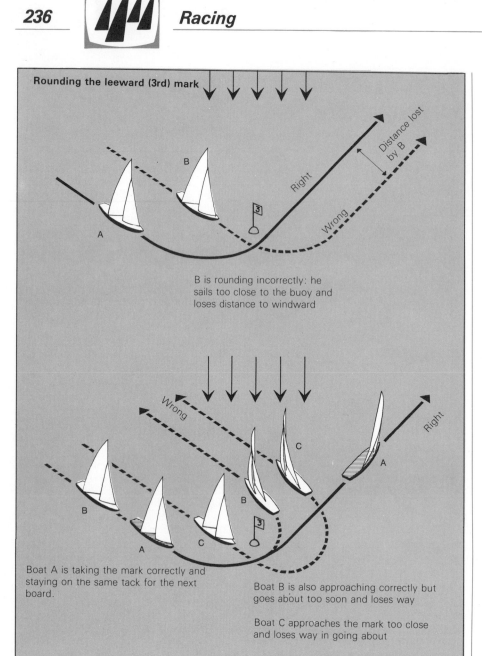

Rounding the leeward (3rd) mark

Distance lost by B

Right

Wrong

3

B

A

B is rounding incorrectly: he sails too close to the buoy and loses distance to windward

Wrong

Right

C

A

B

B

C

A

3

Boat A is taking the mark correctly and staying on the same tack for the next board.

Boat B is also approaching correctly but goes about too soon and loses way

Boat C approaches the mark too close and loses way in going about

The basic principle behind sailing with the swell is to head up when climbing towards the crest and to bear away when dipping into the trough.

Where you have a current on a broad reach leg, you will have to take into account your likely rate of drift. In other words, you don't sail the exact compass course towards the next mark, as you will then be carried downwind and have to make up for the loss to windward. You head up as much as necessary to make the mark.

A current pushing a boat to windward on a beat will always be beneficial. In other words, with a known direction of current and a known course to be sailed in relation to the wind, you should always try to sail the longer tack with the current and the shorter one, if necessary, against it. If you have to buck the stream, it will be worth pointing high, so that you gain a little windward distance although you lose speed. If the current is coming from leeward, it will push the boat higher. If it is coming from the other side, you will be carried downwind by it, so you should bear away and pick up more speed.

Depending on where you sail, the current will be of more or less significance. On lakes and reservoirs it will be less than on the sea and sometimes non-existent. In the Mediterranean and Baltic seas there is little or no tide or significant current. Strong tides can play a very large part in the outcome of a race and should be reckoned as important as wind, especially when the wind is light.

A good sailor will acquaint himself with local tide conditions right from the beginning and plan his tactics accordingly. Much useful data can only be acquired as a result of a longer acquaintance than just a single regatta, and sailors who sail frequently where there are tides and currents will make a special study of the subject. However, when all is said and done, wind conditions take precedence over any others in making tactical decisions.

It is advisable to keep spoiling tactics to a minimum. In fact, it is best to try and sail races without resorting to them at all. That way both you and

your opponent is unable to fetch the mark while you can, you are in luck. Sail on the same tack until you cross the line. The other boat will have to come about but will no longer have right of way, being on the port tack.

Willi Kuhweide has more useful tips about racing for a young aspiring sailor.

Firstly, he ought to check his equipment thoroughly before every race to see that everything is in order. Many sailors come in halfway through a race with something broken, throwing a good position

down the drain simply because they had not carried out a proper inspection of their gear before the race.

In very strong winds you should pay particular attention to the mainsheet traveller. If the main has to be eased, the traveller should be used for the purpose rather than the sheet. Point up farther, so you are almost pinch-

ing, even if this means that half the sail is lifting. Planing dinghies are an exception to this rule, since with these it may be more worthwhile to bear away so as to reach top speed on a semi-plane.

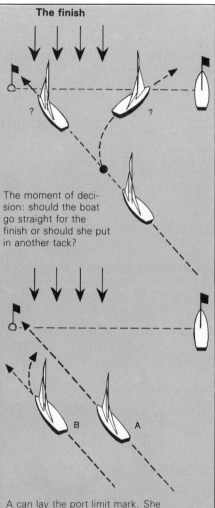

The finish

The moment of decision: should the boat go straight for the finish or should she put in another tack?

A can lay the port limit mark. She should continue as she is and will be able to beat B. B cannot weather the mark and will have to tack. She may not balk A in the manoeuvre, as A has right of way.

your opponents keep your tempers and you will not find yourself in the position of being retaliated against for something you had endeavoured to do to somebody earlier in the race.

Willy Kuhweide is well known in Olympic sailing circles for his unconventional hard sheeting on the wind. It is interesting to find out what the advantages of this technique are.

Seen from astern, his mainsail looks like a straight line. The German Soling trainer said that you can tell his leech three miles away. Even in light winds he hardens both main and jib sheet as far as they will go, cleats

them and leaves them cleated. He does exactly the same in all wind strengths up to the strongest. With the sails sheeted hard in he gets a fantastic increase in speed and exceptional pointing ability, so he is able to sail just that bit faster and higher than the others. In order to get this speed and gain to windward, he has to find the right angle to steer and hold it. With this method there is no room for error. If you don't keep 100% on course, but err ¼° above or ¼° below, you lose way instantly. With conventional sail trim, with slacker sheets, you have a much greater margin of error and can find and hold your course much more easily. Slight deviations will not lose you much speed.

Yardstick racing

A problem faced by many organizers of club and friendly races is in making allowances for the immense variety of boat types. However, a way of making it feasible for different classes of boats to compete with one another is in general use and is known as the yardstick system. This was invented in 1951 by an Englishman, S. Zillwood Milledge. Every boat is given a rating number allied to its speed. The time taken by each boat to sail from the starting line to the finish is adjusted on the basis of the yardstick numbers to give a time handicap on which final results are based.

A variety of handicapping systems has been devised and different places use different ones. For example, the four main ones recognised by the United States Yacht Racing Union are the International Offshore Racing, the Performance Handicap Racing Fleet, the Midget Ocean Racing Club and the Measurement Handicap System. In the United Kingdom and many other areas throughout the world the Portsmouth yardstick tables are both the best known and the most widely used.

Race training afloat

The best practice for a racing sailor, of course, is frequent participation in races. However, a course of training between races, and a similar course at the beginning, is also to be recommended most strongly. The most important manoeuvres should be practised time and again: tacking on a beat and round the marks, gybing both with and without a spinnaker, round a mark and in clear water, setting and handing the spinnaker, weathering gusts and changing sails at speed. In addition, in the case of dinghies, capsize training must not be neglected. Training with other club members, or with neighbouring sailing clubs is also a good idea. A series of practice activities is suitable for this.

- Two or more boats at a time sail together on the same course. Each attempts to increase her speed by carrying out various manoeuvres.
- Several boats together set a close-hauled course and then tack at the instructor's command.
- The boats sail together on a run. At the instructor's command the spinnaker is set (and later handed). This exercise may be repeated several times on a long course.
- Two boats sail together on the wind. One is slightly ahead and to weather of the other and must defend her position by carefully tacking. The other boat then attacks and tries to outwit the opponent by tacking, false tacks and double tacks.
- Sail to a mark from a specified point and round it correctly.
- Sail a short triangular course as frequently as possible. The major purpose of this exercise is to practise rounding the marks.
- Lay out two marks about 150 yd (137m) apart so that they form both a close-hauled and a broad reach course. First sail round the marks clockwise, which will enable you to practise setting the spinnaker while bearing away and subsequently handing it. Then sail

round the marks in a counter-clockwise direction to practise setting the spinnaker after a tack and handing it before a gybe.

- Lay out more marks, close together and in a line at right-angles to the wind. Heading up and bearing away, as well as smooth setting and handing of the spinnaker, may then be practised by slalom sailing between the marks.
- Lay out several marks in a row at relatively short intervals one behind the other in the direction of the wind. Practise tacking by slalom sailing into the wind, and gybing on the return journey before the wind.
- Get as much starting practice as possible with the help of a short starting line. To save time, the normal time intervals for the starting signals may be reduced.
- Practise starting as before, but this time race to a mark 200-300 yd (182-274 m) to windward.
- Pursuit races: start the boats at equal intervals, the slowest first, from a start line or specified point to a mark. This is a good way of practising attack and defence.
- Practise starting and sailing around a small course.
- Hold short races on a small course.

Alongside these exercises and training it is important to have close understanding of the boat's fine tuning. See the chapter on sailing theory.

Keep-fit training

In the varied conditions you are likely to meet, racing is a tough sport and there is little chance of real success if you are not physically fit. Unless they are all in good condition, no crew will be in a position to last a three or four hour race, which may be repeated several days running, with the complete concentration, unfaltering reflexes and sheer physical effort required to win. Many technically, and tactically, able sailors never achieve

good placings in dinghy races ins strong winds because they have neglected to do any bodybuilding and keep-fit training. As a result they are simply not capable of maintaining a hiking position and thus keep the boat up for long periods. Therefore anyone who wishes to be successful in racing must also be physically fit and prepared to begin bodybuilding exercises during the off season. This training should continue throughout the sailing season.

As well as overall fitness, agility, stamina, well-developed powers of concentration, quick reflexes and a certain willpower, a racing sailor needs muscular strength and endurance.

The following muscles are those on which the most stress is placed in sailing, and which must be strengthened by practising, for example, the exercises described below.

Training programme

Even fifteen minutes' exercise at home is worthwhile. In group training in a gymnasium you should allow at least an hour. If games are part of the gym routine we would recommend up to 2 hours. Obviously one should warm up thoroughly beforehand and even at home, running, skipping, turning your arms in a circle, etc. General exercises with the emphasis on bending the trunk backwards are to be recommended. Then follows the main part of the special training scheme, in which a selection of the special exercises should be worked

through one after the other. Circuit training is also a valuable form of exercise. In this form of training 12 (say) exercises are laid out at 12 positions around the gym and must be worked through one after another. The whole thing runs more smoothly if someone blows a whistle to indicate exercise time and rest time. We suggest on average 30 seconds' exercise, 20 seconds' rest before going on to the next position. Shorter intervals, such as 20/10 seconds, are only recommended for general training (for example during the warm-up period) or for those who are out of condition. These short intervals place demands on the circulation for too short a time and give the muscles too little work to do. For the main training schedule for those already in good shape and for the sailor who really wants to get on top form, for example for a championship race, we would recommend 45 seconds' exercise and 30 seconds' rest, during which you can aim for an even but not hectic performance.

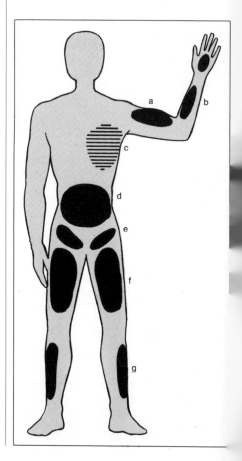

a biceps
b forearm and handmuscles
c shoulder blade muscles
d abdominal muscles
e iliopsoas muscles
f quadriceps
g shin muscles

We consider it useful, (and this applies mainly to the advanced training schedule) to do each exercise on the circuit twice before changing to the next. This will give the muscles more exercise.

After each circuit you should have a short rest (only a few minutes) while you breathe deeply, stretch and relax. One of these circuits should be worked through 2 to 6 times, depending on the stage reached in training and on the time of year.

Muscles used	Use to which muscles are put		Exercises
Upper arm and shoulder muscles, used for bending and pulling (biceps)	Holding and hardening sheets. Weather helm. Trapeze work for the crew. Sheet control when sitting out		1 Climb or hang in an arched position from a climbing rope 2 Do pull-ups from, for example, a horizontal bar 3 Raise a weight above the head
Hand muscles for gripping (long and short muscles of the forearm and hand)	Holding sheets or trapeze. Holding the tiller		1 Squeeze tennis-balls or small dumb-bells in each hand 2 Flex fingers rapidly 3 Climb two climbing ropes
Abdominal muscles and muscles associated with the hip joint	Hiking out, returning inboard from hiking out or trapeze work		1 Sit astride a stool or bench and bend back and forth as if you were on a dinghy 2 Jacknife exercises 3 With feet held under a bar perform sit-ups
Knee-joint extension muscles (quadricep, muscles at lower end of thigh)	Hiking out, crouching, moving while tacking, movement on the trapeze		1 Stand against a wall with legs bent: hold position for 30-90 secs 2 Jump and stretch from crouching position 3 Rock back and forth
Muscles for lifting foot arches (front shin muscles)	Holding the feet in toestraps		1 Walk on your heels 2 In a sitting position, rapidly bend and stretch the feet 3 Sit up with your feet wedged under a cupboard. Hold for 30-60 secs

LEFT ROW FROM TOP TO BOTTOM: a successful start on the port tack. A few seconds before the start all the Flying Dutchmen were ready for a starboard tack start. Then the wind backed, giving an advantage at the port end. Boats H11 and G1280 obviously anticipated the shift and decided on a port tack start, which allowed them to lead the fleet from the start. In the top picture in the right-hand row you can see how far the boats on starboard tack have to bear away, and how FDF155 is experiencing difficulty with the mark . . . Now more and more boats are coming on to port tack . . . while F155 is still caught at the mark and has had to let the boat previously behind him, FD G1131, overtake him to weather

Calendar for shore training

Period and time	Type of training	Training sessions per week
Transition period (northern hemisphere) 15 Sept-15 Nov (southern hemisphere: 21 April-1 May)	General gymnastics, posture exercise, general agility training, general circuit training (20 secs exercise, 10 secs rest)_7, cross-country running, games (such as indoor football and basketball)	Adults — two Teenagers — two
Preparatory period 1 15 Nov-15 Jan (southern hemisphere: 1 May-1 April)	General gymnastics, exercises for overall agility and dexterity, general circuit training, skiing exercises, games	Adults — two Teenagers — two
Preparatory period 2 15 Jan-15 March (southern hemisphere: 1 April 1 Sept)	Special sailing training comes in. In circuit training the intervals should be increased to 30 secs' work, 20 rest	Adults — three Teenagers — two to three
Main preparatory period 15 March-1st May (southern hemisphere: 1 Sept-1 Nov)	Full body-building training. In circuit training, increase to 45 secs' work followed by 30 rest and each position on the circuit should be completed twice	Adults — three — four Teenagers — three Championship sailors — four to five
Completion period 1 May-15 Sept (southern hemisphere: 1 Nov-1 April)	Special keep-fit training now, rather than body-building, even more intensive, combining different types of exercise. Cross-country running, ball games, cycling	Adults, teenagers, and championship sailors: two — five times after the beginning of training afloat

ABOVE: Olympic helmsman Willy Kuhweide with crew Karsten Meyer and Axel May in his Soling Darling. Note the very flat mainsail

BELOW: Flying Dutchmen just before the windward mark

Examples of special circuit training exercises for sailors (12 positions)

1 Pull-ups on a high horizontal bar. After each pull-up jump back down to the floor and start again.
2 Place a bench in front of the wall-bars, lean back in the sitting out position, rock slightly and, if need be, bend back the upper part of the body.
3 As for 2 but with load, pulling on the expander with one hand.
4 Springboard and low bar. Crawl under and then jump over a bench.
5 Climbing-rope. Hang in an arched position or swing.
6 Stretch jumps from a crouching position holding a sandbag on the nape of the neck.
7 Sit or stand in front of the wall-bars. Raise your insteps firmly and hold the position.
8 Crouch on the knot of a climbing-rope (see photograph), hold on to the rope with the left and right hand alternately, touching the floor with the free hand.
9 Jump from side to side over a bench.
10 Sit on a box with a sandbag resting on the ankles and raise them.
11 From a lying position, with a medicine ball held in both hands, sit up and throw the ball at the wall or to a partner.
12 Balance, without using hands, on a sloping ladder, climb up it, turn round and then come back down.
   The order in which the exercises are carried out may have to be changed according to the arrangement of the apparatus in the gym.

Examples of circuit training for sailors at home (8 positions)

1 Rock backwards and forwards in the starting crouch.
2 Adopt a sitting-out posture on a stool, bench or something similar.
3 Sit on front of a cupboard or something similar, with your feet under the edge of the cupboard and lean right back.
4 Squeeze a tennis ball vigorously in each hand.
5 Sit cross-legged with arms folded, then stand up.
6 Lie under a table, grasp the table-top and pull yourself upwards.
7 Sit on the floor, legs slightly apart. Lift your legs slightly and rock gently.
8 Secure a chest expander at one end (for example to a radiator, or alternatively with your foot) and pull it with one hand.

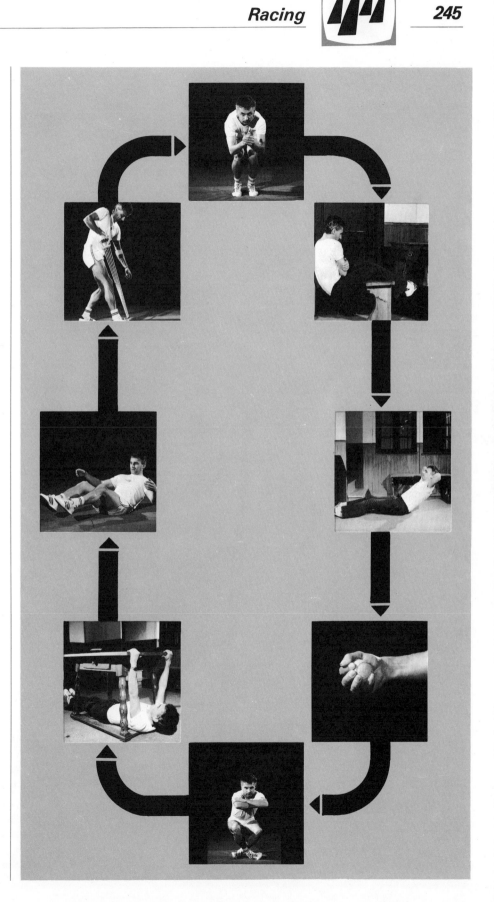

Offshore racing

Offshore races, sometimes over very long distances, are becoming more important and more popular. Most of these events are designed for boats measured under the International Offshore Rule.

Offshore races are also sailed under the IYRU international racing rules, with special rules being laid down by the organizing committee depending on the type of race and where it is being held. The safety restrictions set out in the Offshore Council

November 71 Special Regulation must be adhered to. In cases where the start and finish are in different countries, races are organized jointly by the clubs participating.

Developments in design and construction of offshore yachts have made enormous progress in recent years, so that ever better hull shapes, fittings, rigging and sail-making techniques have been produced. Even brand new types of sails have been invented, the blooper for example. The challenges for the America's Cup and Admiral's Cup are particularly important in furthering the advance of yacht design.

The huge financial outlay required to build the America's Cup 12-metre

boats (which are actually over 20 m long and cost millions each) or the 16-metre Class 1 racers used in the Admiral's Cup may seem absurd at first. But when you consider how advances made in yacht construction in these classes will benefit cruising boats and the whole spectrum of the sport, you must agree that the expense of developing these yachts is justified.

The crew of an offshore racer has to get the best out of their yacht at every stage of the race, day or night. It must be obvious that every action by the crew, such as the many sail changes, has to be performed perfectly. In particular you have to use every favourable wind and cur-

Beating in heavy weather during an offshore race. G15 is on starboard tack, G110 on port. Both yachts are reefed

OPPOSITE: Duel in an offshore race

Some well-known offshore races

Name	Location	Length (nm)	First sailed	Frequency
Bermuda Race (in the Onion Patch Trophy series)	USA/North Atlantic (from Newport to Bermuda)	635	1906	Every 2 yrs
Buenos Aires – Rio de Janeiro	South Atlantic	1200	1947	Every 3 yrs
Fastnet Race (at the end of Cowes Week)	England/North Atlantic	615	1925	Every 2 yrs
California-Honolulu	Pacific	2225	1906	Every 2 yrs
Sydney – Hobart (in the Southern Cross series)	Australia	680	1945	Annual
Chicago – Mackinnac	USA/Great Lakes	333	1898	Annual
St Petersburg – Havana (Fort Lauderdale)	Caribbean	284	1930	Annual
Transatlantic Race	North Atlantic	3500	1866	Irregular intervals
Singlehanded Transatlantic Race (OSTAR)	North Atlantic (from Plymouth to Newport)	3500	1960	Every 4 yrs
Cape Town – Rio Race	South Atlantic	3600	1971	Every 2 yrs
Whitbread Round the World Race	All oceans	26,500	1973/74	Not yet fixed

ent. Navigation, too, is an important aspect of offshore races as it will enable you to reach your destination more quickly. Inaccurate navigation can cause the yacht to take an unnecessarily long route. An efficient navigator is therefore a vital member of the crew.

Other well-known offshore races, in addition to those shown above, are the Transpacific Race (2225 miles: 3560 km from Los Angeles to Diamond Head), the Miami-Montego Bay Race (600 miles: 960 km from Florida to Jamaica, finishing the Southern Ocean Racing Circuit Series), the Channel Race (250 miles: 400 km between Portsmouth and Le Havre, a prelude to Cowes Week), the Skaw Race (290 miles: 464 km in the Skagerrak), the Round-Gotland Race (290 miles: 464 km around the island of Gotland in the Baltic), the Middle Sea Race (613 miles: 9808 km around Sicily, starting and finishing at Malta), the China Sea Race (600 miles: 960 km from Hong Kong to Manila) and the Agulhas Race (500 miles: 800 km off the coast of South Africa).

There are also world championships held in level-rating categories, the most important being the Half-Ton, Ton and Two-Ton Cups.

Two offshore races attracting a great deal of spectator interest are the America's Cup, the Admiral's Cup series and the Single-handed Transatlantic Race (OSTAR), of which we will give brief details.

The start of the Sydney-Hobart race

A 12-metre

The America's Cup

This is a trophy originally called the Queen's Cup and first donated in 1857 by Queen Victoria of England for a race around the Isle of Wight. After the overwhelming victory of the US schooner *America* against powerful British competition, it became the America's Cup. The trophy was given to the New York Yacht Club by the owners' syndicate with the obligation to defend it against any foreign challenge, which first took place in 1870. Since 1958 the America's Cup

challenges have been sailed in 12-metre yachts. They consist of duels, in which two boats sail the course: the challenger and the defender. A maximum of seven races are sailed on a triangular course with a length of 24.3 miles (39 km). The winner is the first yacht to win four races. To date the Cup has always been successfully retained by the Americans. In 1977 the twenty-fourth challenge took place. As this book goes to press, preparations are under way for the next challenge, for which new yachts are being designed and built.

The Admiral's Cup

This trophy was first instituted for off-shore racers in 1957 and is named after Admiral Sir Miles Wyatt of the Royal Ocean Racing Club. It is a national team race series (three yachts in each team) and is part of the un-official Offshore Crew Championship. The series takes place every two years at the same time at Cowes Week and consists of four races: the Channel Race, which is sailed over a 250-mile (400 km) triangular course with the start and finish at Portsmouth (double points), the famous 615-mile (984 km) Fastnet Race (treble points) and two inshore races of 35 miles (56 km) from Cowes, which take place in the Solent and are worth single points. Yachts eligible for entry are those with ratings of 29-45 ft (8.7-13.5 km) under the 10R Mark III regulations, fast ocean racers, for the most part crewed by between nine and eleven.

Since its inception, the Admiral's Cup has usually been won by one of three countries, England, the USA or Australia, although in 1973 the Germans has a sensational win.

Single-handed Trans-Atlantic Race

This race was first sailed in 1960 and takes place every fourth year. It is sailed from Plymouth, England, to Newport, Rhode Island, USA, in boats of any type helmed by one sailor. Winners to date, with their times are: 1960, Francis Chichester, Great Britain, in his 39 ft (12 m) *Gipsy Moth III* in 40 days; there were five contestants. 1964, Eric Tabarly, France in his 44 ft (13.4 m) *Pen Duick III* in 27 days; 15 contestants. 1968, Geoffrey Williams, Great Britain in the 57 ft (17.3 m) *Sir Thomas Lipton* in 25 days, 20 hours and 33 minutes; 35 participants. 1972, Alain Colas, France in the 70 ft (21.3 m) catamaran *Pen Duick IV* in 20 days, 12 hours; 54 contestants. Colas came in 15 minutes before the giant three-master *Vendredi Treize*. 1976, Eric Tabarly, France, in the 74 ft (72.5 m) ketch *Pen Duick VI*; 125 contestants took part.

Navigation

Whether cruising in coastal waters or engaged in offshore racing, the skipper has to know at any moment which course has to be steered and where his yacht is on the chart. It is basically this process of course determination and position finding that navigation is all about. There are three types of navigation.

1 Piloting, which relies on landmarks and navigation marks like buoys and beacons in coastal proximity. It is, in fact, coastal navigation.
2 Navigation by radio aids.
3 Celestial navigation, also known as astro-navigation, which is based on the measurement of angles of altitude and azimuth of celestial bodies and is practised offshore.

The tools of navigation

The compass

The compass is probably the navigator's most important tool. The only type used in yacht navigation is the magnetic compass, which can be either a dry-card compass or a liquid compass, a spherical compass or one with a flat top-plate.

Two types of compass are needed on board: one for steering by — the steering compass — and one for taking bearings, which is usually a hand-bearing compass.

Flat-topped steering compass in gimbals

The steering compass must be installed in the cockpit in a position where it can be clearly seen by the helmsman. It is always a liquid compass. The liquid, which is either a very refined oil or a mixture of water and alcohol with anti-freeze added, has a dampening effect on the movement of the compass-card. To prevent excessive sluggishness liquid compasses used to have stronger magnets than dry-card compasses. Nowadays magnets made of a special alloy are commonly used which, for the same weight, can be magnetized much more strongly than the usual steel magnets. The compass-card is

Modern globe steering compass

suspended on a cap and needle pivot inside the bowl. To cut down wear, the needle point is usually made of hardened steel, platinum or iridium, and the cap centre is a jewel (ruby or sapphire).

Compass cards are almost exclusively marked in black on white or white on black. The graduation used to be in 32 points, each point being 11¼°, but modern compasses use the much more practical graduation by degrees from 0° to 360°.
0° or 360° = north
90° = east
180° = south
270° = west
It is important that a yacht's steering compass should be mounted in gimbals, either single gimbals, which let it pivot in one plane only, or preferably double gimbals consisting of an inner and an outer ring, which allow it to tilt in all directions. But

even without gimbals, a modern spherical yacht compass is so shaped that the card can be tilted to as much as 75° without sticking.

It is also fairly important that the steering compass should be illuminated, either by a conventional bulb light fitted inside the bowl or by a Beta light. This is a fluorescent tritium cell that emits a faint light that cannot be seen in daylight but which illuminates the compass card adequately at night.

Apart from the well-known spherical compass, the grid compass recommends itself for yacht use because it is particularly easy to steer by. It is flat topped and has an outer graduated ring that can be turned. The course to be steered is set on this ring to coincide with the index mark and the course steered to keep the north-south line of the card parallel with the grid lines on the glass.

The following points must be taken into account when installing a steering compass.

1 It must be as far as possible away from large masses of iron such as the keel or the engine and at least 1.2m (4 ft) from any object made of magnetic metal, be it parts of the rigging, the stove or even temporarily stowed gear such as knives, cameras or beer-cans.
2 In steel yachts it must be installed on the centreline to ensure symmetrical distribution of the steel masses of the hull.
3 Electrical cables in its vicinity must be so installed that the positive and negative leads run immediately adjacent to each other. If there is an electrical lead for compass illumination, this should be twisted.
4 Radios and electronic navigation instruments such as an RDF set and depth sounder must be at an adequate distance to ensure non-interference both switched off and on.
5 When not in use the compass must be protected from sun, extreme temperature changes and the weather in general. If it is permanently installed in the cockpit, it should have a cover. The liquid should occasionally be inspected and, if an air bubble has formed, topped up. To do this, the compass has to be opened in a way ap-

propriate to the model — usually turned upside down and the plug on the underside unscrewed. Compasses filled with a water/alcohol mixture can be topped up with a 50/50 mixture of pure alcohol and distilled water. Furthermore, the compass should be protected from knocks and be checked by a reputable compass maker every few years.

The matter of compensating the compass will be discussed in a later section.

Instruments for taking bearings

The instrument most commonly used on yachts for taking bearings is the hand-bearing compass. This is a small compass with incorporated

Hand bearing compass

sight, usually with a handgrip that may house the batteries for illumination. Some types are fitted with a prism which can be pivoted to reflect the card graduation, which can then be read off where the notch above the prism coincides with the lubber line. Being portable, a hand-bearing compass can be used from any position on deck, but again it must be kept at a distance from iron parts and electrical instruments.

For use at night a hand-bearing compass must be illuminated. Some models are fitted with bulb and batteries, others with a Beta light.

On steel yachts the use of a hand-bearing compass is problematic because it may give completely different readings from different positions on deck. In such a case a deviation table must be drawn up for one particular position, although its

Azimuth circle mounted on steering compass

reliability would have to be checked repeatedly. Some skippers claim to have obtained satisfactory results by standing on top of the cabin roof when taking bearings.

On wooden or fibreglass yachts it is not normally necessary to allow for deviation in a hand-bearing compass (see left), although it is advisable to make sure of this from time to time by means of a transit bearing (see p 274). At the same time the best position on deck for taking reliable bearings can be found.

Some hand-bearing compasses can be put in a bracket and used as steering compasses if the need arises, and this is a useful feature since safety regulations for ocean rcing require a second steering compass to be carried on board.

Another method of taking bearings, which is no longer widely used on yachts, is with the help of an azimuth ring. This is a revolving ring with a sight vane which is mounted on the steering compass. It can only be used, of course, if the steering compass is so installed that the view is unobstructed on all sides, which is not usually the case.

The pelorus, too, is not seen much on yachts today. It is a 'dummy compass': a compass-card mounted on a base and fitted with a revolving sight vane. This is installed in an elevated position on deck and in such a way that the north-south line of the card is in line with the centreline of the boat. The angle is measured between the sighted object and that line, and the

Pelorus

resulting bearing is a relative bearing which must be applied to the boat's heading at the moment it is taken. Bearings as such will be discussed in a later section.

The chart

Without a sea chart, or rather a set of charts for the sea area in question, a compass is of no use. An adequate collection of charts is one of the basic requirements of navigation. Charts must meet certain conditions to be suitable for navigation.

1   It must be possible on a sea chart to draw a course line not as a curve but as a straight line and to construct a course triangle with straight sides. The course line is the angle between the boat's centreline and the local meridian, and for this angle to remain the same while the course remains the same the meridians on a chart must be parallel.

2   The chart must be so constructed that every angle on the chart is equal to the corresponding angle on the earth's surface. In other words, the angle of a course steered by the helmsman must correspond to the angle entered in the chart.

3   Areas represented on the chart must be authentic in shape but need not be authentic in size.

4   Distances must be easy to measure. It must be possible to take distances off the side scale of

the chart with dividers and transfer them to the chart.

The pictorial representation of the earth's curved surface on a flat sheet of paper poses obvious problems, and most methods devised by cartographers result in distortion. The projection most suitable for charts, because it meets all the conditions listed above, is Mercator's projection, devised by the German cartographer Gerhard Kremer (*Mercator* in Latin), who lived from 1512 to 1594. The principle is logical. Imagine the globe being scored from pole to pole along the meridians like an orange and the 'skin' being peeled off and laid flat on the table (see diagram). What we get is a number of segments side by side. This is not yet a usable projection because the meridians are not parallel. We now have to 'stretch' the segments at the top and the bottom until their edges meet and we have a solid oblong.

However, we have now introduced a serious mistake. The further away we move from the Equator in a northerly or southerly direction, the greater is the east-west distortion of areas. This is illustrated by the 'island' on the 60th parallel, which was originally circular but is now oval. So we have to stretch our projection in a north-south direction until all circles are once again circles, which means that all angles are accurate. Since more stretch is needed further away from the equator, the areas near the Equator remain virtually the same while those near the poles get 'blown up'. The distance between the parallels of latitude (read off on the right and left margin of the chart) in-

creases towards the poles, whereas the distance between meridians of longitude (read off along the top and bottom edge of the chart) remain the same. Near the Equator, one minute of arc is the same distance in latitude and longitude. The further away from the Equator we measure, the longer one minute of latitude becomes. Since one nautical mile equals one minute of arc, distances taken off with dividers must always be taken off the left- or right-hand margin of the chart at a point that corresponds to the latitude where the plotting is done.

Charts come in different scales. It might be appropriate here to explain the meaning of scale. If a chart has a scale of 1:1,000,000, for example, it means that the relationship of any distance on the chart to the corresponding distance on the earth's surface is one to one million. One inch on the chart equals one million inches (or roughly 13.7 nautical miles) on the earth's surface and one centimetre on the chart equals one million centimetres, or ten kilometres.

The following scales are commonly used for charts.

1 Ocean charts drawn to a scale of 1:5 million or smaller depict a whole ocean without showing much detail and are used mainly for planning sea crossings.
2 Sailing charts drawn to a scale of 1:1 million or smaller are similarly used for passage planning and not for detailed navigation.
3 General coastwise charts drawn to a scale of between 1:400,000 and 1:250,000 show details of coastline and navigation marks and are used

for offshore navigation.
4 Coastal charts and approach charts drawn to a scale of between 1:250,000 and 1:25,000 represent parts of sea areas and coastlines in great detail and are indispensable for coastal navigation.
5 Harbour charts are drawn to a scale of between 1:40,000 and 1:10,000. They contain all the precise information needed for making a landfall and entering a harbour, such as landmarks, leading marks and lights, buoys and depths in channels, anchorages, berths and jetties. Harbour plans are usually drawn to the Gnomonic projection, in which parallels of latitude are concentric circles and meridians straight lines radiating from the chosen tangent point. However, for practical purposes, on so large a scale, they can safely be treated as being straight and at right-angles.

In most countries there are two basic types of chart available. The first type are government publications. In Britain, Admiralty charts are published by the Hydrographic Department of the Ministry of Defence. They cover all parts of the world and are used by shipping everywhere. They are all numbered and are listed, grouped into folios, in the Catalogue of Admiralty Charts, published annually.

In the United States, government charts are published by the National Oceanic and Atmospheric Administration, (NOAA) National Ocean Survey for coastal and offshore waters as well as the Great Lakes. Charts of most rivers (Missisippi, Missouri, Ohio, etc.) are published by the United States Army Corps of Engineers, whereas official charts of foreign waters are published by the Defense Mapping Agency. In Canada, government charts of coastal waters and Great Lakes are published by the Canadian Hydrographic Service. In Australia, coastal charts are published by the Royal Australian Naval Hydrographic Department, while in New Zealand they are published by the Royal New Zealand Naval Hydrographic Department. Catalogues of charts published are issued by the respective offices.

The second type of chart is the commercially produced yachtsman's

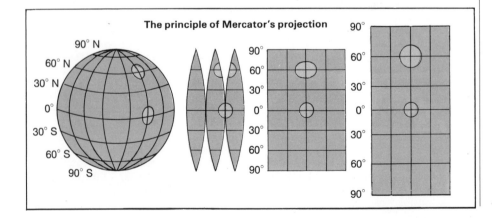

The principle of Mercator's projection

charts or small-craft charts, which may be published by commercial chart publishers, yachting magazines or tourist organizations. These charts are usually smaller and more easily folded than government charts, more colourful, and sometimes contain a considerable amount of ancillary information such as inset harbour plans, facilities available at ports, piloting information, safety regulations, and so on. Similar small-craft charts for United States waters are also published by NOAA.

When sailing in foreign waters it is often advisable to obtain charts published in the particular country, particularly large-scale coastal charts and harbour plans.

Government-published charts usually bear the chart's title, number, scale and source at the top outside the chart margin. On commercially produced charts this information may be found in some other convenient place. The date of the edition of government charts is normally found at the bottom of the chart along the border and the date of the latest printed corrections in the lower left-hand corner.

Both land and sea areas on charts are covered with symbols which describe features such as the nature of the coastline, conspicuous buildings, the nature of the sea bottom, navigational hazards, buoys, beacons, lighthouses, etc. Some of these symbols are self-explanatory, others are not. It is good practice to always refer to an explanation of symbols when reading a chart. Symbols used on US NOAA charts are explained in Chart No. 1, Nautical Chart Symbols and Abbreviations, which is a National Ocean Survey publication. Those used on British Admiralty charts are contained in B.A. Chart No. 5011, Symbols and Abbreviations Used on Admiralty Charts, published by the Hydrographic Department, Ministry of Defence. The corresponding publication in Australia is AUS 5011, published by the RAN Hydrographic Department. In New Zealand it is NZ 200, published by the RNZN Hydrographic Department. Symbols used conform largely to the standard of the International Hydrographic Bureau.

Typical of charts is the profusion of

figures indicating charted depths and depth contour lines, which link places of equal depth. Drying heights (in tidal waters) are indicated by figures which are underlined. On all US charts as well as older Admiralty charts depths and drying heights are given in fathoms, or feet, or a combination of both, and contour lines are fathom lines. On recent Admiralty charts and other European charts depths and drying heights are given in metres.

Depths and drying heights must obviously refer to some fixed level from which they are measured. This is referred to as Chart Datum or Plane of Reference. It is by no means the same for all charts of all parts of the world, and the notes on any chart should be studied carefully to ascertain which plane, or datum, the soundings are referred to.

On United States NOAA charts of the Atantic coast the plane of reference is Mean Low Water, on charts of the Pacific coast as far as the Strait of Juan de Fuca it is the Mean of the Lower Low Waters. From Puget Sound to Alaska it is the Indian Tide Plane, which is roughly that of the Lowest Low Water Observed. In Hydrographic Office charts of the Great Lakes the plane of reference is the mean level of the lake in 1847, and in Lake Survey charts it is the mean elevation of the lake above mean tide of New York. On recent British Admiralty charts the chart datum adopted is that of the Lowest Astronomical Tide, on older Admiralty charts and some other European charts it is Mean Low Water Ordinary Springs. It must be remembered that in all cases (except possibly Indian Tide Plane and Lowest Astronomical Tide) there will be times when the tide falls below the reference plane.

A chart always has a compass rose printed on it; some have more than one in different places. This takes the form of two concentric circles graduated in degrees from 0 to 360, the outer one aligned to geographic north, the inner to magnetic north. The magnetic rose states the local variation for the year in which the chart was first printed and also the annual change in variation (see 'Variation, p 268).

Chart corrections

On newly bought charts all corrections have been made up to date. After that, it is up to the owner to keep the chart up to date by inserting corrections as they occur. The United States Defense Mapping Agency, the Canadian Coast Guard and the Hydrographic Departments in the UK, Australia and New Zeland publish weekly bulletins called Notice to Mariners which, apart from advising on important matters affecting navigational safety, give information for updating the latest editions of charts. These are free publications obtainable from chart agents. In the United States local Notices to Mariners are also issued by each Coast Guard District. Some chart agents undertake to correct charts for a fee. Corrections made are marked alongside the chart's lower margin in the left-hand corner, and the entry should consist of the year and number of the issue of Notices to Mariners in which the correction appeared. When extensive corrections, which are too complex to insert by hand, become necessary, the chart is reprinted.

Publications useful to yachtsmen

Apart from charts and a compass, the navigator needs a number of navigational books and publications to help him. In Britain, many of the essential ones are published by the Hydrographic Department, Ministry of Defence, in the United States by the National Oceanic and Atmospheric Administration, National Ocean Survey, the United States Coast Guard and the Defense Mapping Agency, Hydrographic Centre.

1 **Sailing Directions,** also referred to as Pilots. These are books supplementing the information given on charts. They contain descriptions of coastlines, harbours, dangers, aids, approaches, etc. Volumes in this category are: Admiralty Sailing Directions, published in 75 volumes covering the whole world. These can be purchased in Australia and New Zealand too.

Sailing Directions published by the US Defense Mapping Agency, also covering the whole world.

Coast Pilots, for United States coastal waters, Great Lakes and Intracoastal Waterways, published by the US, National Oceanic and Atmospheric Administration, National Ocean Survey.

Sailing Directions for Australian and New Zealand coastal waters published by the Maritime Services Board of each state.

Pilots for Canadian Waters, published by the Canadian Hydrographic Office.

Apart from these government-issued pilots, which are primarily produced for the benefit of large ships, there are large numbers of commercially produced pilots, guides and handbooks written especially for the cruising sailor. They give rather more detailed information on smaller channels, creeks, anchorages and shore facilities. There are probably very few stetches of water frequented by small craft on which someone has not written a Cruising Guide.

2 **Tide Tables.** These are indispensable when sailing in tidal waters anywhere. They are published annually and give the daily times and heights of High Water and Low Water for selected Standard Ports (or Reference Stations) plus tidal difference tables for a great number of Secondary Ports (or Subordinate Stations). In the United States they are published by the National Ocean Survey in several volumes which cover most parts of the world. The same agency publishes Tidal Current Tables for North America. In Australia and New Zealand, Tide Tables are published by the Naval Hydrographic Service, in Canada by the Canadian Hydrographic Service. In the UK, Admiralty Tide Tables are published by the Hydrographic Department; they come in three volumes and are world wide. Tide Tables are issued annually.

3 **Tidal Stream or Current Charts.** These show the direction and speed of the tidal stream for each hour before and after High Water at specifiec Standard Ports. United States Tidal Current Charts, published by the National Ocean Survey, come in 11 volumes which cover various water areas on both the Atlantic and Pacific Coasts. In Canada, Australia and New Zealand, Tidal Current Charts or Atlases are issued by the Hydrographic Service of each country. British Admiralty Tidal Stream Atlases are published by the Hydrographic Department in 11 volumes covering UK and adjacent European waters.

4 **Lists of lights and fog signals** give details of lighted navigational aids such as lighthouses, lightships and beacons. These details include the name and position of aid, characteristics of its light and sound signals, appearance and dimensions of structure. The United States Coast Guard Light List published in five volumes covers all navigable United States waters and also includes unlighted aids such as buoys and radio beacons. The Admiralty List of Lights and Fog Signals is published by the (British) Hydrographic Department in 12 volumes and covers the whole world. Corresponding lists are published by the Hydrographic Services of Canada, Australia and New Zealand.

5 **Lists of radio signals.** Government publications that contain useful information for small-craft skippers are: a) in the United States: H.O. 117 Radio Navigational Aids, which include radio beacons, marine direction-finding stations, time signals, navigational warnings, Loran, Consol, and regulations on the use of radio in territorial waters. Also H.O. 118 Radio Weather Aids. b) in the UK: Admiralty list of Radio Signals Vol. II listing radio beacons and direction finding stations, Vol. III listing radio weather services and Vol. V giving radio time signals, navigational warnings and position-fixing systems. c) in Canada, Australia and New Zealand, Lists of Radio Signals are issued by the Hydrographic Service of each country.

6 **The Nautical Almanac.** This is produced jointly by H.M. Nautical Almanac Office, Royal Greenwich Observatory, and the Nautical Almanac Office, United States Naval Observatory. The British and American editions are identical and one or other is available in Canada, Australia and New Zealand through chart agents. The Nautical Almanac contains a year's astronomical data for the sun, moon, planets and stars. It is indispensable to any yachtsman practising celestial navigation.

7 **Sight Reduction Tables.** Either tables for marine navigation or tables for air navigation can be used. Sight Reduction Tables for Marine Navigation are published jointly by the United States Naval Oceanographic Office (as H.O.229) and the (British) Hydrographic Department, Ministry of Defence (as NP 401). The equivalent tables for Air Navigation, which are used in this book, are H.O 249 in the United States and A.P. 3270 in the United Kingdom.

8 **Pilot charts** are needed for long ocean passages. They are available for all of the world's oceans and give information on predominant wind strengths and directions for each month of the year. They are published in the United States by the Defense Mapping Agency, Hydrographic Centre, and in the United Kingdom by the Hydrographic Department, Ministry of Defence.

9 **Others.** Two publications should be mentioned here which have become household words in their respective countries: *The American Practical Navigator* by Bowditch, which contains the answer to every possible question on piloting and navigation, and *Reed's Nautical Almanac,* published annually by Thomas Reed Publications Ltd which not only contains a wealth of information on navigation, seamanship, sea signalling, weather forecasting, collision regulations and first aid but also up-to-date tide tables, tidal stream charts, lists of lights and radio beacons, nautical ephemeris and notes on buoyage. There is a European edition, which covers United Kingdom waters

and adjacent European coasts, and an American East Coast edition. In Australia a comprehensive publication called Marine Information Manual is published by the Department of Transport. It covers Australian waters and gives valuable information on all aspects of piloting.

Tools for chartwork

The most important tools needed for chartwork, apart from a soft pencil and an eraser, are a pair of dividers, a pair of pencil compasses and parallel rules. Instead of the latter, some people work with two set-square protractors and the results are identical. When it comes to dividers, there are two basic types: the straight-legged kind and the bowed kind. Opinions differ as to which type is easier to use. The main thing is that they should be workable with one hand and have at least 6in (15 cm) legs.

Parallel rules are used for plotting courses and transferring position lines from one part of the chart to another. They come in two types: the roller type and the hinged type, and they can be made of wood, metal or plastic. Captain Field's pattern is made of transparent plastic, which is useful because the chart can be seen through it. Its upper edge is marked in degrees, from 0° to 180° in one direction and reciprocal, i.e. from 180° to 360° in the other, so that it can be used as a protractor. Other models have no degree markings and can only be used in conjunction with the compass rose printed on the chart.

Depth finding instruments

An instrument for measuring depth is an important aid in navigation. The simplest piece of equipment for this purpose is the lead line. The modern, electronic equivalent is the depth sounder. A yacht doing serious cruising should, ideally, be equipped with both.

The lead line
This consists of a length of very pliant non-kinking line to the end of which is made fast a rocket-shaped, heavy piece of lead. The bottom of the lead is hollowed out and filled, or 'armed', with tallow. A sample of the sea bottom, which sticks to this tallow, can be identified as the lead is recovered and helps to fix the yacht's position. For yacht use the line is normally up to 25 fathoms long and marked at intervals as follows, starting from the lead (1 fathom = 6 feet = 1.83 metres):

1 fathom	1 strip of leather
2 fathoms	2 strips of leather
3 fathoms	3 strips of leather
5 fathoms	a piece of white cloth
7 fathoms	a piece of red cloth
10 fathoms	a piece of leather with a hole in it
13 fathoms	a piece of blue bunting
15 fathoms	same as 5 fathoms
17 fathoms	same as 7 fathoms
20 fathoms	2 strips of leather with holes in them

The intermediate fathoms, called 'deeps', are judged by eye. It is worth knowing that a new line should be soaked and stretched before being marked.

When taking soundings with a lead line from a boat under way the lead is swung and released to land in the water well ahead, on the windward

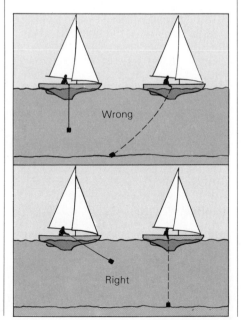

side to avoid sailing over it. The inboard end is made fast on deck.

The weight of leads used on yachts is normally in the region of 5 to 10lb (2.5 to 5 kg) and the line is 25 fathoms at the most. Deep-sea leads used by big ships may weigh between 30 and 100lb (13.5 and 45kg) and the lines be 100 fathoms long.

The depth sounder
This is an electronic instrument that

Modern depth sounder

transmits a supersonic sound impulse towards the sea bottom, from where it is reflected back to a receiver in the boat. The speed of sound through water being known to be (4925 ft/second or 1500 m/second), the instrument measures the time elapsed between transmission and reception and converts it into a depth reading displayed on a scale. The more sophisticated models can be switched to display feet, fathoms and metres. The visual display can be one of three types: rotating light, index finger or digital.

The transducer, which transmits and picks up the sound signal, must be installed on the hull in a well-considered place where there are no air bubbles in the water-flow, because air bubbles interfere with the transmission of sound waves.

Modern depth sounders are fully transistorized and have a very low electricity consumption, so that their operation off the boat's batteries presents no problem.

The log

The log is a device for determining

the boat's speed and distance covered. Except for the ground log, which is hardly used nowadays, logs measure speed through the water. If a yacht sails in a volume of water which is itself moving, for example a tidal current, this will falsify the read-out. If the current is against the yacht the speed recorded will be higher than the actual speed over the ground. If the current is with the yacht, the speed recorded will be lower. The actual speed over the ground can be found approximately by allowing for the current if the rate of flow is known, and by taking bearings of marks if any are in sight.

Distances at sea are measured in nautical miles. A nautical mile equals 6080 feet or 1852 metres and is arrived at by dividing an average great circle of the earth by the minutes of arc (21,600 min). Hence, one nautical mile equals one minute of arc.

Speeds at sea are measured in knots, one knot being one nautical mile per hour. The following equations apply.

Speed S in knots =
$$\frac{\text{Distance D in nautical miles}}{\text{Time t in hours}}$$

or:

Speed S in knots =
$$\frac{\text{Distance D in nautical miles} \times 60}{\text{Time t in minutes}}$$

Example
D = 5 miles   t = 42 minutes
$$S = \frac{5 \times 60}{42} = 7 \text{ knots}$$

Conversely, time can be calculated, say to establish how much longer it will take to the next mark, if the distance is known (from the chart) and the ship's speed has been logged.

Time t in hours =
$$\frac{\text{Distance D in nautical miles}}{\text{Speed S in knots}}$$

or:

Time t in minutes =
$$\frac{\text{Distance D in nautical miles} \times 60}{\text{Speed S in knots}}$$

Example
D = 5 miles   S = 7 knots
$$t \text{ (min)} = \frac{5 \times 60}{7} = 42 \text{ minutes}$$

Distance covered can also be calculated, if speed and time are known.

Distance D in nautical miles =
Speed S in knots × time t in hours

or

Distance D in nautical miles =
$$\frac{\text{Speed S in knots} \times \text{time t in minutes}}{60}$$

Example
S = 5 knots   t = 42 minutes

$$D = \frac{5 \times 42}{60} = 3.5 \text{ nautical miles}$$

There are four basic types of log: the towed log, the Chernikeef log, the pitometer log, and the electronic log. The group of towed logs includes the now antiquated chip log, in which a line is let out from a reel and the knots are counted. Another towed log, still in use today, is the patent log. This consists of a very long, specially plaited line to one end of which is made fast a rotator. As this is let out and towed through the water, the revolving rotator and line transmit the rotary motion to a registering device fitted on the stern of the boat. The patent log registers distance covered, not speed, but speed can easily be calculated using one of the above equations. It is unreliable at high and very low speeds.

The Chernikeef log consists basically of an impeller at the end of a small, through-hull shaft. The impeller's rotary motion, as the vessel moves through the water, is transmitted electrically to a registering device, which

Walker's Patent Log

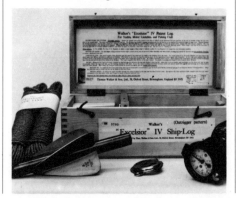

displays distance covered and also converts it to speed.

The pitometer log measures water pressure difference through two ('pitot') tubes projecting through the hull. The measurements are transmitted electrically, and both distance and speed can be registered.

The electronic log measures speed through ultra-high frequency sound waves.

Rotators, impellers and pressure tubes can be fouled by seaweed and floating debris and should therefore be shielded. Electronic logs suffer less from this disadvantage. Any electrically operated log recorder must be installed at least 1m (3 ft) away from the steering compass.

Logs that record speed rather than distance covered are now generally referred to as speedometers.

If, for some reason, the navigator finds himself without any device for measuring speed, he can always resort to the Dutchman's log. This involves marking a spot on the forward part of the rail and another one aft, the two being as far as possible apart, say 6m (20 ft) on a pocket cruiser, 10 or 12m (30 or 40ft) on a larger boat. Stopwatch in hand, the navigator throws an easily visible floating object, such as a ball of newspaper or a plastic bottle, into the water well ahead of the bow. As it passes the forward mark he starts the stop watch, and as it passes the after mark he stops it. Assuming that the distance between the marks is 6m (20ft) and the object takes 5 seconds to cover it, the boat's speed is
$$S = \frac{D}{t} = \frac{20}{5} \text{ ft/sec} = 4 \text{ ft/sec}$$

However, we want to know the speed in knots. Since there are 3600 seconds in an hour and 6080 feet in a nautical mile, the formula for knots (that is, nautical miles per hour) is as follows.
S in knots =
$$\frac{\text{Distance D between marks in ft} \times 3600}{\text{time t in secs} \times 6080}$$

or since $\frac{3600}{6080}$ equals roughly 0.6

$$S \text{ in knots} = \frac{D \text{ in ft}}{t \text{ in secs}} \times 0.6$$

in our case:
$$S = \frac{20}{5} \times 0.6 = 2.4 \text{ knots}$$

The sextant

The sextant is an instrument for measuring angles. Its basic parts are the arc, with the scale engraved on it, the index bar, which moves on it, an index glass, a horizon glass (both with shades) and a telescope. The sextant is the mainstay of celestial navigation, and it is discussed in detail in that section. It is not essential for coastal navigation, although it is useful in position fixing for taking horizontal angles and vertical angles for distance off.

Other navigational instruments

Other useful instruments which the navigator will want to have aboard are a pair of binoculars, an accurate clock or chronometer, a barometer or barograph, and a radio for receiving weather forecasts. The latter does not have to be a special 'yacht radio' as frequently advertised but can be a normal high-quality portable radio, which need not even have VHF. It must, of course, have those frequencies on which weather bulletins are broadcast (see the section on Publications, p.253). A radio that can receive radio beacon frequencies (285 to 415 KHz (or kc/s) on the long wave band) and which is equipped with a directional aerial can even be used for direction finding.

Radio beacons and their use are discussed in a later section.

Buoys and lights

Lights

Coastal navigation by night is made possible by lights situated at important points ashore or off the coast: lighthouses, lightships, lighted beacons and lighted buoys. The light source can be electricity, oil, pressurized or liquid gas, or acetylene. The light is passed through special lenses, made up of a number of prisms. Details of lights such as characteristics, range, sectors, phase, height of structure, etc. are contained in the Light Lists (see the section on Publications, p 253).

Luminous range and geographical range

The luminous range of a light, as given in the Light Lists, is the maximum distance at which a light, theoretically, can be seen, and depends entirely on the intensity of the light. It takes no account of the

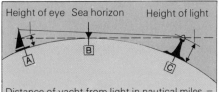

Distance of yacht from light in nautical miles = AB + BC

height of the light, the curvature of the earth or the height of the observer's eye. The distance at which light could actually reach an observer, taking into account the curvature of the earth, the height of the light (above High Water) and assuming an observer's height of eye of 5ft (4.5m) is called the geographical

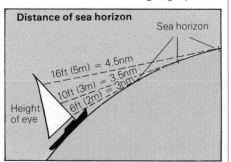

range. The geographical range of lights of any elevation for any height of eye can be extracted from a table usually labelled Distance Off — Lights Rising or Dipping. A light is said to be 'rising' or 'dipping' when it is just visible on the horizon.

Light characteristics

Every light has its own characteristics, i.e. the length of time during which it appears, in what group pattern, at what intervals, what colour the light shows and so on. The characteristics of a light are indicated in charts and Lights Lists.

Key to the identification of light phases	
Fixed (F.)	A continuous steady light
Flashing (Fl.)	Single flash at regular intervals. Duration of light less than periods of darkness.
Fixed and Flashing (F.Fl.)	A steady light varied at regular intervals by a flash of greater brilliance.
Quick Flashing (QkFl.)	Showing about 60 flashes per minute
Interrupted Quick Flashing (I.Qk.Fl.)	Showing quick flashes in groups interrupted by dark periods
Group flashing (Gp.Fl.)	Two or more flashes in groups at regular intervals
Fixed and Group Flashing (F.Gp.Fl.)	Steady light with two or more brilliant flashes in a group at regular intervals
Isophase (Iso) or Equal Interval (E.Int.)	A light where durations of light and darkness are equal
Occulting (Occ.)	Steady light with total eclipse at regular intervals. Duration of darkness less than that of light
Group Occulting (Gp.Occ.)	A light with a group of two or more eclipses at regular intervals.
Morse Code Light (Mo.())	Characteristics are shown by the appropriate letter or figure in brackets.

Thus you may read against a particular light GpFl (2) WRG 10s, which means: flashing in groups of 2 flashes each, either white, red or green depending on the sector, every 10 seconds. Sectors are listed in a separate column in the Lights List. The period of 10 seconds means that 10 seconds elapse from the start of one group of 2 flashes to the start of the next group. For the correct identification of lights it is essential to have a watch with a second hand or a stop watch.

Special use of lights

Sectored lights are mainly found in lighthouses and light beacons where a safe approach from seaward has to be specially marked, i.e. through shallows, rocks or other hazards. The safe sector is usually white, the dangerous sector or sectors red. As soon as the helmsman loses the white light and sees red he knows that he has left the navigable channel. Sectored lights can be fixed, flashing, or have any of the other characteristics listed. In charts and Light Lists they are fully described, including the angles which the different sectors cover. (Bearings of lights are always given from seaward.) Thus, if you read FlWR 10s, W262°-208° (306°), R208°-262° (54°), this means that there is a white and a red sector, the white sector covering an angle of 306°, from 262° to 208° (looking at the light from seaward), the red sector covering an angle of 54°, from 208° to 262°. The lights in both sectors are flashing once every 10 seconds. More often than not all sectors together cover only part of the full 360°. Occasionally the dangerous sector or sectors of a light may not show a different colour but a different rhythm, for example the leading sector may be fixed white, while the dangerous sectors may be flashing.

Leading lights or range lights
Where the width of a navigable channel is critical, for example when approaching a harbour entrance, or in the case of any other approach which leads through hazardous ground, two lights are set up at a distance from each other and at different heights, which, if kept in line, will 'lead' a vessel in. As soon as they 'open up', the helmsman knows that he has to correct his course. The lights may be any colour, fixed or flashing, and their characteristics and bearing are given in Lights Lists and Sailing Directions (Pilots).

Harbour and lock lights Lights installed at the ends of quays and piers to mark a harbour entrance are frequently fixed red. If the entrance is flanked by a pier on either side, the port light (coming from seaward) is often green and the starboard light red (in the United States), or the port light red and the starboard light green (in UK, Australian and European waters). The same goes for lock entrances.

Lights on buoys In the United States Lateral Buoyage System, white or green lights, flashing, occulting or quick flashing, may be fitted to port-side buoys. White lights, short-long flashing, may be fitted to mid-channel buoys, while white lights, interrupted quick flashing, may be fitted to junction buoys. *Red* lights, flashing, occulting or quick flashing, are fitted to *starboard-side* buoys.

From 1981, in United Kingdom, Australian, New Zealand and European waters, lights on buoys, as buoys themselves, will be uniform according to the IALA Buoyage System. Lights on port-hand buoys, if fitted, will be red with any rhythm. Lights on starboard-hand buoys, if fitted, will be green with any rhythm. Lights on isolated danger marks, if fitted, will be white, GpFl (2). Lights on safe water marks, if fitted, will be white isophase, occulting or long flash, 10 seconds. Lights on special marks, if fitted, will be yellow. Lights on cardinal marks, if fitted, will be white. For flashing characteristics see the following section on buoyage.
Note: In the United States, red means starboard (coming from seaward), in UK, Australian, New Zealand and European waters red means port. This goes for lights on buoys and buoys themselves.

Occasional lights If a light is marked 'occas.' or 'privately maintained' it should not be relied on. It means that

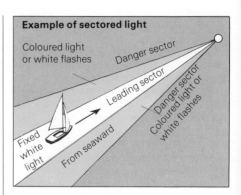

Example of sectored light

it is only lit when convenient, or in certain weather conditions, or on special occasions, such as the fishing fleet coming in.

General notes on lights
1 Coloured lights are less easily distinguished than white ones. Green is more difficult to distinguish than red.
2 The characteristics of a light may appear altered through the influence of dirt, temperature and long distance.
3 On the borderline of visibility the duration of a light flash appears shortened, so that a flash described as long in the Lights List may be interpreted as short.
4 Great distance and poor visibility affect the colour of lights. A white light, for example, may appear reddish.
5 Light buoys may have drifted from their marked position or may have become extinguished.

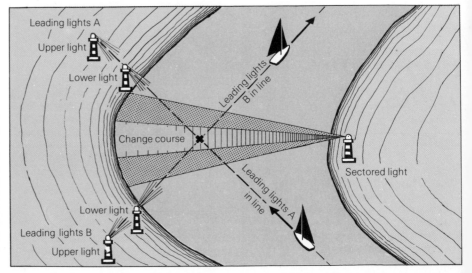

Symbols and abbreviations used on British Admiralty charts

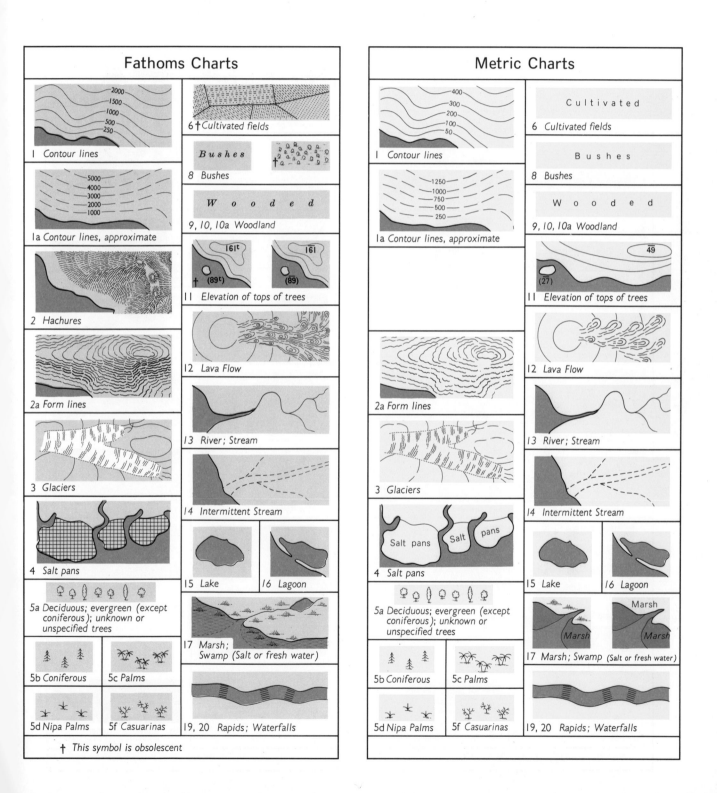

Fathoms Charts

1 Contour lines

1a Contour lines, approximate

2 Hachures

2a Form lines

3 Glaciers

4 Salt pans

5a Deciduous; evergreen (except coniferous); unknown or unspecified trees

5b Coniferous

5c Palms

5d Nipa Palms

5f Casuarinas

† This symbol is obsolescent

6 † Cultivated fields

8 Bushes

9, 10, 10a Woodland

11 Elevation of tops of trees

12 Lava Flow

13 River; Stream

14 Intermittent Stream

15 Lake

16 Lagoon

17 Marsh; Swamp (Salt or fresh water)

19, 20 Rapids; Waterfalls

Metric Charts

1 Contour lines

1a Contour lines, approximate

2a Form lines

3 Glaciers

4 Salt pans

5a Deciduous; evergreen (except coniferous); unknown or unspecified trees

5b Coniferous

5c Palms

5d Nipa Palms

5f Casuarinas

6 Cultivated fields

8 Bushes

9, 10, 10a Woodland

11 Elevation of tops of trees

12 Lava Flow

13 River; Stream

14 Intermittent Stream

15 Lake

16 Lagoon

17 Marsh; Swamp (Salt or fresh water)

19, 20 Rapids; Waterfalls

Fathoms Charts

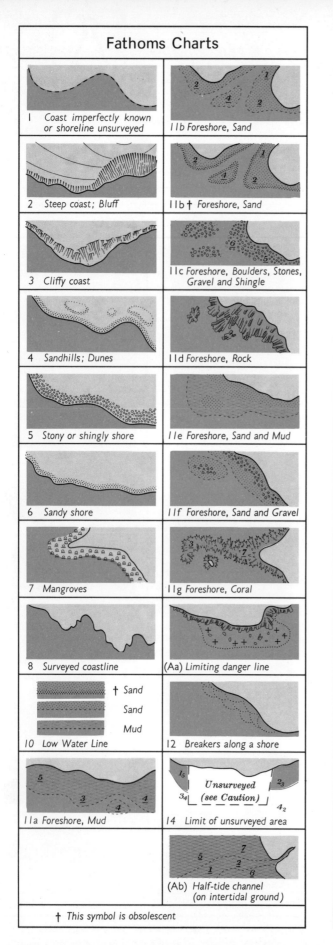

1   Coast imperfectly known or shoreline unsurveyed

11b   Foreshore, Sand

2   Steep coast; Bluff

11b†   Foreshore, Sand

3   Cliffy coast

11c   Foreshore, Boulders, Stones, Gravel and Shingle

4   Sandhills; Dunes

11d   Foreshore, Rock

5   Stony or shingly shore

11e   Foreshore, Sand and Mud

6   Sandy shore

11f   Foreshore, Sand and Gravel

7   Mangroves

11g   Foreshore, Coral

8   Surveyed coastline

(Aa)   Limiting danger line

† Sand
Sand
Mud

10   Low Water Line

12   Breakers along a shore

11a   Foreshore, Mud

14   Limit of unsurveyed area

Unsurveyed (see Caution)

(Ab)   Half-tide channel (on intertidal ground)

† This symbol is obsolescent

Metric Charts

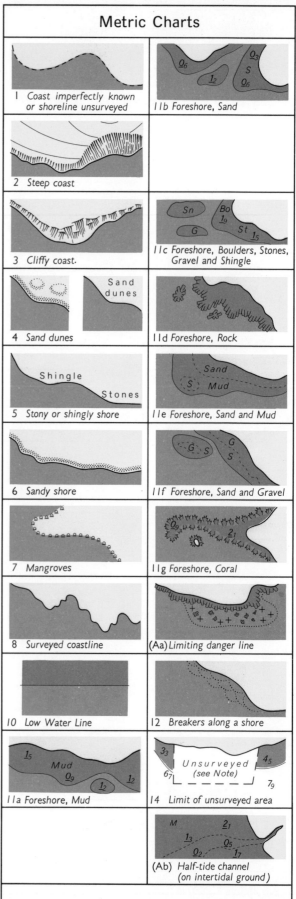

1   Coast imperfectly known or shoreline unsurveyed

11b   Foreshore, Sand

2   Steep coast

3   Cliffy coast.

11c   Foreshore, Boulders, Stones, Gravel and Shingle

4   Sand dunes

Sand dunes

11d   Foreshore, Rock

5   Stony or shingly shore

Shingle   Stones

11e   Foreshore, Sand and Mud

6   Sandy shore

11f   Foreshore, Sand and Gravel

7   Mangroves

11g   Foreshore, Coral

8   Surveyed coastline

(Aa)   Limiting danger line

10   Low Water Line

12   Breakers along a shore

11a   Foreshore, Mud

14   Limit of unsurveyed area

Unsurveyed (see Note)

(Ab)   Half-tide channel (on intertidal ground)

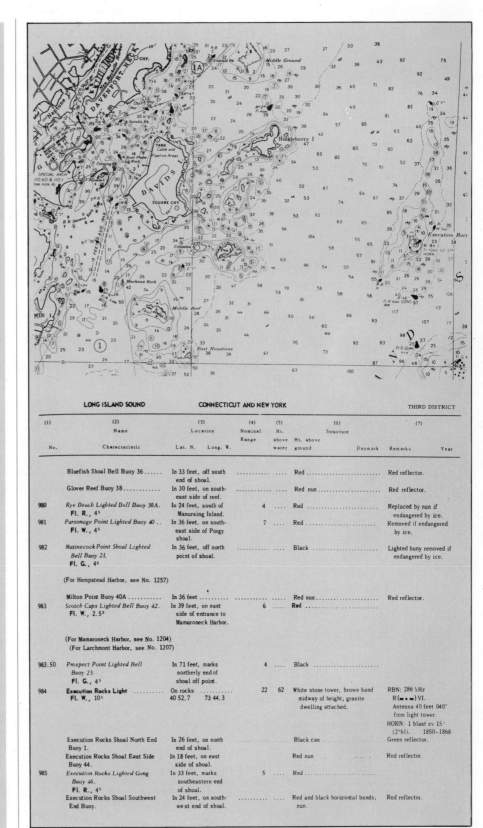

(1)	(2)	(3)	(4)	(5)		(6)		(7)	
No.	Name Characteristic	Location Lat. N. Long. W.	Nominal Range	Ht. above water	Ht. above ground	Structure	Daymark	Remarks	Year
	Bluefish Shoal Bell Buoy 36	In 33 feet, off south end of shoal.	....	....	Red			Red reflector.	
	Glover Reef Buoy 38	In 30 feet, on south- east side of reef.	....	....	Red nun			Red reflector.	
980	*Rye Beach Lighted Bell Buoy 38A.* **Fl. R., 4ˢ**	In 24 feet, south of Manursing Island.	4	....	Red			Replaced by nun if endangered by ice.	
981	*Parsonage Point Lighted Buoy 40 ..* **Fl. W., 4ˢ**	In 36 feet, on south- east side of Porgy shoal.	7	....	Red			Removed if endangered by ice.	
982	*Matinecock Point Shoal Lighted* *Bell Buoy 21.* **Fl. G., 4ˢ**	In 36 feet, off north point of shoal.			Black			Lighted buoy removed if endangered by ice.	
	(For Hempstead Harbor, see No. 1257)								
	Milton Point Buoy 40A	In 36 feet	....	....	Red nun			Red reflector.	
983	*Scotch Caps Lighted Bell Buoy 42.* **Fl. W., 2.5ˢ**	In 39 feet, on east side of entrance to Mamaroneck Harbor.	6	....	**Red**				
	(For Mamaroneck Harbor, see No. 1204) (For Larchmont Harbor, see No. 1207)								
983.50	*Prospect Point Lighted Bell* *Buoy 23.* **Fl. G., 4ˢ**	In 71 feet, marks northerly end of shoal off point.	4	....	Black				
984	**Execution Rocks Light** .... **Fl. W., 10ˢ**	On rocks 40 52.7 73 44.3	22	62	White stone tower, brown band midway of height; granite dwelling attached.			RBN: 286 kHz R(● ● ■) VI. Antenna 40 feet 040° from light tower. HORN: 1 blast ev 15ˢ (2ˢbl). 1850–1868	
	Execution Rocks Shoal North End Buoy 1.	In 26 feet, on north end of shoal.	....	....	Black can			Green reflector.	
	Execution Rocks Shoal East Side Buoy 44.	In 18 feet, on east side of shoal.			Red nun		......	Red reflector.	
985	*Execution Rocks Lighted Gong* *Buoy 46.* **Fl. R., 4ˢ**	In 33 feet, marks southeastern end of shoal.	5	....	Red				
	Execution Rocks Shoal Southwest End Buoy.	In 24 feet, on south- west end of shoal.	....	....	Red and black horizontal bands, nun.			Red reflector.	

LONG ISLAND SOUND   CONNECTICUT AND NEW YORK   THIRD DISTRICT

Previous page:
Mooring might be called part of navigation. Three different ways of mooring cruising yachts: TOP LEFT: This obviously meant to be temporary mooring while the occupants are going for a swim!

TOP RIGHT: One way of lying against a dock with the help of a mooring buoy. The yacht on the left is just dropping astern, having first secured her bow line to the buoy. The yacht on the right also has a bow line out to starboard to keep her clear of her neighbours.

BOTTOM: Moored with her nose up against the dock, this yacht obviously has a stern anchor out.

This page:
TOP: Moored alongside the dock

CENTRE: Moored in a raft

BOTTOM: Of these two yachts, one is lying head to the dock, the other stern to the dock.

Buoys and Beacons
IALA Buoyage System 'A'
The combined Cardinal and Lateral System (Red to Port)

Fathoms and Metric Charts

Where in force, System 'A' applies to all fixed and floating marks other than lighthouses, sector lights and leading-marks, lightships and Lanbys (large navigational buoys). There are no special characteristics reserved for marking wrecks.

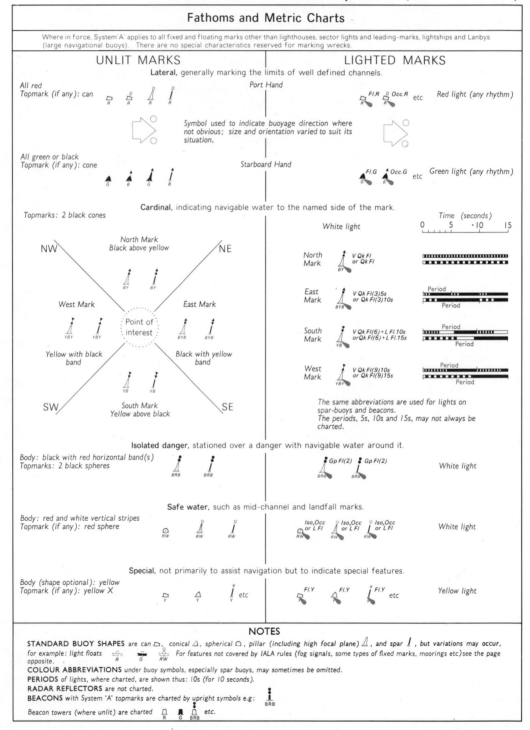

UNLIT MARKS

LIGHTED MARKS

Lateral, generally marking the limits of well defined channels.

Port Hand

All red
Topmark (if any): can

FI.R Occ.R etc — Red light (any rhythm)

Symbol used to indicate buoyage direction where not obvious; size and orientation varied to suit its situation.

Starboard Hand

All green or black
Topmark (if any): cone

FI.G Occ.G etc — Green light (any rhythm)

Cardinal, indicating navigable water to the named side of the mark.

White light

Time (seconds)
0   5   ·10   15

NW

North Mark
Black above yellow

NE

West Mark

Point of interest

East Mark

Yellow with black band

Black with yellow band

SW

South Mark
Yellow above black

SE

Topmarks: 2 black cones

North Mark — *V Qk FI or Qk FI*

East Mark — *V Qk FI(3)5s or Qk FI(3)10s* — Period / Period

South Mark — *V Qk FI(6)+L FI.10s or Qk FI(6)+L FI.15s* — Period / Period

West Mark — *V Qk FI(9)10s or Qk FI(9)15s* — Period / Period

The same abbreviations are used for lights on spar-buoys and beacons.
The periods, 5s, 10s and 15s, may not always be charted.

Isolated danger, stationed over a danger with navigable water around it.

Body: black with red horizontal band(s)
Topmarks: 2 black spheres

Gp FI(2) Gp FI(2) — White light

Safe water, such as mid-channel and landfall marks.

Body: red and white vertical stripes
Topmark (if any): red sphere

Iso,Occ or L FI   Iso,Occ or L FI   Iso,Occ or L FI — White light

Special, not primarily to assist navigation but to indicate special features.

Body (shape optional): yellow
Topmark (if any): yellow X

FI.Y   FI.Y   FI.Y etc — Yellow light

NOTES

STANDARD BUOY SHAPES are can ⬜, conical △, spherical ◯, pillar (including high focal plane) ⬟, and spar ⌶, but variations may occur, for example: light floats ⌁ ⌁ For features not covered by IALA rules (fog signals, some types of fixed marks, moorings etc) see the page opposite.

COLOUR ABBREVIATIONS under buoy symbols, especially spar buoys, may sometimes be omitted.

PERIODS of lights, where charted, are shown thus: 10s (for 10 seconds).

RADAR REFLECTORS are not charted.

BEACONS with System 'A' topmarks are charted by upright symbols e.g:

Beacon towers (where unlit) are charted ⬜ ⬛ ⬟ etc.

Note: On a chart the details reproduced here in blue would appear in magenta.

6 Lightships and light buoys may heel in a sea and not be visible over the stipulated distance.

7 In principle, a helmsman should never have a coloured light dead ahead unless he has been assured by the Sailing Directions that this is correct. As a rule, coloured lights mark an obstacle of some sort.

Buoys and beacons

Navigation marks and landmarks are of the greatest assistance to the sailor when navigating during the day. They are marked on charts and enable him to fix the boat's position. Three categories can be basically distinguished.

1 Landmarks, natural and man made, such as mountains and headlands, large solitary trees, church spires, factory chimneys, radio masts, etc.

2 Fixed navigation marks, such as lighthouses, beacons, stakes.

3 Navigation marks afloat, such as buoys and lightships.

Buoys

In most parts of the world buoys come in a number of basic shapes, the most important ones being can, conical or nun, spar, spherical and

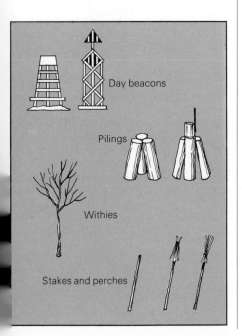

Day beacons

Pilings

Withies

Stakes and perches

various variations. The major colours are black, red, white, yellow and green and combinations of these colours, usually in the form of stripes.

Unfortunately, this is where any effort at generalization has to end, because there is, so far, no uniform buoyage system for the whole world, nor for the western world, nor even for the English-speaking part of the world. In fact, in one respect the rules concerning lateral buoyage in the United States are completely reversed by comparison with those in force in the United Kingdom and other European countries. In the United States red buoys and lights mark starboard, on the other side of the Atlantic they mark port!

However, a uniform buoyage system, known as the IALA Buoyage System 'A', is being introduced to UK and adjacent European waters as well as Australian and New Zealand waters and will be extensively implemented by the end of 1981. This new system provides five types of marks which may be used in any combination.

1 **Lateral marks.** They mark the course to be followed, the rule being red can or spar buoy to port, green conical or spar buoy to starboard. In rivers and estuaries this applies coming from seaward. Elsewhere along the coast the rule is in conjunction with the Conventional Buoyage Direction, which generally means 'when following the main flood stream'.

2 **Cardinal marks.** These are pillar or spar shaped, black and yellow. They are used in conjunction with compass 'sectors' grouped round the obstacle. Four different colour patterns and topmarks indicate in which sector a buoy stands and where navigable water is to be found. A north-sector buoy, for example, indicates that clear water is to the north of it.

3 **Isolated danger marks.** They are pillar or spar shaped, black with red bands. They are used to mark an isolated hazard which has navigable water all round it.

4 **Safe water marks.** They are spherical, pillar, or spar shaped, with red and white vertical stripes. They indicate that there is navigable water all round the mark. They are used mainly as mid-channel marks or in

place of cardinal or lateral marks to mark safe landfall.

5 **Special marks.** They are yellow and of optional shape. They are not primarily intended to assist navigation but indicate special areas of features, for example spoil grounds, military exercise zones or recreation zones.

The United States Coast Guard Buoyage System can be summarized as follows. On entering a channel from seaward, buoys on the starboard side are red, nun or spar shaped, with even numbers. Buoys on the port side are black, can or spar shaped, with odd numbers. Lights on buoys on the starboard side of the channel are red or white, on the port side white or green. Instead of lights, reflective tape of the appropriate colour is often used. Mid-channel buoys are can, nun or spar shaped without shape significance, and have black and white vertical stripes. Obstruction and Junction buoys are green or have red and black horizontal bands. Where the preferred channel is to port, the buoy is spar or nun shaped with a red band uppermost. Where the preferred channel is to starboard, the buoy is spar or can shaped with a black band uppermost. Special buoys that have no lateral significance and which are spar shaped are: orange and white horizontal bands = special purpose; yellow = quarantine anchorage; white = anchorage; white with black horizontal band = fish net; white with green horizontal band = dredging.

Piloting

An essential part of navigation is the determination of the ship's position. This is done by reference to a grid systems, which is, of course, the universally accepted system of parallels of latitude and meridians of longitude. Each meridian is half a great circle around the earth passing through both poles. The meridian that passes through Greenwich has been designated 0°. Both eastward and westward of it, meridians are numbered up to 180°, so that altogether they encompass 360°. The 180th meridian is the Date Line, subject to some small modifications to keep islands in the same group on the same side of the meridian. When crossing the Date Line from east to west, a day is lost, and the date must be advanced one day. When crossing it from west to east, a day is gained and the date must be retarded by one day.

Cutting the meridians at right angles are the parallels of latitude. The parallel mid way between the two poles is the Equator, which is a Great Circle, i.e. it passes through the centre of the earth, and is numbered latitude 0°. On either side of it, towards the poles, the parallels of latitude follow each other at equal distances in ever decreasing Small Circles, i.e. they do not pass through the centre of the earth. They are numbered 0° to 90° on either side of the Equator. 90°N is the North Pole, 90°S is the South Pole.

Every spot on earth can be precisely fixed by latitude and longitude. The geographical longitude of a place is that of the meridian which passes through it, in other words it is the angle between the local meridian and the Greenwich meridian. The geographical latitude of the place is its distance, on the local meridian,

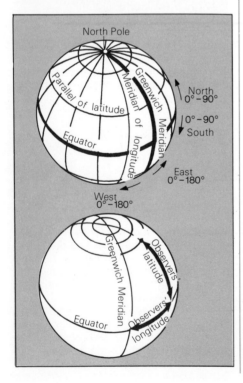

from the Equator. Geographical position is expressed in this way.

For example: Lat. 54° 17′N
                       Long. 10° 19′E

Longitude is marked along the upper and lower chart margins, latitude along the side margins. Each degree (°) of arc is subdivided into 60 minutes (′) of arc, each minute into 60 seconds (″) of arc. In practice, however, seconds are not used but instead decimals of minute, for example 50° 17.5 N instead of 50°17′30″N.

The use of charts, dividers and parallel rules

With the help of a chart, parallel rules and dividers many basic navigational problems can be solved.

1 Determining the geographical position of a given point on the chart.
2 Plotting a point on the chart whose geographical latitude and longitude are known.
3 Plotting the true course from A to B.
4 Plotting a compass course steered from A.
5 Plotting bearings and position lines.
6 Measuring and laying off distances.

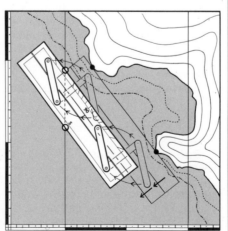

1 Determining the geographical position of a given point

A perpendicular is dropped from the given point on to the upper or lower chart margin and longitude can be read off where it cuts the scale. Another perpendicular is then dropped from the point on to one of the side margins, and latitude can be read off where it cuts that scale. If the point given is near the edges of the chart, a set-square can be used for this purpose. If the point given is too far removed from the edges, two set-squares or parallel rules have to be used. The job can be done equally well with dividers, by measuring the distance of the point from the nearest parallel and the nearest meridian and transferring the distances to the latitude and longitude scales respectively.

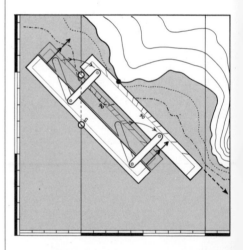

2 Plotting a point on the chart whose geographical position is known

Latitude is found on one of the side scales and the perpendicular raised on it. Longitude is found along the top or bottom scale and the perpendicular raised on it. The intersection of the two perpendiculars is the point in question. Alternatively, the given latitude is laid off with dividers on the nearest meridian and a parallel drawn on the chart. On this parallel the longitude is laid off from the same meridian.

3 Plotting the true course from A to B

The top edge of the parallel rules is

placed along the line AB. If the rules are Captain Field's pattern they are then moved, if possible in one step, until the index mark on the lower

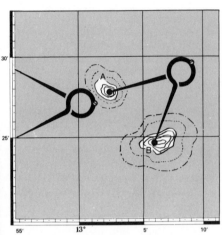

edge is on a meridian. With the index mark held in place, the rules are closed and the bearing read off along the top edge where the meridian cuts the protractor scale. Two sets of figures, 180° apart, are marked in the protractor scale, one being the course, the other being the reciprocal course, BA. Care has to be taken to read the correct one.

If the rules do not incorporate a protractor, the course is measured by stepping the rules across the chart to where a compass rose is printed on it and placing one edge through the centre of the compass rose.

4 Plotting a compass course steered

If a known compass course is steered from point A it can be established where this course will take the yacht. After the compass course has been turned into a true course by applying deviaion and variation (see Correcting the Course, p.269) the parallel rules are so aligned on the chart that the index mark on the bottom edge and the bearing of the true course along the top edge are on the same meridian. If, at the same time, the top edge passes through point A, that line is the course from A. Or, if the rules are simple ones, they are so placed on the (true) compass rose printed on the chart that one edge passes through the centre and the course bearing. The rules are then stepped

across the chart until one edge passes through point A, when a course line can be drawn.

5 Plotting bearings and position lines

Bearings are plotted in the same way as described under 4 above. Say the bearing is 138°, the parallel rules are lined up with the nearest meridian passing through the index mark and through 138°. It is then stepped across until one edge passes through the point of which the bearing was taken. A line drawn along that rule edge is the position line, (see Fix by Bearings, p.273).

6 Measuring and laying off distances

Since one nautical mile on the chart equals one minute of latitude, distances can be taken off the chart with dividers and measured on the latitude scale along the side margins (see The Chart, p.251). Similarly, distances taken off the side margins with dividers can be plotted on the chart. For example, if 8 knots are logged during an hour's sailing on a certain known course, the course is plotted first, as explained above, and then 8 miles laid off along that course to give the dead reckoning position. More will be said about this later.

Hints for chart work

1 Never use ink or ballpoint pen for chartwork. Use a soft, well-sharpened pencil.
2 All notes and lines drawn on the chart must be easily erased.
3 Dividers should be held at a slight angle and not allowed to pierce a hole in the chart.
4 Charts should be placed on a completely level surface and perferably be weighed down with a chart weight to prevent either chart or parallel rules becoming displaced during chart work.
5 Charts must never be folded, because the paper gets worn along folds and difficult to work on. They should not be rolled, either. Ideally, they should be stowed flat.
6 All entries made on a chart during a previous passage must be removed before the chart is used for another trip. At the same time (and well before departure date) it

is advisable to check whether the chart is still up to date or needs correcting.
7 Charts must not get wet or damp. If a chart is used in the cockpit, it is a good idea to put it into a large plastic wallet, which can easily be made at home.

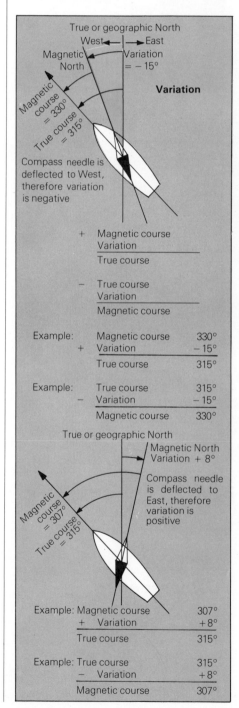

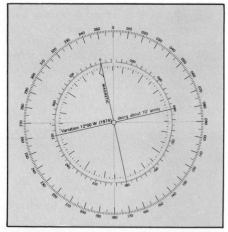

Compass rose as it is printed on Admiralty charts.

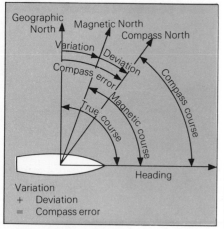

The navigator deals with three different Norths:
1. *True or geographic North, which is the direction of the meridians.*
2. *Magnetic North, which is the North direction determined by the earth's magnetic field. This is the North a compass shows which is free from deviation.*
3. *Compass North, which is the North direction indicated by the steering compass.*

Compass error

Two phenomena affect the ship's magnetic compass: variation and deviation. Both together are termed compass error.

Variation

The needle of the ship's magnetic steering compass aligns itself along the earth's magnetic field, the poles of which do not coincide with the earth's geographic poles. Therefore, the compass needle points to magnetic north, which is not identical with geographic or true north as indicated by the meridians on the chart. Hence two kinds of north are being dealt with: north on the chart = geographic or true north, and north as indicated by the compass = magnetic north. The angle between the two is called variation. Variation is not the same everywhere on the earth's surface, nor does it stay the same in a given place. Annual variation for a given area at a given time, plus the amount by which it increases or decreases annually, is indicated on the compass rose printed on the chart for that area. Variation can be westerly or easterly depending on whether magnetic north is to the west or the east of true north respectively. Westerly variation gets a minus prefix (−), easterly variation a plus prefix (+). It follows that a compass course steered has to be corrected for variation before it can be plotted as a true course on the chart. Similarly a course plotted on the chart as a true course must have variation applied to it before it can be steered as a magnetic course. The angle between the boat's centreline (or 'heading') and true north is the true course. The angle between the boat's heading and magnetic north is the magnetic course.

It should be said here that many sailors do not bother to convert bearings and courses to true but follow the practice of working in magnetic throughout, using the innner, magnetic rose printed on the chart. This method has obvious advantages, but it also has one or two drawbacks. Firstly, the magnetic rose becomes out of date, since variation changes constantly and charts are frequently not reprinted for several years. Secondly, parallel rules of Captain Field's pattern, which are widely favoured for their accuracy, cannot be used with this method because they have to be aligned to true north. Lastly, the direction of tidal currents and bearings printed on charts are always given in true, and this may lead to confusion. Nevertheless, although purists and navigation instructors will always insist on the need for doing chartwork in true, the practice of working in magnetic is well established and considered preferable by many sailors. However, for the purposes of this chapter, we have adhered to the text book method.

Deviation

While variation is a compass error caused by the earth's magnetic field, deviation is an error which is caused by the magnetism of the boat itself i.e. in the large masses of iron such as the keel and the engine, fittings and gear made of ferrous metals and electrical apparatus. It results in the compass needle not pointing to magnetic north, but to compass north. If compass north is west of magnetic north, deviation is negative (−), if it is east of magnetic north, deviation is

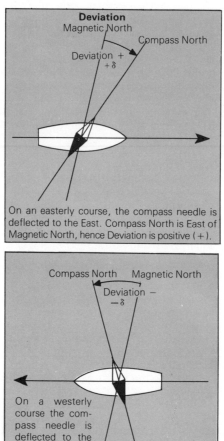

Deviation

On an easterly course, the compass needle is deflected to the East. Compass North is East of Magnetic North, hence Deviation is positive (+).

On a westerly course the compass needle is deflected to the West. Compass North is West of Magnetic North, hence Deviation is negative (−).

positive (+). While variation is the same for every boat in a given area at a given time and does not change with the course of the boat, deviation changes with the heading and differs from boat to boat, since the layout of magnetic material is different on every boat. Thus, if two boats are sailing close to each other on the same heading, they both have to allow for the same variation. Both are dealing with the same true course and the same magnetic course. But since their compasses are subject to different deviation influences, they register different compass courses.

How is deviation recorded? It involves drawing up a deviation table, or having one drawn up by an expert, while 'swinging' the boat through 360° (while moored or anchored) and taking a compass bearing of an object on different headings, say every 10°. The deviation table is based on the comparison of a known magnetic bearing taken from the chart with a compass bearing of the same object, taken on board with the steering

compass. The object can be a charted landmark, while the boat is anchored in a known position or made fast to a fixed beacon, or it can be two objects in line, i.e. a transit. As the boat is swung, the compass readings may be affected by an error which is caused by the compass card not returning to its rest position after each 10° turn. This can be almost completely eliminated by repeating the whole procedure of swinging in the opposite direction and taking the mean of each pair of readings. If deviation on most headings exceeds 4-5°, it is advisable to draw up two deviation tables, or at least two columns, one for compass heading and one for magnetic heading. The first is used when converting compass course to true course, the second when converting true course to compass course.

A deviation table can also be drawn up with the help of a hand-bearing compass, which can be used in a position where it is assumed not to be affected by deviation. This method is

useful in boats where the steering compass is below the cockpit coaming and cannot therefore be used itself for taking bearings. The hand-bearing compass is installed in an elevated, unobscured position aft of the mast on the centreline of the boat and as far as possible removed from any magnetic material and electrical instruments. One good place has been found to be in the middle between the two backstays (if they are non-magnetic stainless steel!) at eye-level of someone standing on the after deck, and aligned with the centre of the mast. The procedure requires three persons. One stands by the hand-bearing compass, one by the steering compass and one at the bow with an oar. The person at the bow swings the boat round very slowly, steadying it every 10°, while the two people at the compasses compare the boat's heading as read off their respective compasses.

A deviation table should be checked for accuracy from time to time, especially in a steel yacht and certainly after structural alterations and changes to equipment and instrumentation have been carried out. If you cannot or don't want to draw up your own deviation table by the methods described, you can employ a qualified compass adjuster to do it for you.

Compensating a compass
If deviation is excessive, the compass has to be compensated, which means corrected. In steel yachts this is always necessary. It involves the placing of compensating magnets in certain positions relative to the compass and is a very skilled job which is best left to a trained compass adjuster. At the time the compass is adjusted all gear normally carried should be aboard and everything stowed in its sea-going position. For any error remaining after compensation, a deviation table has to be drawn up in the normal way.

Correcting the course

Because of variation and deviation, which together account for compass error, the compass course, i.e. the course steered by the compass, must

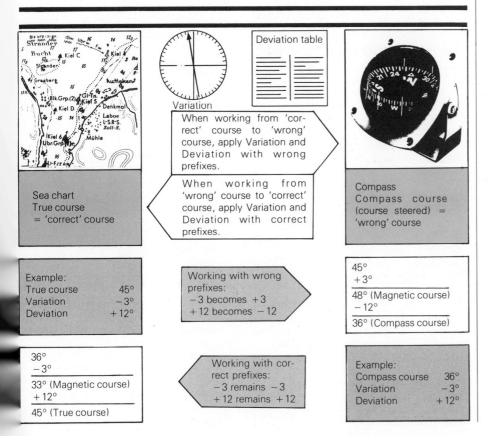

be converted to a true course before it can be plotted on the chart. Similarly, a true course as drawn on a chart must be converted to a compass course before it can be steered. To do this, variation and deviation are either added or subtracted depending on whether they are east or west and on whether you are working from true to compass, or from compass to true.

Remembering that the 'correct' prefixes are west = minus (−) and east = plus (+), there are numerous aids to memory which help the navigator to apply compass error correctly. For example, the *true* course could be called the *correct* course, the *compass* course the *wrong* course. Therefore, when converting from *wrong* course to *correct* course, apply error with the *correct* prefixes. When converting from *correct* course to *wrong* course, apply error with the *wrong* prefixes.

Another method, illustrated by the scheme below can be used in which variation and deviation are always entered with the 'correct' prefixes.

When converting from compass to true, work downwards with an overall positive prefix. When converting from true to compass, work upwards with an overall negative prefix.

In doing so, the mathematical rule concerning two prefixes has to be obeyed: (+) and (+) = (+) (+) and (−) = (−), (−) and (−) = (+). Thus, when −3° is applied downwards, with a (+) prefix, it stays −3°, when it is applied upwards with a (−) prefix, it becomes +3°.

For example:

Compass Course	36°C
Deviation	+12°
Magnetic Course	48° M
Variation	−3°
True Course	45°

+|−

At the same time, the mnemonic **C**an **D**ead **M**en **V**ote **T**wice suggests in which order deviation and variation are applied.

Hints for course correction

1 To simplify matters, variation and deviation can be combined to give one figure for compass error. Using the same figures as before, the calculation then looks as follows.

Deviation	+12°
Variation	−3°
Compass Error	+9°
Compass Course	36°C
Error	+9°
True Course	45°

+|−

2 When sailing on a northerly course, near 0° (= 360°), it can happen that the figure for error exceeds that for course. For example, compass course 6°, error −9°. Since 9 cannot be subtracted from 6, the compass course is called 366°, hence 366° − 9° = 357°. On the other hand, if the end figure exceeds 360°, 360° has to be subtracted: 357° + 9° = 366°, 366° − 360° = 6°.

Exercises for course correction

1 Compass course 48°, variation −4°, deviation +7°. What is the true course?
2 True course 357°, variation −5°, deviation −8°. What is the compass course?
Answer: 1) 51° 2) 10°

Leeway and tidal current

After the application of deviation and variation, course correction is complete only if the boat suffers no leeway and there is no current. In practice, however, both influences are frequently present, and if they are, they must be included in the course correction.

Leeway

Leeway, which is caused by the sideways component of the wind, is the amount by which the boat sideslips, especially when sailing on the wind. It is normally something between 3° and 6°. Leeway can be recognized as the angle between the boat's heading and the direction of the wake. In other words, it is the difference between the direction in which the boat is pointing, which is the course steered, and the direction in which it is actually moving, which is the course made good. If leeway is noticed, it must be allowed for in the course correction by applying the following rule.

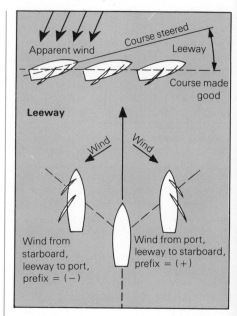

Leeway

Wind from port, leeway to starboard = prefix (+)
Wind from starboard, leeway to port = prefix (−)

Some examples

1 A yacht is steering a compass course of 36°, wind NW, leeway approximately 4°. Which is the course made good if deviation is +12°, variation −3°?

Answer

Compass course	36°
Deviation	+12°
Magnetic course	48°M
Variation	−3°
True course	45°
Leeway to starboard	+4°
Course made good (true)	49°

+

2 The course is to be made good as plotted on the chart is 130°, wind S. The navigator wants to allow for an expected leeway of 6°. Which compass course must he steer if variation is +7°, deviation −5°?

This calculation goes from true to compass, which is in the opposite direction to the first example! The layout is the same.

Answer

Compass course	134°C
Deviation	−5°
Magnetic course	129°M
Variation	+7°
True course	136°

−

Leeway to port   −6° ↓−
Course made good (true)   130° ↓

Tidal current

Since tidal currents are a typical feature of a great many sea areas, all the relevant data are collected in Tide Tables,. Tidal Current Charts, Current Tables and Sailing Directions. The speed of a tidal current is measured in knots (which is the speed per hour). If the current is fair (with the boat), it has to be added to the yacht's own speed, if it is foul (against the boat), it has to be deducted from the yacht's own speed. If it is oblique to the yacht's heading, it will carry her sideways in the direction the current is setting. Once again we have to distinguish between course through the water and course made good, the latter being the actual track over the ground under the influence of the current.

It is important to remember that whereas wind direction is named by the direction *from* which the wind blows, tidal current direction, known as 'set', is named the opposite way: tidal set is the direction *in* which the current sets.

The influence of tidal current on the yacht's course is calculated graphically by drawing a course triangle. This can be drawn for one hour or several hours, depending on the scale of the chart. If two sides of the triangle are known, the third side can be found. If course and speed through the water and speed and set of tidal current are known, then course and speed made good can be found. If, on the other hand, course and speed through the water and course and speed made good are known, then speed and set of tidal current can be found.

Three basic problems have to be solved

1 The course and speed through the water are known, so are the speed and set of the tidal current. What are the course and speed made good?

Answer
From departure point A lay off the course through the water

and mark off one hour's run to point B. From B lay off the speed and set of the tidal current for one hour, to point C. Draw line AC, which represents course and speed made good.

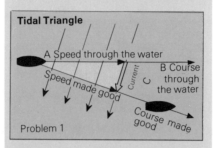

Problem 1

2 The speed and set of the tidal current are known, so are the speed through the water and the point of arrival. Which course through the water has to be steered?

Answer
Draw a line between point of departure A and point of arrival B. This is the course to be made good. From A lay off the speed and set of the tidal current for one hour, to point C. With "iders, lay off from C the boat's known speed through the water. It cuts AB at D. Join C and D, and CD is the course and speed through the water.

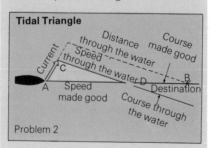

Problem 2

To find the actual compass course to be steered, the course through the water, which is a true course, has to be corrected for variation, deviation and leeway. To find the distance through the water from A to B, line CD is transferred to pass through B and is measured. The estimated time taken to sail from A to B is then calculated as follows:

Time =

$$\frac{\text{Distance through the water}}{\text{Speed through the water}}$$

3 The known quantities are: course through the water, as drawn on the chart, the logged speed through the water, and the yacht's actual (fixed) position, which does not lie on the course-line through the water. How can the speed and set of the tidal current be determined?

Answer
Draw a line from departure point A to actual position B. This is the course made good. Lay off the known course through the water from point A and mark off the distance logged since leaving A, which in this case is in excess of one hour. Point C is the DR position (see the following section on Dead Reckoning), which does not take into account the tidal effect. Join B and C. To find the speed and set of the tidal current, lay off the logged speed through the water (in miles *per hour*)

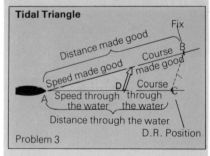

Problem 3

from A to give point D. If line BC is then transferred parallel to pass through D, DE is the speed and set of the tidal current.

Position finding

Dead reckoning

In estimating a yacht's position by dead reckoning, no use is made of landmarks. The DR position is arrived at by allowing only for the boat's true course and speed *through the water* since leaving a given departure point. The DR position is marked on the chart by a small tick across the course

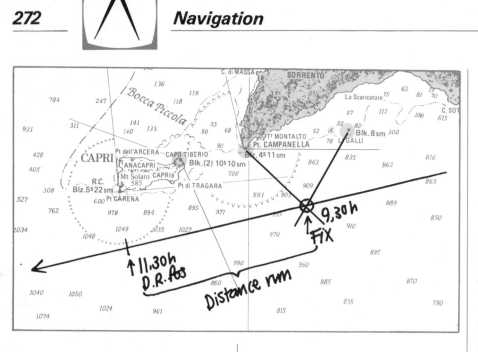

line, with the time written against it. If the estimated influence of tidal current and leeway is applied to this (see the previous section), we get the estimated position (EP). This could be described as the best estimated position made good, allowing for course, speed, current and leeway. It is marked on the chart with a small triangle with a dot inside. The time is written against it, as before. Finally, if the yacht's position can be fixed by observation, the fix is marked on the chart by a circle where the position lines cross. At least two position lines are needed to give a fix.

Position lines in coastal navigation are 'terrestrial position lines'. They are obtained by taking visual bearings of charted objects, by calculating 'distance off', by taking horizontal sextant angles and measuring depth.

Fix by range

If there is a sextant on board, the distance of a charted object ashore can be found by taking a *vertical sex-*

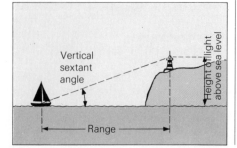

tant angle. Lighthouses are suitable objects, their height being listed in the Lights Lists. The range, which is the distance from the observer, is calculated by the following formula.

Range in naut. miles =
$$\frac{13}{7} \times \frac{\text{Height in metres}}{\text{Vertical sextant angle in minutes}}$$

For example, if the height of a lighthouse is listed as 50 metres and the observed sextant angle is 40', then

Range =
$$\frac{13}{7} \times \frac{50}{40} = 2.3 \text{ nautical miles}$$

The corresponding formula for feet is: Range in naut. miles =
$$0.57 \times \frac{\text{Height in feet}}{\text{Vertical sextant angle in minutes}}$$

For example, if the height of a lighthouse is listed as 164 ft and the measured sextant angle is 40', then

Range =
$$0.57 \times \frac{164}{40} = 2.3 \text{ nautical miles}$$

Lights Lists give the elevation of the centre of the lantern both above the ground and above sea level. Since the base of a lighthouse cannot usually be discerned very clearly, it is recommended to use the elevation above sea level. In tidal waters this is understood to be the High Water Mark, and if exceptional accuracy is required, allowance must be made for this at all other stages of the tide. There are tables for finding distance

off by vertical sextant angles (e.g. Lecky's and similar tables contained in nautical handbooks), in which the answer can be found by inspection and without any calculations whatsoever.

At night, distance off can be determined by observing lights rising and dipping (see p.257). At the moment a charted light just rises above or dips below the horizon, its distance can be found by entering the appropriate table with the known height and the observer's height of eye. This will not yield a straight position line, of course, but a circle with the light as the centre. To get a fix, a second position line must be obtained, for example by taking a bearing of the light. The point of intersection of the two position lines is the yacht's position.

Taking soundings

If there is no other means of getting a fix of a yacht's position, for example in poor visibility and in the absence of radio beacons, the taking of soundings may at least give an approximate position line. This method is only useful where the sea bed is characterized by marked differences of depth. For example, where the bottom is evenly and fairly steeply shelving, even a single sounding may yield a position line, which will be identical with a particular fathom line. If it should subsequently be possible to take a bearing of an object, this will yield a second position line with which to cross the first one and thus obtain a fix.

A single sounding is not usually sufficient, though, and a position line has to be found by a number of successive soundings. While a straight course is steered, soundings are taken at short, regular intervals and noted, together with the time and log reading, on a strip of tracing paper, using the chart scale to measure the distance between soundings. This pattern on tracing paper is then moved around on the chart in the vicinity of the yacht's estimated position until a position is found where the soundings coincide with those on the chart. In tidal waters the soundings taken must first be reduced to Chart Datum.

Fix by horizontal sextant angle

If a sextant is available and two

charted objects are in sight for taking visual bearings, a circular position line can be obtained by measuring the horizontal sextant angle between the two objects as seen from the yacht. The diagram illustrates that the yacht may be anywhere on the arc of the circle, since from any point on the arc the two objects appear under the same angle. To find the centre of the arc, a triangle has to be constructed in which the two objects A and B and the centre M are the corners. The following principles apply.

1 The angle at the centre of a circle is twice the angle α measured on the arc (ie. $2 \times \alpha$).
2 The two angles ß at A and B are equal, and their angle is the difference between angle α and 90°. If angle α is less than 90°, they are $90° - \alpha$ if angle α is greater than 90°, they are $\alpha - 90°$.

Thus, after angle α has been measured with the sextant, its difference to 90° is calculated, which gives angle ß. A and B are joined by a line and angle ß measured on this line at A and B. The intersection of the

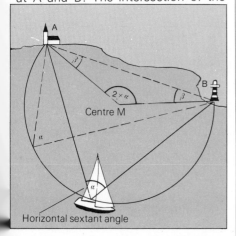

Horizontal sextant angle

two angle radii is the required centre M. With the compasses set at distance MA or MB, an arc is struck with centre at M, which represents the position line.

If three suitable objects offer themselves, then a very precise fix can be obtained by measuring the horizontal angles between A and B, and B and C and proceeding as before. The point of intersection of the two circular position lines is the yacht's position.

Another, and somewhat quicker,

method of obtaining a fix from two horizontal sextant angles is to use a station pointer, which is a three-armed protractor. The measured angles are set on the instrument, which is then positioned on the chart and moved about until the appropriate edges of the three arms pass through the sighted objects. The position can then be marked with a pencil through the centre hole of the station pointer.

Fix by bearings

As discussed earlier in the secton Instruments for Taking Bearings (see p. 251), bearings can be taken with a hand-bearing compass, a steering compass fitted with an azimuth ring, or with a pelorus. Bearings taken with the steering compass are *compass bearings*.

Since compass bearings suffer from deviation and variation, they have to be corrected before they can be plotted on a chart as true bearings. This is done by the same rules that apply to course correction (see p. 269). It is important to remember that deviation depends on the boat's heading, which is the compass course steered.

The following example assumes deviation −2°, variation +3°.

Compass bearing	90°
Deviation	− 2°
Magnetic bearing	88° +
Variation	+ 3°
True bearing	91°

If a pelorus is used, a *relative bearing* is obtained, which means a bearing relative to the boat's heading. It must be converted into a compass bearing

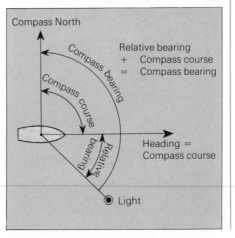

before it can be plotted on the chart: relative bearing + compass course = compass bearing.

In the following example compass course = 80°, relative bearing = 40°, deviation = +4°, variation = −3°.

Compass course	80°C
Relative bearing	40°C
Compass bearing	120°C
Deviation	+ 4° +
Magnetic bearing	124°M
Variation	− 3°
True bearing	121°

If a hand-bearing compass is used for taking bearings, deviation can be ignored as long as the compass is used at a considerable distance from any magnetic material. It is preferable, however, to use it always in the same position and to draw up a deviation table for that position.

The type of fix obtained from bearings depends on the number of suitable objects in sight.

The running fix

This method is used if only one charted object is available of which to take a bearing. As the first bearing is taken, the time and log are noted and the position line obtained is plotted on the chart. After a while, when the bearing of the same object has sufficiently changed, a second bearing is taken and once again the position line is plotted. The course steered, which must be an unaltered course between the two bearings, is then plotted at an estimated distance off the object and the distance run between the two bearings laid off on the course line. The first position line is then transferred, with parallel rules, to pass through the end of the distance run. The intersection of the transferred first position line with the second position line is the fix position at the time the second bearing was taken.

If a second object becomes visible ater the bearing of the first has been taken, and possibly by that time the

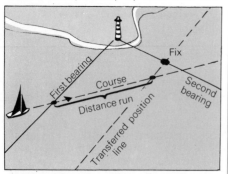

first object is no longer visible, the second object can be used for the second bearing and the first position line transferred to cross it in the normal way.

A variation on the running fix is known as doubling the angle on the bow. Here, the first bearing is taken as before and the angle on the bow, which is the relative bearing to the boat's heading, noted. The second bearing is taken when the angle on the bow is exactly twice that of the first bearing. The distance run between the two bearings is then equal to the boat's distance off the object at the time of the second bearing.

Another variation of the running fix is the four point fix. The first bearing is taken when the object is bearing 4 points, which is 45°, on the bow. The time and log reading are noted. The second bearing is taken when the object is abeam, i.e. is bearing 90° on the bow. Again the time and log are noted and the distance run is calculated. The distance run is then

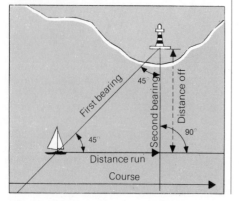

equal to the distance off the object when it is abeam.

Fix by two or more bearings

The two-point fix is the simplest of all fixes. Simultaneous bearings taken of two charted objects produce two position lines. Their point of intersection is the yacht's position. To get an accurate result, the objects should be between 50° and 130° apart. If the

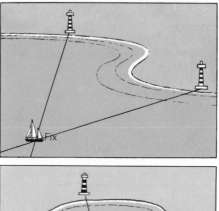

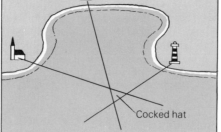

Cocked hat

angle is smaller or larger, the fix is unreliable.

A three-point fix, in which position lines from three bearings are obtained, is to be preferred to a two-point fix for reliability. Three-point fixes frequently come out in a cocked hat, the name given to the triangle of uncertainty which results if the three position lines do not pass through one point. It is normal to assume the yacht's position to be in the centre of the cocked hat. If it is too large, it is advisable to check for an error somewhere. It may be that the bearings were not taken accurately or not accurately plotted, or that the objects were incorrectly identified, or that compass error was wrongly applied.

Fix by transit and bearing

No compass or bearing finder is need-

ed for a transit. At the moment when two clearly visible objects are seen to be in alignment, the yacht must obviously lie on the extension of the line joining them. The objects may be two

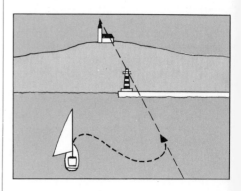

beacons, a lighthouse and a church spire, a chimney and the edge of a headland, and so on. Buoys should never be used for transits since they may have shifted from their charted position.

A transit produces one position line. To get a fix, a second position line must be obtained to cross it by taking a simultaneous bearing of a third object.

Summary of position finding

1 In the absence of any visible charted object the yacht's position can only be estimated by dead reckoning.
2 If one charted object is visible, the following methods can be employed to obtain a fix.
   a) Range (i.e. distance off by vertical sextant angle) + bearing
   b) Soundings and bearing.
   c) Running fix (including doubling the angle on the bow, four point fix).
3 If two charted objects are visible, a fix can be obtained by the following methods.
   a) Two-point fix.
   b) Transit + bearing
   c) Horizontal sextant angle + bearing (or + range)
   d) Two ranges.
4 If three charted objects are visible, a fix can be obtained by the following methods.
   a) Three-point fix
   b) Horizontal sextant angles between three objects.

Tides

Principles

Tides can be described as a vertical movement of the water which causes the rising and lowering of the sea level, as well as a horizontal movement of the water, which creates tidal streams or currents. These movements take place with a regular rhythm.

Tides are a normal phenomenon in many of the world's sea areas. They are caused by gravitational forces between the earth and the moon, and the earth and the sun, the moon's attractive force in this context being the greater. The highest water level in one cycle is called High Water (HW), the lowest Low Water (LW). The stage between LW and HW during which the water rises is the flood, the stage between HW and LW during which the water level falls is the ebb. The difference in height between successive HW and LW is the range. Rise is the difference between the level of any HW and the level of Chart Datum (or Reference Plane).

Ebb and flood together make one tide. If sun and moon are in conjunction and their graviational pull coincides, which is the case at full moon and new moon, tides have their highest rise and lowest fall and are known as Spring Tides. When the moon is in its first or last quarter, tides have their smallest rise and fall and are known as Neap Tides. There is a time lag between full or new moon and the highest Spring Tide, which differs locally and can be anything from one day to three days. The same applies to Neap Tides.

Tideas can be semi-diurnal, mixed or diurnal. Sea areas with semi-diurnal tides, like the Atlantic and European coastal waters, experience two High Waters and two Low Waters in one day, with about 6¼ hours between HW and successive LW, and about 12½ hours between successive High Waters or Low Waters. Both High Waters and both Low Waters are of approximately equal height. The first HW occurs about 50 minutes later each successive day. Sea areas with mixed tides, like large parts of the Australian coast and the Pacific coast of North America, also experience two High Waters and two Low Waters per (lunar) day, but there are marked inequalities between the first High (or Low) Water and the second High (or Low) Water. We therefore have Higher High Water (HHW) and Lower High Water (LHW), Higher Low Water (HLW) and Lower Low Water (LLW). Sea areas with diurnal tides, which are mainly in or just outside the Tropics, experience only one High Water and one Low Water per lunar day, and the range is not usually very large.

Tidal current

Tidal currents are the result of the horizontal movement of the water as caused by the tides. When applied to inshore waters, the inward flow is the flood current, the outward flow is the ebb current. The short time in between, when there is no current, is known as slack water. The change from flood to ebb or vice versa is the turn of the tide. Currents offshore do not necessarily follow this pattern but may have a rotary motion.

Tide tables

Tide tables give the predicted times and heights of High and Low Water for each day of the year for a number of major ports known as Standard Ports or, in the United States, Reference Stations. They also give tabulated information on time and height differences for a large number of Secondary Ports, or Subordinate Stations. For example, Southampton, Portsmouth and Dover are some of the Standard Ports on the south coast of England, while Boston, Newport and Sandy Hook are among the various Reference Stations on the east coast of North America.

As mentioned in the section on Publications (see p. 254), British Admiralty Tide Tables are published in three volumes to cover the whole world, while United States Tide Tables are published by the National Oceanic and Atmospheric Administration (NOAA), also in several volumes, and cover all the coasts of North and South America as well as United States possessions.

Information on tidal currents is found in the Tidal Stream Atlases published by the British Admiralty in 11 volumes covering UK and adjacent European waters, the Tidal Current Tables and Tidal Current Charts published by the NOAA, and similar publications in other countries. *Reed's Nautical Almanac*, of which there is a European and an American East Coast edition, contains both Tide Tables and Tidal Current Charts.

Chart Datum or Plane of Reference

All heights given in Tide Tables refer to Chart Datum, the US equivalent to which is Plane of Reference; they have to be added to the charted depths. Charted depth is the depth of

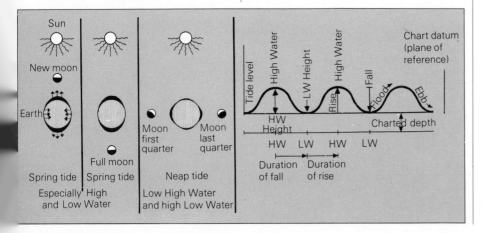

Sun

New moon

Earth

Spring tide — Especially High and Low Water

Full moon

Spring tide

Moon first quarter   Moon last quarter

Neap tide — Low High Water and high Low Water

Tide level — High Water — LW Height — Rise — High Water — Fall — Flood — Ebb — Chart datum (plane of reference)

HW Height — Charted depth

HW   LW   HW   LW

Duration of fall   Duration of rise

water at Chart Datum, or below the Plane of Reference, as printed on the chart. Height of tide is the amount of water *above* Chart Datum or Plane of Reference. The actual *depth of water* at any time is made up of Charted Depth + Height of Tide. As explained in the section on charts (see p.253) the Plane of Reference, or Chart Datum, is not the same for all charts nor for all parts of the world. The notes on the chart in use should always be carefully read.

Effect of weather

The predicted heights of tide as listed in the Tide Tables do not take into account the influence of weather conditions. Strong winds and low barometric pressure can have a marked influence on predicted heights and times, especially during Spring Tides.

Spring and neap tide lag

The days of the month during which Spring or Neap Tides will occur can be established by consulting the Phases of the Moon table in the Nautical Almanac. In theory, Spring Tides occur from two days before to two days after Full or New Moon, Neap Tides occur from two days before to two days after the first and last quarter. In practice, however, there is a time lag between the actual moon phase and the corresponding tide phase of anything between one day and three days, depending on location.

Basic tide problems

When navigating in tidal waters, the following basic questions confront the navigator.
- What are the times of HW and LW for a Standard Port (Reference Station) or Secondary Port (Subordinate Station)?
- What are the heights of HW and LW?
- What is the depth of water at a given spot at a particular time between HW and LW?
- How much water is there under the keel at LW at a given place?
- What is the direction and speed of the tidal stream at a given time and place?

Examples

1 What are the times and heights of HW and LW at Portsmouth on 17 September 1974?

Answer by reference to the table for Standard Port Portsmouth (see illustration) not forgetting to add 1 hour for British summer-time.

First HW	0030 hrs	4.8 m
Second HW	1301 hrs	5.0 m
First LW	0556 hrs	0.4 m
Second LW	1817 hrs	0.5 m

2 What are the times and heights of first LW and second HW at Calshot Castle on 3 September 1974?

Answer by reference to Standard Port Portsmouth, and Table of Tidal Differences on Portsmouth (see illustration), Calshot Castle being a Secondary Port. Add 1 hour for

B.S.T.

First LW Portsmouth	0616 hrs	0.9 m
Difference Calshot Castle	0010 hrs	0.0 m
First LW Calshot Castle	0606 hrs	0.9 m
Second HW Portsmouth	1318 hrs	4.5 m
Difference Calshot Castle	+0000 hrs	0.3 m
Second HW Calshot Castle	1318 hrs	4.2 m

3 A yacht reaches Lymington late in the afternoon on 4 September 1974 and wants to anchor in a spot where, according to the chart, there are 2 m of water at Chart Datum. The yacht draws 1.6 m. Can she anchor here or will she go aground at Low Water?

Answer
First, the height of tide at next LW has to be established and then the depth of water calculated by the formula: Depth of Water = Height of Tide + Charted Depth. Add 1 hour for B.S.T.

Second LW Portsmouth 1906 hrs	0.9 m
Difference for Lymington Springs)	−0.1 m
Second LW Lymington	0.8 m

Depth of water = 2 m + 0.8 m = 2.8 m. The yacht can anchor at the chosen spot without drying out at LW.

4 On 4 September 1974 at about 1600 hrs a yacht anchors off Portsmouth after having sounded 7 m. Can she anchor in this spot if her draft is 1.5 m?

This problem can be solved by the Admiralty method of finding the height of tide at times between high and low water, which involves the use of a tidal curve. (See page 278)

Answer
First find the range of the day (= HW − LW): 4.5m − 09m = 3.6m. Enter the Tidal Curve for Portsmouth with time after HW = 2 hrs (BW being at 1351 hrs), along the horizontal scale, and where it meets the curve, in this case the

PHASES OF THE MOON											
New Moon			**First Quarter**			**Full Moon**			**Last Quarter**		
d	h	m	d	h	m	d	h	m	d	h	m
									Jan. 4	19	04
Jan. 12	10	20	Jan. 20	15	14	Jan. 27	15	09	Feb. 3	06	23
Feb. 11	05	17	Feb. 19	07	39	Feb. 26	01	15	Mar. 4	20	20
Mar. 12	23	47	Mar. 20	20	05	Mar. 27	10	36	Apr. 3	12	25
Apr. 11	16	39	Apr. 19	04	41	Apr. 25	19	55	May 3	05	44
May 11	07	05	May 18	10	29	May 25	05	51	June 1	23	23
June 9	18	49	June 16	14	58	June 23	16	54	July 1	16	37
July 9	04	10	July 15	19	47	July 23	05	28	July 31	08	48
Aug. 7	11	57	Aug. 14	02	24	Aug. 21	19	48	Aug. 29	23	20
Sept. 5	19	19	Sept. 12	11	59	Sept. 20	11	50	Sept. 28	11	46
Oct. 5	03	23	Oct. 12	01	15	Oct. 20	05	06	Oct. 27	22	07
Nov. 3	13	05	Nov. 10	18	21	Nov. 18	22	28	Nov. 26	06	52
Dec. 3	00	50	Dec. 10	14	39	Dec. 18	14	40	Dec. 25	14	52

ENGLAND, SOUTH COAST — PORTSMOUTH
Lat. 50° 48′ N. Long. 1° 07′ W.

20

TIME ZONE: G.M.T.   TIMES AND HEIGHTS OF HIGH AND LOW WATERS   YEAR 1974

JULY

Time	m	Ft.		Time	m	Ft.
1 M 0156	1·4	4·5	16 Tu	0055	1·5	5·0
0908	4·1	13·4		0803	4·0	13·1
1421	1·5	4·8		1327	1·4	4·5
2123	4·2	13·9		2031	4·2	13·9
2 Tu 0248	1·2	4·0	17 W	0201	1·2	4·1
0959	4·2	13·9		0910	4·2	13·9
1509	1·4	4·5		1430	1·2	4·0
2209	4·3	14·2		2133	4·5	14·6
3 W 0334	1·1	3·7	18 Th	0300	1·0	3·2
1045	4·3	14·2		1009	4·5	14·7
1552	1·3	4·2		1526	1·0	3·5
2252	4·4	14·4		2230	4·6	15·1
4 Th 0415	1·0	3·3	19 F	0353	0·7	2·4
1126	4·4	14·4		1103	4·7	15·4
1632	1·2	3·8		1618	0·8	2·6
2331	4·4	14·4		2321	4·7	15·5

AUGUST

Time	m	Ft.		Time	m	Ft.
1 Th 0324	1·3	4·2	16 F	0248	1·0	3·2
1034	4·2	13·9		0956	4·5	14·7
1541	1·3	4·1		1515	1·0	3·2
2239	4·4	14·1		2216	4·6	15·1
2 F 0403	1·1	3·7	17 Sa	0342	0·7	2·2
1111	4·4	14·3		1049	4·8	15·6
1618	1·2	3·8		1606	0·7	2·4
2316	4·4	14·3		2305	4·8	15·6
3 Sa 0437	1·0	3·2	18 Su	0430	0·5	1·5
1144	4·4	14·4		1137	4·9	16·1
1652	1·0	3·5		1652	0·6	2·0
2348	4·3	14·2		2352	4·8	15·9
4 Su 0509	0·9	3·0	19 M	0515	0·3	1·1
1215	4·4	14·5		1224	5·0	16·3
1726	1·0	3·3		1737	0·6	1·9

SEPTEMBER

Time	m	Ft.		Time	m	Ft.
1 Su 0415	1·0	3·3	16 M	0411	0·4	1·4
1118	4·5	14·6		1116	5·0	16·3
1630	1·0	3·4		1633	0·6	1·9
2324	4·4	14·4		2330	4·8	15·9
2 M 0445	0·9	3·0	17 Tu	0456	0·4	1·3
1147	4·5	14·8		1201	5·0	16·4
1702	1·0	3·3		1717	0·5	1·8
2354	4·4	14·4				
3 Tu 0516	0·9	2·8	18 W	0015	4·9	16·1
1218	4·5	14·8		0539	0·5	1·5
1734	0·9	3·1		1245	5·0	16·4
				1759	0·6	2·0
4 W 0025	4·4	14·4	19 Th	0059	4·9	16·0
0548	0·8	2·6		0620	0·6	2·0
1251	4·4	14·7		1326	4·9	16·2
1806	0·9	2·9		1839	0·7	2·4

---

350   **ENGLAND, SOUTH COAST**

No.	PLACE	Lat. N.	Long. W.	High Water at 0000 and 1200	High Water at 0600 and 1800	Low Water at 0500 and 1700	Low Water at 1100 and 2300	MHWS	MHWN	MLWN	MLWS
	STANDARD PORT										
65	PORTSMOUTH	(see page 17)						15·4	12·5	5·8	2·0
	SECONDARY PORTS			TIME DIFFERENCES (Zone G.M.T.)				HEIGHT DIFFERENCES			
35	Swanage*	50 37	1 57	−0250 / +0110	−0530§ / +0105	−0105	−0105	−9·0 / −10·6	−7·3 / −7·9	−2·3	−0·9
36	Poole (Entrance)*	50 40	1 56	−0240 / +0115	−0510§ / +0105	−0100	−0030	−8·8 / −10·5	−7·2 / −7·9	−2·3	−0·9
36a	Poole (Bridge)*	50 43	1 59	−0215 / +0210	−0430§ / +0130	−0015	0000	−8·1 / −9·9	−6·5 / −7·5	−2·0	−0·6
37	Bournemouth*	50 43	1 52	−0240 / +0135	−0500§ / +0055	−0050	−0030	−8·7 / −10·3	−7·1 / −7·7	−2·4	−0·9
38	Christchurch**	50 43	1 45	−0230 / +0050	+0030	−0035	−0035	−9·4 / −10·6	−7·9	−3·7	−0·8
39	Hurst Point†	50 42	1 33	−0115 / +0045	−0005	−0030	−0025	−6·4 / −7·1	−4·9	−1·6	−0·4
40	Lymington†	50 46	1 32	−0055 / +0045	+0005	−0020	−0020	−5·4 / −6·0	−4·1	−1·4	−0·4
41	Solent Bank†	50 44	1 26	−0100 / +0045	0000	−0015	−0020	−4·2 / −4·5	−3·3	−1·0	−0·4
	Isle of Wight										
45	Yarmouth†	50 42	1 30	−0105 / +0050	+0005	−0025	−0030	−5·3 / −6·1	−4·2	−1·2	−0·1
45	Totland Bay*	50 41	1 33	−0130 / +0105	−0045 / +0045	−0040	−0040	−6·5 / −7·2	−4·9 / −5·0	−1·6	−0·2
48	Freshwater*	50 40	1 31	−0205 / +0040	+0015	−0050	−0055	−6·9 / −7·1	−5·1	−1·7	−0·3
51	Ventnor	50 36	1 12	−0025	−0030	−0025	−0030	−2·5	−1·9	−0·4	+0·5
53	Sandown	50 39	1 09	0000	+0005	+0010	+0025	−2·0	−1·6	−0·6	0·0
54	Brading	50 42	1 06	−0010	+0005	+0020	0000	−5·3	−4·9	−4·5	−2·1
58	Ryde	50 44	1 07	−0010	+0010	−0005	−0010	−0·5	−0·3	+0·2	+0·5
	Medina River										
60	Cowes†	50 46	1 18	−0015	+0015	0000	−0020	−1·5	−1·1	−0·2	−0·1
60a	Folly Inn	50 44	1 17	◊	◊	◊	◊	−1·8	−1·2	−0·1	+0·5
60b	Newport	50 42	1 17	◊	◊	◊	◊	−1·8	−1·2	+0·4	+4·2
61	Calshot Castle†	50 49	1 18	0000	+0020	−0010	−0020	−0·9	−0·5	+0·1	+0·1
62	SOUTHAMPTON‡	50 54	1 24	STANDARD PORT				See Table V			
64	Lee-on-Solent†	50 48	1 12	+0005	−0005	−0010	−0015	−0·5	−0·3	+0·3	+0·6

CAUTION. Owing to the complicated variations in the tide between Portland and Portsmouth, the time and height differences on this page will only give approximate predictions. A more accurate representation of the tidal curves at these places can be obtained from a plot of hourly heights, using Table IIIa (p. xxii).
* From Swanage to Christchurch and from Totland Bay to Freshwater double high waters occur except at neaps; at neaps the time differences marked § may represent only the beginning of a "stand" or a point at which the rate of rise decreases noticeably.
** Tidal Levels at Christchurch are for a position inside the bar; outside the bar the tide falls about 2 ft. lower at Springs.
† Within the Western Solent double high waters may occur at or near springs; on other occasions there is a stand which lasts about 2 hours. Where two high water time differences are given these may, therefore, represent the *beginning* and *end* of the stand; where only one H.W. time difference is given, this represents approximately the *middle* of the stand.
‡ Meteorological effects at SOUTHAMPTON. With a N.E. gale and a high barometer, tidal heights may be as much as TWO FEET less than predictions.
◊ No data.

---

curve for Springs, read the factor off the vertical scale: 0.88. Multiply the range of the day by the factor: 3.6 × 0.88 = 3.17. This is the height of tide in metres above LW. Add to this the LW height: 3.17 + 0.9 = 4.07 m. This is the height of tide, round it up to 4.1 m. Now apply the formula:

Charted Depth = Depth of Water − Height of Tide

= 7m − 4.1 m = 2.9 m

This means that the yacht, which draws 1.5 m, can anchor in this spot.

If working without the help of a Tidal Curve, the height of tide at any time before or after High or Low Water can be determined from an appropriate Height of Tide table. There are several of these, either included in Tide Tables or found in nautical handbooks (such as Reed's), and each one works with slightly different arguments. The usual arguments entered are duration of rise or fall, interval from HW, and either range, or HW less mean level, or a constant. They all give the answer to the question: What is the height of tide at a given spot at a certain time between HW and LW? Once this is known, and the depth of water has been established, as in the previous example, by taking soundings, the charted depth can be calculated by the formula: Charted Depth = Depth of Water − Height of Tide. Or if the charted depth is known from the chart and the navigator wants to know how much water there will be at a given time, he can calculate the depth of water by the formula: Depth of Water = Charted Depth + Height of Tide.

The two tables on this page and the diagram on the following page are produced from portions of Admiralty Tide Tables for 1974 with the sanction of the Controller, H.M. Stationery Office and of the Hydrographer of the Navy.

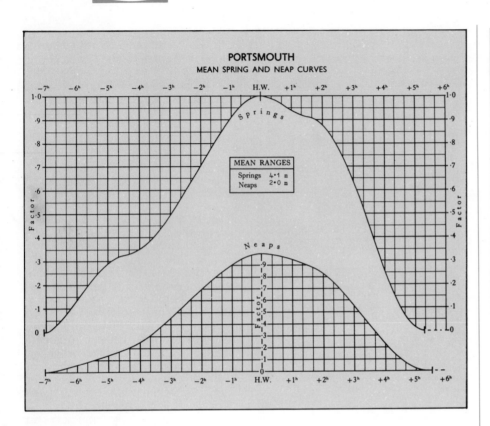

PORTSMOUTH
MEAN SPRING AND NEAP CURVES

MEAN RANGES

Springs	4·1	m
Neaps	2·0	m

Celestial navigation

A crash course

Basic principles

The purpose of celestial, or astro-navigation, as that of piloting or coastal navigation, is to fix a vessel's position at sea. This position is always obtained by the intersection of two or more position lines. While in coastal navigation bearings are taken of charted objects, in celestial navigation sights are taken of celestial bodies, mostly the sun. Thus, celestial navigation is not a secret science but is based on the same principles as coastal navigation. In many respects it may even be said to be easier, for while it is often difficult to identify landmarks accurately, there can be no doubt about the identity of the sun, the moon and some of the planets. With the help of modern navigation tables or pocket calculators, the reduction of sights,

which means their conversion into position lines, is no longer a problem. While years ago the astro-navigator had to be thoroughly familiar with the intricacies of trigonometry, today he needs no mathematical knowledge other than that of adding and subtracting degrees, minutes and seconds.

What is more, a position line might even be worked out quite mechanically by feeding figures into a pre-digested formula, but it is doubtful that this would give any navigator great satisfaction. Moreover, it would put him at the total mercy of the end result without any means of checking error. After all, the basic principles of astro-navigation are so simple that it would be a pity to obliterate all trace of them completely and reduce the navigator to an unskilled pen-pusher. In any case, there is very little in astro-navigation that has to be or indeed *can* be learned from books, except for a few definitions that must be memorized.

The principles for obtaining a position line are the same in celestial navigation as they are in coastal

Admiral's Cup yachts at the start of an ocean race

Anyone crossing the oceans in a yacht like this one must have a thorough knowledge of navigation.

navigation. Go back to the section on Fix by Range (p. 272) and the diagram that illustrates the taking of a vertical sextant angle. The angle is measured between lighthouse lantern, observer and sea level at lighthouse and according to the following formula.

Distance in naut. miles

$= 0.57 \times \dfrac{\text{Height in feet}}{\text{Vertical sextant angle in mins.}}$

The distance of the yacht from the lighthouse can be calculated and, with compasses set to that distance, a circle can be drawn round the lighthouse. This circle is the position line.

We can say that we need the following information to obtain this position line.

1 The exact angle: light, observer, sea level.
2 The height of the light above sea level.
3 The exact position of the light.

So far, we have probably not realized that position of the light is part of the information needed to draw a position line, because we do not usually have difficulties in finding a light on the chart. It is, of course, the point where we place the tip of our compasses as we draw the circular position line.

The formula above is not applicable when the yacht is so far removed from the light that, due to the curvature of the earth, the sea level directly below the light cannot be seen and the angle to it cannot be observed. What can be seen is the horizon, which is the dividing line between water and sky. At sea, this is often very clearly defined.

In this case, what is measured is not the angle
    Light, observer, sea level
but the angle
    Light, observer, sea horizon.
Although this new formula is not so straightforward, it is nevertheless

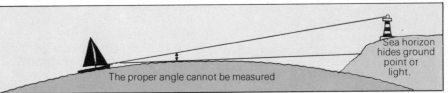

The proper angle cannot be measured — Sea horizon hides ground point or light.

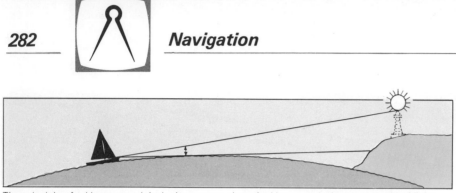

The principle of taking a sun sight is the same as that of taking a vertical sextant angle of light.

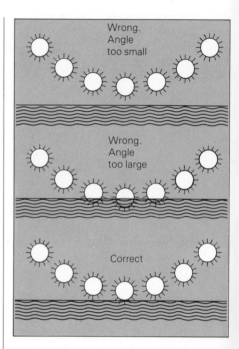

Wrong.
Angle
too small

Wrong.
Angle
too large

Correct

possible to use the observed angle and the known height of the light above sea level to calculate the distance of the light from the observer and get a position line in the usual way.

We can say that in this case the following information is needed to obtain a position line.

1 The observed angle.
2 The height of the light above sea level.
3 The position of the ground point of the light.

In exactly the same way a position line can be obtained from the sun, which could be imagined to be the lantern in a lighthouse. Although a very much more complicated formula is used to calculate a position line from sun observation, the navigator does not actually have to know this formula because he can use tables that have done all the work for him.

Again, the following information is needed to obtain a position line from the sun.

1 The height of the sun above sea level.
2 The observed angle.
3 The position of the ground point of the sun, this being the point on the earth's surface perpendicularly below the sun.

Height of sun (or other observed body) above sea level

A beginner might think that this is an important point, but in fact, in celestial navigation it can be altogether ignored. The distance of the sun, or indeed any other observed body, from the earth is so enormous, that for all practical purposes it can be called 'infinite'. The very welcome result of this is the total absence of the quantity 'height above sea level'.

The observed angle

The sextant

It is advisable to use a precision instrument, either a sextant or an octant, for measuring angles. Cheap plastic sextants may be adequate for taking angles in coastal navigation but they are not sufficiently accurate for serious astro-navigation. A yacht sextant should have the following basic parts.
Telescope (maximum 5 times magnification)
Shades
Micrometer drum
Illumination

Possibly a star telescope
A bubble sextant with an artificial horizon cannot be used on a yacht.

The observed angle — celestial body, observer, sea horizon — must be accurate to within one minute of arc. The technique of taking very accurate sights can only be acquired by practice.

Sighting errors

The most common cause of considerable error with beginners is failure to hold the sextant completely vertically at the moment of taking the sight. This results in the observed angle being greater than it should be. It can be avoided by rotating the sextant back and forth about the telescope axis while taking the sight so that the body observed is seen moving in a curve against the horizon. When it is closest to the horizon, the sextant is held steady and the fine adjustment made until the lower limb (= edge) of the sun just touches the horizon. It is only by this procedure that the observer can be certain of the accuracy of the angle he has measured. There is no other way of checking whether the sextant is vertical at the moment of taking the sight. Any sight taken without following this procedure is unreliable and should be discarded.

Corrections

The angle measured with the sextant has to be corrected before it can be used for sight reductions.

1 The *index error* is no error in the sense that it is a mistake made by the observer. With the index bar clamped at zero and the sextant held vertically, the true and the reflected images of a straight, vertical or horizontal line (such as the horizon) at a distance of at least three kilometres (two miles) must together form an unbroken line. I

they don't, there is index error. The micrometer screw is then turned until the line is continuous, when the index error can be read off the micrometer screw. Unless it is more than two minutes of arc, in which case the sextant has to be adjusted, it should be allowed for at each observation. A simpler method is to find the index error at the beginning of a voyage and re-mark the index on the micrometer screw with an indelible felt-tip pen. Index error must be checked from time to time.

2 *Correction for sun's lower limb.* The observed altitude as read off the sextant must also be corrected for a number of falsifications. One is refraction, which is due to the light rays being bent as they pass through the earth's atmosphere. Another is the dip of the horizon, which is a function of the observer's height of eye at the time of taking the observation. Then there are corrections for the sun's semi-diameter because the edge of the sun and not its centre are sighted, and for parallax because the observer is not at the centre of the earth. The correction is taken from the Sun Altitude Correction Table, which in the official Nautical Almanac, both American and British editions, is in two parts but in other almanacs, such as Reed's, is a Total Correction Table. The obtained correction is always additive. If the average observer's height of eye on a yacht is taken as being about 1.8 m (6 ft), the following corrections can be taken as average for the sun's lower limb.

Observed altitude	Total correction
from 20°	+ 11 minutes
from 25°	+ 12 minutes
from 40°	+ 13 minutes

Geographical position of body

The equivalent of the base point of the lighthouse is the geographical

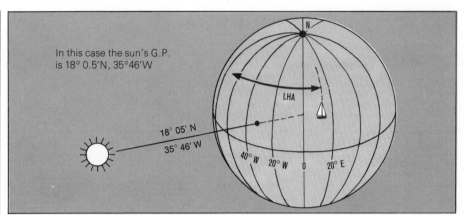

In this case the sun's G.P. is 18° 0.5'N, 35°46'W

position of a celestial body observed. It is the point on the earth's surface through which a line drawn from the body to the centre of the earth would pass. This concept is the key to all celestial navigation and makes it possible to project any position up in the heavens on to the earth's surface. The system of terrestrial co-ordinates of latitude and longitude can therefore be directly applied to celestial navigation.

The latitude of a celestial body is its declination. The longitude of a celestial body is its Greenwich Hour Angle (GHA).

In the illustration, the sun's declination is 12° 14' N. While declination is measured north and south of the Equator in exactly the same way as latitude, GHA is measured from 0° to 360° westward from the Greenwich meridian, instead of eastward and westward from it from 0° to 180°. Thus, if the sun's GHA is longitude 35° 46' W by terrestrial coordinates, this is GHA 35° 46' without the suffix W or E. If it is 170° E by the earth's coordinates, it is GHA 190°.

We could compare the sun's geographical position to the sun's ground point. As the sun, it travels once round the earth from east to west in 24 hours. It does so at a speed of over 1600 km per hour (900 miles per hour), which explains why it is so essential that the geographical position of the sun is known precisely for the very second in which the altitude is measured.

Time

Celestial navigation involves only

GMT (Greenwich Mean Time). For reasonably accurate navigation, time must be known to the second. While not so long ago expensive ship's chronometers were needed for this, we can now achieve the same results by using radio time-signals to check a simple wristwatch. It should be mentioned here that even quartz watches need to be checked, since they are sensitive to changes in temperature. There are time-signal stations all over the world which transmit time-signals during 24 hours, some of them with a spoken announcement. The frequencies are: 2.5 MHz (or Mc/s), 5MHz, 10 MHz, 15MHz, 20MHz, 25MHz, 30MHz.

The nautical almanac

This is published annually as a joint British/American edition and lists in easily extracted, tabulated form, the geographical position of sun, moon, planets and stars for every hour, minute and second of every day of the year.

Example
On 1 August 1975 a yacht is in the Mediterranean, approximate position 40° 40'N, 13°33'E. Precisely at 14h29m22s GMT a sight is taken of the sun (height of observer's eye 1.8 m (6 ft.). The observed altitude is 42°18'. What is the sun's geographical position at the moment the sight is taken?
Answer
On the page for 1 August 1975, in the column headed Sun, are given the Greenwich Hour Angle (GHA) and Declination

1975 JULY 30, 31, AUG. 1 (WED., THURS., FRI.) 151

Day	G.M.T. h	SUN G.H.A. ° ′	SUN Dec. ° ′	MOON G.H.A. ° ′	MOON v ′	MOON Dec. ° ′	MOON d ′	MOON H.P. ′
30	00	178 23.8	N18 43.0	288 43.9	14.5	N11 03.5	9.3	54.5
	01	193 23.8	42.4	303 17.4	14.5	11 12.8	9.2	54.5
	02	208 23.8	41.8	317 50.9	14.4	11 22.0	9.3	54.5
	03	223 23.9	·· 41.2	332 24.3	14.3	11 31.3	9.2	54.6
	04	238 23.9	40.6	346 57.6	14.3	11 40.5	9.1	54.6
	05	253 23.9	40.0	1 30.9	14.3	11 49.6	9.1	54.6
	06	268 23.9	N18 39.4	16 04.2	14.2	N11 58.7	9.0	54.6
W	07	283 24.0	38.8	30 37.4	14.1	12 07.7	9.0	54.6
E	08	298 24.0	38.2	45 10.5	14.2	12 16.7	9.0	54.6
D	09	313 24.0	·· 37.6	59 43.7	14.0	12 25.7	8.9	54.7
N	10	328 24.0	37.0	74 16.7	14.0	12 34.6	8.9	54.7
E	11	343 24.0	36.4	88 49.7	14.0	12 43.5	8.8	54.7
S	12	358 24.1	N18 35.8	103 22.7	13.9	N12 52.3	8.8	54.7
D	13	13 24.1	35.2	117 55.6	13.8	13 01.1	8.7	54.7
A	14	28 24.1	34.6	132 28.4	13.8	13 09.8	8.6	54.7
Y	15	43 24.1	·· 34.0	147 01.2	13.7	13 18.4	8.7	54.8
	16	58 24.2	33.4	161 33.9	13.7	13 27.1	8.5	54.8
	17	73 24.2	32.8	176 06.6	13.6	13 35.6	8.5	54.8
	18	88 24.2	N18 32.2	190 39.2	13.6	N13 44.1	8.5	54.8
	19	103 24.2	31.6	205 11.8	13.5	13 52.6	8.4	54.8
	20	118 24.3	31.0	219 44.3	13.4	14 01.0	8.3	54.9
	21	133 24.3	·· 30.4	234 16.7	13.4	14 09.3	8.3	54.9
	22	148 24.3	29.8	248 49.1	13.3	14 17.6	8.2	54.9
	23	163 24.3	29.2	263 21.4	13.3	14 25.8	8.2	54.9
31	00	178 24.4	N18 28.6	277 53.7	13.2	N14 34.0	8.1	55.0
	01	193 24.4	28.0	292 25.9	13.1	14 42.1	8.1	55.0
	02	208 24.4	27.4	306 58.0	13.1	14 50.2	8.0	55.0
	03	223 24.4	·· 26.7	321 30.1	13.0	14 58.2	7.9	55.0
	04	238 24.5	26.1	336 02.1	13.0	15 06.1	7.9	55.0
	05	253 24.5	25.5	350 34.1	12.9	15 14.0	7.8	55.1
	06	268 24.5	N18 24.9	5 06.0	12.8	N15 21.8	7.8	55.1
	07	283 24.5	24.3	19 37.8	12.8	15 29.6	7.6	55.1
T	08	298 24.6	23.7	34 09.6	12.7	15 37.2	7.7	55.1
H	09	313 24.6	·· 23.1	48 41.3	12.6	15 44.9	7.5	55.2
U	10	328 24.6	22.5	63 12.9	12.6	15 52.4	7.5	55.2
R	11	343 24.7	21.9	77 44.5	12.5	15 59.9	7.4	55.2
S	12	358 24.7	N18 21.3	92 16.0	12.4	N16 07.3	7.4	55.2
D	13	13 24.7	20.6	106 47.4	12.4	16 14.7	7.3	55.3
A	14	28 24.7	20.0	121 18.8	12.3	16 22.0	7.2	55.3
Y	15	43 24.8	·· 19.4	135 50.1	12.2	16 29.2	7.1	55.3
	16	58 24.8	18.8	150 21.3	12.1	16 36.3	7.1	55.3
	17	73 24.8	18.2	164 52.4	12.1	16 43.4	7.0	55.4
	18	88 24.9	N18 17.6	179 23.5	12.1	N16 50.4	6.9	55.4
	19	103 24.9	17.0	193 54.6	11.9	16 57.3	6.9	55.4
	20	118 24.9	16.3	208 25.5	11.9	17 04.2	6.8	55.4
	21	133 25.0	·· 15.7	222 56.4	11.8	17 11.0	6.7	55.5
	22	148 25.0	15.1	237 27.2	11.7	17 17.7	6.6	55.5
	23	163 25.0	14.5	251 57.9	11.7	17 24.3	6.6	55.5
1	00	178 25.1	N18 13.9	266 28.6	11.6	N17 30.9	6.5	55.6
	01	193 25.1	13.2	280 59.2	11.5	17 37.4	6.4	55.6
	02	208 25.1	12.6	295 29.7	11.5	17 43.8	6.3	55.6
	03	223 25.2	·· 12.0	310 00.2	11.4	17 50.1	6.2	55.6
	04	238 25.2	11.4	324 30.6	11.3	17 56.3	6.2	55.7
	05	253 25.2	10.8	339 00.9	11.2	18 02.5	6.0	55.7
	06	268 25.3	N18 10.1	353 31.1	11.2	N18 08.5	6.0	55.7
	07	283 25.3	09.5	8 01.3	11.1	18 14.5	5.9	55.8
	08	298 25.3	08.9	22 31.4	11.0	18 20.4	5.9	55.8
F	09	313 25.4	·· 08.3	37 01.4	10.9	18 26.3	5.7	55.8
R	10	328 25.4	07.7	51 31.3	10.9	18 32.0	5.7	55.9
I	11	343 25.4	07.0	66 01.2	10.8	18 37.7	5.5	55.9
D	12	358 25.5	N18 06.4	80 31.0	10.7	N18 43.2	5.5	55.9
A	13	13 25.5	05.8	95 00.7	10.7	18 48.7	5.4	55.9
Y	14	28 25.5	05.2	109 30.4	10.6	18 54.1	5.3	56.0
	15	43 25.6	·· 04.5	124 00.0	10.5	18 59.4	5.2	56.0
	16	58 25.6	03.9	138 29.5	10.4	19 04.6	5.1	56.0
	17	73 25.6	03.3	152 58.9	10.4	19 09.7	5.0	56.1
	18	88 25.7	N18 02.6	167 28.3	10.3	N19 14.7	5.0	56.1
	19	103 25.7	02.0	181 57.6	10.2	19 19.7	4.8	56.1
	20	118 25.7	01.4	196 26.8	10.1	19 24.5	4.7	56.2
	21	133 25.8	·· 00.8	210 55.9	10.1	19 29.2	4.7	56.2
	22	148 25.8	18 00.1	225 25.0	10.0	19 33.9	4.5	56.2
	23	163 25.9	17 59.5	239 54.0	9.9	19 38.4	4.5	56.3
		S.D. 15.8	d 0.6	S.D. 14.9		15.1		15.2

Lat. °	Twilight Naut. h m	Twilight Civil h m	Sunrise h m	Moonrise 30 h m	Moonrise 31 h m	Moonrise 1 h m	Moonrise 2 h m
N 72	□	□	□	20 02	19 28	□	□
N 70	////	////	01 09	20 29	20 18	19 58	□
68	////	////	02 06	20 50	20 50	20 54	21 09
66	////	////	02 38	21 06	21 14	21 28	21 55
64	////	01 28	03 02	21 20	21 33	21 53	22 26
62	////	02 08	03 21	21 31	21 48	22 12	22 49
60	////	02 34	03 36	21 41	22 01	22 28	23 07
N 58	01 20	02 55	03 49	21 49	22 12	22 42	23 22
56	01 56	03 11	04 00	21 57	22 22	22 53	23 35
54	02 21	03 25	04 10	22 03	22 30	23 04	23 47
52	02 40	03 37	04 19	22 09	22 38	23 13	23 57
50	02 56	03 47	04 27	22 15	22 45	23 21	24 06
45	03 26	04 09	04 43	22 27	23 00	23 39	24 25
N 40	03 48	04 26	04 56	22 37	23 12	23 53	24 41
35	04 06	04 40	05 08	22 45	23 23	24 05	00 05
30	04 20	04 52	05 18	22 53	23 32	24 16	00 16
20	04 43	05 11	05 35	23 06	23 48	24 34	00 34
N 10	05 01	05 27	05 49	23 17	24 02	00 02	00 50
0	05 16	05 41	06 03	23 28	24 15	00 15	01 05
S 10	05 29	05 54	06 16	23 39	24 28	00 28	01 20
20	05 41	06 07	06 31	23 50	24 42	00 42	01 37
30	05 52	06 21	06 47	24 04	00 04	00 59	01 55
35	05 59	06 29	06 56	24 11	00 11	01 08	02 06
40	06 05	06 38	07 06	24 20	00 20	01 19	02 19
45	06 12	06 47	07 19	24 31	00 31	01 32	02 33
S 50	06 19	06 58	07 34	24 43	00 43	01 48	02 52
52	06 23	07 04	07 41	24 49	00 49	01 55	03 00
54	06 26	07 09	07 49	24 56	00 56	02 03	03 10
56	06 30	07 15	07 58	25 03	01 03	02 13	03 21
58	06 34	07 22	08 07	25 11	01 11	02 23	03 33
S 60	06 38	07 30	08 19	00 05	01 20	02 35	03 48

Lat. °	Sunset h m	Twilight Civil h m	Twilight Naut. h m	Moonset 30 h m	Moonset 31 h m	Moonset 1 h m	Moonset 2 h m
N 72	□	□	□	14 13	16 24	□	□
N 70	22 55	////	////	13 48	15 35	17 38	□
68	22 03	////	////	13 28	15 04	16 42	18 16
66	21 31	////	////	13 13	14 41	16 08	17 30
64	21 08	22 39	////	13 00	14 23	15 44	17 00
62	20 50	22 02	////	12 50	14 08	15 25	16 37
60	20 35	21 36	////	12 41	13 56	15 10	16 19
N 58	20 22	21 16	22 48	12 33	13 45	14 56	16 04
56	20 11	21 00	22 13	12 26	13 36	14 45	15 51
54	20 01	20 46	21 50	12 20	13 28	14 35	15 39
52	19 53	20 34	21 31	12 14	13 21	14 26	15 30
50	19 45	20 24	21 15	12 09	13 14	14 18	15 21
45	19 29	20 03	20 46	11 59	13 00	14 01	15 02
N 40	19 16	19 46	20 23	11 50	12 48	13 48	14 47
35	19 04	19 32	20 06	11 42	12 39	13 36	14 34
30	18 55	19 20	19 52	11 35	12 30	13 26	14 22
20	18 38	19 01	19 29	11 24	12 15	13 08	14 03
N 10	18 23	18 45	19 12	11 14	12 02	12 53	13 46
0	18 10	18 32	18 57	11 04	11 50	12 39	13 30
S 10	17 56	18 19	18 44	10 55	11 38	12 25	13 15
20	17 42	18 06	18 32	10 45	11 25	12 09	12 58
30	17 27	17 52	18 21	10 34	11 11	11 52	12 39
35	17 17	17 44	18 15	10 27	11 02	11 42	12 27
40	17 07	17 36	18 08	10 20	10 53	11 30	12 14
45	16 54	17 26	18 02	10 11	10 41	11 17	11 59
S 50	16 39	17 15	17 54	10 01	10 28	11 00	11 41
52	16 32	17 10	17 51	09 56	10 21	10 53	11 32
54	16 24	17 04	17 47	09 51	10 14	10 44	11 22
56	16 16	16 58	17 44	09 45	10 07	10 34	11 11
58	16 06	16 51	17 40	09 38	09 58	10 24	10 58
S 60	15 55	16 43	17 35	09 31	09 48	10 11	10 43

Day	SUN Eqn. of Time 00ʰ m s	SUN Eqn. of Time 12ʰ m s	SUN Mer. Pass. h m	MOON Mer. Pass. Upper h m	MOON Mer. Pass. Lower h m	MOON Age d	MOON Phase
30	06 25	06 24	12 06	04 54	17 16	21	◑
31	06 23	06 21	12 06	05 39	18 03	22	
1	06 20	06 18	12 06	06 27	18 52	23	

28ᵐ INCREMENTS AND CORRECTIONS 29ᵐ

28ᵐ s	SUN PLANETS ° ′	ARIES ° ′	MOON ° ′	v or d ′	Corrⁿ ′	v or d ′	Corrⁿ ′	v or d ′	Corrⁿ ′
00	7 00·0	7 01·1	6 40·9	0·0	0·0	6·0	2·9	12·0	5·7
01	7 00·3	7 01·4	6 41·1	0·1	0·0	6·1	2·9	12·1	5·7
02	7 00·5	7 01·7	6 41·3	0·2	0·1	6·2	2·9	12·2	5·8
03	7 00·8	7 01·9	6 41·6	0·3	0·1	6·3	3·0	12·3	5·8
04	7 01·0	7 02·2	6 41·8	0·4	0·2	6·4	3·0	12·4	5·9
05	7 01·3	7 02·4	6 42·1	0·5	0·2	6·5	3·1	12·5	5·9
06	7 01·5	7 02·7	6 42·3	0·6	0·3	6·6	3·1	12·6	6·0
07	7 01·8	7 02·9	6 42·5	0·7	0·3	6·7	3·2	12·7	6·0
08	7 02·0	7 03·2	6 42·8	0·8	0·4	6·8	3·2	12·8	6·1
09	7 02·3	7 03·4	6 43·0	0·9	0·4	6·9	3·3	12·9	6·1
10	7 02·5	7 03·7	6 43·3	1·0	0·5	7·0	3·3	13·0	6·2
11	7 02·8	7 03·9	6 43·5	1·1	0·5	7·1	3·4	13·1	6·2
12	7 03·0	7 04·2	6 43·7	1·2	0·6	7·2	3·4	13·2	6·3
13	7 03·3	7 04·4	6 44·0	1·3	0·6	7·3	3·5	13·3	6·3
14	7 03·5	7 04·7	6 44·2	1·4	0·7	7·4	3·5	13·4	6·4
15	7 03·8	7 04·9	6 44·4	1·5	0·7	7·5	3·6	13·5	6·4
16	7 04·0	7 05·2	6 44·7	1·6	0·8	7·6	3·6	13·6	6·5
17	7 04·3	7 05·4	6 44·9	1·7	0·8	7·7	3·7	13·7	6·5
18	7 04·5	7 05·7	6 45·2	1·8	0·9	7·8	3·7	13·8	6·6
19	7 04·8	7 05·9	6 45·4	1·9	0·9	7·9	3·8	13·9	6·6
20	7 05·0	7 06·2	6 45·6	2·0	1·0	8·0	3·8	14·0	6·7
21	7 05·3	7 06·4	6 45·9	2·1	1·0	8·1	3·8	14·1	6·7
22	7 05·5	7 06·7	6 46·1	2·2	1·0	8·2	3·9	14·2	6·7
23	7 05·8	7 06·9	6 46·4	2·3	1·1	8·3	3·9	14·3	6·8
24	7 06·0	7 07·2	6 46·6	2·4	1·1	8·4	4·0	14·4	6·8
25	7 06·3	7 07·4	6 46·8	2·5	1·2	8·5	4·0	14·5	6·9
26	7 06·5	7 07·7	6 47·1	2·6	1·2	8·6	4·1	14·6	6·9
27	7 06·8	7 07·9	6 47·3	2·7	1·3	8·7	4·1	14·7	7·0
28	7 07·0	7 08·2	6 47·5	2·8	1·3	8·8	4·2	14·8	7·0
29	7 07·3	7 08·4	6 47·8	2·9	1·4	8·9	4·2	14·9	7·1
30	7 07·5	7 08·7	6 48·0	3·0	1·4	9·0	4·3	15·0	7·1
31	7 07·8	7 08·9	6 48·3	3·1	1·5	9·1	4·3	15·1	7·2
32	7 08·0	7 09·2	6 48·5	3·2	1·5	9·2	4·4	15·2	7·2
33	7 08·3	7 09·4	6 48·7	3·3	1·6	9·3	4·4	15·3	7·3
34	7 08·5	7 09·7	6 49·0	3·4	1·6	9·4	4·5	15·4	7·3
35	7 08·8	7 09·9	6 49·2	3·5	1·7	9·5	4·5	15·5	7·4
36	7 09·0	7 10·2	6 49·5	3·6	1·7	9·6	4·6	15·6	7·4
37	7 09·3	7 10·4	6 49·7	3·7	1·8	9·7	4·6	15·7	7·5
38	7 09·5	7 10·7	6 49·9	3·8	1·8	9·8	4·7	15·8	7·5
39	7 09·8	7 10·9	6 50·2	3·9	1·9	9·9	4·7	15·9	7·6
40	7 10·0	7 11·2	6 50·4	4·0	1·9	10·0	4·8	16·0	7·6
41	7 10·3	7 11·4	6 50·6	4·1	1·9	10·1	4·8	16·1	7·6
42	7 10·5	7 11·7	6 50·9	4·2	2·0	10·2	4·8	16·2	7·7
43	7 10·8	7 11·9	6 51·1	4·3	2·0	10·3	4·9	16·3	7·7
44	7 11·0	7 12·2	6 51·4	4·4	2·1	10·4	4·9	16·4	7·8
45	7 11·3	7 12·4	6 51·6	4·5	2·1	10·5	5·0	16·5	7·8
46	7 11·5	7 12·7	6 51·8	4·6	2·2	10·6	5·0	16·6	7·9
47	7 11·8	7 12·9	6 52·1	4·7	2·2	10·7	5·1	16·7	7·9
48	7 12·0	7 13·2	6 52·3	4·8	2·3	10·8	5·1	16·8	8·0
49	7 12·3	7 13·4	6 52·6	4·9	2·3	10·9	5·2	16·9	8·0
50	7 12·5	7 13·7	6 52·8	5·0	2·4	11·0	5·2	17·0	8·1
51	7 12·8	7 13·9	6 53·0	5·1	2·4	11·1	5·3	17·1	8·1
52	7 13·0	7 14·2	6 53·3	5·2	2·5	11·2	5·3	17·2	8·2
53	7 13·3	7 14·4	6 53·5	5·3	2·5	11·3	5·4	17·3	8·2
54	7 13·5	7 14·7	6 53·8	5·4	2·6	11·4	5·4	17·4	8·3
55	7 13·8	7 14·9	6 54·0	5·5	2·6	11·5	5·5	17·5	8·3
56	7 14·0	7 15·2	6 54·2	5·6	2·7	11·6	5·5	17·6	8·4
57	7 14·3	7 15·4	6 54·5	5·7	2·7	11·7	5·6	17·7	8·4
58	7 14·5	7 15·7	6 54·7	5·8	2·8	11·8	5·6	17·8	8·5
59	7 14·8	7 15·9	6 54·9	5·9	2·8	11·9	5·7	17·9	8·5
60	7 15·0	7 16·2	6 55·2	6·0	2·9	12·0	5·7	18·0	8·6

29ᵐ s	SUN PLANETS ° ′	ARIES ° ′	MOON ° ′	v or d ′	Corrⁿ ′	v or d ′	Corrⁿ ′	v or d ′	Corrⁿ ′
00	7 15·0	7 16·2	6 55·2	0·0	0·0	6·0	3·0	12·0	5·9
01	7 15·3	7 16·4	6 55·4	0·1	0·0	6·1	3·0	12·1	5·9
02	7 15·5	7 16·7	6 55·7	0·2	0·1	6·2	3·0	12·2	6·0
03	7 15·8	7 16·9	6 55·9	0·3	0·1	6·3	3·1	12·3	6·0
04	7 16·0	7 17·2	6 56·1	0·4	0·2	6·4	3·1	12·4	6·1
05	7 16·3	7 17·4	6 56·4	0·5	0·2	6·5	3·2	12·5	6·1
06	7 16·5	7 17·7	6 56·6	0·6	0·3	6·6	3·2	12·6	6·2
07	7 16·8	7 17·9	6 56·9	0·7	0·3	6·7	3·3	12·7	6·2
08	7 17·0	7 18·2	6 57·1	0·8	0·4	6·8	3·3	12·8	6·3
09	7 17·3	7 18·4	6 57·3	0·9	0·4	6·9	3·4	12·9	6·3
10	7 17·5	7 18·7	6 57·6	1·0	0·5	7·0	3·4	13·0	6·4
11	7 17·8	7 18·9	6 57·8	1·1	0·5	7·1	3·5	13·1	6·4
12	7 18·0	7 19·2	6 58·0	1·2	0·6	7·2	3·5	13·2	6·5
13	7 18·3	7 19·4	6 58·3	1·3	0·6	7·3	3·6	13·3	6·5
14	7 18·5	7 19·7	6 58·5	1·4	0·7	7·4	3·6	13·4	6·6
15	7 18·8	7 20·0	6 58·8	1·5	0·7	7·5	3·7	13·5	6·6
16	7 19·0	7 20·2	6 59·0	1·6	0·8	7·6	3·7	13·6	6·7
17	7 19·3	7 20·5	6 59·2	1·7	0·8	7·7	3·8	13·7	6·7
18	7 19·5	7 20·7	6 59·5	1·8	0·9	7·8	3·8	13·8	6·8
19	7 19·8	7 21·0	6 59·7	1·9	0·9	7·9	3·9	13·9	6·8
20	7 20·0	7 21·2	7 00·0	2·0	1·0	8·0	3·9	14·0	6·9
21	7 20·3	7 21·5	7 00·2	2·1	1·0	8·1	4·0	14·1	6·9
22	7 20·5	7 21·7	7 00·4	2·2	1·1	8·2	4·0	14·2	7·0
23	7 20·8	7 22·0	7 00·7	2·3	1·1	8·3	4·1	14·3	7·0
24	7 21·0	7 22·2	7 00·9	2·4	1·2	8·4	4·1	14·4	7·1
25	7 21·3	7 22·5	7 01·1	2·5	1·2	8·5	4·2	14·5	7·1
26	7 21·5	7 22·7	7 01·4	2·6	1·3	8·6	4·2	14·6	7·2
27	7 21·8	7 23·0	7 01·6	2·7	1·3	8·7	4·3	14·7	7·2
28	7 22·0	7 23·2	7 01·9	2·8	1·4	8·8	4·3	14·8	7·3
29	7 22·3	7 23·5	7 02·1	2·9	1·4	8·9	4·4	14·9	7·3
30	7 22·5	7 23·7	7 02·3	3·0	1·5	9·0	4·4	15·0	7·4
31	7 22·8	7 24·0	7 02·6	3·1	1·5	9·1	4·5	15·1	7·4
32	7 23·0	7 24·2	7 02·8	3·2	1·6	9·2	4·5	15·2	7·5
33	7 23·3	7 24·5	7 03·1	3·3	1·6	9·3	4·6	15·3	7·5
34	7 23·5	7 24·7	7 03·3	3·4	1·7	9·4	4·6	15·4	7·6
35	7 23·8	7 25·0	7 03·5	3·5	1·7	9·5	4·7	15·5	7·6
36	7 24·0	7 25·2	7 03·8	3·6	1·8	9·6	4·7	15·6	7·7
37	7 24·3	7 25·5	7 04·0	3·7	1·8	9·7	4·8	15·7	7·7
38	7 24·5	7 25·7	7 04·3	3·8	1·9	9·8	4·8	15·8	7·8
39	7 24·8	7 26·0	7 04·5	3·9	1·9	9·9	4·9	15·9	7·8
40	7 25·0	7 26·2	7 04·7	4·0	2·0	10·0	4·9	16·0	7·9
41	7 25·3	7 26·5	7 05·0	4·1	2·0	10·1	5·0	16·1	7·9
42	7 25·5	7 26·7	7 05·2	4·2	2·1	10·2	5·0	16·2	8·0
43	7 25·8	7 27·0	7 05·4	4·3	2·1	10·3	5·1	16·3	8·0
44	7 26·0	7 27·2	7 05·7	4·4	2·2	10·4	5·1	16·4	8·1
45	7 26·3	7 27·5	7 05·9	4·5	2·2	10·5	5·2	16·5	8·1
46	7 26·5	7 27·7	7 06·2	4·6	2·3	10·6	5·2	16·6	8·2
47	7 26·8	7 28·0	7 06·4	4·7	2·3	10·7	5·3	16·7	8·2
48	7 27·0	7 28·2	7 06·6	4·8	2·4	10·8	5·3	16·8	8·3
49	7 27·3	7 28·5	7 06·9	4·9	2·4	10·9	5·4	16·9	8·3
50	7 27·5	7 28·7	7 07·1	5·0	2·5	11·0	5·4	17·0	8·4
51	7 27·8	7 29·0	7 07·4	5·1	2·5	11·1	5·5	17·1	8·4
52	7 28·0	7 29·2	7 07·6	5·2	2·6	11·2	5·5	17·2	8·5
53	7 28·3	7 29·5	7 07·8	5·3	2·6	11·3	5·6	17·3	8·5
54	7 28·5	7 29·7	7 08·1	5·4	2·7	11·4	5·6	17·4	8·6
55	7 28·8	7 30·0	7 08·3	5·5	2·7	11·5	5·7	17·5	8·6
56	7 29·0	7 30·2	7 08·5	5·6	2·8	11·6	5·7	17·6	8·7
57	7 29·3	7 30·5	7 08·8	5·7	2·8	11·7	5·8	17·7	8·7
58	7 29·5	7 30·7	7 09·0	5·8	2·9	11·8	5·8	17·8	8·8
59	7 29·8	7 31·0	7 09·3	5·9	2·9	11·9	5·9	17·9	8·8
60	7 30·0	7 31·2	7 09·5	6·0	3·0	12·0	5·9	18·0	8·9

for every full hour. At 1400h the GHA is 28°25′.5. To find out by how much the GHA has increased in the remaining 29m22s turn to the tables Increments and Corrections towards the end of the Almanac. In the table marked 29m follow the left-hand column down until you get to 22s and read off immediately to the right of it, in the column Sun, Planets, the increment 7°20′.5. Thus, at 14h29m22s

the exact GHA is 28°25′.5
+ 7°20′.5
GHA 35°46′.0

The intercept method

Now that we know the height of the sun above sea level (infinite), the observed altitude (the angle) and the sun's geographical position, we could, with the help of a very complicated formula, calculate the distance between the yacht's position and the sun's geographical position. This would be about 2912 nautical miles. If we tried to draw a circle round the sun's geographical position with a radius of 2912 miles, we would find that this is not possible on a chart. For if a chart were to contain both the yacht's position and the sun's geographical position it would be of so small a scale as to be useless for navigation purposes. On the other hand, if it were a normal chart used for navigation, the sun's geographial position would be far beyond its edge. So in practice this method, logical as it may appear, cannot be used. A trick is therefore introduced: if the sun's geographical position and the observed altitude give us the observer's distance from the sun's geographical position, then conversely it should be possible to calculate the sun's altitude if its position and the observer's position (hence his distance from the sun's GP) are known. The yacht's position is not known, of course, as we want to fix i

by taking sun sights. But we must have at least an approximate idea of its DR position. If we used this for our calculations and it turned out that the observed altitude and the calculated altitude were identical, this would mean that our DR position was at the same distance from the sun's GP as our true position. It is more likely, however, that the observed altitude differs from the calculated altitude. If it is greater, which means that the sun is in fact higher, it means that we are closer to it than we thought. If it is smaller, it means that we are further away from the sun than our DR position had us believe. (DR position, see p.271)

> Repeat: We calculate the altitude that our sextant *would* measure if the yacht were precisely in our estimated DR position. If the altitude which we actually *do* measure with the sextant is smaller, the yacht is further away from the sun's GP; if it is greater, the yacht is closer to the sun's GP.

If the calculated altitude and the observed altitude are identical, the yacht is on a circular position line which passes through the DR position. Since our distance from the sun's GP, and therefore the radius of this circle, is so enormous, we can, for chartwork purposes, straighten out its curvature. Our position line is therefore a straight line. It must be at right-angles to the sun's bearing, which is called azimuth. This is important, since the sun's GP, which is the point where we would place the tip of our compasses, is not actually on the chart and we consequently have no other way of establishing the direction of the position line.

Normally, the calculated altitude and the observed altitude are not identical and the position line does not pass through the DR position, but is either closer to the sun's GP or is further away.

The amount by which the position line has to be moved towards or away from the sun is the difference between the calculated altitude and the observed altitude, one minute of arc equalling one nautical mile.

We can now proceed to calculate altitude and azimuth by using the following formula.

$Hc = \sin^{-1}$
$(\cos LHA)\,(\cos dec)\,(\cos L) + (\sin dec)\,(\sin L)$

$$Z = \cos^{-1} \frac{\sin dec - (\sin Hc)\,(\sin L)}{(\cos Hc)\,(\cos L)}$$

where Hc = Calculated altitude
dec = Declination
L = DR latitude
Z = Azimuth angle

Azimuth Zn =
N. Latitudes
    Z, when sin LHA less than 0
360° − Z, when sin LHA greater than 0
S. Latitudes
180° − Z, when sin LHA less than 0
180° + Z, when sin LHA greater than 0

All parts of the equations are known, except LHA which is explained in the following section.

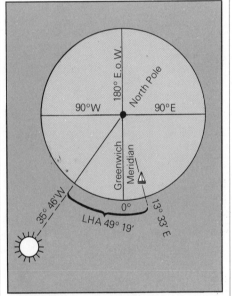

Local hour angle (LHA)
This angle is nothing more than the difference between the (DR) longitude of the observer and the GHA of the celestial body.

> Note: LHA is always measured westward from the observer. It is found by using the formulae:
> LHA = GHA + Longitude east
> LHA = GHA − Longitude west

In our example on p. 283 LHA is
      35°46′
   + 13°33′ (Longitude east!)
LHA   49°19′

How to calculate altitude and azimuth

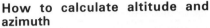

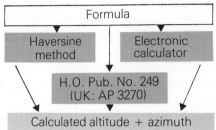

Whichever method is used, the principle remains the same, and the result is always calculated altitude and azimuth.

1 Haversine method. This is a method once used. Since it involves the use of logarithm tables it is laborious and incorporates a very great error potential.
2 Electronic calculator with trigonometric functions. With an electronic calculator, sine and cosine are no longer mathematical problems but simply a matter of pushing buttons. Since there is a danger of pressing the wrong button, programmed calculators are to be preferred. The operating sequence is:
1 Key in the programme
2 Check the programme with test data
3 Run the actual problem.
There are calculators for which the programme can be stored on magnetic card and recalled as

Programmed pocket calculator

Pub. No. 249, Band III

DECLINATION (15°-29°)
SAME NAME AS LATITUDE

N. Lat. {LHA greater than 180°....... Zn=Z; LHA less than 180°........... Zn=360−Z}

LHA	15° Hc	d	Z	16° Hc	d	Z	17° Hc	d	Z
	° ′	′	°	° ′	′	°	° ′	′	°
0	64 00	+60	180	65 00	+60	180	66 00	+60	180
1	63 59	60	178	64 59	60	178	65 59	60	178
2	63 57	59	176	64 56	60	176	65 56	60	175
3	63 52	60	173	64 52	60	173	65 52	59	173
4	63 46	60	171	64 46	59	171	65 45	60	171
5	63 38	+60	169	64 38	+59	169	65 37	+59	168
6	63 29	59	167	64 28	59	167	65 27	59	166
7	63 18	59	165	64 17	58	164	65 15	59	164
8	63 05	59	163	64 04	58	162	65 02	58	162
9	62 51	58	161	63 49	58	160	64 47	57	159
10	62 35	+58	159	63 33	+57	158	64 30	+57	157
11	62 18	57	157	63 15	57	156	64 12	56	155
12	61 59	57	155	62 56	56	154	63 52	56	153
13	61 39	56	153	62 35	56	152	63 31	55	151
14	61 18	55	151	62 13	55	150	63 08	55	149
15	60 55	+55	149	61 50	+55	148	62 45	+54	147
16	60 31	55	147	61 26	53	146	62 19	54	145
17	60 06	54	146	61 00	53	145	61 53	53	144
18	59 40	53	144	60 33	53	143	61 26	52	142
19	59 13	52	142	60 05	52	141	60 57	52	140
20	58 45	+51	141	59 36	+52	140	60 28	+51	138
21	58 15	51	139	59 06	51	138	59 57	50	137
22	57 45	51	137	58 36	50	136	59 26	49	135
23	57 14	50	136	58 04	49	135	58 53	49	134
24	56 42	49	134	57 31	49	133	58 20	49	132
25	56 09	+49	133	56 58	+48	132	57 46	+48	131
26	55 35	49	132	56 24	48	130	57 12	47	129
27	55 01	48	130	55 49	47	129	56 36	47	128
28	54 26	47	129	55 13	47	128	56 00	46	127
29	53 51	46	128	54 37	47	126	55 24	45	125
30	53 14	+47	126	54 01	+45	125	54 46	+45	124
31	52 37	46	125	53 23	45	124	54 08	45	123
32	52 00	45	124	52 45	45	123	53 30	44	122
33	51 22	45	123	52 07	44	122	52 51	44	120
34	50 44	44	121	51 28	44	120	52 12	43	119
35	50 05	+44	120	50 49	+43	119	51 32	+43	118
36	49 26	43	119	50 09	43	118	50 52	43	117
37	48 46	43	118	49 29	43	117	50 12	42	116
38	48 06	43	117	48 49	42	116	49 31	41	115
39	47 25	43	116	48 08	42	115	48 50	41	114
40	46 44	+42	115	47 26	+42	114	48 08	+41	113
41	46 03	42	114	46 45	41	113	47 26	41	112
42	45 22	41	113	46 03	41	112	46 44	40	111
43	44 40	41	112	45 21	41	111	46 02	40	110
44	43 58	41	111	44 39	40	110	45 19	40	109
45	43 15	+41	110	43 56	+40	109	44 36	+39	108
46	42 33	40	109	43 13	40	108	43 53	39	107
47	41 50	40	109	42 30	40	108	43 10	39	107
48	41 07	40	108	41 47	39	107	42 26	39	106
49	40 24	39	107	41 03	39	106	41 42	39	105
50	39 40	+40	106	40 20	+39	105	40 59	+38	104
51	38 57	39	105	39 36	39	104	40 15	38	103
52	38 13	39	104	38 52	38	103	39 30	38	102
53	37 29	39	104	38 08	38	103	38 46	38	102
54	36 45	39	103	37 24	38	102	38 02	37	101
55	36 01	+38	102	36 39	+38	101	37 17	+38	100
56	35 16	39	101	35 55	38	100	36 33	37	99
57	34 32	38	101	35 10	38	100	35 48	37	99
58	33 47	38	100	34 25	38	99	35 03	37	98
59	33 03	38	99	33 41	37	98	34 18	37	97
60	32 18	+38	98	32 56	+37	97	33 33	+37	96
61	31 33	38	98	32 11	37	97	32 48	37	96
62	30 48	38	97	31 26	37	96	32 03	37	95
63	30 03	38	96	30 41	37	95	31 18	37	94
64	29 18	38	95	29 56	37	95	30 33	36	94
65	28 33	+37	95	29 10	+37	94	29 47	+37	93
66	27 48	37	94	28 25	37	93	29 02	37	92
67	27 03	37	93	27 40	37	93	28 17	37	92
68	26 17	38	93	26 55	37	92	27 32	36	91
69	25 32	37	92	26 09	37	91	26 46	37	90
	15°			16°			17°		

LHA	18° Hc	d	Z	19° Hc	d	Z	20° Hc	d	Z	21° Hc	d	Z
	° ′	′	°	° ′	′	°	° ′	′	°	° ′	′	°
0	67 00	+60	180	68 00	+60	180	69 00	+60	180	70 00	+60	180
1	66 59	60	178	67 59	60	178	68 59	60	177	69 59	60	177
2	66 56	60	175	67 56	60	175	68 56	60	175	69 56	60	175
3	66 51	60	173	67 51	60	173	68 51	59	172	69 50	60	172
4	66 45	59	170	67 44	60	170	68 44	59	170	69 43	59	169
5	66 36	+59	168	67 35	+59	168	68 34	+59	167	69 33	+59	167
6	66 26	59	166	67 25	58	165	68 23	59	165	69 22	58	164
7	66 14	58	163	67 12	58	163	68 10	58	162	69 08	58	161
8	66 00	58	161	66 58	57	160	67 55	58	160	68 53	57	159
9	65 44	58	159	66 42	57	158	67 39	57	157	68 36	56	156
10	65 27	+57	157	66 24	+56	156	67 20	+57	155	68 17	+56	154
11	65 08	57	154	66 05	55	154	67 00	56	153	67 56	55	152
12	64 48	56	152	65 44	55	151	66 39	55	151	67 34	54	149
13	64 26	55	150	65 21	55	149	66 16	54	148	67 10	54	147
14	64 03	54	148	64 57	54	147	65 51	54	146	66 45	53	145
15	63 39	+53	146	64 32	+54	145	65 26	+52	144	66 18	+52	143
16	63 13	53	144	64 06	52	143	64 58	52	142	65 50	52	141
17	62 46	52	143	63 38	52	142	64 30	51	140	65 21	51	139
18	62 18	52	141	63 10	51	140	64 01	50	139	64 51	50	137
19	61 49	51	139	62 40	50	138	63 30	50	137	64 20	49	135
20	61 19	+50	137	62 09	+50	136	62 59	+49	135	63 48	+48	134
21	60 47	50	136	61 37	49	135	62 26	48	133	63 14	48	132
22	60 15	49	134	61 04	49	133	61 53	47	132	62 40	47	130
23	59 42	49	133	60 31	47	131	61 18	47	130	62 05	47	129
24	59 09	47	131	59 56	47	130	60 43	47	129	61 30	45	127
25	58 34	+47	130	59 21	+47	128	60 08	+45	127	60 53	+45	126
26	57 59	46	128	58 45	46	127	59 31	45	126	60 16	45	124
27	57 23	46	127	58 09	45	126	58 54	45	124	59 39	43	123
28	56 46	46	125	57 32	44	124	58 16	44	123	59 00	44	122
29	56 09	45	124	56 54	44	123	57 38	44	122	58 22	42	120
30	55 31	+45	123	56 16	+43	122	56 59	+43	120	57 42	+42	119
31	54 53	44	122	55 37	43	120	56 20	42	119	57 02	42	118
32	54 14	44	120	54 58	42	119	55 40	42	118	56 22	41	117
33	53 35	43	119	54 18	42	118	55 00	42	117	55 42	40	116
34	52 55	43	118	53 38	42	117	54 20	41	116	55 01	40	114
35	52 15	+42	117	52 57	+42	116	53 39	+40	115	54 19	+40	113
36	51 35	41	116	52 16	41	115	52 57	40	114	53 37	40	112
37	50 54	41	115	51 35	41	114	52 16	39	113	52 55	39	111
38	50 12	41	114	50 53	41	113	51 34	39	112	52 13	39	110
39	49 31	40	113	50 11	40	112	50 51	39	111	51 30	39	109
40	48 49	+40	112	49 29	+40	111	50 09	+39	110	50 48	+38	108
41	48 07	40	111	48 47	39	110	49 26	38	109	50 04	38	107
42	47 24	40	110	48 04	39	109	48 43	38	108	49 21	38	107
43	46 42	39	109	47 21	39	108	48 00	38	107	48 38	37	106
44	45 59	39	108	46 38	38	107	47 16	38	106	47 54	37	105
45	45 15	+39	107	45 54	+38	106	46 32	+38	105	47 10	+37	104
46	44 32	39	106	45 11	38	105	45 49	37	104	46 26	37	103
47	43 49	38	106	44 27	38	104	45 05	37	103	45 42	36	102
48	43 05	38	105	43 43	38	104	44 21	36	103	44 57	37	101
49	42 21	38	104	42 59	37	103	43 36	37	102	44 13	36	101
50	41 37	+38	103	42 15	+37	102	42 52	+36	101	43 28	+36	100
51	40 53	37	102	41 30	37	101	42 07	37	100	42 44	36	99
52	40 08	38	101	40 46	37	100	41 23	36	99	41 59	36	98
53	39 24	37	101	40 01	37	100	40 38	36	99	41 14	36	98
54	38 39	37	100	39 16	37	99	39 53	36	98	40 29	36	97
55	37 55	+37	99	38 32	+36	98	39 08	+36	97	39 44	+36	96
56	37 10	37	98	37 47	36	97	38 23	36	96	38 59	35	95
57	36 25	37	98	37 02	36	97	37 38	36	96	38 14	35	95
58	35 40	37	97	36 17	36	96	36 53	36	95	37 29	35	94
59	34 55	37	96	35 32	36	95	36 08	36	94	36 44	35	93
60	34 10	+37	96	34 47	+36	95	35 23	+35	94	35 58	+36	93
61	33 25	37	95	34 02	36	94	34 38	35	93	35 13	35	92
62	32 40	36	94	33 16	36	93	33 52	36	92	34 28	35	91
63	31 55	36	93	32 31	36	92	33 07	36	92	33 43	35	91
64	31 09	37	93	31 46	36	92	32 22	35	91	32 57	35	90
65	30 24	+37	92	31 01	+36	91	31 37	+35	90	32 12	+35	89
66	29 39	36	91	30 15	36	90	30 51	36	90	31 27	35	89
67	28 54	36	91	29 30	36	90	30 06	36	89	30 42	35	88
68	28 08	37	90	28 45	36	89	29 21	35	88	29 56	35	87
69	27 23	36	89	27 59	36	89	28 35	36	88	29 11	35	87
	18°			19°			20°			21°		

S. Lat. {LHA greater than 180°....... Zn=180−Z; LHA less than 180°........... Zn=180+Z}

desired. These are ideal but expensive.

3 Sight Reduction Tables H.O.Pub.No. 249. These are published in the United States by the US Naval Oceanographic Office. The identical British edition is AP 3270 published by the Air Ministry. The method of calculating altitude and azimuth with the help of these tables has by no means been superceded by the electronic calculator. It is a quick and easy method which, with practice, yields a position line in five minutes.

How to work with tables H.O.249

Since it is impossible to tabulate altitude and azimuth of every single point on earth, the tables give solutions for whole degrees only. The tables are used by entering not the DR position as an argument but the 'chosen' or 'assumed' latitude nearest the DR latitude, which must be in whole degrees, and a 'chosen' longitude which will result in a LHA of whole degrees when subtracted from or added to the GHA. This is of no importance to the accuracy of the result, since the DR position is not the yacht's true position anyway. It is important, however, that the 'chosen' position is as close as possible to the DR position. The chosen position must meet the following conditions.

1 Its latitude must be in whole degrees.
2 Its longitude must be so chosen that when added to or subtracted from the GHA it results in a LHA of whole degrees.

In other words, the DR position is used purely to determine the nearest suitable chosen position. From then on, only the chosen position is used in calculations and in plotting the position line.

In the example on p 283 the chosen position would be 41°N (DR latitude 40°40′N), 13°14′E (DR longitude 13°33′E), because only 13°14′ results in a LHA of whole degrees when added to the GHA of 35°46′. Thus, the LHA is 49°. There are now two arguments for entering the tables. The third entry is the declination, which in this case is 18°05′N.

TABLE 5.—Correction to Tabulated Altitude for Minutes of Declination

d'	1 2 3	4 5 6	7 8 9	10 11 12	13 14 15	16 17 18	19 20 21	22 23 24	25 26 27	28 29 30	31 32 33	34 35 36	37 38 39	40 41 42	43 44 45	46 47 48	49 50 51	52 53 54	55 56 57	58 59 60	d'
0	0 0 0	0 0 0	0 0 0	0 0 0	0 0 0	0 0 0	0 0 0	0 0 0	0 0 0	0 0 0	0 0 0	0 0 0	0 0 0	0 0 0	0 0 0	0 0 0	0 0 0	0 0 0	0 0 0	0 0 0	0
1	0 0 0	0 0 0	0 0 0	0 0 0	0 0 0	0 0 0	0 0 0	0 0 0	0 0 0	0 0 0	1 1 1	1 1 1	1 1 1	1 1 1	1 1 1	1 1 1	1 1 1	1 1 1	1 1 1	1 1 1	1
2	0 0 0	0 0 0	0 0 0	0 0 0	0 0 0	1 1 1	1 1 1	1 1 1	1 1 1	1 1 1	1 1 1	1 1 1	1 1 1	1 1 1	1 1 1	2 2 2	2 2 2	2 2 2	2 2 2	2 2 2	2
3	0 0 0	0 0 0	0 0 0	0 1 1	1 1 1	1 1 1	1 1 1	1 1 1	1 1 1	1 1 1	2 2 2	2 2 2	2 2 2	2 2 2	2 2 2	2 2 2	2 2 3	3 3 3	3 3 3	3 3 3	3
4	0 0 0	0 0 0	0 1 1	1 1 1	1 1 1	1 1 1	1 1 1	1 2 2	2 2 2	2 2 2	2 2 2	2 2 2	2 3 3	3 3 3	3 3 3	3 3 3	3 3 3	3 4 4	4 4 4	4 4 4	4
5	0 0 0	0 0 0	1 1 1	1 1 1	1 1 1	1 1 1	2 2 2	2 2 2	2 2 2	2 2 2	3 3 3	3 3 3	3 3 3	3 3 4	4 4 4	4 4 4	4 4 4	4 4 4	5 5 5	5 5 5	5
6	0 0 0	0 0 1	1 1 1	1 1 1	1 1 1	2 2 2	2 2 2	2 2 2	2 3 3	3 3 3	3 3 3	3 3 4	4 4 4	4 4 4	4 4 4	5 5 5	5 5 5	5 5 5	5 6 6	6 6 6	6
7	0 0 0	0 1 1	1 1 1	1 1 1	2 2 2	2 2 2	2 2 2	3 3 3	3 3 3	3 3 3	4 4 4	4 4 4	4 4 5	5 5 5	5 5 5	5 5 6	6 6 6	6 6 6	6 7 7	7 7 7	7
8	0 0 0	1 1 1	1 1 1	1 1 2	2 2 2	2 2 2	3 3 3	3 3 3	3 3 4	4 4 4	4 4 4	5 5 5	5 5 5	5 5 6	6 6 6	6 6 6	7 7 7	7 7 7	7 7 8	8 8 8	8
9	0 0 0	1 1 1	1 1 1	1 2 2	2 2 2	2 3 3	3 3 3	3 3 4	4 4 4	4 4 4	5 5 5	5 5 5	6 6 6	6 6 6	6 7 7	7 7 7	7 8 8	8 8 8	8 8 9	9 9 9	9
10	0 0 0	1 1 1	1 1 1	2 2 2	2 2 2	3 3 3	3 3 3	4 4 4	4 4 4	5 5 5	5 5 5	6 6 6	6 6 6	7 7 7	7 7 7	8 8 8	8 8 8	9 9 9	9 9 9	10 10 10	10
11	0 0 1	1 1 1	1 1 2	2 2 2	2 3 3	3 3 3	3 4 4	4 4 4	5 5 5	5 5 5	6 6 6	6 7 7	7 7 7	7 8 8	8 8 8	8 9 9	9 9 9	10 10 10	10 10 10	11 11 11	11
12	0 0 1	1 1 1	1 2 2	2 2 2	3 3 3	3 3 4	4 4 4	4 5 5	5 5 5	6 6 6	6 6 7	7 7 7	7 8 8	8 8 8	9 9 9	9 10 10	10 10 10	10 11 11	11 11 11	12 12 12	12
13	0 0 1	1 1 1	2 2 2	2 2 3	3 3 3	3 4 4	4 4 5	5 5 5	5 6 6	6 6 6	7 7 7	7 8 8	8 8 9	9 9 9	9 10 10	10 10 10	11 11 11	11 11 12	12 12 12	13 13 13	13
14	0 0 1	1 1 1	2 2 2	2 3 3	3 3 3	4 4 4	4 5 5	5 6 6	6 6 6	7 7 7	7 7 8	8 8 8	9 9 9	9 10 10	10 10 10	11 11 11	11 12 12	12 13 13	13 13 13	14 14 14	14
15	0 0 1	1 1 1	2 2 2	2 3 3	3 4 4	4 4 5	5 5 5	6 6 6	6 7 7	7 7 8	8 8 8	9 9 9	9 10 10	10 10 11	11 11 11	12 12 12	12 13 13	13 13 14	14 14 14	15 15 15	15
16	0 1 1	1 1 2	2 2 2	3 3 3	3 4 4	4 5 5	5 5 6	6 6 7	7 7 7	7 8 8	8 9 9	9 10 10	10 10 11	11 11 11	12 12 12	12 13 13	13 14 14	14 14 15	15 15 15	16 16 16	16
17	0 1 1	1 1 2	2 2 3	3 3 3	4 4 4	5 5 5	5 6 6	6 7 7	7 8 8	8 8 8	9 9 9	10 10 10	10 11 11	11 12 12	12 13 13	13 13 14	14 14 14	15 15 15	16 16 16	16 17 17	17
18	0 1 1	1 1 2	2 2 3	3 3 4	4 4 4	5 5 5	6 6 6	7 7 7	7 8 8	8 9 9	9 10 10	10 11 11	11 12 12	12 13 13	13 13 14	14 14 15	15 15 16	16 16 16	16 17 17	17 18 18	18
19	0 1 1	1 2 2	2 3 3	3 3 4	4 4 5	5 5 6	6 6 7	7 7 8	8 8 9	9 9 9	10 10 10	11 11 11	12 12 12	13 13 13	14 14 14	15 15 15	16 16 16	16 17 17	17 18 18	18 19 19	19
20	0 1 1	1 2 2	2 3 3	3 4 4	4 5 5	5 6 6	6 7 7	7 8 8	8 9 9	9 10 10	10 11 11	11 12 12	12 13 13	13 14 14	14 15 15	15 16 16	16 17 17	17 18 18	18 19 19	19 20 20	20
21	0 1 1	1 2 2	2 3 3	3 4 4	5 5 5	6 6 6	7 7 7	8 8 8	9 9 9	10 10 10	11 11 12	12 12 13	13 13 14	14 14 15	15 15 16	16 16 17	17 17 18	18 19 19	19 20 20	20 21 21	21
22	0 1 1	1 2 2	3 3 3	4 4 4	5 5 5	6 6 7	7 7 8	8 8 9	9 10 10	10 11 11	11 12 12	12 13 13	14 14 14	15 15 15	16 16 16	17 17 18	18 18 19	19 19 20	20 21 21	21 22 22	22
23	0 1 1	2 2 2	3 3 3	4 4 5	5 5 6	6 7 7	7 8 8	8 9 9	10 10 10	11 11 11	12 12 13	13 13 14	14 15 15	15 16 16	16 17 17	18 18 18	19 19 20	20 20 21	21 21 22	22 23 23	23
24	0 1 1	2 2 2	3 3 4	4 4 5	5 6 6	6 7 7	8 8 8	9 9 10	10 10 11	11 12 12	12 13 13	14 14 14	15 15 16	16 16 17	17 18 18	18 19 19	20 20 20	21 21 22	22 22 23	23 24 24	24

See the page taken from H.O.249 (shown left) headed Lat. 41° Declination (15°-29°), Same Name as Latitude (because both declination and latitude are northerly).

The extreme left- and right-hand columns of the table are entered with the LHA. In this case we enter the left-hand column and at 49 we follow through horizontally into the column for 18° which is the declination. The remainder of 05' will be dealt with later by a correction table. If the declination were 18°59', the same column for 18° would have to be used.

The answer from the table

If we enter the table with the arguments LHA 49°, Lat. 41° and Dec 18° we get an answer which consists of three sets of figures:

42°21' 38' 104°

The figure on the left is the calculated altitude (Hc) for a declination of 18°. However, since the declination was 18°05', a correction must be applied. The key for the correction is given by the figure in the middle: 38' (the sign, always given in the first line of each block, being +). With this correction factor of +38 we now enter Table 5: Correction to Tabulated Altitude for Minutes of Declination. The answer for 38 (read down the left edge) and 5 (05' of declination, read off along the top) gives a correction of 3', which is added to the calculated altitude of 42°21'. This gives a final calculated altitude HC of 42°24'.

The third figure 104° which is the Tabular Azimuth Angle Z is the key to the azimuth. The rules are found on every page of the Sight Reduction Tables: N. Lat.: LHA greater than 180°... $Zn = Z$, LHA less than 180° ... $Zn = 360 - Z$. S. Lat.: LHA greater than 180°... $Zn = 180 - Z$, LHA less than 180° ... $Zn = 180 + Z$. Zn is the azimuth we want, Z is the Tabular Azimuth Angle. Since, in our example, we are in the northern hemisphere and our LHA is less than 180°, the calculation goes:

Azimuth $Zn = 360° - 104° = 256°$

The last calculation remaining is the comparison of Calculated Altitude Hc and Observed Altitude Ho (including the Total Correction, see p.288):

Observed altitude Ho	42°18'
Total correction	+ 13'
	42°31'
Calculated altitude Hc	−42°24'
Intercept	0°07'

Since the observed altitude is greater by 07' it means that the yacht's position is closer to the sun than estimated. The intercept is 'towards'.

Plotting the position line

In plotting the position line it is important to remember that the reference point is not the DR position but the chosen position.

The procedure for plotting the position line is:

1 Plot the chosen position.
2 Through the chosen position, draw the azimuth of the observed body.
3 Perpendicular to the azimuth and passing through the chosen position draw a line and move it by the amount of the intercept (07') towards the sun's GP, i.e. towards 257°. This line is the position line.

Meridian altitude

Even in the age of electronic calculators and Reduction Tables, latitude by meridian altitude (noon sight) is still popular because it is simple and quick procedure that gives the observer's latitude without the need for plotting a position line. Meridian altitude can only be taken at local noon, which is the moment the sun passes the observer's meridian, when GHA is identical with the observer's longitude. The exact moment of transit need not even be calculated; it can be established by observing the sun and taking the sight when it is at its highest point (culmination). However, rather than spend an unnecessarily long time on deck anticipating this moment, it is better to calculate the sun's meridian passage (also called 'transit') with the help of the Nautical Almanac and the DR longitude. An error of up to 20 nautical miles is unimportant here,

ALTITUDE CORRECTION TABLES 0°–35°—MOON

App. Alt.	0°–4° Corrⁿ	5°–9° Corrⁿ	10°–14° Corrⁿ	15°–19° Corrⁿ	20°–24° Corrⁿ	25°–29° Corrⁿ	30°–34° Corrⁿ	App. Alt.
00	0 33.8	5 58.2	10 62.1	15 62.8	20 62.2	25 60.8	30 58.9	00
10	35.9	58.5	62.2	62.8	62.1	60.8	58.8	10
20	37.8	58.7	62.2	62.8	62.1	60.7	58.8	20
30	39.6	58.9	62.3	62.8	62.1	60.7	58.7	30
40	41.2	59.1	62.3	62.8	62.0	60.6	58.6	40
50	42.6	59.3	62.4	62.7	62.0	60.6	58.5	50
00	1 44.0	6 59.5	11 62.4	16 62.7	21 62.0	26 60.5	31 58.5	00
10	45.2	59.7	62.5	62.7	61.9	60.4	58.4	10
20	46.3	59.9	62.5	62.7	61.9	60.4	58.3	20
30	47.3	60.0	62.5	62.7	61.9	60.3	58.2	30
40	48.3	60.2	62.6	62.7	61.8	60.3	58.2	40
50	49.2	60.3	62.6	62.7	61.8	60.2	58.1	50
00	2 50.0	7 60.5	12 62.6	17 62.7	22 61.7	27 60.1	32 58.0	00
10	50.8	60.6	62.6	62.6	61.7	60.1	57.9	10
20	51.4	60.7	62.6	62.6	61.6	60.0	57.8	20
30	52.1	60.9	62.7	62.6	61.6	59.9	57.8	30
40	52.7	61.0	62.7	62.6	61.5	59.9	57.7	40
50	53.3	61.1	62.7	62.6	61.5	59.8	57.6	50
00	3 53.8	8 61.2	13 62.7	18 62.5	23 61.5	28 59.7	33 57.5	00
10	54.3	61.3	62.7	62.5	61.4	59.7	57.4	10
20	54.8	61.4	62.7	62.5	61.4	59.6	57.4	20
30	55.2	61.5	62.8	62.5	61.3	59.6	57.3	30
40	55.6	61.6	62.8	62.4	61.3	59.5	57.2	40
50	56.0	61.6	62.8	62.4	61.2	59.4	57.1	50
00	4 56.4	9 61.7	14 62.8	19 62.4	24 61.2	29 59.3	34 57.0	00
10	56.7	61.8	62.8	62.3	61.1	59.3	56.9	10
20	57.1	61.9	62.8	62.3	61.1	59.2	56.9	20
30	57.4	61.9	62.8	62.3	61.0	59.1	56.8	30
40	57.7	62.0	62.8	62.2	60.9	59.1	56.7	40
50	57.9	62.1	62.8	62.2	60.9	59.0	56.6	50

H.P.	L U	L U	L U	L U	L U	L U	L U	H.P.
54.0	0.3 0.9	0.3 0.9	0.4 1.0	0.5 1.1	0.6 1.2	0.7 1.3	0.9 1.5	54.0
54.3	0.7 1.1	0.7 1.2	0.7 1.2	0.8 1.3	0.9 1.4	1.1 1.5	1.2 1.7	54.3
54.6	1.1 1.4	1.1 1.4	1.1 1.4	1.2 1.5	1.3 1.6	1.4 1.7	1.5 1.8	54.6
54.9	1.4 1.6	1.5 1.6	1.5 1.6	1.6 1.7	1.6 1.8	1.8 1.9	1.9 2.0	54.9
55.2	1.8 1.8	1.8 1.8	1.9 1.9	1.9 1.9	2.0 2.0	2.1 2.1	2.2 2.2	55.2
55.5	2.2 2.0	2.2 2.0	2.3 2.1	2.3 2.1	2.4 2.2	2.4 2.3	2.5 2.4	55.5
55.8	2.6 2.2	2.6 2.2	2.6 2.3	2.7 2.3	2.7 2.4	2.8 2.4	2.9 2.5	55.8
56.1	3.0 2.4	3.0 2.5	3.0 2.5	3.0 2.5	3.1 2.6	3.1 2.6	3.2 2.7	56.1
56.4	3.4 2.7	3.4 2.7	3.4 2.7	3.4 2.7	3.4 2.8	3.5 2.8	3.5 2.9	56.4
56.7	3.7 2.9	3.8 2.9	3.8 2.9	3.8 2.9	3.8 3.0	3.8 3.0	3.9 3.0	56.7
57.0	4.1 3.1	4.1 3.1	4.1 3.1	4.1 3.1	4.2 3.1	4.2 3.1	4.2 3.2	57.0
57.3	4.5 3.3	4.5 3.3	4.5 3.3	4.5 3.3	4.5 3.3	4.5 3.4	4.6 3.4	57.3
57.6	4.9 3.5	4.9 3.5	4.9 3.5	4.9 3.5	4.9 3.5	4.9 3.5	4.9 3.6	57.6
57.9	5.3 3.8	5.3 3.8	5.2 3.8	5.2 3.7	5.2 3.7	5.2 3.7	5.2 3.7	57.9
58.2	5.6 4.0	5.6 4.0	5.6 4.0	5.6 4.0	5.6 3.9	5.6 3.9	5.6 3.9	58.2
58.5	6.0 4.2	6.0 4.2	6.0 4.2	6.0 4.2	6.0 4.1	5.9 4.1	5.9 4.1	58.5
58.8	6.4 4.4	6.4 4.4	6.4 4.4	6.3 4.4	6.3 4.3	6.3 4.3	6.2 4.2	58.8
59.1	6.8 4.6	6.8 4.6	6.7 4.6	6.7 4.5	6.7 4.5	6.6 4.5	6.6 4.4	59.1
59.4	7.2 4.8	7.1 4.8	7.1 4.8	7.1 4.8	7.0 4.7	7.0 4.7	6.9 4.6	59.4
59.7	7.5 5.1	7.5 5.0	7.5 5.0	7.5 5.0	7.4 4.9	7.3 4.8	7.2 4.7	59.7
60.0	7.9 5.3	7.9 5.3	7.9 5.2	7.8 5.2	7.8 5.1	7.7 5.0	7.6 4.9	60.0
60.3	8.3 5.5	8.3 5.5	8.2 5.4	8.2 5.4	8.1 5.3	8.0 5.2	7.9 5.1	60.3
60.6	8.7 5.7	8.7 5.7	8.6 5.7	8.6 5.6	8.5 5.5	8.4 5.4	8.2 5.3	60.6
60.9	9.1 5.9	9.0 5.9	9.0 5.9	8.9 5.8	8.8 5.7	8.7 5.6	8.6 5.4	60.9
61.2	9.5 6.2	9.4 6.1	9.4 6.1	9.3 6.0	9.2 5.9	9.1 5.8	8.9 5.6	61.2
61.5	9.8 6.4	9.8 6.3	9.7 6.3	9.7 6.2	9.5 6.1	9.4 5.9	9.2 5.8	61.5

xxxiv

DIP

Ht. of Eye (m)	Ht. of Eye (ft)	Corrⁿ	Ht. of Eye (m)	Ht. of Eye (ft)	Corrⁿ
2.4	8.0	−2.8	9.5	31.5	−5.5
2.6	8.6	−2.9	9.9	32.7	−5.6
2.8	9.2	−3.0	10.3	33.9	−5.7
3.0	9.8	−3.1	10.6	35.1	−5.8
3.2	10.5	−3.2	11.0	36.3	−5.9
3.4	11.2	−3.3	11.4	37.6	−6.0
3.6	11.9	−3.4	11.8	38.9	−6.1
3.8	12.6	−3.5	12.2	40.1	−6.2
4.0	13.3	−3.6	12.6	41.5	−6.3
4.3	14.1	−3.7	13.0	42.8	−6.4
4.5	14.9	−3.8	13.4	44.2	−6.5
4.7	15.7	−3.9	13.8	45.5	−6.6
5.0	16.5	−4.0	14.2	46.9	−6.7
5.2	17.4	−4.1	14.7	48.4	−6.8
5.5	18.3	−4.2	15.1	49.8	−6.9
5.8	19.1	−4.3	15.5	51.3	−7.0
6.1	20.1	−4.4	16.0	52.8	−7.1
6.3	21.0	−4.5	16.5	54.3	−7.2
6.6	22.0	−4.6	16.9	55.8	−7.3
6.9	22.9	−4.7	17.4	57.4	−7.4
7.2	23.9	−4.8	17.9	58.9	−7.5
7.5	24.9	−4.9	18.4	60.5	−7.6
7.9	26.0	−5.0	18.8	62.1	−7.7
8.2	27.1	−5.1	19.3	63.8	−7.8
8.5	28.1	−5.2	19.8	65.4	−7.9
8.8	29.2	−5.3	20.4	67.1	−8.0
9.2	30.4	−5.4	20.9	68.8	−8.1
9.5	31.5		21.4	70.5	

MOON CORRECTION TABLE

The correction is in two parts; the first correction is taken from the upper part of the table with argument apparent altitude, and the second from the lower part, with argument H.P., in the same column as that from which the first correction was taken. Separate corrections are given in the lower part for lower (L) and upper (U) limbs. All corrections are to be **added** to apparent altitude, *but 30' is to be subtracted from the altitude of the upper limb.*

For corrections for pressure and temperature see page A4.

For bubble sextant observations ignore dip, take the mean of upper and lower limb corrections and subtract 15' from the altitude.

App. Alt. = Apparent altitude = Sextant altitude corrected for index error and dip.

---

minutes. It follows that the sun will pass the observer's meridian (22°W) 1 hour 28 minutes after passing the Greenwich meridian:
Mer. Pass. Greenwich

Mer. Pass. Greenwich	12hrs 06min
15°W +	1hr 0min
7°W +	28 min
Meridian Passage, 22°W	13 hrs 34 min G.M.T.

'Mer.Pass.Greenwich' is taken from the daily pages of the Nautical Almanac, where it will be found in the bottom righthand corner under the heading 'Mer.Pass.' This is the sun's Meridian Passage at the Greenwich Meridian. To it we have to apply our longitude, in time, to obtain the time at which the sun passes our meridian. This can be sooner, if our longitude is east, or later, if our longitude is west. The rules for Meridian Passage are simple:

1. Declination north, sun bears south (in the northern hemisphere), or declination south, sun bears north (in the southern hemisphere):
Latitude = 90° + Dec − Corrected altitude
2. Declination south, sun bears south (in the northern hemisphere) or declination north, sun bears north (in the southern hemisphere):
Latitude = 0° − Dec. − Corrected altitude
3. Declination north, sun bears north (northern hemisphere) or declination south, sun bears south (southern hemisphere):
Latitude = Dec. + Corrected Altitude − 90°

Example
On 1 August 1975 at 13h34min a sun sight is taken at meridian passage. The observed altitude is 67°24' sun bearing south. What is the latitude?
Declination
90°
+ 18°05'
108°05'

Corr. altitude
−67°41' (67°24' + 13')
Latitude 40°24'N

Meridian altitude is a useful sight not only because it is easy but because the position line obtained from it can

---

because at noon the sun — apparently — remains at the same altitude for several minutes.
Example:
On 1 August 1975 the DR longitude is 22°W. At what time is sun's meridian passage?

The sun moves through 360° in 24 hours, through 15° in one hour, through 1° in 4 minutes. Thus, one hour after passing the Greenwich meridian it will pass 15°W. The remaining 7° it will cover in 7 × 4 = 28

moon, on the other hand, is very useful for day observations because a sun sight can be taken almost simultaneously and an immediate fix obtained from the two position lines. Not only do the two lines cut at a good angle, but there is no need to transfer a position line, which is always a source of uncertainty. During the full phase, the moon cannot be used during the day because its azimuth is almost opposite to that of the sun, so that the two position lines cut at an unusable angle. The reduction of moon sights differs in some points from that of sun sights.

Altitude correction

The corrections are for semi-diameter, refraction, parallax and dip, and are found in a two-part Altitude Correction Table towards the end of the Nautical Almanac. The argument for the top half of the table is Apparent Altitude, which is sextant altitude corrected for index error and dip. Dip is found in a separate little table on the same page. Degrees of App.Alt. are read across, minutes down. The argument for the second half of the table is Horizontal Parallax (HP), and the answer is read off in the same column as that from which the first correction was taken. HP is found in the Moon column of the daily pages. Both corrections are additive. In the second part of the table values are given for both L (Lower Limb) and U (Upper Limb). If the Upper Limb is observed, 30' must be subtracted from the altitude.

Greenwich hour angle

The speed of the sun's movement relative to the earth is uniform and the values for GHA from hour to hour, based on the sun's speed of 15° per hour, can easily be tabulated. The moon's speed, on the other hand, varies from day to day. The moon's GHA, as tabulated in the daily pages, is based on its minimum speed. Since its speed on most days is different from this minimum, a 'v' correction has to be applied. 'v' is found alongside GHA in the Moon column of the daily pages, and the correction for the particular value of 'v' is found in the table Increments and Corrections headed by the number of minutes past the hour.

Aptel Novice DDF 3000 Direction Finder (see page 291)

be crossed conveniently with a morning or afternoon sight. Since the yacht will have covered a certain distance between the taking of the first and second sight, the first position line must be transferred by that distance along the course line.

The moon

It cannot be stressed enough that moon sights at night must not be taken since the horizon, due to glare, is inadequately defined. The half-

Example
GHA moon on 1 August 1975 at
10h28m10s:
GHA for 10h   51°31′.3
Incr. for 28m10s   + 6°43′.3
v-correction for v = 10.9
                     + 5′.2
GHA   58°19′.8

Declination

While the sun's declination changes very slowly and intervals between full hours can be allowed for roughly by mental interpolation, this is not possible in the case of the moon, whose declination changes very rapidly. The necessary correction is quite easy, though. The key to it is 'd' in the Moon column of the daily pages. With the value of 'd' we enter the appropriate Increments and Corrections table (in our case the one for 28m) to extract the 'd-correction':

Moon's dec. 10h   18°32′.0
d-correction for d = 5.7
                       + 2′.7
Declination   18°34′.7

Note: While the increment and v-correction for GHA are always additive, the d-correction may be subtractive. Comparison of the declination for the previous and following hours, as listed in the column, will provide the answer.

The calculation of altitude and azimuth is the same for the moon as it is for the sun, and the plotting of the position line is identical.

Planets

Planets are useful for observation if the horizon is clearly visible. The reduction of the sights is the same as that for the sun, and the plotting of the position line is identical. In the daily pages of the Nautical Almanac the columns to be used are individually headed Venus, Mars, Jupiter and Saturn. In the Altitude Correction Tables, in the front of the Almanac, and in the Increments and Correction Tables they figure collectively as Planets.

Stars

Star sights should only be taken at the moment the star has just become visible and the horizon is still visible, or when the horizon has just become visible and the star is still visible. In other words, either at dusk or at dawn. Many may be fooled into taking star sights on a bright night, but these sights will be unreliable since the horizon is not clearly discernible, usually because of moon glare.

The navigator need not be able to identify individual stars. All he needs is Vol. I of H.O.249 Seven Selected Stars, from which he can pre-calculate altitude and azimuth of any of the seven stars at a given time. He will then set his sextant to this altitude and at the chosen moment point it in the right direction (azimuth), when he should see the star in his telescope (though not necessarily with his bare eye). Errors are not very likely and would be revealed by startling results when plotting the position line.

With the help of H.O.249, Vol.I, the reduction of star sights is easier than the reduction of sun sights. These tables for Seven Selected Stars are so far pre-calculated that declination is no longer needed, only the latitude of the chosen position in whole degrees and the LHA Aries in whole degrees. The First Point of Aries (♈) is not a star but an imaginary point in the celestial sphere used for calculations. (It is, in fact, the point where the sun's ecliptic crosses the equator.) LHA Aries is

GHA Aries + Longitude. GHA Aries for the day and time is found in the daily pages of the Nautical Almanac. Once we know LHA Aries we enter the table for our chosen, whole-degree latitude of Seven Selected Stars and simply read off altitude and azimuth (Hc and Zn). At the selected time the sextant is pointed at the star, using the obtained altitude and azimuth, and the star should appear in the telescope, or not very far off. The sight is then taken, the time recorded, the sextant altitude corrected from Altitude Correction Tables, column Stars and Planets, and the position line worked out as for the sun.

H.O.249, Vol.I, Seven Selected Stars is published annually and only valid for that year. It can, however, be used during the year before and the year after by applying corrections taken from Table 5 in the Annex to Vol.I.

Direction-finding systems–radio navigation

Direction-finding by radio beacon (RDF)

Nearly all antennae (aerials) used for receiving radio waves are to some ex-

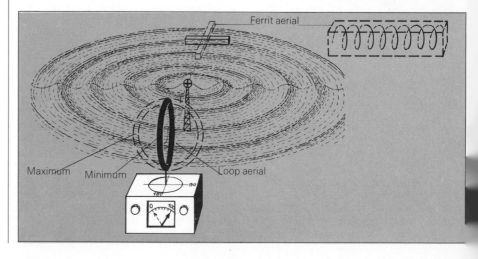

Ferrit aerial

Maximum   Minimum   Loop aerial

tent directional, which means they pick up more or less energy depending on their orientation relative to the transmitter. If we rotate the antenna of an ordinary portable radio set, we notice the signal alternately fading and increasing. RDF sets use antennae with very pronounced directional characteristics, and instead of using the maximum signal for locating the radio beacon, they use the 'null', or 'zero', because this is more easily identified by the human ear. The principle behind RDF sets is a loop or bar antenna linked to a compass or a disc graduated from 0° to 360° like a compass-card. When the null has been found by rotating the aerial, the bearing, which is either direct or relative depending on the particular model, is read off this compass or compass-card and can then be plotted as a position line after the appropriate corrections.

RDF sets are used in connection with marine radio beacons and aeronautical beacons, which are found on most of the world's coasts and are marked on charts. A complete list of the world's radio beacons, both marine and aeronautical, is found in the Admiralty List of Radio Signals, Vol.2, Radio Navigational Aids. The appropriate US Oceanographic Office publication is H.O.117: Radio Navigational Aids. All radio beacons operate on frequencies between 285 and 415 kHz (kc/s) on the long wave band, which is one reason why ordinary radio sets are not normally suitable for RDF. The maximum range of radio beacons is in the order of 200 nautical miles, but they should not be used at a distance exceeding 50 miles.

Some marine radio beacons are linked in groups with a common frequency which differs from that of any adjoining group. Thus, all beacon signals in one group can be listened to in turn on the same frequency and a number of bearings obtained within minutes. The difficulty, especially for beginners, lies in identifying the correct beacon if several can be heard on the same frequency. As with most things, competence comes with practice. Each beacon has a call sign (station identification signal), which is named in the List of Radio Signals and which usually consists of one or

two letters in Morse Code. At the listed times, this signal is transmitted in two groups, with one long 'dash' in between (beacons north of latitude 46°), or in three groups with one long dash between each group (beacons south of latitude 46°).

Aeronautical beacons, which are particularly useful in parts of the world where there are no marine radio beacons, usually transmit continuously. They, too, have call signs (station identification signals) which consist of two or more Morse Code letters. Since they are subject to greater change than marine radio beacons, they should not be relied on in the same way. Inland aeronautical radio beacons should be avoided altogether.

Procedure for taking RDF bearings

Earphones should be used in preference to a loudspeaker. In instruments with Beat Frequency Oscillator (BFO) this should be switched on. The receiver is then tuned to the frequency of the selected beacon or group of beacons and the call-sign identified. As soon as the long dash is heard, the antenna, or in some models the whole set, is rotated until the signal fades and then cuts out. The null is midway between the two points where the signal fades. The bearing obtained at that moment is read off the graduated disc mounted on top of the instrument, or off the compass, depending on the type of set.

There are basically two types of RDF set in common use on yachts: one is the loop- or bar-type set, which is usually a complete radio set with several wave-bands and is installed in a fixed position, normally in the cabin or wheelhouse. It must be aligned to the yacht's centreline, and the bearing obtained from it is a 'relative' bearing, i.e. relative to the ship's head. The other type incorporates a magnetic compass, is portable and waterproof so that it can be used in any position on deck, and gives a direct bearing. Well-known models of this type are the Seafarer Seafix, the Brooke & Gatehouse Homer/Heron, and the DDF 3000 by Aptel Marine, which is a comparatively recent, digital instrument.

RDF sets in the first group may have a visual read-out and a null meter that considerably facilitates the location of the null. Some instruments have a gionometer instead of a manually operated loop antenna. With this arrangement the antenna can be installed in an interference-free spot at a distance from the set (for example, the masthead) and is remote-controlled from the set.

ADF (Automatic Direction Finding) sets as used in aero-navigation have made small inroads in yacht use. They work on basically the same principle except that the manually operated antenna is replaced by an electro-magnetically controlled pointer.

RDF error (quadrantal error)

Radio waves are deflected by the yacht's standing rigging or, in metal yachts, by the metal of her hull. even when precautions are taken such as installing an RDF set as far away as possible from rigging wires and the boat's sides, the RDF is likely to suffer from Quadrantal Error and should not be relied on until its accuracy has been checked and if necessary a correction table drawn up. Portable sets incorporating a compass are less likely to suffer significant Quadrantal Error because they can be used in positions well clear of metal parts, which is essential in any case to avoid compass deviation.

A correction table for an RDF set can be compiled by anchoring the yacht within sight of a radio beacon. While swinging the yacht very slowly through 360°, simultaneous RDF and visual bearings are taken every 10°. The visual bearings by hand-bearing or steering compass must, of course, be corrected for variation and deviation, if any. In RDF sets that incorporate a magnetic compass and give direct bearings, the RDF error can be immediately established as the difference between the (corrected) visual bearing and the radio bearing as observed on the same instrument. Corrections can be recorded in a table, in a curve, or both (see illustration).

Consol/Consolan

Consol, or Consolan in the United

States, is a long-range navigation aid intended mainly for aircraft but also used by ships. The only equipment needed is an RDF set with frequencies as low as 192 kHz (kc/s), preferably equipped with a B.F.O. for clear reception, and a Consol(an) chart of the area. There are three Consol stations in Europe, at Stavanger (Norway), Lugo (Spain) and Ploneis (France). The two Consolan stations on the eastern seaboard of the United States, on Nantucket Island and at San Francisco, are being discontinued. The system is not used in Australia.

In a simplified way, the principle could be explained as follows: the Consol(an) station transmits a radiation pattern of alternate dot and dash groups. Of a total of 24 sectors, 12 are A-sectors, in which the transmission begins with dots, and 12 are B-sectors, in which the transmission begins with dashes. In each operating cycle a total of 60 dot-dash characters are transmitted. For example, in an A-sector the transmission will begin with dots, which will gradually change into a continuous note, the equisignal, and then into dashes. During the equisignal of the transmission, where dots and dashes merge, a number of characters are lost and must be re-added to bring the total character count back to 60. If the observed count is 14 dots and

RDF deviation table and curve

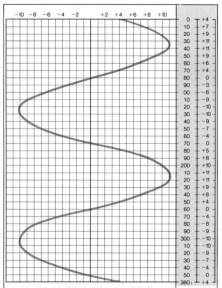

40 dashes, 6 characters are missing. These are equally divided between dots and dashes, so that the final count is 17 dots and 43 dashes. It is the type of character transmitted before the equisignal that determines the position line, in this case dots. All the navigator has to do now is to refer to the Consol(an) chart and find the lattice line for his beacon, in the sector of his D.R. position, which is marked with 17 dots.

Consol(an) bearings are primarily useful for ocean navigation, having a range of 1600 kilometres (1000 miles) or more, but they are not accurate enough for landfalls or coastal navigation.

Radar

While at one time radar was the privilege of commercial shipping, in recent years the dimensions of units has shrunk and their cost diminished sufficiently to make it a realistic proposition for yachts. Radar has two principal applications. It is not only an anti-collision device but also an aid to navigation, especially at night and under conditions of reduced visibility. A radar set sends out brief pulses of super-high frequency radio waves that are reflected back by objects at a distance. The time it takes for the pulse to go out and for the echo to come back is a measure of the distance to the reflecting object, which shows up on the screen as a

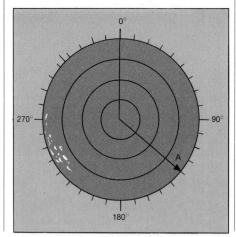

spot or patch of light. On most radars, concentric luminous circles are used as range markers, so that distance is not difficult to determine. The relative bearing of the object is indicated directly on the screen, 12 o'clock being directly ahead. The main difficulty of the radar readout lies in the uncertainty with which echoes can be identified as certain objects.

Hyperbolic line systems

Loran C

This is a long-range navigation system, at present only available on the east coast of the United States. During the next few years more stations will be built, eventually to cover the whole of the US coastal waters and the Great Lakes. Loran C has a range of 650 miles (1000 kilometres) by day, 1500 miles (2400 kilometres)

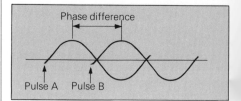

Phase difference

Pulse A   Pulse B

at night, and an accuracy of as close as 500 yards (450 metres). A special receiver is needed, which is an expensive piece of equipment, and a Loran C latticed chart. The system is based on a principle of pairs of stations transmitting synchronized radio pulses with a fixed delay between the 'master' and the 'slave'. The receiver measures the time difference between the reception of the two pulses. On the chart, all points with the same

An Omega receiver

time difference are linked by a hyperbolic line. A fix is obtained by receiving a second pair of stations and again measuring the time difference between the two pulses, which produces a second position line.

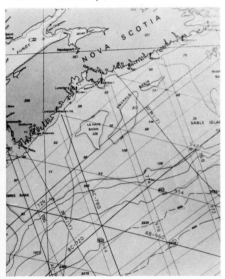

Section of an Omega chart

In working out the position line, RDF error is applied according to the same principles by which deviation is applied to a compass bearing. Once the true radio bearing has been determined, the position line can be plotted on the chart in the usual way. Assuming the observed radio bearing is 224°, RDF error +11°, variation −3° and deviation −5°, the calculation looks like this:

Radio bearing, relative	224°
D/F error	+ 11°
Ship's head	110°
Deviation	− 5°
Magnetic bearing	340°
Variation	− 3°
True radio bearing	337°

A word of warning
Bearings by radio beacon are very popular among yachtsmen because they are convenient. In foul weather the navigator does not even have to go on deck. It cannot be stressed enough, though, that radio bearings must be treated with extreme caution and that RDF error must be accurately recorded and allowed for.

Twilight effect (also known as sky-wave effect or night effect)
Radio bearings should never be taken between one hour before sunset and one hour after sunrise, because serious errors (up to 90°) may occur in bearings. The effect is most marked within one hour before and after sunset and sunrise, and bearings should not even be taken in an emergency during those times. The effect is not as marked at night, but even then bearings should not be considered reliable.

Land effect
If a radio signal travels overland for a considerable distance and does not cut the coastline at right-angles, it will be bent as it passes the borderline between land and sea. Land effect has not been sufficiently researched to make it predictable, and for this reason bearings of beacons which pass across land for some distance should be considered unreliable.

Falsification of RDF correction table
Any change in the arrangement of metal parts on deck and in the rigging may make the RDF correction table invalid. This can happen at great angles of heel or on certain points of sailing (for example through the spinnaker pole's being rigged). The possibility of this happening must be taken into account.

Ambiguity
Unless an RDF set is equipped with a sense-finding circuit, readings have a 180° ambiguity, which means that two nulls, 180° apart, are obtained. In most cases this does not present a problem because the navigator will know at least roughly on which side of the beacon he is.

Conclusion
Considering the many possibilities of error inherent in RDF bearings, the question inevitably arises whether radio beacons should be regarded as a valid aid to yacht navigation. One can only reply to this that radio navigation cannot replace any of the classic methods of coastal and celestial navigation, but it can be a valuable aid when these fail. During an offshore passage in thick fog an

RDF position line, however unreliable, can make all the difference to several days of dead reckoning.

Loran C is an updated version of Loran A, which will eventually be phased out.

Decca
This is a widely used medium-range system that also works by the principle of equal phase-difference lines. Its accuracy is remarkable and allows it to be used for coastal navigation. A special receiver, hired from Decca Navigator Co Ltd, must be used in conjunction with groups of Decca shore transmitters and Decca latticed charts. The system is available in Europe, where there is total coverage, in South Africa, Canada, Japan, the Persian Gulf and N-W Australia. It is not used in the United States.

Omega
This is another hyperbolic line system that provides a radio position anywhere on the earth's surface to an accuracy of at least 1.6 kilometres (1 mile). It operates from eight stations set up in Japan, Trinidad, Argentina, Le Reunion, North Dakota, Hawaii, Libera and Norway. If the special receiver is fed the ship's position at the beginning of the voyage, it gives a continuous digital readout of the hyperbolic lines that are being crossed, giving three position lines simultaneously. The disadvantages of the Omega system for yachts are obvious: the receiver is expensive and has to be run continuously. Even if modern electronics have produced instruments not only more reasonably priced but also more modest in their consumption of electricity, the system has not yet found wide popularity among yachtsmen.

The future

It is thinkable that at some time in the future modern technology will bring highly sophisticated navigation systems within the reach of yacht navigators by making the necessary instruments cheaper, smaller and more economical in their use of electricity. At the moment, the Inertial

Navigation System, as tested and used on warships, appears sheer utopia, and so does navigation by satellites, but the day may come when they will be considered as commonplace as the hend-bearing compass today.

Radiotelephones

For yachts over 30ft (9m) overall, which have an adequate power supply, a radiotelephone is a very desirable extra and, if long voyages are undertaken, an additional safety feature. Most radiotelephones used on yachts operate in the MF band on frequencies between 1605 and 3800 kHz (kc/s) and have an output of between 30 and 50 watts, which under average conditions gives a range of about 50 nautical miles, more under exceptional conditions. They enable the skipper to make contact with other boats, shore radio stations worldwide and, via them, with any subscriber of a national telephone network.

Emergency messages are broadcast and received on the international distress frequency of 2182 kHz (kc/s). This frequency is constantly monitored by Coastguards, by lighthouses, commercial shore stations and other vessels.

As most coastal radio stations of the world have installed or are installing VHF/FM transmitters and as VHF sets are getting cheaper, they are being used more and more aboard yachts. The main advantage on the VHF band is interference-free reception and freedom from static, while the rather more limited range of about 20 miles (32 kilometres) is a slight disadvantage. The distress frequency on VHF is 156.80 MHz (Mc/s), which is Channel 16.

The installation of a radiotelephone aboard a yacht must be checked in the United States by a person holding a first or second class licence, who will make certain tests prescribed by the FCC; in the United Kingdom by a person holding a Ministry of Posts and Telecommunications Certificate of Competency in Radiotelephony. Also, an operator's licence and a station licence are required for the use of a radiotelephony installation. In the UK this is obtained by application to the Home Office, in the US from the FCC (Federal Communications Commission). Furthermore, every station (= transmitter) in the US must have a copy and current amendments of Vol. IV of FCC Rules and Regulations, obtainable from the Government Printing Office in Washington.

The UK equivalent is Handbooks for Radio Operators, issued by the Post Office and published by Her Majesty's Stationery Office. Furthermore, in the United States the keeping of a radio log is obligatory.

Citizens band

Citizens Band (CB) radios have become highly popular in the United States, and in view of the number of boats fitted with CB using inshore waters the US Coast Guard stations do intermittently monitor CB channel 9. However, the USCG does regard CB as a secondary broadcast system and considers VHF as the primary marine communications system. In distress conditions a call over CB channel 9 would, if received, be given the same priority as the same call over VHF. However, the amount of CB radio traffic, the limited range of CB and the need for the Coast Guard to use the base CB station to coordinate a search and rescue mission do make CB less dependable than VHF.

Weather

The structure of weather

The wind is the driving-force of the sailing-boat. Unforeseen changes in the weather can be dangerous in the open sea. In sailing, as in mountain-climbing, you have to judge for yourself what your weather limits are. Everything we refer to as weather has its origin in the atmosphere: wind, rain, clouds, fog, thunderstorms, hail or snow. Without the atmosphere, we would also be deprived of the blue of the sky, the colours of the rainbow, and the red skies at morning or night.

Observers as early as Aristotle tried to work out the connection between the rays of the sun and the wind systems of the earth. They were right — the sun is indeed the energy-source for the entire weather structure. But the physical process is far from simple. It is complicated by various factors:

- The effects of the sun's position depending on the latitude, the time of day, and the season of the year.
- The relative amounts of land and sea on the earth's surface.
- The reflection and absorption of the sun's rays in the stratosphere and the atmosphere.

If the earth were a stationary planet it would be heated only at the equator by the rays of the sun. The result would be rising warm air that would be replaced by cold air from the poles. In these circumstances we would have only north or south winds. In fact, however, the earth rotates about its axis once every 24 hours. The cold air from the poles is deflected westwards by the rotation, creating the basic wind-system:

- In lower latitudes (equatorial): east winds.
- In higher latitudes (temperate): west winds.

The fact that on the earth areas of water alternate with irregularly distributed land masses explains the disturbances that produce our constantly changing weather patterns. The east wind in tropical latitudes (trade winds, monsoon) is slowed down when it meets the continental coasts. The girdle of westerlies in the middle latitudes of the northern hemisphere is broken up by the land masses of North America, Europe and Asia. Only the west winds in the middle latitudes of the southern hemisphere remain unaffected by the intrusion of land.

Most weather activities take place in the lower layers of the atmosphere, in the so-called troposphere. That is the layer from the surface of the earth to an altitude of about 26,000 ft (8000 m). The majority of meteorological phenomena can be explained by an examination of relatively few factors. The most important are:

1 Atmospheric pressure
2 Air temperature
3 Wind
4 Humidity

The measurement of a meteorological factor, e.g. barometric pressure, gives information about the situation at a given moment. From data gathered over a longer period, records of diurnal, monthly and yearly averages can be built up. Thus for a particular district the connection between changes in the observed factors and alterations in weather behaviour can be determined. Long-term research in this field is part of the science of climatology.

Atmospheric pressure

The earth's envelope of air exercises a surprisingly strong pressure on the surface of the planet. Toricelli, a pupil of Galileo, already knew that the column of air on every square centimetre of the earth's surface exerted a force of about one kilogramme. He made this measurement by observing the height of a column of mercury that could be supported by the pressure of air, and even today it remains common practice to measure atmospheric pressure in terms of millimetres of the mercury column that the air pressure being measured will support. In these units, the average pressure of the atmosphere at sea level is 760 mm mercury.

An enchanting cruising mood

International Code and other flags used in racing

	P Preparatory sign		**S** Shorten course signal
	N Abandonment signal		**Y** Lifejacket signal
N over first substitute Cancellation signal			**First substitute** General recall sign
	I Round the ends starting rule		**Blue flag or shape** Finishing signal
	L Come within hail or Follow me		**B** Protest signal
	Red flag Leave all marks to port		**Green flag** Leave all marks to starboard
	X Individual recall		For code flag and answering pennant see page 317
N over X Abandonment and Re-sail signal			**M** Mark signal

Some of the most important code flag signals

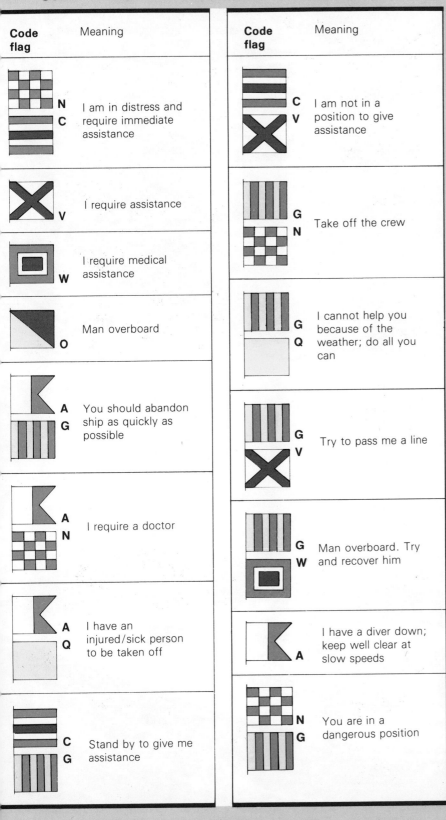

Code flag		Meaning
	N C	I am in distress and require immediate assistance
	V	I require assistance
	W	I require medical assistance
	O	Man overboard
	A G	You should abandon ship as quickly as possible
	A N	I require a doctor
	A Q	I have an injured/sick person to be taken off
	C G	Stand by to give me assistance
	C V	I am not in a position to give assistance
	G N	Take off the crew
	G Q	I cannot help you because of the weather; do all you can
	G V	Try to pass me a line
	G W	Man overboard. Try and recover him
	A	I have a diver down; keep well clear at slow speeds
	N G	You are in a dangerous position

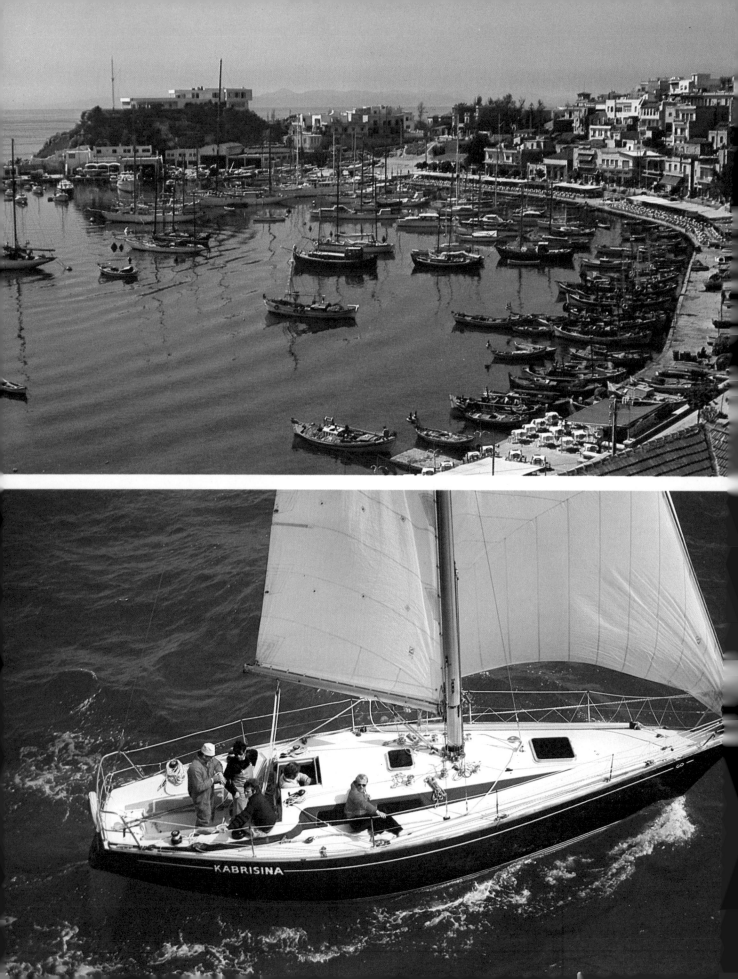

Nowadays it is more usual to express barometric pressure in millibars. In the metric system of physical measurements, 1 bar is the pressure exerted by a force of one megadyne acting on an area of one square centimetre. The force that produces an acceleration of 1 cm/sec when acting on a mass of 1 gramme is one dyne: a megadyne is one million dynes. The bar is divided into 100 millibars.
1000 mb = 750 mm mercury
760 mm mercury = 1013 mb

mb	mm
980	735
985	739
990	742,5
995	746,5
1000	750
1005	754
1010	757,5
1015	761,5
1020	765
1025	769
1030	772,5
1035	776,5
1040	780

Some barometers are graduated in millimetres, others in millibars. The above table facilitates conversion from one to the other.

Barometric pressure falls with increasing altitude, roughly by one millibar for every 8 m of height; from this follows the fact that a barometer can be used as an altimeter and an altimeter as a barometer.

The most widely used type of barometer is the aneroid barometer. This consists of a circular metal case out of which most of the air has been evacuated. One side is a diaphragm which is pushed outwards by a spring, while the atmospheric pressure

Barograph

tends to push it in. The small changes caused by variations in air pressure are tranferred to a pointer which can rotate, allowing the barometric pressure to be read off a dial. This is often calibrated in both mb and mm. The reading can usually be set by adjusting a screw on the back of the instrument.

The mercury barometer is too cumbersome and fragile for use on a small boat. For long-distance sailors the recording aneroid (or barograph) can be useful as it enables the timing and rate of pressure changes to be studied. It should be remembered that the barograph reacts sensitively to all the ship's movements. A well-padded or gimballed stowage place is therefore very necessary. The average sailor will usually make do with the ordinary aneroid barometer, but whatever he chooses there should be some sort of reliable barometer on board. The barometer is an essential part of every ship's equipment. Rises and falls in the atmospheric pressure are the most important warning signs of weather changes.

Air temperature

The temperature of the air has a considerable influence on weather patterns. The heating of the atmosphere does not result primarily from direct radiation but from the heating of the earth's surface by the sun's rays. This explains why air temperature falls with increasing altitude, although this rule only holds good up to a height of 9000 m (30,000 ft).

It is not only the air pressure that is affected by temperature changes. Differences in temperature in neighbouring air masses lead to bodily movement of air. In fact, they produce wind.

The air temperature of a place depends on its latitude (length of night and day, time of year, amount of sunshine and altitude of the sun) and the state of the weather and climatic conditions.

The land warms up rapidly during the day and causes the air above it to

TOP: A typical Mediterranean scene — the yacht harbour at Piraeus, Greece

BOTTOM: A typical modern cruiser racer. In this picture she is racing, which is indicated by the missing national ensign and the fact that the helmsman is checking his watch, obviously prior to the start.

warm up too. Similarly, it cools quickly at night and the temperature of the lower air layers falls. In lakes and at sea, the warmth penetrates deeper. The daytime temperature rises more slowly, but the mass of matter that has been warmed is greater. By night (and in winter) the air temperature over water therefore does not drop as low as it does over land.

Maximum daily and yearly temperatures are not reached, therefore, at the time of greatest solar radiation. On a summer's day, maximum temperature usually occurs about two hours after local solar noon, while the hottest days of summer are not usually until July to August in the northern hemisphere and January to February in the southern. Similarly, the coldest days of winter are usually January (northern hemisphere) or July (southern hemisphere).

Air temperature is measured by the thermometer, which consists of a thin, closed glass tube with a bulb at the bottom containing mercury or alcohol. The remaining space in the tube is a vacuum. The mercury or alcohol expands with increasing temperature, and the level reached by the liquid in the tube is read off against a graduated scale, giving the temperature in degrees.

There are two principal scales for the measurement of temperature. The centigrade (or Celsius) scale is used in most European countries and in scientific work all over the world. It takes the freezing point of water as 0° and its boiling point (at a barometric pressure of 760 mm mercury) as 100°. The system is abbreviated C, which will be found above the scale on the thermometer.

The other important scale is Fahrenheit, used in the United States and largely in England and Australia, although the use of centigrade in the United Kingdom, at least, is becoming more widespread. Here the freezing point of water is taken as 32° (F) and the boiling point as 212°F, so there are 180 degrees between the two fixed points instead of 100. Thus 1°F is 5/9°C, or conversely 1°C is 1.8°F. The two scales may be inter-converted with the help of the following table.

Certain old thermometers still exist, mainly in continental Europe, that are graduated on the Réamur scale (abbreviated R), on which 0° is the freezing point of water and 80° its boiling point. They are of historic interest but no practical use!

° centigrade	° farenheit
+ 30	+ 86
+ 20	+ 68
+ 16	+ 61
+ 10	+ 50
+ 6	+ 43
+ 2	+ 35,5
0	+ 32
− 2	+ 28,5
− 6	+ 21
− 10	+ 14

Important rules for the measurement of air temperature

Never measure the temperature with the thermometer exposed to the direct rays of the sun. It should always be kept in a shady position. Body heat (warming the thermometer with the hand) can also lead to false readings. Do not take temperature readings below deck, where the temperature will also be affected by body heat, sun through cabin windows, and perhaps even cooking.

For an ocean cruiser, a water thermometer can be almost as useful as one for air temperature. With its help, cold and warm ocean currents can be located, which can help in establishing the boat's position.

Atmospheric humidity

The air always contains some water vapour, but the proportion varies. Atmospheric water vapour leads to cloud formation, and so to precipitation. This may evaporate immediately, or prolong the cycle by making its own way over the land by streams and rivers to the lakes or the sea, the main source of evaporation.

Water vapour condenses as a consequence of the cooling of the air. Air at a certain temperature can only hold a certain proportion of water vapour. When it can hold no more, one speaks of air saturated with water vapour, or a relative humidity of 100%.

Temperature (°C)	-20°	0°	+20°
Maximum water vapour content, (g per cubic metre)	1.1	4.8	17.3

This shows that as the air cools, less and less water vapour can be contained before saturation point is reached. On the other hand, as the temperature rises, the air can absorb more water vapour.

A cubic metre of air holds 17.3 g of water vapour at 20°C when the relative humidity is 100%. If, at this temperature, the actual water vapour content is only 4.8 g, then the relative humidity is 4.8 ÷ 17.3 = 0.28 (approx.) or, in other words, the relative humidity is 28%.

The air would reach its saturation point in these circumstances when the temperature falls to 0°C. So, for air at a temperature of 20°C and a relative humidity of 28%, the dew point is 0°C. At that temperature it will deposit dew or rather, as the temperature is 0°C, hoar frost.

Air which is getting warmer becomes relatively drier, air which is getting cooler relatively moister. These are two important factors in the understanding of weather behaviour.

The measurement of humidity is carried out with a hygrometer. One form is the hair hygrometer, which takes advantage of the fact that a grease-free human hair absorbs water vapour from the atmosphere and lengthens in the process. Another method of measuring humidity consists of observing the difference in reading between a thermometer with a dry bulb and one whose bulb is encased in damp muslin. By the use of tables it is simple to get a direct reading of the relative humidity from these figures.

There is no need for the ordinary cruising sailor, be he inshore or offshore, to make a habit of measuring and recording relative humidity.

The wind

Naturally, this subject interests the sailor most of all. In meteorological terms, wind is the movement of air that results when air flows from an area of higher pressure to one of lower pressure. The uneven heating of different air masses creates important differences in pressure. For example, the temperature differences between the air over land and sea explain the well-known diurnal alternation between land- and sea-breezes.

To determine the probable future behaviour of the wind it is important to know the pattern of barometric pressure in the area in question.

An H on the weather map denotes an area of high pressure and an L one of low pressure, referred to, for short, as High and Low respectively. All places where the barometric pressure is the same are joined by lines known as isobars. An area of high pressure on the weather-map looks like an island surrounded by isobars, which denote successively lower pressures the further they are from the high pressure centre. With low pressure areas it is the other way round. The isobars indicate higher pressures the further they are from the low. Weather maps generally show the isobars at intervals of 5mb. Yachtsmen should remember that steep pressure gradients are shown by areas where the isobars lie close together, and here strong and rising winds must be expected. As a rule of thumb it can be said that if high and low are close together, the pressure gradient is steep and winds are strong. Gentle pressure gradients are shown by widely separated isobars and lighter winds are then to be expected.

Wind is described by direction and strength and force. The direction is always that *from which* the wind blows. The strength of the wind depends on the speed of the air movement. It is given in metres per second, miles per hour, or knots (nautical miles per hour). In practice, the most important measurement used by seamen is the Beaufort Scale, which divides wind speeds into twelve forces.

The scale is named after a hydrographer to the British navy, Admiral Sir Francis Beaufort, who devised it in 1805. It received international recognition in 1874, and during the Second World War the scale was extended by the US navy from its original twelve forces to seventeen. This extension has no practical value to yachtsmen, as it is impossible to measure the higher forces with normal equipment, but it does permit a more accurate description of the very high wind velocities that are met in revolving storms such as tornadoes and hurricanes. In a hurricane, wind speeds of up to 75 knots and more may be experienced. The sailing man is concerned only with the forces from 0-12, which are set out in detail in the table on the next page.

Closely linked to the wind force is the state of the sea. This has two components. There are wind-formed waves caused by the wind blowing at the time in the particular sea area, and there is swell, which is transmitted wave action caused by wind which is, or has been, blowing elsewhere. The waves formed by swell are not steep and are therefore reatively long; this distinguishes them from the wind-formed waves, which are steeper. Steepness is determined by the proportion of wave height to wave length. It is a striking fact that in the open sea wave length often increases with rising wind more rapidly than wave height.

For a sailing-boat a particularly dangerous phenomenon is a cross-sea. This occurs when the direction of the wind-formed waves conflicts with that of the underlying swell.

In shallow water the wave crests are forced closer together, resulting in an increase in wave height and steepness. This tendency results in breakers, whose height can reach 14m (45 ft) or more.

Deep-sea wave heights are given in the table on the Beaufort Scale. As an interesting comparison, here are some statistics for the shallower seas of northern Europe. The figures are maxima during gale-force winds. As a comparison, the steepness coefficient in the open sea would be about 3.

Windspeed is measured with an anemometer. Larger yachts often carry one as a permanent fixture, usually on a fitting at the masthead. This is connected electrically to a deck-level dial. For smaller yachts, there are a number of hand-held instruments which will give readings of fair accuracy, though naturally less than that of a fitted instrument.

One problem that arises when the yachtsman tries to assess the wind force or direction is that a vessel under way experiences not the true but the apparent wind. This consists, as already set out in detail on page 89, of two components: the true wind that would be observed if the vessel were stationary, and the induced wind caused by the progress of the boat.

The wind indicator on a moving yacht thus indicates only the apparent wind. You can, however, estimate the direction of the true wind by observing the direction of the waves, and also, perhaps, by signs on or near the shore, such as smoke trails, flags, or the burgees on moored yachts.

At sea, in particular, it is by no means easy to deduce the direction of the true wind from the look of the sea. Here are a few points to note.
1 The direction of foam-streaks helps to ascertain wind direction.
2 The combination of wind-formed waves and swell can mislead the observer.
3 Wave direction does not follow a change in the wind immediately.

On no account should the observer use the direction of cloud movement as a guide to the true wind. The wind at cloud level often differs markedly in direction, as well as speed, from that at the surface.

Important: The occurrence of squalls in association with showers or thunderstorms, and also in fine sunny weather as a result of intense local heating of the ground, leads to variations in the apparent wind direction, even though the true wind direction has not changed. The temporary increase in the wind velocity automatically causes a change in the direction of the apparent wind.

Weather

Beaufort wind scale

Beafort number	Limits of wind speed in knots†	Descriptive terms	Weather map symbol	Sea criterion	Probable height of waves in metres*	Probable maximum wave height in metres
0	Less than 1	Calm		Like a mirror	—	—
1	1-3	Light air		Ripples with the appearance of scales are formed but without foam crests.	—	—
2	4-6	Light breeze		Small wavelets, still short but more pronounced. Crests have glassy appearance.	0.15	0.30
3	7-10	Gentle breeze		Large wavelets. Crests begin to break. Foam of glassy appearance. Perhaps scattered white horses.	0.60	1.0
4	11-16	Moderate breeze		Small waves becoming longer: fairly frequent white horses.	1.0	1.50
5	17-21	Fresh breeze		Moderate waves, taking a more pronounced long form, many white horses are formed. (Chance of some spray.)	1.80	2.50
6	22-27	Strong breeze		Large waves begin to form; the white foam crests are more extensive everywhere. (Probably some spray.)	3.0	4.0
7	28-33	Near gale		Sea heaps up and white foam from breaking waves begins to be blown in streaks along the direction of the wind.	4.0	6.0
8	34-40	Gale		Moderately high waves of greater length; edges of crests begin to break into spindrift. The foam is blown in streaks along the direction of the wind.	5.50	7.50
9	41-47	Strong gale		High waves. Dense streaks of foam along the direction of the wind. Crests of waves begin to toplle, tumble and roll over. Spray may affect visibility.	7.0	9.75
10	48-55	Storm		Very high waves with long overhanging crests. The resulting foam in great patches is blown in dense white streaks along the direction of the wind. On the whole the surface of the sea takes a white appearance. The tumbling of the sea becomes heavy and shocklike. Visibility affected.	9.0	12.50
11	56-63	Violent storm		Exceptionally high waves. (Small and medium-sized ships might be for a time lost to view behind the waves.) The sea is completely covered with long white patches of foam lying along the direction of the wind. Everywhere the edges of the wave crests are blown into froth. Visibility affected.	11.30	16.0
12	64 +	Hurricane		The air is filled with foam and spray. Sea completely white with driving spray. Visibility very seriously affected.	13.70	—

*Wave heights in open sea with established wind strength.
†Measured at a height of 10m. above sea level.

Weather development and wind

In the middle latitudes of the northern hemisphere, the weather pattern can largely be considered as a continuing struggle between cold and warm air masses. The so-called temperate latitudes lie between the high of the horse latitudes and the polar high. From both sides, air masses arrive in the depression corridor of the temperate latitudes, thus producing a zone of highly changeable weather that affects both the North American Atlantic and European coasts. On the other hand, during the summer the American Pacific coast, apart from Alska, is normally in the circulation of an anti-cyclone (high) centred over the North Pacific, producing relatively settled weather.

In the southern hemisphere, the westerly belt lies south of all land except southern South America, the south coast of Australia, and the South Island of New Zealand. Between these two belts lie the areas of trade winds and doldrums dealt with below. In local summer (January) Australia is mostly divided between the south-east trades and the southern end of the north-west monsoon.

In the northern hemisphere, there are four main types of air-mass:
1 Polar-maritime air (P_m). Originating in polar latitudes, it has picked up moisture and warmth from its passage over the sea. Tendency to clouds or showers. Comes from the north-east on the eastern coast of the USA, north-west or north in Europe or western USA.
2 Polar-continental (P_c). Similar source, but has passed over land, so remains dry. Warm in summer, very cold in winter. From north-east or north in Europe or western USA, north-west or north in eastern USA.
3 Tropical-maritime (T_m). Moist and warm, producing cloud, drizzle and sometimes fog. From south-west or south in Europe and western USA, south-east or south in eastern USA.
4 Tropical-continental (T_c). Warm, dry air producing very fine, often cloudless weather, sometimes with poor visibility. From south or south-east in Europe and western USA, south-west in eastern USA.

These differing air masses tend to remain separate, divided by boundary surfaces known as fronts. It is along the line of these fronts that depressions first form when a salient of warm air pushes into the cold air. This interaction of cold and warm air is often marked by sudden variations in atmospheric pressure, temperature and wind direction. Once a depression is formed, it tends to drift from west to east, with a mass of warm air (warm front) pressing on stationary cold air, followed by cold air (cold front) overtaking the slower warm air. The track of a depression is influenced by surface obstructions and stationary or slow-moving anti-cyclones.

The strongest winds in a depression occur closely behind the cold front. As the front passes, the pressure begins to rise. If it does not, you have a trough, which sometimes builds up behind a cold front and is associated with gale-force winds. It is worth remembering that if a pressure rise does not occur with the passage of a cold front, a sharp rise in the wind may be expected.

In the depression corridor, ridges of high pressure often occur. They are preceded by fresh west to north-west winds, scattered showers and moderate visibility, quickly followed by fine weather and light winds (lasting from a few hours to a couple of days). The appearance of cirrus clouds heralds the approach of the next depression.

Particularly in autumn or winter, stationary highs can build up over land masses, accompanied by exceptionally high barometric pressure, and often lasting for a week or more. Such a high can also occur in summer, when it causes a long-lasting

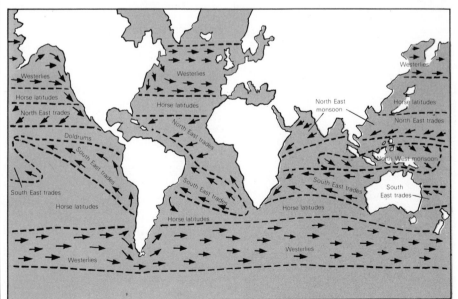

Main wind systems of the earth, January to March

heatwave. As the air is mainly dry in such conditions, thunderstorms are rare.

As has already been mentioned elsewhere, high and low pressure areas are built up as a result of warming and cooling of the earth's surface.

- A low occurs when part of the surface becomes warmer than the surrounding areas.
- A high results when part of the surface becomes cooler than surrounding areas.

In an attempt to equalize the atmospheric pressure, air is constantly on the move. It pours into the low and out of the high. The rotation of the earth causes deflection of the moving air. This is due to the Coriolis Force, sometimes called the Geostrophic Force, through which the earth's rotation causes a moving body to be deflected to its right in the northern hemisphere and to its left in the southern. The effect of this deflection is at its greatest in the temperate latitudes. Wind velocity increases with altitude. Furthermore, winds are stronger over the open sea than over land.

The wind-pattern around a high or low is a spiral. In the northern hemisphere the spiral is clockwise and outwards round a high, counterclockwise and inwards around a low. In the southern hemisphere, because of the reversal of the Coriolis effect, the direction of rotation is the opposite.

The shape of the land masses, above all steep coasts and mountains, contribute to the greater or lesser strength of the wind.

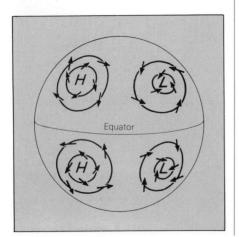

- A vertical component is introduced. The air rises. Build-up of cloud and precipitation.
- If the wind begins parallel to a coast or mountain range, the rotation of the earth will deflect it either towards or away from the geographical barrier. In the first case there is again cloud formation and precipitation. In the latter, a suction effect develops, which can on occasion cause a build-up of locally strong wind at sea or inland.
- Where the wind's path is restricted, e.g. between mountains, the wind velocity is increased.

For coastal or inland water sailing, these effects can produce tricky situations arising out of local phenomena in a generally fine weather area.

Types of wind and wind systems

Different sea areas have their own individual wind systems. Among the most important of these are the following.

Trade winds

Winds of this type occur only over or near the sea, and they are a main feature of the planetary wind system. They arise from a broad belt of moving air, lying approximately between latitude 30° and 35° N and S. The trade wind is distinguished by a high degree of reliability (which used to be important for sea trade, hence the name) and is generally associated with fine weather. Average windspeed is 7-21 knots, Beaufort Scale 3-5.

Monsoons

Wind systems covering a large area, with half-yearly changes of direction, caused by the distribution of land and sea (in the vicinity of the Indian sub-

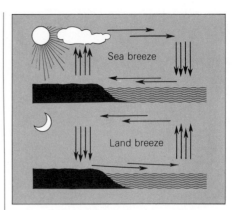

continent). The cooling of the land mass in winter leads to the build-up of a high pressure zone over the land, from which air flows outwards to the sea.

Conversely, the heating of the land mass in summer leads to the formation of a low pressure area centred over north-west India, and an inflow of air from the sea. The summer south-west monsoon in the Arabian Sea reaches a wind speed of 38 knots (Force 8). It is very moist, and when it is forced to rise as it crosses the Asiatic coasts, cloud formation and precipitation occur, bringing about the seasonal rains typical of this part of the world. The winter north-east monsoon is very dry, coming as it does from the continental air mass. It only reaches an average speed of 14 knots (Force 4).

Such seasonal wind changes are to be found all over the world.

Examples include the eastern North Sea and Baltic (north winds in early summer, sometimes extremely squally, and southerlies in late autumn), the north coast of Australia (north-west winds in summer, south-east in winter), or the eastern coast of North America between San Francisco and Vancouver (mainly northerlies in summer, south-west in winter).

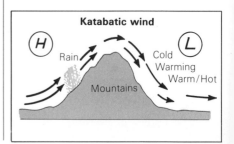

Typical cloud formation associated with Katabatic winds (in this case the Föhn)

Land and sea breezes

The seasonal change in the direction of the monsoon is mirrored in miniature by the diurnal rhythm of the land and sea breezes along the coasts. In fine weather, a local low builds up over the land as a result of heating, and air streams in from the sea, creating the sea breeze. In the evening the breeze dies away as the temperature difference between the air over land and sea equalizes. During the night, the more rapid cooling of the land produces a local high, and the wind flows out over the sea, the land breeze. Entering coastal harbours under sail is therefore easier during the daytime, while it is easier to leave during the night or, at least, before dawn.

The sea and land breeze effect is only perceptible when the overall weather situation is such as to produce only light or moderate winds, and it can be overriden in direction by the general wind. Thus if the wind over the whole area is westerly Force 4, then on a west-facing coast the result of the land and sea breeze effect would be to increase the daytime wind along the coastal strip to Force 6, and to reduce the wind at night to Force 2, but still westerly.

Katabatic winds

This type of wind is caused when the general airflow passes over a high range of mountains. On the way up, any moisture content is precipitated on the windward slopes of the mountains. Cooled by passing over the cold upper slopes, the air near the summit is colder than that further from the peaks. It therefore develops a tendency to sink, which causes it to drop down the lee slopes at an accelerating speed. The air heats up rapidly, partly through adiabatic heating due to the greater pressure as it descends, but also, in many cases, to a greater degree for reasons not yet fully understood. Finally it pours out over the plains or the sea in the form of a strong wind of low relative humidity, often abnormally hot. Typical associated weather is dry and bright with exceptional visibility.

Winds of this kind are found all over the world: the Föhn north of the Swiss, German and Italian Alps, the Bora, Mistral and Sirocco in the Mediterranean, the Chinook in the Rockies, the Santa Ana in California, the Williwaw in Argentina, the Norwester in New Zealand and the Fallvaer in Norway.

Winds of this type can be caused by a relatively small change in pressure distribution, causing a light breeze to begin passing over the mountains. On the lee side of the range, however, the gravitational effect can convert this unimportant

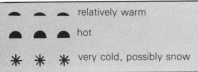

breeze into a strong or gale-force wind. In areas subject to this type of weather (mainly coasts close to mountains) a sharp lookout must be kept at all times, as katabatic winds often strike without warning.

Thunderstorms

These mostly occur as a result of the intense heating of the land surface in summer. Mountains also cause the build-up of thunderstorms by bringing about a rapid ascent of air masses. In both cases, the humidity of the air must be high. So-called frontal storms are caused by the incursion of a wedge of cold air under a body of stationary moist warm air,

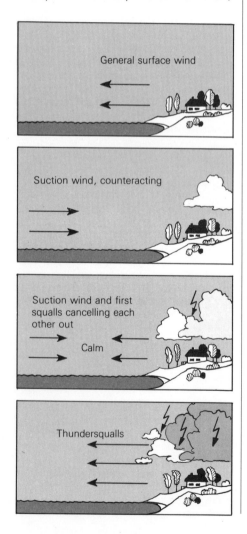

General surface wind

Suction wind, counteracting

Suction wind and first squalls cancelling each other out

Calm

Thundersqualls

which is forced rapidly upwards. This type of thunderstorm can occur in summer or winter.

The sudden uplifting of moist, warm air and the resulting heavy rain (or in some circumstances hail or snow) is associated with the build-up of an electric charge. When the potential difference between two cloud areas which are oppositely charged, or between a cloud and the earth (in which an opposite charge is locally induced) becomes too great, lightning occurs.

The distance of a thunderstorm from the observer can be judged by the time interval between a flash of lightning and its associated thunderclap. At sea level, sound travels at approx. 1100 ft (335 m) per second, so roughly speaking every three-second interval denotes one kilometre distance from the storm and every five-second interval denotes one mile distance.

It is important to be aware of one feature of thunderstorms, namely the suction wind. A thunderstorm draws air into itself while building up, but the process is reversed later by the squalls that occur during the storm itself. If the storm is forming upwind of the observer, the effect of the suction wind can be to cancel out the general wind, producing a short calm. As the storm builds, squalls develop from the direction of the storm, usually after a second calm (calm before the storm!) when the suction and squall winds temporarily cancel each other out again.

When the storm is forming downwind from the observer, the first calm cannot occur. The suction wind causes a freshening of the general wind, followed by a brief calm before the storm, as the increasing squall momentarily balances the combined forces of the general and suction winds.

Short sharp gusts of wind often occur at the beginning of thunderstorms. Thunder is, as a rule, associated with heavy squalls, but on inland waters the wind speed does not rise above 40 knots (Force 8). To this is often added torrential rain.

A true summer storm normally lasts between ½ and 1 hour and is followed by a steady improvement to fine weather. On the other hand, a

Name	Area	Description
Baguio	Phillipines	Tropical revolving storm
Blizzard	North America	Snowstorm due to incursion of cold air
Bora	Adriatic	Cold katabatic wind
Chinook	Rocky Mts	Warm katabatic wind
Cordonazo	Central America	Tropical revolving storm
Cyclone	Indian Ocean	Tropical revolving storm
Etesian	Aegean	Regular summer dry NW wind
Fallvaer	Norway (fjords)	Violent katabatic squall
Föhn	European Alps	Warm katabatic wind
Gregale	S Italy	Moist, blustery NE wind
Harmattan	Guinea Coast	Very dry NE trade
Hurricane	W Indies/G. of Mexico,	Tropical revolving storm
Khamsin	Egypt	Hot desert wind from SE
Meltemi	Greece	Strong N wind
Mistral	Gulf of Lyons	Cold katabatic wind: often gale force
Monsoon	Indian Ocean	Biannual land/sea wind
Norther	N and C America	Northerly gale from polar air incursion
Norwester	S Island N.Z. (east coast)	Katabatic wind
Pampero	S America	Gale resulting from incursion of S polar air
Santa Ana	California	Katabatic wind
Simoom	N Africa	Revolving sandstorm
Sirocco	Mediterranean	S wind, dry or humid according to area
Sumatra	Malacca Straits	Katabatic wind (from Sumatra)
South Sea hurricane	S Pacific	Tropical revolving storm
Southerly buster	Australia/N.Z.	Gale from S polar air incursion
Typhoon	N Pacific	Tropical revolving storm

Name	Area	Description
Tornado	1 N America	Small but violent whirlwind
	2 W Africa	Thunderstorm
Trade wind	30°N to 30°S	Steady NE or SE winds blowing with great reliability
Tramontana	W Mediterranean	Cold N wind
Waterspout	All oceans	Small violent whirlwind over sea
Williwaw	Argentina/ Chile	Katabatic squall, often violent
Willy-willy	NW Australia	Tropical revolving storm
Zonda	Argentina	Katabatic wind

frontal thunderstorm may well be the precursor of a permanent deterioration in the weather.

Tropical revolving storms (hurricane, typhoon, etc.)

A model of a tropical storm may be observed in the form of the sharply delineated dust-storms that often occur over strongly heated ground. The full-scale version is an intensely deep depression, generally between 50 and 250 miles (80-400 km) across (as compared with 1000 miles (1600 km) for an average depression in temperate latitudes), and almost exactly circular. Pressure can be as low as 950 mb in the centre of one of these systems, and winds of 150 knots and more have been recorded, more than twice the speed at which Beaufort first describes the wind as being of hurricane force.

Storms of this kind are normally confined to tropical latitudes, although Caribbean hurricanes sometimes get across the Atlantic and appear in northern European waters as larger, but still intense, depressions, which can give rise to exceptionally strong winds, sometimes reaching Force 12, in the east Atlantic and North Sea.

Very small revolving storms, with a diameter of only 660 ft (200 m) or so sometimes occur at sea. These give

rise to water spouts, often seen in tropical waters, and visible because of the thin column of cloud sucked down by the low pressure in the centre. Although of purely local extent, such systems can give rise to wind speeds which exceed 150 knots.

High clouds: Altitude 5000-13,000m (1600-45,000 ft) (temperate latitudes)

Cirrus (Ci)	Ice clouds, feathery, fibrous formations. Mares tails.
Cirrocumulus (Cc)	Flocks of sheep. High ice clouds, taking on intense colours at sunset. Mackerel sky.
Cirrostratus (Cs)	High ice-composed sheet cloud. A transparent veil often producing a halo. A build-up of this cloud warns of approaching bad weather.

Intermediate clouds: 2000-7000m (6500-23,000 ft) (temperate latitudes)

Altocumulus (Al)	A layer of small globular or flattened clouds. Lenticular Al is typical of warm katabatic wind conditions.
Altostratus (As)	Thin sheet cloud, usually grey. A rain warning, giving notice of the approach of bad weather.
Nimbostratus (ns)	Sheet rain-cloud; amorphous.

Lower clouds: Below 2000m (7000 ft)

Stratocumulus (Sc)	Flocks of sheep transitional between a heaped and a sheet form. Can cover the entire sky. Grey, sometimes with white.
Stratus (St)	Lowest sheet-cloud, often with shreds extending to the surface. Related to fog. May produce drizzle.
Cumulus (Cu)	Heaped cloud. Often seen on fine days, but can also develop into thundercloud.
Cumulonimbus (Cb)	Towering heaped cloud: thundercloud. Often anvil-shaped. The higher the cloud extends, the more severe the possible storm.

Thunderstorm: Typical anvil-shaped cloud.

Named winds

In many parts of the world, important or recurring winds have special names. The table on page 308-9 explains some of these names, which recur regularly in literature or weather reports.

Clouds as weather indicators

The cooling of air produces condensation and thus creates cloud or fog. The sight of clouds actually forming indicates an area of rising air. Clouds consist of water droplets. Their three basic forms are:

- Cumulus, or heaped clouds (abbr. Cu)
- Stratus, or layered clouds (abbr. St)
- Cirrus, or feathery clouds (abbr. Ci)

The most important subdivisions are shown in the table.

Individual cloud forms have typical originating causes. The formation and behaviour of clouds is a vital link in the development of weather patterns.

Rapidly expanding strongly heated air leads to cumulus formation. Such clouds have, therefore, also been called expansion clouds or thermal clouds. They occur more frequently in summer than in winter.

We often see stratocumulus, which are rolls of clouds, covering a wide area of sky. The vertical thickness of this type of cloud is relatively small and it produces no precipitation. Strong cooling after heat irradiation or a widespread rising of warm air produce the often un-broken sheets of stratus cloud. Cirrus is composed of ice particles and is therefore only found in the higher levels of the troposphere. This type of cloud provides data about wind conditions in the upper atmosphere and often gives warning of an impending deterioration in the weather.

Cloud forms often alter confusingly quickly, particularly on hot summer days. Here is an example of what can happen.

1 A July morning. Cloudless sky.
2 In the course of the morning, small cottonwool clouds develop.
3 If these clouds remain shallow and small, fine weather is to be expected all day.
4 A continual break up of these little clouds is also evidence that no thunderstorm will develop. But a fresh sea breeze may be expected (see page 307).
5 The development of cloud pillars in the course of the late morning deserves attention. These can grow into thunderheads. The more quickly they dissipate, the less the danger of storm.
6 If, however, the clouds mushroom rapidly, lose their sharp edges and appear to smoke, a storm must be expected.

General Rule

It is not threatening black clouds that introduce a change in the weather. Far more important indicators are extensive fibrous or scale-like white or greyish clouds (feather or sheet clouds). They herald the approach of a deterioration in the weather, which will arrive the more quickly if the warning clouds are moving rapidly.

Forecasting, weather reports and weather maps

Forecasting

The foregoing section has already covered a number of points about weather observation and should have given the reader an idea about the recognition of impending weather changes. The thermometer and barometer enable the basic sequence of events to be followed.

Temperature
● In summer, falling temperature indicates bad weather, rising temperature indicates good weather.
● In winter, falling temperature indicates fine weather, rising temperature indicates bad weather.

Pressure
● Slowly falling pressure shows the approach of a large depression (low). Bad weather.
● Rapidly falling pressure (1 mb or more per hour) indicates danger of gales and possible thunderstorms.
● Slowly rising pressure shows the approach or build-up of an extensive anticyclone (high). Good weather.
● A fast rise (1 mb or more per hour) denotes the passage of a ridge or col; it does not necessarily mean good weather.

Further possible observations
● Heavy dew formation after a hot day means a high probability of continued good weather.
● Mist formation: possible deterioration in good weather.
● Very red sky at sunset: continuing good weather.
● Very red sky at dawn: bad weather to come.
● Halo round the sun and/or moon: deterioration possible.
● Stars noticeably twinkling: deterioration possible.
● Streaks of yellow and green in the sky at dawn or dusk: bad weather possible.

All these and similar indications must be regarded with a degree of caution – note the words 'possible', 'expect', etc. Accurate knowledge of what causes weather is required to produce a more certain forecast. So as a rule you will add study of the local weather report and weather map to your own observations.

Weather reports and forecasts

This book is intended for an international readership, so it would clearly be impossible to give details of weather reports available by radio and other means all over the world. Certainly for the passage-making sailor or the serious cruising man, the radio forecast is likely to remain the primary source of weather information, so a reliable radio (and preferably a spare) should be carried aboard every seagoing yacht. The actual times and radio frequencies of shipping and other forecasts must be found out locally. Most nautical handbooks give full details. If a VHF radiotelephone is installed, it is also often possible to get weather information direct from a shore station.

Weather maps

The observations of many hundreds of weather stations are combined in the daily weather map, which is published in simplified form in many daily newspapers. More detailed maps are usually to be found on display in harbourmasters' offices, marinas and other suitable locations around the coast, very often being divided into a general charting of a large area, e.g. the north Atantic, and a more detailed chart of a smaller local area. This might be a square three or four hundred miles (480-650 km) across.

Professional forecasters also make use of an upper air chart, giving the weather-creating factors for the whole of the troposphere. This is necessary because the distribution and movement of high and low pressure areas at higher altitudes have a considerable influence on surface weather. On these maps, the principal lines are those joining places where 500 mb of pressure occurs at equal altitude (isohypses). The air temperature at this level is recorded. Wind direction is indicated by arrows on the isohypse or 500 mb contour.

On the normal weather map, the most prominent lines are those connecting places of equal barometric pressure reduced to sea level, the isobars. The numbers written against them, eg 1025, denote the pressure in millibars. Other symbols are used internationally as shown in the diagram below.

Alternatively, in English-speaking countries Beaufort notation may be used.

When reading a weather map, remember that it depicts the situation as it was several hours ago. Only by analysing a series of successive weather maps can you build up a picture of a developing weather pattern.

A few important rules

- A low always moves towards the area where the air pressure falls most rapidly.
- A low intensifies when the air pressure in front of it falls more than it rises behind it.

- A low fills when the air pressure ahead of it falls less than it rises behind it.
- Depressions (lows) slow down their east-west progress over land. As a result they can even become stationary.
- Anticyclones (highs) determine the paths of lows. A low (or several, one after the other) passes the strongest high in the direction of its circulation, i.e. on the side nearest the pole.
- A high always moves towards the area where the pressure rises most strongly.

The evaluation of weather maps

All available weather information should be recorded during a passage and the skipper should complete as accurate a weather map as he can at least twice a day, making use of the most recent map he has as a starter and updating it with new information.

If this routine is used, it is often possible to predict and allow for the approach of a front and its passage.

In any case, the study of a weather map before sailing, and its retention for reference during the passage, enables the observer to understand and interpret what he sees and to

L	Low
H	High
⌐⌐	Warm front
▲▲	Cold front
▲⌐	Occluded front
○	Clear sky
◔	1/8 cloud cover
◑	2/8 cloud cover
◑	3/8 cloud cover
◑	4/8 cloud cover
◕	5/8 cloud cover
◕	6/8 cloud cover
◕	7/8 cloud cover
●	8/8 cloud cover

⊗	Sky obscured
•	Slight rain
••	Moderate rain
••	Continuous moderate rain
•••	Heavy rain
••••	Continuous heavy rain
,	Drizzle
✳	Snow
▽	Shower
△	Hail
⌐⌐	Thunderstorm
=	Mist
≡	Fog
•⊡	Rain in past hour

Meteorological terms

Anabatic wind	Wind caused by air heated in a valley during the day, flowing up a hillside at night, replaced by colder air from above.
Anticyclone	Area of relatively high pressure: a high.
Backing (wind)	Wind direction changing counter-clockwise.
Beaufort Scale	Scale of wind forces devised by Admiral Sir Francis Beaufort, and now internationally used.
Cloud cover	Proportion of the sky covered. Estimated in eighths or (esp. by military observers) tenths.

Col	The ridge of high pressure joining two anticyclones.
Cold front	The boundary between the cold air at the rear of a depression, and the warmer air it is overtaking.
Cyclone	Tropical revolving storm. Also obsolete term for depression.
Depression	Area of relatively low pressure: a low.
Doldrums	Area of calms near the equator, dividing the NE and SE Trade Wind belts.
Halo	Visible circle of light appearing round the sun or moon, resulting from diffraction by ice crystals in high altitude cloud. Often a sign of impending bad weather.
Horse latitudes	Belts of calms between the Trade Winds and westerly belts.
Inversion	Situation where the air temperature rises with increasing altitude, instead of falling as it normally does. Often results in fog when occurring at sea level.
Katabatic wind	Wind caused by cold air accelerating down a slope, often warming rapidly as it goes.
Line squall	Squall accompanying the passing of a cold front. The hard line of black cloud often visible gives it its name.
Occluded front (or occlusion)	When the cold sector of a depression catches up with itself, pushing the warm sector up, the boundary between the advancing and retreating cold air masses is called an occluded front.
Precipitation	Any form of deposit of water from the air such as rain, snow, frost or dew.
Ridge	An extension of high pressure from a high into a low pressure area.
St. Elmo's Fire	Technically a brush discharge, this phenomenon appears as a violet light at masthead, spreaders etc. Caused by high potential charges in the air in thundery conditions.
Trough	An extension of low pressure from a low into an area of higher pressure.

The Mistral at Marseille (Mediterranean Sea)

Clouds building up for a thunderstorm.

Meteorological terms

Veering (wind) Wind direction changing clockwise.

Visibility Maximum distance at which a suitable object can be seen. Haze and fog reduce visibility. Not to be confused with the distance to the horizon (dipping distance) or the theoretical visibility of lights.

Warm front The boundary between the advancing edge of the warm sector of a depression and the retreating cold air.

Unstable Air is said to be unstable when, owing to a steep temperature gradient, a body of hot air rising remains warmer than its surroundings in spite of the cooling it suffers by expansion (adiabatic cooling). These are the circumstances in which thunderstorms develop.

revise the forecast in the light of actual developments. Notice should be taken of the direction and speed of movement of weather features. This information can be used to correct the map or construct a fresh one for the sea areas in which the yacht is or will be sailing. Here are two important facts for the sailor to bear in mind:

1 The direction in which a low is moving in relation to the future position of the yacht.
2 The spacing of the isobars, and thus the probable wind force. In the northern hemipshere, the wind veers if a depression passes to the north of the observer, and backs if it passes to the south. In the southern hemisphere the opposite is the case. If the distance between the isobars increases, the wind will normally decrease. On the other hand, if the isobars become more closely spaced, this normally indicates a rise in wind force.

The preparation of a weather map from information provided by the shipping forecast is quite an art and requires some practice. It is strongly recommended that you familiarize yourself with the proper procedure by studying one of the books that specialize on the subject (see Bibliography).

Finally, for the ocean sailor, who may be unable to pick up useful forecasts, there is Buys Ballot's Law which states that in the northern hemisphere an observer standing with his back to the wind has the centre of the depression on his left, and in the southern hemisphere on his right. From this law you may deduce that if you are running before a gale in the open sea you should keep the wind on the starboard quarter in the northern hemisphere and on the port quarter in the southern, to ensure that the boat is sailing out of the depression.

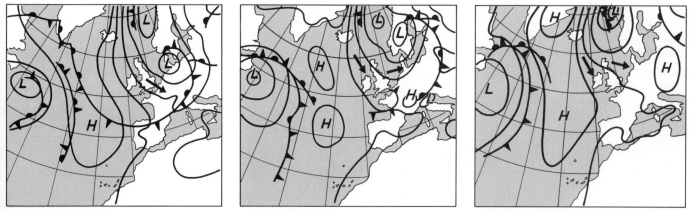

A sequence of three days of Atlantic weather showing a stationary low off the western seaboard of North America and a stationary high in mid-North Atlantic, with a complex series of lows over NW Europe

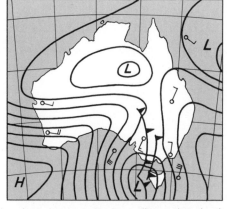
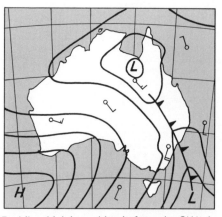

Three-day sequence of Australian weather, showing a low over N. Australia moving slowly NE while a high is pushing in from the SW. A cold front is moving west to east.

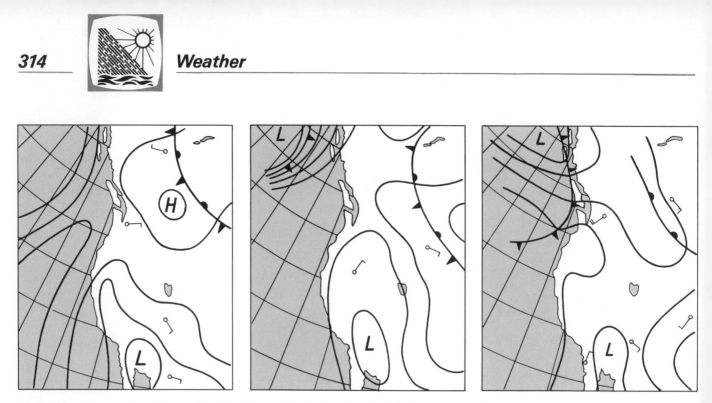

Three-day sequence of weather on the West Coast of North America showing the progress of a cold front from the NW.

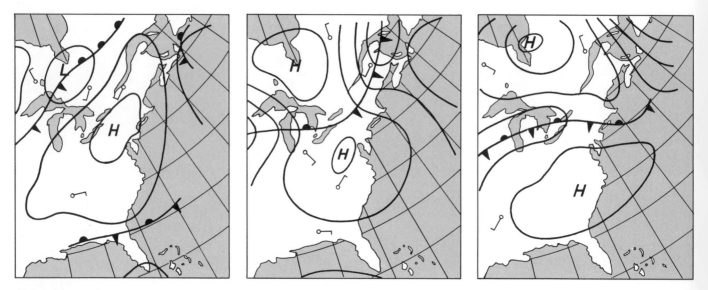

Three-day weather sequence on the eastern seaboard of North America, showing a 'backdoor cold front' approaching from the north west and pushing south.

The proper conduct of vessels at sea is governed by the International Regulations for the Prevention of Collisions at Sea, a copy of which should be carried on board all cruising yachts. The rules should be thoroughly understood by all yachtsmen, wherever they sail, as they are as fundamental to safety at sea as the rules that apply to motorists are essential to safety on the road. The most important rules from the small-boat sailor's point of view are reproduced in this section. They include internationally agreed light and sound signals. In all parts of the world there are local regulations as well, but these are not dealt with in this book as they are too extensive and too detailed. They can be found in publications of harbour authorities, river boards and the like. Enquire where you sail if there are local regulations which must be observed. It is important to note that the International Regulations are never superceded by any local rules.

In the United States of America there are special navigation requirements for certain inland waters. These are all set out and the areas clearly defined in Publication CG-169 of the US Department of Transportation, entitled Navigation Rules. These rules apply to ports and harbours, sounds and islands of the Atlantic, Gulf and Pacific seaboards, as well as Hawaii, Puerto Rico, the Virgin Islands and Alaska.

An important development in some parts of the world is the introduction of the Sea Traffic Separation Schemes, which are included in the Collision Regulations. These have been introduced by international agreement to try to reduce the incidence of collisions in shipping lanes which are particularly well used and where the size of vessels is often large, e.g. supertankers. It is very important that all small boat sailors should be aware of the presence and position of the Separation Lanes and obey explicitly the rules of navigation that apply to them. These are set out later in this chapter.

With the increase in shipping traffic in recent years the sailboat owner has had to accept more and more that he has no real privileges as a vessel under sail, except perhaps where other yachts are concerned. The impossibility of asking large vessels like supertankers to give way to small sailboats in congested and restricted waters has made it imperative to introduce rules in favour of the power-driven vessels. A wise sailor will keep well out of the way of shipping or give way to it, even if the rules are in his favour, unless, of course, such an action puts him in danger. Always bear in mind the very serious consequences of a collision with another, larger vessel even if she is no bigger than a coaster. You could have an awkward time too, if you were the cause of a large ship running aground as the result of such a collision.

Sound, shape and light signals are important for the positive identification of types of vessels in different situations. This is a particularly important part of the rules if you sail frequently in congested waters, but they are difficult to remember and an illustrated checklist is a useful thing to have on board. A good book for the purpose is *International Light, Shape and Sound Signals* by D.A. Moore (Stanford Maritime in UK).

In certain countries, Germany for example, certificates of competency are obligatory for small boat sailors. These certainly ensure that the persons concerned have had to learn the rules thoroughly as well as be competent navigators. In other countries voluntary certificates, like the Yachtmaster's Certificate (Offshore) in the UK, can be obtained by study. They are to be highly recommended as a contribution to safety afloat.

Navigation in open waters

In open waters the regulations are entirely international. On pages 322-24 we set out Rules 1-19 in full, as they are fundamental to an understanding of the correct way in which all vessels are expected to behave. Rule 10, concerning Separation Schemes, is dealt with separately on page 325.

RIGHT: The International Code of Signals

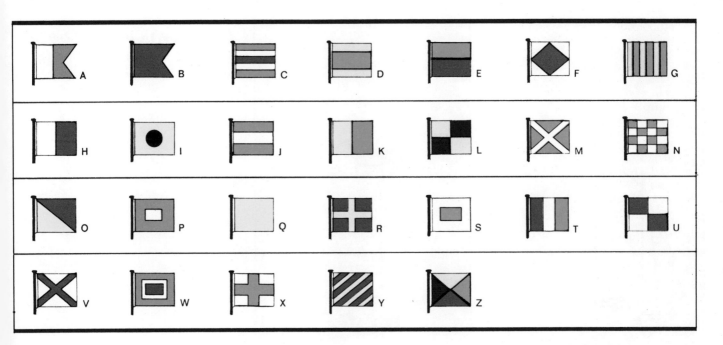

Substitutes or repeaters

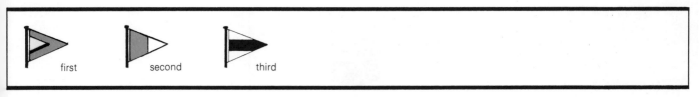

first   second   third

Numeral pendants

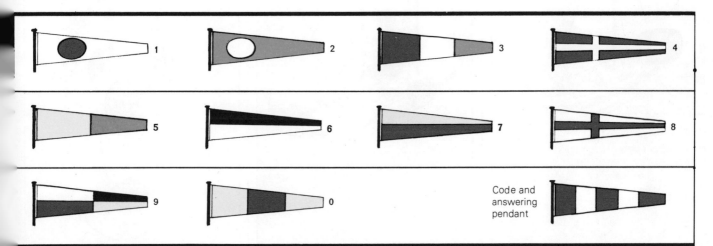

1   2   3   4

5   6   7   8

9   0

Code and
answering
pendant

Lights which must be carried by sailing boats

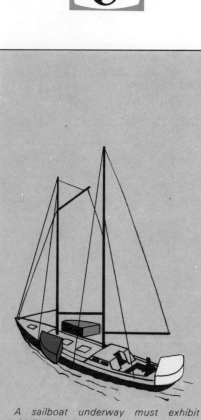

A sailboat underway must exhibit sidelights and sternlight

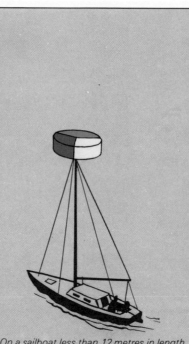

On a sailboat less than 12 metres in length a tricolour lantern can be exhibited at the masthead

A sailboat under 20 metres in length can have its sidelights combined in one lamp, shown here mounted on the pulpit

A sailboat underway can, in addition to the prescribed lights, exhibit two all-round lights in a vertical line, the upper one red and the lower one green, at the masthead. These lights cannot be exhibited together with a tricolour lantern.

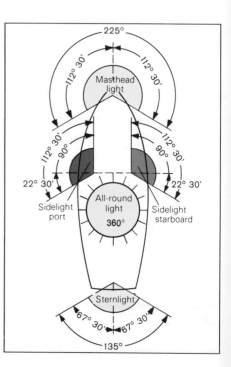

In this illustration is a variety of craft showing lights to indicate their type and situation. This is typical of the kind of range of craft likely to be met at night in coastal waters. Some of the vessels shown are very common indeed, like fishing vessels and large tankers or coasters.

1 A group of vessels at anchor. The one in the foreground is over 100 metres in length as she is exhibiting her working lights to illuminate her decks, as required in the rules. Behind her, to the left, is

a yacht of less than 50 metres in length and therefore showing only a single all-round anchorlight forward, while to the right of her is a vessel less than 100 metres in length showing, as required, two all-round white lights, one fore and one aft, but not exercising her right to use her working lights to illuminate the deck.

2 This vessel is engaged in dredging operations and is restricted in her ability to manoeuvre so she is exhibiting three all-round lights in a

vertical line where they can best be seen. The highest and lowest of these lights have to be red and the middle white. In addition the vessel shows two all-round red lights in a vertical line to indicate the side on which the obstruction is (in this case a barge into which the spoil is being discharged) and two green lights similarly displayed on the side on which another vessel may pass.

3 This is a power-driven vessel towing and unable to deviate from her

course, the tow exceeding 200 metres. Seen from ahead, the vertical arrangement of lights would be, from top to bottom, three white lights over one red, over one white, over one red. Port and starboard lights would also be seen. The tow is exhibiting normal sidelights and is lit by working lights to indicate the unusual size and nature of the vessel.

4 This is a power-driven vessel under 50 metres in length, showing starboard sidelight and masthead light. She could also show a second masthead light abaft of and higher than the forward one, but this is only obligatory for power-driven vessels over 50 metres in length. Due to the angle of her course the sternlight cannot be seen and will only appear when she has passed the observer.

5 Here is a power-driven vessel under 7 metres in length whose maximum speed does not exceed 7 knots. She is required only to display an all-round white light. It is recommended that such vessels should exhibit sidelights if possible.

6 A boat under oars must have an electric torch or lighted lantern showing a white light, which shall be exhibited in sufficient time to prevent a collision. Such a boat can, if she wishes, display the same lights as prescribed ·for sailboats under way, i.e. sidelights and sternlight.

7 This is a pilot vessel at anchor. While on duty a pilot vessel shall display at or near the masthead two all-round lights in a vertical line, the upper white and the lower red. In this case the anchorlight is being displayed as well, but if she were underway she would have sidelights and sternlight.

8 Here is a group of sailboats. To the left, the boat is under 12 metres in length and permitted to use a tricolour (combined) lantern at the masthead instead of separate sidelights and sternlight. Moving in a clockwise direction, the next boat is motor-sailing and therefore counts as a power-driven vessel, exhibiting masthead light, sidelights and sternlight. At two o'clock is a sailboat under 12 metres in length under way and us-

ing a two-colour combined lantern mounted on the pulpit. The sailboat at four o'clock is exercising her option to carry two all-round lights at or near the top of her mast, the upper red and the lower green, as well as normal sidelights, and sternlight to indicate that she is under way. Finally, at six o'clock is again the combined tricolour light at the masthead seen from the port side.

9 A power-driven vessel over 50 metres in length must exhibit a second masthead light abaft of and higher than the forward one. A shorter vessel *may* carry such a light if she wishes but is not compelled to do so. Therefore, the appearance of the lights in this case is no guarantee of the size of the vessel.

10 Here we have two fishing boats pair trawling. Each vessel displays two all-round lights in a vertical line, the upper green and the lower white, and, if making her way through the water, sidelights and sternlight. As required by the rules, each vessel is also directing a searchlight forward and in the direction of the other vessel of the pair to indicate that they are working together and that there is an obstruction between them.

11 A fishing vessel that is not trawling must display two all-round lights in a vertical line, the upper red and the lower white. If she is not moving through the water, sidelights and sternlight need not be displayed.

12 A fishing vessel whose outlying gear extends over 150 metres horizontally from the vessel is required to show an all-round white light in the direction of the gear.

13 A vessel whose manoeuvrability is restricted must exhibit three all-round lights in a vertical line, the upper and lower ones red, the middle one white. When making way through the water she must also show sidelights, mastheadlight(s) and sternlight.

14 A vessel engaged in trawling must exhibit two all-round lights in a vertical line, the upper green and the lower white. If the vessel is longer than 50 metres and making way through the water, as this one is, she must display an after-

masthead light as well as sidelights and sternlight.

15 This is a power-driven vessel towing. As stipulated, she is exhibiting two masthead lights forward in a vertical line. If the length of the tow exceeds 200 metres, three such lights in a vertical line must be shown. If she is making way through the water, she must also show sidelights, a sternlight, and a yellow towing light in a vertical line above the sternlight. The vessel being towed must exhibit sidelights and a sternlight.

16 This is a power-driven vessel towing but not making way through the water. The towing vessel is exhibiting two masthead lights in a vertical line, because the tow does not exceed 200 metres.

17 A vessel whose manoeuvrability is restricted by her draft must display three all-round red lights in a vertical line in addition to the usual lights prescribed for power-driven vessels.

18 A vessel not under command (not making way through the water) must show two all-round red lights in a vertical line.

A sailboat making way through the water under sail must exhibit sidelights and sternlight.

Sailboats under 20 metres in length can have their sidelights in a combined lantern. A good place for this is on the pulpit.

A sailboat less than 12 metres in length can have its sidelights and sternlight combined in a single tricolour lantern at the masthead.

A sailboat under way using sail alone can display all-round red and green lights at the masthead in addition to the side and sternlights prescribed. The lights shall be mounted vertically, red over green, and must not be combined with a tricolour masthead light.

(See also section on lights on page 327.)

Part A — General

RULE 1
Application

(a) These Rules shall apply to all vessels upon the high seas and in all waters connected therewith navigable by seagoing vessels.

(b) Nothing in these Rules shall interfere with the operation of special rules made by an appropriate authority for roadsteads, harbours, rivers, lakes or inland waterways connected with the high seas and navigable by seagoing vessels. Such special rules shall conform as closely as possible to these Rules.

(c) Nothing in these Rules shall interfere with the operation of any special rules made by the Government of any State with respect to additional station or signal lights or whistle signals for ships of war and vessels proceeding under convoy, or with respect to additional station or signal lights for fishing vessels engaged in fishing as a fleet. These additional station or signal lights or whistle signals shall, so far as possible, be such that they cannot be mistaken for any light or signal authorized elsewhere under these Rules.

(d) Traffic separation schemes may be adopted by the Organization for the purpose of these Rules.

(e) Whenever the Government concerned shall have determined that a vessel of special construction or purpose cannot comply fully with the provisions of any of these Rules with respect to the number, position, range or arc of visibility of lights or shapes, as well as to the disposition and characteristics of sound-signalling appliances, without interfering with the special function of the vessel, such vessel shall comply with such other provisions in regard to the number, position, range or arc of visibility of lights or shapes as well as to the disposition and characteristics of sound-signalling appliances, as her Government shall have determined to be the closest possible compliance with these rules in respect to that vessel.

RULE 2
Responsibility

(a) Nothing in these Rules shall ex-onerate any vessel, or the owner, master or crew thereof, from the consequences of any neglect to comply with these Rules or of the neglect of any precaution which may be required by the ordinary practice of seamen, or by the special circumstances of the case.

(b) In construing and complying with these Rules due regard shall be had to all dangers of navigation and collision and to any special circumstances, including the limitations of the vessels involved, which may make a departure from these Rules necessary to avoid immediate danger.

RULE 3
General definitions

For the purpose of these Rules, except where the context otherwise requires:

(a) The word 'vessel' includes every description of water craft, including nondisplacement craft and seaplanes, used or capable of being used as a means of transportation on water.

(b) The term 'power-driven vessel' means any vessel propelled by machinery.

(c) The term 'sailing vessel' means any vessel under sail provided that propelling machinery, if fitted, is not being used.

(d) The term 'vessel engaged in fishing' means any vessel fishing with nets, lines, trawls or other fishing apparatus which restrict manoeuvrability, but does not include a vessel fishing with trolling lines or other fishing apparatus which do not restrict manoeuvrability.

(e) The word 'seaplane' includes any aircraft designed to manoeuvre on the water.

(f) The term 'vessel not under command' means a vessel which through some exceptional circumstance is unable to manoeuvre as required by these Rules and is therefore unable to keep out of the way of another vessel.

(g) The term 'vessel restricted in her ability to manoeuvre' means a vessel which from the nature of her work is restricted in her ability to manoeuvre as required by these Rules and is therefore unable to keep out of the way of another vessel.

The following vessels shall be regarded as vessels restricted in their ability to manoeuvre:

(i) a vessel engaged in laying, servicing or picking up a navigation mark, submarine cable or pipeline:

(ii) a vessel engaged in dredging, surveying or underwater operations;

(iii) a vessel engaged in replenishment or transferring persons, provisions or cargo while underway;

(iv) a vessel engaged in the launching or recovery of aircraft;

(v) a vessel engaged in minesweeping operations;

(vi) a vessel engaged in a towing operation such as severely restricts the towing vessel and her tow in their ability to deviate from their course.

(h) The term 'vessel constrained by her draft' means a power-driven vessel which because of her draft in relation to the available depth of water is severely restricted in her ability to deviate from the course she is following.

(i) The word 'underway' means that a vessel is not at anchor or made fast to the shore, or aground.

(j) The words 'length' and 'breadth' of a vessel means her length overall and greatest breadth.

(k) Vessels shall be deemed to be in sight of one another only when one can be observed visually from the other.

(l) The term 'restricted visibility' means any condition in which visibility is restricted by fog, mist, falling snow, heavy rainstorms, sandstorms or any other similar causes.

Part B — Steering and sailing rules

Section I — Conduct of vessels in any condition of visibility

RULE 4
Application

Rules in this Section apply to any condition of visibility.

RULE 5
Look-out

Every vessel shall at all times maintain a proper look-out by sight and hearing as well as by all available means appropriate in the prevailing

circumstances and conditions so as to make a full appraisal of the situation and of the risk of collision.

RULE 6
Safe speed

Every vessel shall at all times proceed at a safe speed so that she can take proper and effective action to avoid collision and be stopped within a distance appropriate to the prevailing circumstances and conditions.

In determining a safe speed the following factors shall be among those taken into account:

(a) By all vessels:

(i) the state of visibility;

(ii) the traffic density including concentrations of fishing vessels or any other vessels;

(iii) the manoeuvrability of the vessel with special reference to stopping distance and turning ability in the prevailing conditions;

(iv) at night the presence of background light such as from shore lights or from back scatter of her own lights;

(v) the state of wind, sea and current, and the proximity of navigational hazards;

(vi) the draft in relation to the available depth of water.

(b) Additionally, by vessels with operational radar:

(i) the characteristics, efficiency and limitations of the radar equipment:

(ii) any constraints imposed by the radar range scale in use;

(iii) the effect on radar detection of the sea state, weather and other sources of interference;

(iv) the possibility that small vessels, ice and other floating objects may not be detected by radar at an adequate range;

(v) the number, location and movement of vessels detected by radar;

(vi) the more exact assessment of the visibility that may be possible when radar is used to determine the range of vessels or other objects in the vicinity.

RULE 7
Risk of collision

(a) Every vessel shall use all available means appropriate to the prevailing circumstances and conditions to determine if risk of collision exists. If there is any doubt such risk shall be deemed to exist.

(b) Proper use shall be made of radar equipment if fitted and operational, including long-range scanning to obtain early warning of risk of collision and radar plotting or equivalent systematic observation of detected objects.

(c) Assumptions shall not be made on the basis of scanty information, especially scanty radar information.

(d) In determining if risk of collision exists the following considerations shall be among those taken into account.

(i) such risk shall be deemed to exist if the compass bearing of an approaching vessel does not appreciably change;

(ii) such risk may sometimes exist even when an appreciable bearing change is evident, particularly when approaching a very large vessel or a tow or when approaching a vessel at close range.

RULE 8
Action to avoid collision

(a) Any action taken to avoid collision shall, if the circumstances of the case admit, be positive, made in ample time and with due regard to the observance of good seamanship.

(b) Any alteration of course and/or speed to avoid collision shall, if the circumstances of the case admit, be large enough to be readily apparent to another vessel observing visually or by radar: a succession of small alterations of course and/or speed should be avoided.

(c) If there is sufficient sea room, alteration of course alone may be the most effective action to avoid a close-quarters situation provided that it is made in good time, is substantial and does not result in another close-quarters situation.

(d) Action taken to avoid collision with another vessel shall be such as to result in passing at a safe distance. The effectiveness of the action shall be carefully checked until the other vessel is finally past and clear.

(e) If necessary to avoid collision or allow more time to assess the situation, a vessel shall slacken her speed or take all way off by stopping or reversing her means of propulsion.

RULE 9
Narrow channels

(a) A vessel proceeding along the course of a narrow channel or fairway shall keep as near to the outer limit of the channel or fairway which lies on her starboard side as is safe and practicable.

(b) A vessel of less than 20 metres in length or a sailing vessel shall not impede the passage of a vessel which can safely navigate only with a narrow channel or fairway.

(c) A vessel engaged in fishing shall not impede the passage of any other vessel navigating within a narrow channel or fairway.

(d) A vessel shall not cross a narrow channel or fairway if such crossing impedes the passage of a vessel which can safely navigate only within such channel or fairway. The latter vessel may use the sound signal prescribed in Rule 34 (d) if in doubt as to the intention of the crossing vessel.

(e) (i) In a narrow channel or fairway when overtaking can take place only if the vessel to be overtaken has to take action to permit safe passing, the vessel intending to overtake shall indicate her intention by sounding the appropriate signal prescribed in Rule 34 (c) (i). The vessel to be overtaken shall, if in agreement, sound the appropriate signal prescribed in Rule 34 (c) (ii) and take steps to permit safe passing. If in doubt she may sound the signals prescribed in Rule 34 (d).

(ii) This Rule does not relieve the overtaking vessel of her obligation under Rule 13.

(f) A vessel nearing a bend or an area of a narrow channel or fairway where other vessels may be obscured by an intervening obstruction shall navigate with particular alertness and caution and shall sound the appropriate signal prescribed in Rule 34 (e).

(g) Any vessel shall, if the circumstances of the case admit, avoid anchoring in a narrow channel.

RULE 10
This is dealt with separately on page 325.

Section II — Conduct of vessels in sight of one another

RULE 11
Application
Rules in this section apply to vessels in sight of one another.

RULE 12
Sailing vessels
(a) When two sailing vessels are approaching one another, so as to involve risk of collision, one of them shall keep out of the way of the other as follows:

(i) when each has the wind on a different side, the vessel which has the wind on the port side shall keep out of the way of the other;

(ii) when both have the wind on the same side, the vessel which is to windward shall keep out of the way of the vessel which is to leeward;

(iii) if a vessel with the wind on the port side sees a vessel to windward and cannot determine with certainty whether the other vessel has the wind on the port or on the starboard side, she shall keep out of the way of the other.

(b) For the purposes of this Rule the windward side shall be deemed to be the side opposite to that on which the mainsail is carried or, in the case of a square-rigged vessel, the side opposite to that on which the largest fore-and-aft sail is carried.

RULE 13
Overtaking
(a) Notwithstanding anything contained in the Rules of this Section any vessel overtaking any other shall keep out of the way of the vessel being overtaken.

(b) A vessel shall be deemed to be overtaking when coming up with another vessel from a direction more than 22.5 degrees abaft her beam, that is, in such a position with reference to the vessel she is overtaking, that at night she would be able to see only the sternlight of that vessel but neither of her sidelights.

Dover Strait separation lane (see section on traffic separation on facing page)

Routes indicated by arrows Seaward Limits for coastal traffic indicated by unbroken lines.

(c) When a vessel is in any doubt as to whether she is overtaking another, she shall assume that this is the case and act accordingly.

(d) Any subsequent alteration of the bearing between the two vessels shall not make the overtaking vessel a crossing vessel within the meaning of these Rules or relieve her of the duty of keeping clear of the overtaken vessel until she is finally past and clear.

RULE 14
Head-on situation
(a) When two power-driven vessels are meeting on reciprocal or nearly reciprocal courses so as to involve risk of collision each shall alter her course to starboard so that each shall pass on the port side of the other.

(b) Such a situation shall be deemed to exist when a vessel sees the other ahead or nearly ahead and by night she could see the masthead lights of the other in a line or nearly in a line and/or both sidelights and by day she observes the corresponding aspect of the other vessel.

(c) When a vessel is in any doubt as to whether such a situation exists she shall assume that it does exist and act accordingly.

RULE 15
Crossing situation
When two power-driven vessels are crossing so as to involve risk of collision, the vessel which has the other on her own starboard side shall keep out of the way and shall, if the circumstances of the case admit, avoid crossing ahead of the other vessel.

RULE 16
Action by give-way vessel
Every vessel which is directed to keep out of the way of another vessel shall, so far as possible, take early and substantial action to keep well clear.

RULE 17
Action by stand-on vessel
(a) (i) Where one of two vessels is to keep out of the way the other shall keep her course and speed.

(ii) The latter vessel may however take action to avoid collision by her manoeuvre alone, as soon as it becomes apparent to her that the vessel required to keep out of the way is not taking appropriate action in compliance with these Rules.

(b) When, from any cause, the vessel required to keep her course

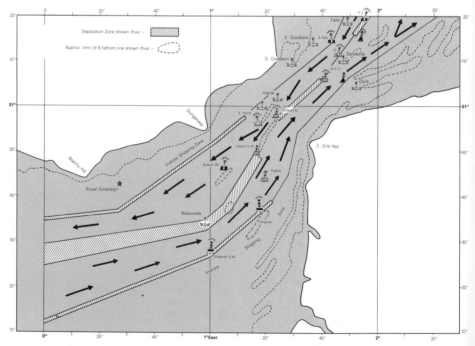

and speed finds herself so close that collision cannot be avoided by the action of the give-way vessel alone, she shall take such action as will best aid to avoid collision.

(c) A power-driven vessel which takes action in a crossing situation in accordance with sub-paragraph (a)(ii) of this Rule to avoid collision with another power-driven vessel shall, if the circumstances of the case admit, not alter course to port for a vessel on her own port side.

(d) This Rule does not relieve the give-way vessel of her obligation to keep out of the way.

RULE 18
Responsibilities between vessels
Except where Rules 9, 10 and 13 otherwise require:

(a) A power-driven vessel underway shall keep out of the way of:

(i) a vessel not under command;

(ii) a vessel restricted in her ability to manoeuvre;

(iii) a vessel engaged in fishing;

(iv) a sailing vessel.

(b) A sailing vessel underway shall keep out of the way of:

(i) a vessel not under command;

(ii) a vessel restricted in her ability to manoeuvre;

(iii) a vessel engaged in fishing.

(c) A vessel engaged in fishing when underway shall, so far as possible, keep out of the way of:

(i) a vessel not under command;

(ii) a vessel restricted in her ability to manoeuvre.

(d) (i) Any vessel other than a vessel not under command or a vessel restricted in her ability to manoeuvre shall, if the circumstances of the case admit, avoid impeding the safe passage of a vessel constrained by her draft, exhibiting the signals in Rule 28.

(ii) A vessel constrained by her draft shall navigate with particular caution having full regard to her special condition.

(e) A seaplane on the water shall, in general, keep well clear of all vessels and avoid impeding their navigation. In circumstances, however, where risk of collision exists, she shall comply with the Rules of this Part.

Section III — Conduct of vessels in restricted visibility

RULE 19
Conduct of vessels in restricted visibility

(a) This Rule applies to vessels not in sight of one another when navigating in or near an area of restricted visibility.

(b) Every vessel shall proceed at a safe speed adapted to the prevailing circumstances and conditions of restricted visibility. A power-dirven vessel shall have her engines ready for immediate manoeuvre.

(c) Every vessel shall have due regard to the prevailing circumstances and conditions of restricted visibility when complying with the Rules of Section I of this Part.

(d) A vessel which detects by radar alone the presence of another vessel shall determine if a close-quarters situation is developing and/or risk of collision exists. If so, she shall take avoiding action in ample time, provided that when such action consists of an alteration of course, so far as possible, the following shall be avoided:

(i) an alteration of course to port for a vessel forward of the beam, other than for a vessel being overtaken;

(ii) an alteration of course towards a vessel abeam or abaft the beam.

(e) Except where it has been determined that a risk of collision does not exist, every vessel which hears apparently forward of her beam the fog signal of another vessel, or which cannot avoid a close-quarters situation with another vessel forward of her beam, shall reduce her speed to the minimum at which she can be kept on her course. She shall if necessary take all her way off and in any event navigate with extreme caution until danger of collision is over.

Sea traffic separation schemes

Due to the very heavy shipping traffic on certain shipping routes it has been agreed internationally to introduce a system by which traffic going in one direction is separated from traffic going in the other. The aim is to reduce the risk of collision. The lanes cannot, obviously, be demarcated physically and so the lanes are entered on charts and their limits defined by distances and the use of existing navigation marks. This is best seen in the example on the facing page, which shows the Straits of Dover, the world's busiest shipping lane. The chief comment to make on the schemes is that small boat sailors must obey to the letter the special regulations attaching to them. The law does not take kindly to a sailboat using the lanes as though they were open water in the normal sense and transgressors are dealt with swiftly. Several British yachtsmen have already been prosecuted for infringements and fines imposed. It is better to cross the lanes in the prescribed way than to attempt to sail in them even if the wind direction is such that you can do so without breaking the law. If you must proceed down one of the lanes then do so under power. Here are the special rules that apply to the separation schemes.

RULE 10
Traffic separation schemes

(a) This Rule applies to traffic separation schemes adopted by the organization.

(b) A vessel using a traffic separation scheme shall:

(i) proceed in the appropriate traffic lane in the general direction flow for that lane;

(ii) so far as practicable keep clear of a traffic separation line or separation zone;

(iii) normally join or leave a traffic lane at the termination of the lane, but when joining or leaving from the side shall do so at as small an angle to the general direction of traffic flow as practicable.

(c) A vessel shall so far as practicable avoid crossing traffic lanes, but if obliged to do so shall cross as nearly as practicable at right angles to the general direction of traffic flow.

(d) Inshore traffic zones shall not normally be used by through traffic which can safely use the appropriate traffic lane within the adjacent traffic separation scheme.

(e) A vessel, other than a crossing vessel, shall not normally enter a separation zone or cross a separation line except:

(i) in cases of emergency to avoid immediate danger;

(ii) to engage in fishing within a separation zone.

(f) A vessel navigating in areas near the terminations of traffic separation schemes shall do so with particula caution.

(g) A vessel shall so far as practicable avoid anchoring in a traffic separation scheme or in areas near its terminations.

(h) A vessel not using a traffic separation scheme shall avoid it by as wide a margin as is practicable.

(I) A vessel engaged in fishing shall not impede the passage of any vessel following a traffic lane.

(j) A vessel of less than 20 metres in length or a sailing vessel shall not impede the safe passage of a power-driven vessel following a traffic lane.

Sound signals

Sound signals are used to call attention to a vessel's intended manoeuvres or to warn of the presence of a vessel in fog or very restricted visibility. Some of these are of particular importance to small boat sailors and the rules for these are reproduced here.

Part D — Sound and light signals

RULE 32
Definitions

(a) The word 'whistle' means any sound signalling appliance capable of producing the prescribed blasts and which complies with the specifications in Annex III to these Regulations.

(b) The term 'short blast' means a blast of about one second's duration.

(c) The term 'prolonged blast' means a blast of from four to six seconds' duration.

RULE 33
Equipment for sound signals

(a) A vessel of 12 metres or more in length shall be provided with a whistle and a bell and a vessel of 100 metres or more in length shall, in addition, be provided with a gong, the tone and sound of which cannot be confused with that of the bell. The whistle, bell and gong shall comply with the specifications in Annex III to these Regulations. The bell or gong or both may be replaced by other equipment having the same respective sound characteristics, provided that manual sounding of the required signals shall always be possible.

(b) A vessel of less than 12 metres in length shall not be obliged to carry the sound signalling appliances prescribed in paragraph (a) of this Rule but if she does not, she shall be provided with some other means of making an efficient sound signal.

RULE 34
Manoeuvring and warning signals

(a) When vessels are in sight of one another, a power-driven vessel underway, when manoeuvring as authorized or required by these Rules, shall indicate that manoeuvr by the following signals on her whistle:

— one short blast to mean 'I am altering my course to starboard';

— two short blasts to mean 'I am altering my course to port';

— three short blasts to mean 'I am operating astern propulsion'.

(b) Any vessel may supplement the whistle signals prescribed in paragraph (a) of this Rule by light

signals, repeated as appropriate, whilst the manoeuvre is being carried out:

(i) these light signals shall have the following significance:

— one flash to mean 'I am altering my course to starboard';

— two flashes to mean 'I am altering my course to port';

— three flashes to mean 'I am operating astern propulsion';

(ii) the duration of each flash shall be about one second, the interval between flashes shall be about one second, and the interval between successive signals shall be not less than ten seconds;

(iii) the light used for this signal shall, if fitted, be an all-round white light, visible at a minimum range of 5 miles, and shall comply with the provisions of Annex I.

(c) When in sight of one another in a narrow channel or fairway:

(i) a vessel intending to overtake another shall in compliance with Rule 9(e)(i) indicate her intention by the following signals on her whistle:

— two prolonged blasts followed by one short blast to mean 'I intend to overtake you on your starboard side';

— two prolonged blasts followed by two short blasts to mean 'I intend to overtake you on your port side'.

(ii) the vessel about to be overtaken when acting in accordance with Rule 9(e)(i) shall indicate her agreement by the following signal on her whistle:

one prolonged, one short, one prolonged and one short blast in that order.

(d) When vessels in sight of one another are approaching each other and from any cause either vessel fails to understand the intentions or actions of the other, or is in doubt whether sufficient action is being taken by the other to avoid collision, the vessel in doubt shall immediately indicate such doubt by giving at least five short and rapid blasts on the whistle. Such signal may be supplemented by a light signal of at least five short and rapid flashes.

(e) A vessel nearing a bend or an area of a channel or fairway where other vessels may be obscured by an intervening obstruction shall sound one prolonged blast. Such signal shall be answered with a prolonged blast by any approaching vessel that may be within hearing around the bend or behind the intervening obstruction.

(f) If whistles are fitted on a vessel at a distance apart of more than 100 metres, one whistle only shall be used for giving manoeuvring and warning signals.

RULE 35
Sound signals in restricted visibility

In or near an area of restricted visibility, whether by day or night, the signals prescribed in the Rule shall be used as follows:

(a) A power-driven vessel making way through the water shall sound at intervals of not more than 2 minutes one prolonged blast.

(b) A power-driven vessel underway but stopped and making no way through the water shall sound at intervals of not more than 2 minutes two prolonged blasts in succession with an interval of about 2 seconds between them.

(c) A vessel not under command, a vessel restricted in her ability to manoeuvre, a vessel constrained by her draft, a sailing vessel, a vessel engaged in fishing and a vessel engaged in towing or pushing another vessel shall, instead of the signals prescribed in paragraphs (a) or (b) of this Rule, sound at intervals of not more than 2 minutes three blasts in succession, namely one prolonged followed by two short blasts.

(d) A vessel towed or if more than one vessel is towed the last vessel of the tow, if manned, shall at intervals of not more than 2 minutes sound four blasts in succession, namely one prolonged followed by three short blasts. When practicable, this signal shall be made immediately after the signal made by the towing vessel.

(e) When a pushing vessel and a vessel being pushed ahead are rigidly connected in a composite unit they shall be regarded as a power-driven vessel and shall give the signals prescribed in paragraphs (a) or (b) of this Rule.

(f) A vessel at anchor shall at intervals of not more than one minute ring the bell rapidly for about 5 seconds. In a vessel of 100 metres or more in length the bell shall be sounded in the forepart of the vessel and immediately after the ringing of the bell the

gong shall be sounded rapidly for about 5 seconds in the after part of the vessel. A vessel at anchor may in addition sound three blasts in succession, namely one short, one prolonged and one short blast, to give warning of her position and of the possibility of collision to an approaching vessel.

(g) A vessel aground shall give the bell signal and if required the gong signal prescribed in paragraph (f) of this Rule and shall, in addition, give three separate and distinct strokes on the bell immediately before and after the rapid ringing of the bell. A vessel aground may in addition sound an appropriate whistle signal.

(h) A vessel of less than 12 metres in length shall not be obliged to give the above-mentioned signals but, if she does not, shall make some other efficient sound signal at intervals of not more than 2 minutes.

(i) A pilot vessel when engaged on pilotage duty may in addition to the signals prescribed in paragraphs (a), (b) or (f) of this Rule sound an identity signal consisting of four short blasts.

RULE 36
Signals to attract attention

If necessary to attract the attention of another vessel, any vessel may make light or sound signals that cannot be mistaken for any signal authorized elsewhere in these Rules or may direct the beam of her searchlight in the direction of the danger, in such a way as not to embarass any vessel.

Lights and shapes

Lights may be used at any time, both day and night, but since they are not easily seen in daylight a system of shapes has been devised which may be used at the same time or by themselves.

This is a very important part of the Collision Regulations, but only a few of the signals are reproduced here

since they are so numerous and detailed that they are best learned from visual reference in colour. A recommended book for this purpose is mentioned on page 316.

The lights that should be on a sailboat are port and starboard lights, sternlight and masthead light. The latter is not required if the sailboat is not equipped with an engine and will not, therefore, proceed under power. The diagram on page 318 shows clearly the arcs of visibility that the individual lights must have. You will note that, for good measure, it shows an all-round light, which is referred to frequently in connection with various vessels. The rules also lay down the distance at which lights shall be seen for various vessels and, therefore, the intensity of the light source. The distances are as follows.

1. In vessels of 50 metres or more in length:
   a masthead light, 6 miles;
   a sidelight, 3 miles;
   a sternlight, 3 miles;
   a towing light, 3 miles;
   a white, red, green or yellow all-round light, 3 miles.
2. In vessels of 12 metres or more in length but less than 50 metres in length;
   a masthead light, 5 miles; except that where the length of the vessel is less than 20 metres, 3 miles;
   a sidelight, 2 miles;
   a sternlight, 2 miles;
   a towing light, 2 miles;
   a white, red, green or yellow all-round light, 2 miles;
3. In vessels of less than 12 metres in length:
   a masthead light, 2 miles;
   a sidelight, 1 mile;
   a sternlight, 2 miles;
   a towing light, 2 miles;
   a white, red, green or yellow all-round light, 2 miles.

The distances are minimum ones and sailboat owners are advised, for additional safety, to try to display lights with a greater intensity than the minimum required. The problem is usually that battery capacity on a sailboat is very restricted and quickly exhausted. It is a sound plan to have two batteries, one for starting the engine and one for the lights. This eliminates the risk of being unable to start the engine to recharge the battery which has been run down by the lights. Try to estimate the amount of current likely to be needed at the worst and then buy batteries that will meet this drain with some to spare.

The lights that must be displayed by a sailboat under way are set out in Rule 25 of the Collision Regulations which is reproduced here.

RULE 25
Sailing vessels underway and vessels under oars

(a) A sailing vessel underway shall exhibit:

(i) sidelights;

(ii) a sternlight.

(b) In a sailing vessel of less than 12 metres in length the lights prescribed in paragraph (a) of this Rule may be combined in one lantern carried at or near the top of the mast where it can best be seen.

(c) A sailing vessel underway may, in addition to the lights prescribed in paragraph (a) of this Rule, exhibit at or near the top of the mast, where they can best be seen two all-round lights in a vertical line, the upper being red and the lower green, but these lights shall not be exhibited in conjunction with the combined lantern permitted by paragraph (b) of this Rule.

(d) (i) A sailing vessel of less than 7 metres in length shall, if practicable, exhibit the lights prescribed in paragraph (a) or (b) of this Rule, but if she does not, she shall have ready at hand an electric torch or lighted lantern showing a white light which shall be exhibited in sufficient time to prevent collision.

(ii) A vessel under oars may exhibit the lights prescribed in this Rule for sailing vessels, but if she does not, she shall have ready at hand an electric torch or lighted lantern showing a white light which shall be exhibited in sufficient time to prevent collision.

(e) A vessel proceeding under sail when also being propelled by machinery shall exhibit forward where it can best be seen a conical shape, apex downwards.

Lights on vessels are also subject to regulations governing their vertical and horizontal placing. These rules apply primarily to large power vessels and the only one which concerns the small sailboat is that which lays down that in all circumstances the masthead light or lights shall be placed as to be above and clear of all other lights and obstructions.

In the diagram on page 318 can be seen the four possibilities for lights on sailboats as laid down in the regulations. Note that the masthead light is carried on the higher of the two masts if the vessel is a ketch, yawl or schooner.

Sailboats of less than 7 metres in length do not have to carry the prescribed lights, but we urge that they be fitted to any boat which is likely to venture into congested waters in the dark. The statutory requirement is to carry a flashlight or lantern which has to be displayed in time to prevent a collision. A strong flashlight shone on the sails of a sailboat at night is a good way of drawing attention to the craft.

Lastly, a word about shapes. These are used to · indicate situations in daylight when the appropriate light signals would not be easily seen. Six common examples of the use of shapes are illustrated here. Sadly, very few sailors seem to observe the rule that when a sailboat is motoring while still under sail an inverted cone must be displayed. This is a dangerous practice because it can cause other sailboats to seriously misjudge the speed of the yacht, for example, going to windward under sail with the engine to assist her.

Some important day signals

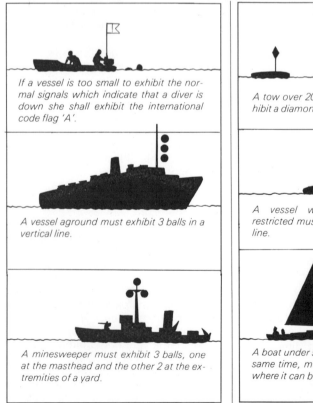

If a vessel is too small to exhibit the normal signals which indicate that a diver is down she shall exhibit the international code flag 'A'.

A vessel aground must exhibit 3 balls in a vertical line.

A minesweeper must exhibit 3 balls, one at the masthead and the other 2 at the extremities of a yard.

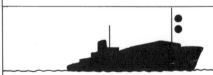

A tow over 200 metres in length must exhibit a diamond on the fore mast.

A vessel whose manoeuvrability is restricted must exhibit 2 balls in a vertical line.

A boat under sail, using her engines at the same time, must exhibit an inverted cone where it can best be seen.

Glossary

Aback When the wind strikes the leeward side of the sail it is said to be aback; it is also said to be aback when it is deliberately sheeted to windward

Abaft On the after side of

Abeam On one side or the other of a vessel at right-angles to the boat's centreline

About To go about, to tack (*qv*)

Abreast Alongside a vessel

Aft Near the stern, towards the stern

Aground Touching the bottom

Ahead In front of a vessel

Ahull, to lie To lie wth no sails set, helm lashed down

Aloft Up the mast, above the deck

Alongside Lying side by side with another vessel, or at a dock or jetty

Amidships In the middle of the ship

Anchor Any object lowered to the bottom to keep the vessel in place

Anchor rode Anchor cable

Anemometer Instrument for measuring wind speed

Apparent wind Wind felt on a moving vessel

Astern Behind the vessel

Athwart, athwartships At right-angles to the vessel; from one side of the vessel to the other

Back Said of the wind when it changes counter-clockwise (opp. lift or veer)

Backstay Stay that supports the mast from aft

Bail To remove water from a boat by hand

Ballast Any weight used to incease the stability of a vessel

Bare poles Underway with no sail set on the masts

Barber hauler Device for moving jib-sheet leads in an athwartships direction

Battens Wood, metal or plastic supports inserted in the leech of the sail

Beaufort scale Scale of wind strengths used internationally.

Beam Breadth of vessel at widest point; deck support athwartships

Bear away To turn away from the wind

Beat To sail to windward close-hauled

Before the wind Running with the wind from astern

Belay To make a rope fast

Bend A knot used to fasten the ends of two lines together or to tie a line to itself

Bendy mast A mast which can be made to take up a desired curvature by deliberately bending it or letting it bend

Bight That part of the rope between the two ends

Board One leg of a beat to windward

Bolt rope Rope sewn to or into the edges of a sail

Bottlescrew *See* Turnbuckle

Bermuda rig Triangular fore and aft sail set on a tall mast

Brightwork That part of a boat which is varnished

Broach To come round broadside on to the seas, at the same time heeling over to an extreme angle

By the lee Running with the wind coming from slightly to leeward and tending to get behind the sail

Camber The curvature of a sail

Capsize To turn a boat over so that she will not right by herself

Cast off To let go a line

Catspaw A very light puff of wind that just disturbs the surface of the water

Caulk To fill the seams of a boat with oakum or cotton to make her watertight

Centreboard/centre plate Metal or wooden board, which is lowered through the boat's bottom by way of a slot in order to reduce leeway

Centre of effort (CE) Centre point of the sail area, where all the forces of wind pressure can be said to be concentrated

Centre of gravity Point at which the total weight of the hull can be said to be concentrated

Centre of lateral resistance Centre point of the underwater area of the hull where the hull's lateral resistance can be said to be concentrated

Clipper bow, *also* **schooner bow** Bow that has a concave curvature

Chain locker Place where the anchor chain is stowed

Clear wind Wind that reaches the sailboat without interference

Clew Lower after corner of a fore and aft sail

Clew outhaul Line or tackle for tensioning the foot of the sail

Close hauled Sailing as close as possible to the wind

Close-reach Slightly freer than close-hauled

Close-reefed All reefs taken in

Close-winded Said of a boat that sails particularly close to the wind

Cockpit Part of the boat where the helmsman and crew work

Companionway The access to the main cabin

Composite construction Said of a vessel made of more than one material, i.e. wood planking, steel frames

Coach roof Structure of the cabin above the deck

Counter A stern that overhangs

Course Direction in which the vessel is being steered

Crazing Fine hairline cracks in paint or gel coat which resemble a jig saw pattern

Cringle Eye in a sail

Cunningham hole or cringle Eye in the luff or at the bottom of the leech of a sail through which a line is passed, one end of which is made fast to the mast or boom and whose purpose is flatten the sail by tightening the luff or foot

Cutter Single-masted sailboat with two or more jibs

Crutch Support for boom when sails are stowed

Dagger board Centreplate which moves vertically up and down

Dinette Arrangement in a cruiser where the table in the main cabin has settees on three sides

Dinghy Small open boat for either sailing or rowing

Dirty wind Turbulent air left by a sailboat

Dismasted Mast lost

Dock Place to which or alongside which you can moor

Downhaul Line or tackle used to put downward pressure on a sail or spar

Down helm To push the tiller to leeward so that the vessel comes up into the wind

Downwind To leeward; running before the wind

Draft Depth of camber of a sail; depth of vessel from bottom of keel to waterline

Drag When the anchor does not hold the vessel's drags

Drift A boat's leeway

Ease To let go a line or sheet gradually

Ebb The falling tide

Even keel When the vessel is floating exactly upright

Eye of the wind The exact point from which the true wind is coming

Eyelets Small brass or stainless steel cringles

Fair wind A favourable wind from the point of view of the course required

Fall off When the head or bow of a vessel moves away from the wind

False tack Misleading an opponent while racing by pretending to tack and instead remaining on the same tack

Fast, make To belay a line or sheet

Fend off To push another vessel away or hold vessel off dock

Fetch The distance a wind-induced sea has to travel across open water; also to reach to, or make a mark

Floatation bags Inflatable bags used to give a boat buoyancy if she gets waterlogged

Flood Rising tide

Foot The bottom edge of a sail from tack to clew

Fore Forward

Fore and aft Lengthwise, along the boat's centreline, hence fore and aft rig

Fore triangle The triangle measured for rating purposes and formed by the mast, forestay and deck

Forward Near or towards the bow

Foul Opposite to clear, e.g. a foul wind; to get the propeller fouled in a rope

Free The wind is said to be free when it moves further aft, opposite to head

Freeboard The distance between the waterline and the deck

Full Said of a sail with plenty of draft

Furl To gather a sail on or round a spar or stay

Flaw Gust of wind

Flying A jib that is set without being hanked to a forestay is said to be flying

Gather way Start to move through the water

Gel coat The external coat of resin on fibreglass boat which has a high gloss

Genoa A very large jib that overlaps the mainsail considerably

Ghosting Moving through the water gently in a very light wind

Give way To allow another vessel right of way

Go about To tack (qv)

Gooseneck Fitting on the mast to which the boom is attached and which has a universal joint

Gripe To have a tendency to pull hard up into the wind

Ground tackle The equipment for anchoring: anchors, rode, etc

Guy Rope used for steadying a spar

Gybe To change from one tack to the other with the wind from aft

Halyards Lines used for hoisting sails

Hand To take a sail down

Hard Hard up/hard down refers to the tiller being put to weather or leeward respectively as far as it will go, thus putting the rudder hard over

Hawser Heavy rope used for towing, mooring etc.

Heading Direction in which the vessel is pointing

Head to wind With the bow directly into the wind

Heave to To stop the boat with the jib backed and the tiller lashed to leeward

Heel Very bottom of the mast; also said of a vessel when she is inclined either to port or starboard by the action of the wind and/or sea

Helm General description of the means of steering, i.e. tiller or wheel

Hike, hike out (N. America) To sit on the side deck and lean outboard to add to the stability of the boat

Hitch A knot used to make a line fast to an object

Horse Bar that takes the traveller (qv)

Headfoil Solid forestay with groove to take jib luff

Head The topmost part of the sail; the wind is said to head when it moves further forward forcing the boat to change direction to leeward or, alternatively, to harden in the sheets

Heads Toilet on a boat

Heave To throw, e.g. heave a line

Inboard In the vessel, also nearer the middle of the vessel

In irons Said of a sailing vessel which is head to wind and is unable to turn one way or the other

Inshore Near to the shore

In stays Said of a sailing vessel when she is on the point of going through the eye of the wind as she tacks; also lying head to wind without steerage way

Jib Sail set forward of the mast

Jib sheet Line that controls the set of a headsail/jib

Jury rig Temporary rig set up after an

accident

Jumpers Stays led over struts which project from the front of the mast (above the crosstrees) and serve to support the mast fore and aft

Kedge General term for stock anchor of the fisherman type. Small anchor used for kedging

Kedging Putting out a small anchor for the purpose of either remaining stationary when becalmed or for hauling the boat off after grounding

Knot A nautical mile per hour

Knock A heading wind (N. America, Australia)

Kicking strap *See* Vang

Lacing Light line used for attaching sails to spars, awnings to framework etc

Lash To secure with a line

Lay To be able to steer a chosen course without diverting from the straight line; the direction of twist in the strands of a rope

Lee The side away from the wind direction
In the lee of = sheltered from the wind by land, another vessel, etc

Leech After-edge of a fore and aft sail

Leeboards Boards rigged on either side of a sailing craft and acting in the same way as a centreboard

Lee helm When the natural tendency of a boat is to turn away from the wind unless rudder correction is applied

Lee shore Shore on to which the wind blows

Leeward Direction away from the wind; downwind

Leeway The drift of a boat sideways due to the side force of the wind

Let fly Let a sheet go completely

Life vest Buoyancy aid (N. America)

Lift A sail lifts when the wind strikes the leeward side so that it is no longer full

List A boat is said to list when she leans to one side, usually as a result of a shift in weight

LOA Length overall, the extreme measurements of a boat including all extensions

Log Device for measuring distance sailed; also detailed account of a boat's day by day happenings and progress

Luff Forward edge of a fore and aft sail; said of a sail (N. America) that is set too close to the wind and is beginning to lift

Luff up Come up towards the wind; *see* Head up

Main boom The spar to which the foot of the mainsail is attached

Mainsail Sail set on the mast; set on the mainmast if there is more than one mast

Mainsheet Sheet used to control the mainsail

Make fast Secure

Marconi rig Bermuda rig (*qv*)

Mark Buoy on racing course

Marline spike Tapered spike used in splicing

Masthead rig Rig in which the jibs/headsails are set from the top of the mast

Mizzenmast The aftermast of a ketch or yawl; mizzen = sail used on mizzen mast

Monohull Vessel with one hull

Moor Tie up a vessel so that she cannot drift free

Multihull Vessel with more than one hull, i.e. catamaran, trimaran

Nautical mile Equivalent of 11/16th land miles or 6080 ft, equal to one minute of longitude

Neap tide Tide whose range is at a minimum

Off the wind Said of a vessel when she is not sailing close hauled

Offshore Away from the land, e.g. offshore wind

Onshore Towards the land, e.g. onshore wind

Outhaul Line or tackle used to pull the foot of the sail out to its fullest extent

Outpoint Said of a sailboat that sails closer to the wind than its competitor

Outrigger Small hull on one or both sides of the main hull and attached to it by booms

Overboard Over the side, into the water

Overstand To remain too long on one tack so that you go beyond the point you had intended

Pay off When the boat's head turns away from the wind

Pile Wooden or concrete post driven into the sea bottom used for mooring or as part of a jetty or dock

Pinch To sail too close to the wind so that the sails start to luff

Pitch When the bow moves violently up and down; also the angle of the propeller blades to the shaft

Plane When a sailboat rises up on its own bow wave and reaches speeds far in excess of those normally associated with its waterline length

Point The ability of a sailboat to sail close to the wind well or badly

Pooped When the stern of a boat is overwhelmed by an overtaking wave and water comes on board

Port Left-hand side of the boat facing forward

Port tack When the wind comes from the port side and the boom is on the starboard side. Port tack vessels give way to starboard tack vessels

Preventer Stay used to keep spar in place (N. America); stay used to support mast from aft (UK)

Pulpit Metal guardrail at the bow

Pushpit Colloquial term for stern pulpit

Quarter Aft part of a vessel on one side or the other; on the quarter refers to anything at an angle of 45° forward of dead astern

Race Turbulent water caused by strong tidal streams

Rafting Vessels moored in groups alongside each other (N. America/Australia)

Rake Fore and aft angle of the mast

Rating The handicap given to a sailboat to enable her to race against dissimilar sailboats under a system of time allowance

Reach Any point of sailing between close hauled and running

Reef To reduce the working area of a sail

Reef pennants Pieces of line used to secure the loose part of a sail when reefed

Reeve To pass a line through a cringle or block

Rig General term for spars, sails and rigging; also the way the masts and sails are arranged, i.e. sloop rig, ketch rig, cutter rig, etc.

Rigging *See* Running riggings, Standing rigging

Rigging screw *See* Turnbuckle

Roach Curved part of the leech of a Bermuda sail, which is supported by the sail battens

Round up Come head to wind

Running Sailing with the wind from aft

Runners Backstays that can be slackened off or taken in at will

Running rigging Rope or wire used in setting and adjusting sails as opposed to standing rigging, i.e. halyards, sheets, guys, topping lifts, etc

Sag Said of a boat that falls off to leeward

Sail track Track on mast or boom to which sail is attached by slides

Sampson post Strong post on foredeck for attaching mooring lines

Scandalize To reduce the effective area of a mainsail by raising the boom or lowering the peak (in a gaff sail) until the sail holds very little wind

Scope Length of chain paid out when anchored

Sea breeze Wind that blows from sea to land

Sea room Room to manoeuvre without danger

Seize Bind firmly together with lashing

Self bailers Ports in the bottom of a dinghy hull or in the transom; if they are opened when the dinghy is underway, any water in the bilges is automatically drained out by suction

Set To hoist and trim sails

Sheer about Swing, usually violently, from side to side on a mooring as a result of the interaction of wind and current

Sheets Lines that control the trim of the sails

Sheet in Haul the sheets in

Shift, wind Change in wind direction

Ship Take into or on the boat, e.g. ship water

Shrouds Rigging that supports the mast athwartships

Shy Said of a spinnaker when it is set as close to the wind as possible

Slat Said of a sail that flaps or flogs in the wind

Slot The gap between the jib and the mainsail through which the wind is funnelled

Sounding Depth of water taken at a particular spot

Spill the wind Let the sails deliberately shake and not use the wind

Split tacks To sail on opposite tack to an opponent in a race

Spoon bow Bow with a convex curvature

Stall A sail stalls when the airflow is so disturbed that the sail ceases to operate efficiently as an aerofoil and produces no lift over the whole or part of its surface

Standing rigging Permanent wire supports for the masts

Starboard tack When the wind comes from the starboard side and the boom is to port

Start sheets To ease the sheets by a very small amount

Stays Rigging that supports the mast fore and aft

Steerage way When the boat has just sufficient movement through the water to enable the helmsman to steer a course

Stem To hold your own against the tide; timber at the bow from keel to deck level

Step Place in which the mast stands; to step the mast is to raise it into position

Sternway Movement of the boat backwards

Stiff A yacht which is stiff has a high resistance to heeling (opposite tender)

Straight stem Bow which is vertical between deck and keel

Swell Wave motion caused by weather in a distant sea area

Tabernacle Support for the mast which is stepped on deck; often the mast will pivot in it for lowering

Tack Lower forward corner of a sail; go about head to wind

Tack downwind To sail first on one broad reach and then the other, gybing each time tacks are changed

Tackle Line and blocks to make a purchase

Take in Reduce or take down sail

Tall boy Long, narrow sail set inside the spinnaker

Tender A boat that has a low resistance to heeling is said to be tender (opposite stiff); also dinghy used for ferrying between shore and moored boat

Topping lift Halyard used to take the weight of the main boom or spinnaker boom

Trapeze To enable the crew member to extend his weight as far outboard as possible, a wire is attached to the hounds from which the crew member suspends himself

Traveller Device for altering the position of the mainsheet lead athwartships to suit varying weather conditions

Trim The attitude of a boat in the water; to adjust the sails to get the

best performance from them

Turtle Bag from which the spinnaker can be set

Trunk Cabin above deck level (N. America)

Turnbuckle Screw device for adjusting the tension of the rigging (N. America)

Underway When a yacht is moving through the water

Up helm Pull the tiller to windward

Upwind In the direction of the wind, to windward

Vang Tackle to prevent boom rising, kicking strap

Veer Said of the wind when it changes direction; to let out more cable

Warp Heavy rope for towing or mooring

Way Movement of a boat through the water

Weather The side from which the wind is blowing; windward; also to go past a boat or obstacle on the windward side

Weather helm When a sailboat has a natural tendency to come up into the wind unless rudder correction is applied (opposite lee helm)

Weather shore Coastline upwind of a boat, from which the wind is blowing

Weigh anchor Take the anchor up

Whip Fasten the end of a rope with twine to prevent the lay from unwinding

Whisker pole Small boom for winging out jib, sometimes called jib stick

Wide berth To keep well clear of another boat

Wind over tide Wind and tide moving in contrary directions

Wind shadow The area affected by the turbulent air from a sailboat's sails

Wing and wing To set the jib on the opposite side to the main when running

Yaw Failing to keep on course by swinging from side to side

Glossary of terms used in navigation

Astro-navigation Navigating by the sun, moon. stars and planets
Bearing The measured angle of an object from the observer
Binnacle Mounting for the compass in the cockpit

Cardinal points The four main points of the compass: north, south, east and west
Cardinal system Of buoyage; the practice of placing buoys to mark the cardinal points of obstacles to navigation
Chart datum The level from which soundings on a chart are taken (N. America); Plane of Reference
Chronometer A timepiece of special accuracy essential to navigation
Compass An instrument for indicating magnetic north in the case of a magnetic compass, and true north in the case of a gyro compass
Compass bearing Direction of an object as indicated by the compass reading, in degrees
Compass course Course followed by vessel as indicated by compass
Compass error The amount by which the compass is inaccurate in its indication of true north due to variation and deviation (*qv*)

Daymarks (N. America) marks on buoys by which their purpose can be identified
Deviation Error induced in compass by the proximity of ferrous metals on board. Deviation can be established for various headings by swinging the vessel through 360° and recording the results on a deviation card
Drift The speed of the current in knots
Dutchman's log (Chip log) method of measuring speed by dropping a small object over the bow and measuring

the time that it takes to reach the stern

Eddy Water flowing against the main stream

Fathom Measure of depth of water equal to 6 ft
Fix Point where at least two lines of position cross

Heeling error Error in compass reading due to the effects of heeling
High water The highest point reached by any individual tide

Knot Measure of speed per hour equal to 1.9 km (1 1/16 land miles)

Latitude The distance from the equator either north or south, measured in degrees
Leading line When two leading marks are in line, the line which joins them is so-called; used when entering harbour or a channel
Line of position (LOP) Line on chart, established by one navigational method or another, somewhere on which the vessel is situated
Log Instrument for measuring distance sailed
Longitude The distance from Greenwich meridian, either east or west, measured in degrees

Magnetic bearing Bearing read off magnetic compass
Magnetic compass Compass whose needle is attracted by magnetic north and is not corrected for variation
Magnetic course Course after application of deviation to compass reading
Magnetic meridian Imaginary line of longitude passing through the magnetic poles and cutting the equator at right angles
Meridian Imaginary line of longitude passing through geographic (true) north and south poles and cutting the equator at right angles

Nautical mile Equal to 1.9 km (1 1/16 land miles); the measurement of one minute of longitude at the equator
Neap tide Tide with the least range

Offing Distance from a coastline or object

Position line *See* Line of position
Parallel A line of latitude; a circle parallel to the equator
Plane of reference *See* Chart datum

Range Distance between successive high and low waters
Relative bearing Angle between the boat's head and an object of which a bearing is taken
Run Distance travelled in a determined period of time

Sextant Instrument for measuring angles
Slack water The period when a tide ceases ebbing or flooding preparatory to changing direction
Sights Angles measured with a sextant
Spring tides Tides with the greatest range, occurring usually when the moon is new or full
Set Direction of tidal current

Tidal current (USA), **stream** (UK) The horizontal flow of water caused by the rise and fall of the tide
Top marks *See* Daymarks
Tide Vertical and horizontal movement of a mass of water brought about by the gravitational pull of the moon and sun

Variation Amount in degrees by which magnetic north varies from true north; variation differs from one point on the earth's surface to another and changes constantly

Lateral system Of buoyage, when the buoys have to be left to port or starboard, e.g. when marking the sides of a channel

Commands used in sailing

Sailing has a language all of its own, which has been developed over the centuries. It is usual for orders on a sailboat to be given in that language so that there can be no mistake about what is meant.

Usually, and if time permits, two commands are given for each action to be performed. The first is to tell the crew to prepare themselves and the boat for whatever is to be done, the second to tell them to perform the action. The expression 'Stand by', followed by a description of the action (like 'to hoist the main'), warns the crew to get ready to do something. In this case they will uncleat the main halyard and hold it in their hand to await the order to hoist. The correct reply to give, so that the skipper knows that he has been heard and understood, is 'Ready'. When the order to perform the action is given it can be acknowledged by the crew by repeating the word. The skipper then knows that the order has been heard and understood.

Here are some useful commands:

Tacking
'Stand by to go about' or 'Ready about'
'Hard alee' (in the UK, 'Lee-o')

Gybing
'Stand by to gybe'
'Gybe-o'

Mooring and unmooring
'Make fast' (secure a line)
'Let go forward/aft'
'Fend off'

Hoisting and lowering sails
'Up main' or 'Hoist main'
'Down jib/main'

Trimming sails
'Trim the sheets' (adjust the sheets using your own initiative)
'Let fly' (ease the sheets with a run)
'Harden in jib/main' (take in all the slack in sheets)
'Ease sheets' (let sheets off by a small amount or as necessary for a new course)
'Back the jib/main' (accompanied by the word port or starboard, push or pull the sail aback)

Anchoring
'Let go the anchor'
'Break out the anchor' (detach from the bottom)
'Haul up the anchor' or 'Weigh the anchor'

Steering
'Helm up' (bear away)
'Helm down' (come up, luff up)
'Hold her', 'Steady' (keep steering as you are)
'Head up' (come up, luff up)
'Bear away'

Flags and flag etiquette

Flags are rectangular and are distinguished from each other by their colour and design. Burgees are triangular, with a length about twice their width. Pennants, usually confined to the International Code numerals and answering pennants, are longer and slimmer than burgees and, moreover, have square ends.

The most important flag flown on a sailboat is the ensign, which denotes her nationality. This is carried on a staff at the stern, but on a yawl or ketch it may be flown from the mizzen truck at sea, while gaff-rigged vessels can fly it from the peak. In many countries the maritime ensign is different from the national flag. In the UK it is the Red Ensign, while the US has a special yacht ensign.

A burgee is used to display the insignia of a yacht club and is flown from the head of the mainmast. If it is rigged on a short staff it can also perform the useful function of indicating the direction of the wind.

It is considered courteous when in foreign waters to fly the ensign of the country being visited from the starboard spreader. Ensigns should be lowered at sunset and hoisted at 08.00 hrs in summer and 09.00 hrs in winter. The burgee may be left flying at night and when the boat is in use.

Saluting other vessels, a courtesy at sea, is done by lowering the ensign half way from its fully hoisted position. It is kept in that position until the vessel being saluted has lowered her ensign and begun to raise it again. Yachts should salute naval vessels, except in naval harbours, royal yachts and any vessel met far from land.

International Code of Signals

The flags for letters and numerals are illustrated on page 317. The code is standard to all countries and was introduced in the nineteenth century.

There are 26 letter flags, ten numeral pennants, three repeater fags, and a code or answering pennant. All single letter flags except R have a distinct message when flown alone. Messages are spelled out by flying combinations of flags one above the other and read from top to bottom. the message is called a hoist, each group of flags on the same halyard being separated by a tackline, which is a length of halyard about 6½ ft (2m) long.

The flags of the International Code of Signals have been specially designed so that they are never confused with each other and so that they can be identified positively even when partly obscured.

For the complete list of signals which can be sent in the code you need to buy the International Code of Signals, which can be obtained from good nautical bookshops. However, the small-boat sailor will not find it necessary to have such a large volume on board and will find practically all the signals he is likely to want to use set out in a nautical almanac or boatman's manual. In this book, on page 299, are set out signals for distress and there is also a table on page 298 showing the international code flags that are used in racing.

The International Code of Signals can also be sent in Morse Code and it is a requirement of any examination for a certificate of competency to know both the flag and Morse Codes. There is no easy way to learn these codes, but there are books devoted to the subject, such as *Sea Signalling Simplified* by Capt. P.J. Russell (Adlard Coles Ltd.).

It is common on special occasions like the visit of a head of state or the birthday of a monarch to dress vessels overall. This can be done with a yacht, using the international code flags displayed in any order you wish.

Bibliography

There are a considerable number of books on the various aspects of sailing — so many, in fact, that we can only mention a small selection. We have limited ourselves to listing those which we consider to be especially good in their field.

General

Sailing from Start to Finish, Ives-Louis Pinaud, Adlard Coles Ltd.
The Sailing Yacht — Juan Baader. Adlard Coles Ltd., W.W. Norton & Co. Inc.
Starting Sailing — James Moore & Alan Turvey. David & Charles; Doubleday & Co. Inc.; Reed.
Piloting, Seamanship and Small Boat Handling — Charles F. Chapman. The Hearst Corporation, Motorboating and Sailing Book Division.
Fundamentals of Sailing, Cruising and Racing — Stephen Colegate. W.W. Norton & Co. Inc.
The New Glénans Sailing Manual — Sail Books; David & Charles.
The Theory and Practice of Seamanship — Graham Danton. Routledge & Kegan Paul.
The Seawife's Handbook — Joyce Sleightholme. Angus & Robertson.
Heavy Weather Sailing — K. Adlard Coles. Adlard Coles Ltd.
Reed's Nautical Almanac — Capt. O.M. Watts. Thomas Reed Publications Ltd.
Reed's Nautical Almanac, American East Coast Edition. As above.

Racing

Expert Dinghy & Keelboat Racing — Paul Elvström. Richard Creagh-Osborne & Partners.
Paul Elvström Explains the Yacht Racing Rules. Richard Creagh-Osborne & Partners.
Ocean Racing — Peter Johnson. Nautical Publishing.
This is Racing — Richard Creagh-Osborne. Nautical Publishing; Sail Books.
This is Competitive Sailing — Fred Imhoff and Lex Pranger. Nautical Publishing; Sail Books.
Tuning a Racing Yacht — Mike Fletcher and Bob Ross. Angus & Robertson.

Cruising

This is Sailboat Cruising — J.D. Sleightholme. Nautical Publishing; Sail Books.
Cruising Under Sail — Eric Hiscock, Oxford University Press.
The Complete Yachtsman — Bobby Schenk. Macdonald & Jane's.
Just Cruising — Alan Licas. Horwitz Books, Australia.

Navigation

Celestial Navigation — Mary Blewitt. Stanford Maritime.
Dead Reckoning Navigation — John Wright. Adlard Coles Ltd.
Practical Yacht Navigator —

Kenneth Wilkes, Nautical
Publishing Co. Ltd.
Reed's Ocean Navigator — John
F. Kemp. Thomas Reed Publica-
tions Ltd.
The Sextant Simplified — Capt.
O.M. Watts. Thomas Reed
Publications Ltd.
Manual of Yacht Navigation —
Jeff Toghill, K.G. Murray
Publishing Co., Australia.

Yacht design and building

The Proper Yacht — Arthur Beiser.
International Marine Publishing
Co.; Adlard Coles Ltd.
Skene's Elements of Yacht Design.
Dodd, Mead and Co. Inc.
Sailing Yacht Design — Douglas
Philips-Birt. Adlard Coles Ltd.
Fibreglass Boats — Hugo de Plessis.
Adlard Coles Ltd.
Illustrated Custom Boatbuilding —
Bruce Roberts. Bruce Roberts In-
ternational, Australia.

Multihulls

Catamaran Sailing to Win —
Chris Wilson & Max Press,
Kayne, Methuen of Australia.
Multihull Seamanship — Michael
McMullen. Nautical Publishing
Co. Ltd.

Sails

Sail Power — Wallace Ross. Alfred
A. Knopf, Inc. Adlard Coles Ltd.
Sails — Jeremy Howard-Williams.
Adlard Coles Ltd.

Maintenance

Fitting Out — J.D. Sleightholme.
Adlard Coles Ltd.
Boat Carpentry — Hervey Garrett
Smith. Van Nostrand Reinhold,
Inc.
Maintenance — Time-Life Books.

Knots and Splices

Knots and Splices — Cyrus Day.
Adlard Coles Ltd.; John de Graaf
Inc.
The Ashley Book of Knots —
Lawrence Ashley. Faber & Faber.
The Marlinspike Sailor — Hervey
Garrett Smith. D. Van Nostrand
Co. Inc.

Weather

Instant Weather Forecasting — Alan
Watts. Adlard Coles Ltd: Dodd,
Mead & Co.
The Weather Guide — A.G.
Forsdyke. Hamlyn Books.
Meteorology — Charles Roberts.
Thomas Reed Publications Ltd.
Your Own Weather Map — C.E.
Wallington. Royal Meteorological
Society, Bracknell.

Sailboarding

Sailboarding — Peter Brockhaus &
Ulrich Stanciu. Adlard Coles Ltd.

Marine engines

*Marine Engines and Boating
Mechanics* — Dermot Wright.
David & Charles.

Index

lying ahull 214
lying to 129-30
lying to at anchor 213-14

M

mainsail 31
  shape of 35
maintenance 61-70
  tools for 61-2, 67
making fast 105
Marine Information Manual 255
marks: *see* buoys
massage, heart 211
masts 25-7, 31, 38, 64, 66, 96-7,
  101, 106, 148, 180, 181, 200
  damage to 200
mast ram 24
medicine chest 214-15
meridians: *see* longitude
metric charts 259-60
Miami-Montego Bay Race 247
Middle Sea Race 247
Mistral 307
mizzen 31
monohulls 12
monsoons 306, 307
mooring 105-7, 177
  leaving a 15, 136-9, 177
motors: *see* engines
motor sailer 16
multihulls 12, 166-78; *see also*
  catamarans

N

Nautical Almanac, the 254, 276,
  283-4, 287, 288, 289, 290
nautical miles 256
navigation 250-94
  rules of 316, 322-8
Norwester 307

O

Offshore Crew Championship 248
oil on water, pouring 214
Opus III 167
oscillation 101
outhaul 23
overboard, man 130-1, 208-11
overhang 16
overlap 219

P

painting 62-3, 64-7, 68
parachute flare 199
parallels: *see* latitude
pelorus 251, 273
Pen Duick III 248
Pen Duick IV 248
Pen Duick VI 248
piers 106
pilot charts 254
piloting 250, 265-74
pilots 253-4
pistol, very 199
Plane of Reference 275-6
planing 102, 114-15, 118, 120, 153
planks 16
position finding 271-4; *see also*
  navigation
power boxes 24
pressure, atmospheric 296-301,
  303, 305-6, 309, 310, 311, 312
proas 166
projecter, flare 199
publications for yachtsmen 253-5

R

racer, ocean 16
racing
  beating in 229-30
  course of 218-19
  finishing line of 235-7
  gybing in 230, 232, 233
  handicap and yardstick 217-18,
  237
  keep-fit programme for 238-40,
  243-5
  ocean 217-18
  offshore 246-8
  preparation for 101-3
  reaching in 230-2
  rounding the marks in 233-4
  round-the-buoys 217, 218
  rules and points of 218, 219-27,
  246
  running in 232
  signals of 219, 227-8
  starting gate of 228-9
  starting line of 227-8
  tacking in 229, 230, 232, 233,
  234, 235
  training for 237-8
  types of 217
  yardstick 237
racing yachts 15, 156, 159, 217
  classes of 53-7
  masts of 25-6, 27
  one-design 217
  sails of 31-2, 36-7, 39-40
  special fittings for 22-4, 30, 47
radar 292
radios 50, 250, 290-1, 292, 294;
  see also direction finders

radio signals, lists of 254
radiotelephones 294
rafting 106-7
range, fixing position by 272
reaching 110, 111, 112, 113, 114-
  15, 118, 153, 173-4, 204, 218,
  230-2
  beam 110, 171
  broad 110, 120, 130, 171, 173,
  184, 190, 191, 232, 236
  close 110, 184
Reed's Nautical Almanac 254-5,
  275
reefing 211-12
regattas 218
repairs 61-70
  tools for 61-2, 67
rescuing man overboard 130-1,
  208-11
resistance 91-3
  form 91-3
  heeling 92
  leeway 93
  skin 91
  water 93
  wind 93
resuscitation 210-11
rigging 25-30, 51-2, 64, 158, 200
  damage to 200
  see also sails
righting a capsize 162-4, 207-8
roller jib 23
ropes 45-6, 105
RORC 54
Round-Gotland Race 247
rounding up 130
rudder 16, 17, 95-6, 101, 108,
  115-18, 125, 126, 127-8, 162,
  201
rules of navigation 316-28
running 110, 111, 113, 118, 125,
  184, 185, 191, 204, 218, 232
running fix, the 273-4
running under bare poles 213

S

Safety 85-6
  equipment 196-9
safety harnesses 198-9
sailboards: *see* windsurfing
sailing directions 253-4
sails
  area of (catamarans') 167
  camber of 33-8, 90-1, 96, 97,
  98, 101, 109
  cloth for 33
  cut of 33-8
  fittings of 38
  handling 25-30, 156-61
  in use today 39-40
  lowering 109, 158
  setting 108-9, 158-9
  treatment and care of 43-4, 64
  trimming 96-8, 102, 103, 109,

Acknowledgments

The publishers would like to thank:

Beken of Cowes for the front jacket photograph; Christopher Cunningham for the photograph of a Hobie Cat on page 224; Fairways Marine for the photograph on page 15; Gowan Sails for the photographs on pages 96 and 97; Guy Gurney for the endpaper photograph and the photographs on pages 56, 57, 95, 132, 239, 243 and 247; Halmatic Ltd for the photograph of fibreglass hull construction on page 19 (copyright Peter Fothergill); The Hydrographic Department, Ministry of Defence, Taunton, England for the symbols from Admiralty charts on pages 258 and 260, the compass rose on page 268 and the IALA Buoyage guide on page 264, and for the three sections produced from portions of Admiralty Tide Tables for 1974 with the sanction of the Controller, HM Stationery Office and the Hydrographer of the Navy, on pages 277 and 278; David Jenkins, who drew a number of the diagrams throughout the book; Brian Manby Photography for the photograph of Berthon Marina, Lymington, England on page 135; the Miami-Metro Department of Publicity and Tourism for the photograph on page 211; Roy Montgomery (Industrial and Marine Photography) for the photograph on page 55. The photograph on page 50 was provided by courtesy of A.H. Moody & Son Ltd. The following were reproduced from the Nautical Almanac, with the permission of the Controller of Her Majesty's Stationery Office: The Phases of the Moon on page 276, the August 1st sun on page 284, the table of Increments and Corrections 28 minutes – 29 minutes on page 284 and the Altitude Correction Tables for 0°–35° Moon on page 288. The section from a chart on page 263 comes from NOAA Chart no. 12366 (Long Island Sound and East River) published by the US Department of Commerce. The accompanying key was reproduced from the US Coast Guard Light List, Vol 1 (the Atlantic Coast from St Croix). We would like to thank Reed's Nautical Almanac for the Beaufort Scale on page 304; Patrick Roach for the back jacket photograph; Simpson Lawrence for the photograph of their SL400 marine head on page 49; the US Naval Academy for the photograph on page 104; Alan Watts for the photographs on pages 295 and 312; Tom Willis for the series of photographs on page 46; Tom Witherspoon (Long Beach News) for the photograph on page 25; Yachting World for the photograph on page 12.